The royal manors of medieval Co. Dublin

The royal manors of medieval Co. Dublin

Crown and community

Áine Foley

FOUR COURTS PRESS

Set in 10.5 on 12.5 point Ehrhardt for
FOUR COURTS PRESS LTD
7 Malpas Street, Dublin 8, Ireland
www.fourcourtspress.ie
and in North America for
FOUR COURTS PRESS
c/o ISBS, 920 N.E. 58th Street, Suite 300, Portland, OR 97213.

A catalogue record for this title
is available from the British Library.

ISBN 978–1–84682–388–6

Printed in England
by Antony Rowe, Chippenham, Wilts.

*In memory of my mother, Ann 'Nan' Foley,
and my father, Dan Foley*

Contents

Abbreviations

Admin. Ire.	H.G. Richardson and G.O. Sayles, *The administration of Ireland, 1172–1377* (Dublin, 1963)
Affairs Ire.	G.O. Sayles (ed.), *Documents on the affairs of Ireland before the king's council* (Dublin, 1979)
AFM	*Annála ríoghachta Éireann: Annals of the kingdom of Ireland by the Four Masters from the earliest period to the year 1616*, ed. and trans. John O'Donovan (7 vols, Dublin, 1851, repr. New York, 1966)
Alen's reg.	*Calendar of Archbishop Alen's register, c.1172–1534; prepared and edited from the original in the registry of the united dioceses of Dublin and Glendalough and Kildare*, Charles MacNeill (ed.); index by Liam Price (Dublin, 1950)
Anal. Hib.	*Analecta Hibernica, including the reports of the Irish Manuscripts Commission* (Dublin, 1930–)
CARD	J.T. Gilbert (ed.), *Calendar of ancient records of Dublin* (19 vols, Dublin, 1889–1944)
CCD	M.J. McEnery and Raymond Refaussé (eds), *Christ Church deeds* (Dublin, 2001)
CCM	Calendar of the Carew Manuscripts preserved in the archiepiscopal library at Lambeth, 1515–74 [etc.] (6 vols, London, 1867–73)
CCR	*Calendar of the close rolls preserved in the Public Record Office, 1272–[1509]* (47 vols, London, 1892–1963)
CDI	H.S. Sweetman and G.F. Handcock (eds), *Calendar of documents relating to Ireland* (5 vols, London, 1875–86)
CFR	*Calendar of the fine rolls ... 1272–[1509]* (22 vols, London, 1911–62)
CICD	Margaret C. Griffith (ed.), *Calendar of inquisitions formerly in the office of the chief remembrancer of the exchequer prepared from the mss of the Irish record commission* (Dublin, 1991)
CIRCLE	Peter Crooks (ed.), *A calendar of Irish chancery letters, c.1244–1509*
CJR	James Mills and M.C. Griffith (eds), *Calendar of the justiciary rolls, or proceedings in the court of the justiciar of Ireland ... 1295–[1314]* (3 vols, Dublin, 1905, 1914, 1956)
CPL	*Calendars of entries in the papal registers relating to Great Britain and Ireland: papal letters, 1198–1304* [etc.] (London, 1893–)

CPR	*Calendar of the patent rolls preserved in the public record office, 1232–[1509]* (53 vols, London, 1911)
CSMA	J.T. Gilbert (ed.), *Chartularies of St Mary's Abbey, Dublin* [...] (2 vols, London, 1884–6)
DGMR	*The Dublin guild merchant roll, c.1190–1265*, ed. Philomena Connolly and Geoffrey Martin (Dublin, 1992)
DHR	*Dublin Historical Record* (Dublin, 1938–)
EFP	Estate and Family Papers, NAI
EHR	*English Historical Review* (London, 1886–)
Giraldus, *Topographia*	Giraldus Cambrensis, *The history and topography of Ireland*, ed. J.J. O'Meara (Mountrath and London, 1982)
Gormanston reg.	*Calendar of the Gormanston register*, ed. James Mills and M.J. McEnery (Dublin, 1916)
HMDI	*Historic and municipal documents of Ireland, 1172–1320*, ed. J.T. Gilbert (London, 1870)
IEMI	*Inquisitions and extents of medieval Ireland*, ed. Paul Dryburgh and Brendan Smith (Kew, 2007)
IHS	*Irish Historical Studies: the joint journal of the Irish Historical Society and the Ulster Society for Irish Historical Studies* (Dublin, 1938–)
JMH	*Journal of Medieval History* (London, 1975–)
JRSAI	*Journal of the Royal Society of Antiquaries of Ireland* (Dublin, 1892–)
JSH	*Journal of Social History*
Knights' fees	*Knights' fees in Counties Wexford, Carlow and Kilkenny*, ed. Eric St John Brooks (Dublin, 1950)
NAI	National Archives of Ireland [includes former PROI] (Dublin)
NHI, ii	Art Cosgrove (ed.), *A new history of Ireland*, ii: *Medieval Ireland, 1169–1534* (Oxford, 1987; repr. with bibliographical supplement, 1993)
NHI, ix	T.W. Moody, F.X. Martin and F.J. Byrne (eds), *A new history of Ireland*, ix: *Maps, genealogies, lists – a companion to Irish history, part II* (Oxford, 1984; repr. 2002)
ODNB	*Oxford dictionary of national biography*
Ormond deeds, 1172–1350 [etc.]	*Calendar of Ormond deeds, 1172–1350* [etc.], ed. Edmund Curtis (6 vols, Dublin, 1932–43)

PBA	*Proceedings of the British Academy* (London, 1903–)
PKCI, 1392–3	*A roll of the proceedings of the king's council in Ireland, for a portion of the sixteenth year of the reign of Richard the second, AD1392–3; with an appendix*, ed. James Graves (London, 1877)
PR 14 John	Oliver Davies and D.B. Quinn (eds), 'The Irish pipe roll of 14 John, 1211–1212', *UJA*, 3rd ser., 4, supp. (July 1941)
PRIA	*Proceedings of the Royal Irish Academy* (Dublin, 1836–)
RAST	J.T. Gilbert (ed.), *Register of the abbey of St Thomas* (Dublin, 1889)
RDKPRI	*Report of the deputy keeper of the public records of Ireland*
RHSJ	Eric St John Brooks (ed.), *Register of the hospital of S. John the Baptist without the Newgate* (Dublin, 1936)
SCSMI	Paul Dryburgh and Brendan Smith (eds), *Handbook and select calendar of sources for medieval Ireland in the National Archives of the United Kingdom* (Dublin, 2005)
ser.	series
Stat. Ire., 1–12 Edw. IV	*Statute rolls of the parliament of Ireland, first to twelfth years of the reign of King Edward IV*, ed. H.F. Berry (Dublin, 1914)
Stat. Ire., 12–22 Edw. IV	*Statute rolls of the parliament of Ireland, 12th to 22nd years of the reign of King Edward IV*, ed. J.F. Morrisey (Dublin, 1939)
Stat. Ire., Hen. VI	*Statute rolls of the parliament of Ireland, reign of King Henry VI*, ed. H.F. Berry (Dublin, 1910)
Stat. Ire., John–Hen. V	*Statutes and ordinances and acts of the parliament of Ireland, King John to Henry V*, ed. H.F. Berry (Dublin, 1907)
supp.	supplement
TNA	The National Archives of the United Kingdom [formerly PRO] (London)
TRHS	*Transactions of the Royal Historical Society* (London, 1872–)
UJA	*Ulster Journal of Archaeology*
VCH	*The Victoria county history of the counties of England* (London, 1900–)

Acknowledgments

One of my earliest memories is of my mother taking me on a walk to the medieval church in Esker late one evening when I could not sleep. The old ruin, still at that time surrounded by fields, was bathed in moonlight. My mother, quite unintentionally, had awakened in me an enthusiasm for the medieval period. When my love affair with the fourteenth century flags under the weight of exchequer receipts and memoranda rolls, I like to think of that evening. What follows, for better or worse, is dedicated to her, and to my father.

I owe a great debt to very many individuals but especially to Seán Duffy. His junior freshman course on medieval Ireland and, later, his special subjects on medieval Dublin and the Irish Sea region were pivotal in my decision to embark on further research. I truly could not have asked for a more supportive supervisor. Peter Crooks has always been incredibly generous in sharing his knowledge and giving me a swift kick whenever it was needed. As much as I have always appreciated his help academically, I appreciate his friendship even more. Thank you for putting up with me! I was very fortunate to have been given the opportunity to work with Robin Frame in the first year of my research; I am very grateful for all his kindness and encouragement.

A generous grant from the Grace Lawless Lee fund in 2007 meant that I was able to spend some time in the National Archives in Kew. Thanks to the archivists there who offered great assistance in locating material. I am also very appreciative to Michael Potterton and Four Courts Press for all their help and patience in transforming my thesis into a book. Thanks to Rosaleen Dwyer of South Dublin County Council and Charles Duggan of Dublin City Council for a subvention towards the cost of publication. Over the course of my research, I was employed by the Examinations Office in Trinity College Dublin and the Centre for Academic Practice and Student Learning (CAPSL). The work they offered me on a regular basis enabled me to finish my thesis, and for that, I am very appreciative.

I am most indebted to friends and colleagues who have helped me in one way or another with this book, particularly the staff of the history department of Trinity College Dublin and my fellow postgrads, past and present. Thanks in particular to all the 'Duffians' (including Linzi Simpson and Sadhbh!). The weekly postgraduate seminars have been especially useful in terms of presenting some of my ideas and I would like to thank David Ditchburn for allowing me to inflict the royal manors onto my fellow students on so many occasions. Thanks to Howard Clarke and Mark Hennessy for their very useful feedback on my thesis; the implementation of some of their suggestions has led to a much better book. This book was born out of my doctoral research and I would especially like to thank all my friends for keeping me (sort of) sane in the last few months of that research. I am also grateful to my sister Margo and brother Joe for all their support. My nephew Adam and niece Anna were not even born when I started researching the royal manors, but somehow these very small beings have managed to wrap me around their little fingers. Thank you for being such wonderful diversions.

Áine Foley
April 2013

The royal demesne in Ireland: settlement and sources

The impression is that the tenants of both manors formed a community having some responsibilities but many profits and privileges in
common ...

Edmund Curtis[1]

INTRODUCTION

This book explores the relationship between the English crown and the four
'royal manors' in the hinterland of the city of Dublin in the late medieval period.
The manors in question, which came into being during the reign of King John
(1199–1216), are Esker, Crumlin, Newcastle Lyons and Saggart.[2] A primary aim
is to test the 'impression' formed by Edmund Curtis, on the basis of manorial
court rolls of the late sixteenth century, that the tenants of these manors formed
a distinctive community.[3] Although there are no similar court rolls surviving for
the royal manors during the Middle Ages, other sources can be used to build up
a picture of cooperative spirit and identity between the tenants here. A central
theme of this work is the relationship between crown and community during the
late medieval period, seen most clearly through patronage. With regard to these
four royal manors, both the king's favourites in London and local administrators
in Dublin benefited through grants of land and annuities, as well as offices on
the manors. This patronage permeated through all levels of society and was the
bond that held it together. Patronage was linked intrinsically to social status and
the sponsorship of a more powerful individual could help smooth the path to
social acceptance. Indeed, most aspects of medieval life were to some degree
'sponsored'.[4] The social composition of the royal manors is examined. Many of

1 Edmund Curtis, 'The court book of Esker and Crumlin, 1592–1600', *JRSAI*, 60 (1930), 146;
for a critical assessment of Curtis' work, see James Lydon, 'Historical revisit: Edmund Curtis, *A
history of medieval Ireland* (Dublin, 1923, 1938)', *IHS*, 31:124 (1999), 535–48; see also Peter
Crooks, 'The Lecky professors' in idem (ed.), *Government, war and society*, pp 25–36. 2
Throughout this book, where I use the term 'the royal manors', unless otherwise noted, it is in
reference to the manors of Esker, Crumlin, Newcastle Lyons and Saggart. 3 The court rolls in
question cover the years 1592 to 1600 and only concern two of the royal manors under review:
Esker and Crumlin. Curtis' introductory remarks, however, refer to all four manors. 4 Michael
J. Bennett, *Community, class and careerism: Cheshire and Lancashire society in the age of Sir Gawain
and the Green Knight* (Cambridge, 1983), p. 192.

the leading families of Dublin city and county held lands here. Some of the royal tenants had administrative and clerical backgrounds, while a significant section of the populace were members of the merchant class. Additionally, the Irish who remained here after the invasion made up a sizeable segment of local society. Rather than being pushed out of the locality by the new colonists, they integrated into the new order with surprising ease and many became English, at least in a legal sense.

Though the royal manors did not come into being until the reign of King John, this locality was an important power centre in the pre-invasion period. In early medieval Ireland, the River Liffey marked the boundary between two great over-kingdoms, that of the Leinstermen to the south and, north of the river, the territory of the Southern Uí Néill. The Leinstermen who controlled this area were the Uí Dúnchada. They were the final Irish dynasty to rule in what is now south-west Co. Dublin before the invasion.[5] The Uí Dúnchada represented the last remnants of the Uí Dúnlainge, who were the most powerful dynasty in Leinster from the seventh to the eleventh century.[6] They were based at Liamhain, which was later transformed into the royal manor of Newcastle Lyons.[7] This frontier zone became more volatile with the emergence of the settlement of Dublin in the Viking Age, which included a large hinterland that the Irish called Fine Gall (the Territory of the Foreigners). By the time of the English intervention in Ireland in the late twelfth century, Dublin had taken its place as the country's capital in all but name.[8] It played a critical role in the events surrounding Diarmait Mac Murchada's infamous expulsion and Strongbow's controversial succession to his kingdom of Leinster, so that when Henry II intervened personally in Ireland in 1171, it was only to be expected that the implications for the city of Dublin and its hinterland would be great.[9] The English king took, among other choice pickings, Dublin and its subordinate territory into his own hands and retained it as royal demesne. In the meantime, the original inhabitants of this territory, the Meic Gilla Mo-Cholmóc (the lineal descendants of the Uí Dúnchada), held on to much of their old property, though now held of the king, for at least another generation; however, they would lose much of their property in the early thirteenth century.

---

5 John Bradley, 'The interpretation of Scandinavian settlement in Ireland' in John Bradley (ed.), *Settlement and society in medieval Ireland: studies presented to F.X. Martin OSA* (Kilkenny, 1988), p. 56; Alfred P. Smyth, *Celtic Leinster: towards an historical geography of early Irish civilization, AD500–1600* (Blackrock, 1982), p. 44; Paul McCotter, *Medieval Ireland: territorial, political and economic divisions* (Dublin, 2008), pp 162–4. See the following chapter for a more in-depth exploration of this area in the pre-invasion period.   6 Smyth, *Celtic Leinster*, p. 39.   7 G.H. Orpen, 'Liamhain, now represented by Lyons, near Newcastle Lyons', *JRSAI*, 36 (1906), 76–8.   8 See Seán Duffy, 'Irishmen and Islesmen in the kingdoms of Dublin and Man, 1052–1171', *Ériu*, 43 (1992), 93–133.   9 See F.X. Martin, 'Allies and an overlord' in *NHI*, ii, pp 67–97 for a general overview of this tumultuous period in Irish history and ch. 2, below, for the effects of the invasion on the locality.

THE ROYAL MANORS: SITUATION AND SETTLEMENT PATTERNS

When these lands in south Co. Dublin passed out of the hands of the Meic Gilla Mo-Cholmóc, the royal manors were established. The two largest manors, Saggart and Newcastle Lyons, were closer to the mountains than Crumlin and Esker and were therefore more vulnerable. Yet, because they were larger, they could also potentially yield the most revenue. As the Middle Ages progressed, they became increasingly important because they formed part of the line of defence against the Irish in the mountains. The two smaller manors were closer to the city and were for that reason better able to maintain their value. Nonetheless, all four manors were more important to the crown as a means of rewarding royal servants, both in the locality and within the royal household, than for the revenues they could potentially generate.

Newcastle Lyons is situated 16 km south-west of Dublin city, close to the border with Kildare. It was composed of a collection of sub-manors, rather than being a single unit. Many of these sub-manors can be identified as modern townlands and it is possible that they defined a single farmstead.[10] These included the central *caput* of Newcastle as well as Calgan,[11] Loghton,[12] Milltown, Kilmactalway, Fyddanston, Jordanstown, Colmanstown, Athgoe and Marshallsrath.[13] The main settlement of Newcastle Lyons had the most tenants, about half of whom were burgesses, and the rest held their property in free socage, which meant they did not have to perform services for their lord. There were no burgage tenements on any of the other sub-manors here. Three of them – Fyddanston, Jordanstown and Marshallsrath – had just a single tenant each. At least two of these can be identified: the Jordans and the Marshals were prominent tenants on this manor in the fourteenth century. The tenants of Calgan owed a rent of 6os. and nine hens. The native Irish tenants on the royal manors often paid their rent in the form of food in the thirteenth century and it is

10 In reference to the various smaller settlements within the royal manors, the term *villatae* is used by Raymond Gillespie, 'Small worlds: settlement and society in the royal manors of sixteenth-century Dublin' in Howard B. Clarke, Jacinta Prunty and Mark Hennessy (eds), *Surveying Ireland's past: multidisciplinary essays in honour of Anngret Simms* (Dublin, 2004), pp 207–8, and Paul MacCotter equates the vill with, among other things, the townland: *Medieval Ireland, territorial, political and economic divisions* (Dublin, 2008), p. 58. Anngret Simms refers to these settlements within the manor as townlands: 'Newcastle as a medieval settlement' in O'Sullivan (ed.), *Newcastle Lyons*, p. 15. They could also be described as granges, though Kenneth Nicholls finds this term problematic and he believes historians have been using *gráig* and *grangia* interchangeably without clearly understanding the different etymology of both words. According to Nicholls, *gráig* was possibly a stock-farm or cattle-steading, while the grange was primarily a tillage establishment: 'Anglo-French Ireland and after', *Peritia*, 1 (1982), 380–1. For the sake of clarity and consistency, smaller units of land within the manors are referred to as sub-manors or simply settlements in this book.   11 Now known as Colganstown.   12 Now called Loughtown, in the modern parish of Kilmactalway.   13 TNA, SC 11/934, this extent dates from 1540 but all these place-names date from a much earlier period.

possible that this sub-manor was originally a betagh settlement. This manor needed more than one reeve to administer it because of its large size and scattered settlements.[14] Before 1321–2, for example, Warin Owen served as reeve of the central *caput* of Newcastle Lyons, while John Aylmer was provost of Ballycolman.[15]

The manor of Saggart, situated 14km south-west of Dublin city, consisted of one central settlement rather than the dispersed settlement structure found at Newcastle Lyons. Saggart was more remote and closer to the mountains and therefore probably never had an adequate population for the establishment of satellite caputs. Nonetheless, the extent from 1540 indicates that the vill of Ballinteer was an external appendage of this manor.[16] The pipe rolls from the fourteenth century indicate that Saggart also had more than one reeve, one being responsible for the manor of Saggart and the other was responsible for collecting the external rents. In 1337–8, the external parts of the manor included not only Ballinteer but also Bothircolyn and other property probably in the same vicinity.[17] It is possible that the land administered by the external reeve of Saggart was the remnants of the manor of Okelly, discussed below.

The manor of Crumlin, though smaller than Saggart, was similar in structure and the settlement here was centralized. It was the manor closest to the city of Dublin, only 3km outside the city walls, and therefore defence was not as much of an issue here as on the other manors. This is possibly the reason it retained its value throughout the medieval period and was worth more than the other manors in the early sixteenth century. In 1540, the manor was valued at 9*d.* an acre, as opposed to Esker which was worth 7*d.* an acre even though it too was relatively secure compared to the outer manors.[18] The Russell family, who will feature prominently in this work, adopted the name Crumlin as their own.

The royal manor of Esker, situated 11km west of the city, was similar in structure to Newcastle Lyons, insofar as it had more than one settlement. In the thirteenth century, this manor was administered in a different way from the other three. While Crumlin, Saggart and Newcastle Lyons were farmed out to a group of small tenants', one individual held Esker. In 1229, the manor was leased to William fitz Wido, dean of St Patrick's.[19] Almost twenty years later in 1248, it was granted to Peter Bermingham in order that he could support himself in the king's service and it remained within his family for the next century.[20] At the time that John Bermingham, the earl of Louth, was murdered in 1329, this manor was in his possession. In 1334, Agnes, widow of Henry Kissok, was granted dower out of twenty acres that Henry had held of John in Esker.[21] It is likely that the manor passed out of the hands of the Bermingham family at the

14 *RDKPRI*, 35, p. 21.   15 *RDKPRI*, 42, p. 52; Ballycolman is Colmanstown in the 1540 extent.   16 TNA, SC 11/934.   17 *RDKPRI*, 45, p. 56.   18 Gillespie, 'Small worlds', p. 200. 19 *CDI, 1171–1251*, §1731.   20 NAI, EFP/Lindsay Papers 10, §5; *CIRCLE*, Hen. III, §3. 21 *CIRCLE*, CR 8 Edw. III, §112.

time of the earl's death and certainly by the end of the Middle Ages this manor too was held by small farmers. As well as the central, and largest, settlement of Esker, it was composed of Ballydowd, Finnstown, Kissoge and Ballyowen.[22] Similarly to Newcastle Lyons, this manor's central caput also had the most tenants, but only one of the sub-manors, Finnstown, had a single tenant. The Bagot family owned this tenement in the sixteenth century and it may have always been a single tenement as it is relatively modest in size, being just 110 acres. Two of these settlements were named after two prominent manorial families. The Owens gave Ballyowen its name and Kissoge was either named after the Kissok family, or it provided this family with its name.

THE ROYAL DEMESNE IN MEDIEVAL ENGLAND AND IRELAND

Its English counterpart indisputably influenced the establishment and development of a royal demesne in Ireland. Initially, the king's policy in Ireland was reactive; the first instinct of Henry II was to make sure his vassal Strongbow did not grow too powerful. There were larger trends at play here too, however, and the retention of a royal demesne in Ireland by Henry could equally be considered an extension of his policy in England. In order to appreciate fully the establishment of the royal demesne in Ireland, it is important to understand the development of the royal demesne in England both before and after 1171. Since the time of William I, successive kings granted away large portions of the crown lands of England to family members and other followers. When Henry II ascended the throne, he was anxious to reverse this policy. In England, the inhabitants of newly emerging urban settlements were potentially lucrative sources of income for the king because taxes could be imposed on them. Increasingly, the inhabitants of these settlements were willing to pay for their economic independence. The crown must have been just as aware of the economic potential of the rural areas of their royal demesne as they were of the urban areas. As a result, while there were undoubtedly strategic reasons for the king to retain lands around his newly acquired city of Dublin, they paled into insignificance when the economic potential of this settlement and its hinterland is considered.

In *The royal demesne in English constitutional history*, R.S. Hoyt assumed that the *terra regis* referred to in the Domesday Book was the same entity as the royal demesne, though, as he pointed out himself, the forests and highways that were part of the royal demesne were never included as part of this *terra regis*.[23] B.P.

22 Anngret Simms, 'Rural settlement in medieval Ireland: the example of the royal manors of Newcastle Lyons and Esker in south county Dublin' in B.K. Roberts and R.E. Glasscock (eds), *Villages, farms and frontiers* (Oxford, 1983), p. 144. 23 Robert S. Hoyt, *The royal demesne in English constitutional history, 1066–1272* (New York, 1950), pp 2–3, 75; he does, however,

Wolffe, writing two decades after him, questioned Hoyt's conclusions as the earliest reference to a royal demesne in England dates to *c.*1187–9. Moreover, there is no mention of an ancient demesne before 1241.[24] It would appear then that the royal demesne in England was consolidated around, or shortly before, the time of the invasion of Ireland and therefore probably does not significantly pre-date the royal demesne of this study. This would mean that, as far as the Irish royal demesne was concerned, the English were not introducing a ready-made or completely evolved administrative organization into Ireland. With this in mind, it might be worthwhile to investigate how the royal demesnes on both sides of the Irish Sea developed to see if they continued to progress along similar lines or if royal policy relating to crown lands in Ireland was radically different from that in England.

In England, the royal demesne as a distinct entity seems to have come into being during the reign of Henry II. Unquestionably, crown lands existed in England before the conquest, but it took at least another century for these lands as a group to acquire political and legal definition. Wolffe theorizes that the development of royal demesne was due to the expanding administrative, judicial and financial control of the Angevin kings.[25] Once Henry II became king, the exchequer took a more 'hands on' approach to exploiting the royal demesne. This policy continued during the reigns of his sons and the royal demesne became associated with the office of the king, rather than being considered his own personal property that he could dispose of at will.[26] Previously, the sheriff had custody of the royal manors of his shire but the bailiffs and farmers who had up to now answered to him now accounted for the revenues directly to the exchequer.[27] The sheriff was not completely excluded from the administration of the royal demesne, however. He had the duty of distraining any keepers or farmers who failed to pay their revenues into the exchequer and he could also be called upon to hold inquests.[28] Furthermore, it was at this time that the king's itinerant justices brought his influence to bear on his boroughs, vills and manors. Not only was it their responsibility to impose royal justice on the king's subjects but it was also their duty to assess a royal tax known as tallage and inquire into the value of royal lands and privileges.[29]

The introduction of royal bailiffs and royal justices into the localities meant that central government had effective control over the financial and judicial aspects of the lives of the royal tenants. Eventually, these administrators were assimilated into local society and locals, in their turn, were drawn into the sphere of government when they were appointed as royal officials. Moreover, many of those appointed to positions in the locality often appointed a deputy to carry out

acknowledge that the royal demesne changed in character in the thirteenth century: p. 134. **24** B.P. Wolffe, *The royal demesne in English history: the crown estate in the governance of the realm from the Conquest to 1509* (London, 1971), p. 17.   **25** Ibid., p. 25.   **26** Hoyt, *Royal demesne*, p. 143.   **27** Ibid., pp 94–5.   **28** Ibid., p. 95.   **29** Wolffe, *Royal demesne*, p. 25.

the practical aspects of the office. These processes created a close bond between core and periphery. This experience was replicated in Dublin and is discussed in chapter three.

Constitutional historians of medieval England writing at the end of the nineteenth and the beginning of the twentieth century believed that the king held lands primarily because he was expected to support himself and his household on their revenues. The earliest evidence of this, however, dates to as late as 1765. William Stubbs applied this eighteenth-century concept to medieval England and subsequent historians accepted this theory until it became sacrosanct.[30] Furthermore, historians accused successive kings of dissipating this form of revenue by granting large portions of their crown lands away. Wolffe successfully demolished this theory in his study on the royal demesne in England. There is no evidence that medieval kings were expected to live off the resources of their own lands. Complaints made by his subjects that the king should 'live of his own', which first arose in the fourteenth century, were in fact a protest against purveyance. Medieval kings were by nature nomadic and their presence, along with a large royal household and various hangers-on, could put considerable pressure on the resources of a locality. Moreover, there were often complaints that purveyors did not pay a fair market price for goods, if they paid anything at all. This was the real cause of dissatisfaction.

The truth of the matter is that the royal demesne simply could not have been exploited directly. Royal influence was not omnipotent, and the kind of administrative infrastructure that was required to exploit the crown lands directly just did not exist in the medieval period. In many cases, the solution was to farm out the royal manors to middlemen. Land granted to farmers for a fixed amount for a set period meant that the crown would receive a guaranteed annual fee and the lands would eventually revert back to the royal demesne. Occasionally, the farm of the manor was granted directly to the tenants already living on the manor as a group.[31] In fact, it looks as if the crown preferred farming the manors to their own tenants.[32] In Dublin, there is evidence that the tenants of the royal manors held the manors themselves. In 1290, when Henry Compton was granted the demesne lands of the royal manor of Crumlin, he met with fierce opposition from the tenants of Crumlin who had previously held the farm of the manor. Moreover, the tenants of the royal manors of Newcastle Lyons and Saggart also impeded Compton from enjoying the pleas and perquisites of their courts – which were granted to him – and this would suggest that they had previously received these revenues.[33] That tenants recognized the advantages of holding royal lands is also demonstrated in another case involving the manor of Leixlip. Leixlip, in Co. Kildare, had been a royal manor during the thirteenth century

30 William Stubbs, *The constitutional history of England in its origin and development* (3 vols, Oxford, 1896), ii, pp 541–3. 31 Hoyt, *Royal demesne*, p. 138. 32 Ibid., p. 160. 33 *CDI, 1285–92*, §855.

though it eventually passed into the hands of the Knights Hospitallers. A close letter from 1359 demonstrates that the native Irish tenants living here remembered their special privileged position as king's betaghs when they argued that they did not have to pay the subsidy in Co. Kildare as they had never been accustomed to paying such subsidies in the past.[34] Although the manor had passed out of the king's hands, the customs and rights associated with it remained.

In England, the crown's ever-expanding control over its rural royal demesne went hand-in-hand with its growing influence over its urban boroughs.[35] As mentioned above, during the twelfth century, the royal administration realized how financially lucrative the developing towns and cities could be in supplementing royal income, and a tallage was imposed on royal boroughs. Hoyt believed that, at least initially, royal tallage was mostly restricted to these royal boroughs but was eventually extended to the royal manors and other lands temporarily held by the crown.[36] Wolffe agreed that tallage was a tax levied upon the royal demesne but he viewed the royal demesne as being a much broader entity than Hoyt perceived it to be. He considered it to be all land never enfeoffed by knight service, 'ancient demesne' lands – which included property once belonging to the king but now permanently alienated away from him – and lands in the king's hands due to the minority of heirs, escheat or forfeiture.[37] In fact, the royal demesne may have been born out of developments in the area of royal taxation and it conceivably included all those landholders who did not hold their property by military tenure.[38] This royal levy was an important source of income for the Angevin kings but in the later thirteenth century, other forms of taxation, particularly new duties imposed on movable property, superseded it. It appears that the king's tenants would have preferred to pay the old tallage and the motivation for this change came from central government.[39]

On 3 July 1215, King John issued a charter to the citizens of Dublin granting them the fee-farm of the city, which was valued at two hundred marks.[40] In return for paying this sum, the citizens were exempt from paying tallage; however, this privilege would not have extended to the rural royal demesne surrounding the city. There is also evidence for the payment of royal tallage in Ireland in 1252, though the royal manors are not mentioned specifically. In that year, the king ordered that a tax be assessed and levied on his vills, boroughs and demesne lands in Ireland just as had recently been done in England.[41] It is possible that tenants living on the royal manors who were also citizens of the city of Dublin were not tallaged, because in 1247 the burgesses of Drogheda were given a grant of liberties that included freedom throughout the king's demesnes from tallage.[42] It is likely that the citizens of Dublin sought similar liberties.

---

34 *CIRCLE*, CR 33 Edw. III, §131.   35 Hoyt, *Royal demesne*, p. 92.   36 Ibid., pp 119, 121.
37 Wolffe, *Royal demesne*, p. 21.   38 Ibid., p. 22.   39 Wolffe, *Royal demesne*, p. 27.
40 *HMDI*, pp 63–4.   41 *CDI, 1252–84*, §108.   42 *CDI, 1171–1251*, §2881.

The royal manors in this study appear to have held a privileged place even within the royal demesne and at least two of them, Newcastle Lyons and Saggart, were royal boroughs. Furthermore, John Bradley is of the opinion that Crumlin may have had borough status too, though the evidence for this is unforthcoming.[43] Crumlin, Newcastle Lyons and Saggart do share one distinction that sets them apart from the rest of the royal demesne, however, because all three were described as being ancient demesne in contemporary sources. In England, the tenants who lived on the king's ancient demesne were a particularly privileged group, though, paradoxically, the concept of an ancient demesne was not ancient at all. Whereas Hoyt and Wolffe appear to be at odds in terms of establishing when the royal demesne came into being, they both agree that the ancient demesne was an invention of the thirteenth century.[44] None of the royal estates recorded in the Domesday Book bear any similarities to the ancient demesne because they did not enjoy any of the same immunities or privileges associated with it – they were simply lands held by the king.[45] The term ancient demesne only began to appear in the records in the 1240s.[46] In spite of this late date, however, the ancient demesne was generally, though not always, based on lands that were held by the king at the time the Domesday Book was compiled. During the thirteenth century, when there was a question of whether a particular manor was ancient demesne, this book would occasionally be consulted, though often the judgment of the jury was enough to establish its status as ancient demesne. As time went on, it became more common to consult the Domesday Book.[47]

The concept of an ancient demesne came early to Ireland. In 1253, Stephen Bauzan acquired extensive lands in Cork on the proviso that they were not part of the king's ancient demesne. In this case, the lands were eventually granted to Stephen and this confirms that they were not part of the ancient demesne.[48] In 1331, a close letter reveals Saggart to have been an 'ancient ferm' and a decade later Crumlin and Newcastle Lyons were described as being 'of the king's ancient demesne'.[49] These three manors appear to be the only lands in Ireland that can conclusively be categorized as ancient demesne. Nevertheless, even though it is never explicitly described as being of the ancient demesne until the very end of the medieval period,[50] Esker could arguably be added to this group since it was often associated with the other three royal manors. For instance, the seneschal of the royal demesne was always responsible for all four manors, or a combination of these four. The classification of these manors as ancient demesne may indicate that they were part of the demesne lands of the Norse

---

43 John Bradley, 'The medieval boroughs of County Dublin' in Con Manning (ed.), *Dublin and beyond the Pale: studies in honour of Patrick Healy* (Dublin, 1998), p. 129. 44 Hoyt, *Royal demesne*, p. vii; Wolffe, *Royal demesne*, p. 17. 45 Hoyt, *Royal demesne*, p. 50. 46 Ibid., pp 177–9. 47 Ibid., pp 174–6. 48 CDI, *1252–84*, §§204, 387. 49 CCR, *1330–3*, p. 196; CCR, *1339–41*, pp 609–10; CCR, *1341–3*, pp 380–1. 50 TNA, SP 46/183/41.

kings of Dublin in the period before the invasion. Certainly, their description as
ancient demesne indicates that they were considered a distinct and separate
entity within the greater royal demesne. Just like boroughs, there were certain
privileges and immunities attached to the ancient demesne and it is possible that
the borough status of Newcastle and Saggart was identical to their status as
ancient demesne.

While the inhabitants of the royal demesne enjoyed certain freedoms, those
individuals living on the ancient demesne were a particularly 'privileged
species'.[51] Even those of villein status in England felt the benefits of living on
the ancient demesne. Technically, as legally unfree men, they could not appeal to
the royal courts, but the royal justices were willing to intervene on their behalf
and investigate any complaints or concerns they may have had.[52] A villein would
legally become a freeman if he lived on the ancient demesne for more than a year
and a day and could not be subsequently removed by his previous lord.[53] The
same privileges extended to Ireland, and a villein living on the king's rural
demesnes or within one of the royal towns, including Dublin, could claim
freedom from his former lord if he lived there for more than a year and a day.[54]
Interestingly, there is evidence that betaghs, the native Irish peasantry, who
resided on the king's rural lands, enjoyed the same royal protection and could
not be taken back by their former lords. In 1283, William Deveneys, who was
keeper of the king's demesne lands in Dublin, was granted three carucates and
forty-five acres of land in the tenement of Brownstown, adjacent to the royal
manor of Newcastle Lyons, for seven pounds of silver.[55] He was given permission to seek out and bring back the betaghs who had previously occupied these
lands on condition that any now resident on the king's demesne would be left
unmolested. This would suggest that legally they were considered to have been
of similar status to the villeins of England and that they were under the king's
protection. In England, this concession does not appear to have been extended
to villeins who lived in all parts of royal demesne and may have been reserved to
those who resided on the ancient demesne. It is possible that this order to
Deveneys was referring to betaghs residing on the ancient demesne lands in
Dublin.

In England by 1334, the royal demesne was no longer important as a means
of taxation, which meant that revenue was no longer the primary reason for the
crown to retain these lands.[56] The tenants living here had the weight of custom
on their side however, and once this form of land tenure became enshrined in law
there was little the administration could do to reverse the process. From a financial and legal perspective, royal tenants had much to gain by the preservation of

51 Hoyt, *Royal demesne*, p. 171.   52 Ibid., p. 198.   53 Marjorie Keniston McIntosh, *Autonomy and community: the royal manor of Havering, 1200–1500* (Cambridge, 1986), p. 187.   54 *CARD*, 1, p. 224.   55 *CDI, 1252–84*, §2070; *CIRCLE, Antiquissime* roll, §1.   56 Wolffe, *Royal demesne*, p. 29.

a royal demesne. There were certain privileges attached to being a tenant of the king and these rights once gained were jealously protected. Among these privileges were freedom of toll and, though they paid the royal tallage, they could expect exemption from other forms of taxation.[57] Moreover, the rents and farms of manors often remained at the same fixed amount for a considerable period. For example, the value of the farms of the royal manors of England listed in the pipe rolls in 1130 almost without exception stayed at the same level for the remainder of the century. Nonetheless, the entry fines for those wishing to acquire tenure of royal lands could be considerable, which reflects how attractive these lands were as an investment to their new owners.[58] This additional revenue flowing into the exchequer was, obviously, useful to the crown and it is important to note that tenants on royal manors received the immunities and privileges they enjoyed because they were willing to lobby and pay for them. The farms of the king's Dublin manors rose steadily during the first half of the thirteenth century, before becoming fixed in 1261–2.[59] These manors ran into arrears from the 1270s onwards because of the more unsettled conditions. In England during the prosperous twelfth and thirteenth centuries, a fixed farm was a distinct advantage. This was not the Irish experience because, even before the tumultuous events that affected all areas of these islands in the fourteenth century, the residents of the Dublin manors were already feeling the pressure. This was because they had their own unique set of problems to contend with – namely the threat of attack from the Irish living in the nearby mountains.

In England, tenants on royal manors also acquired legal privileges including freedom from jury duty outside the manor, which in essence meant that they did not have to attend their county and hundred courts. They also had freedom from the sheriff's jurisdiction and they were not obliged to contribute to the costs when knights of the shire were sent to parliament.[60] On some royal manors, like Havering in Essex, tenants could marry without obtaining royal permission.[61] The privileges were similar to those enjoyed in chartered boroughs and included, for instance, the right to travel and the right to be tried in court before one's peers.[62] The borough status of at least two of the royal manors in Dublin indicates that the king was proactive in terms of attracting and retaining tenants on his lands. Though the earliest reference to Saggart being a borough comes from 1332 and there is no evidence for Newcastle Lyons being a borough earlier than the late fifteenth century, it is likely that they attained their privileged status at an early date.[63] Even if they were not granted borough status at the time of their inception, the unsettled conditions from the last quarter of the thirteenth

57 Frederick Pollock and Frederic William Maitland, *The history of English law* (Cambridge, 1923), p. 384. **58** Wolffe, *Royal demesne*, p. 36. **59** Mary C. Lyons, 'Manorial administration and the manorial economy of Ireland, *c.*1200–1377' (PhD, TCD, 1984), p. 21. **60** Wolffe, *Royal demesne*, p. 25. **61** McIntosh, *Autonomy and community*, p. 39. **62** Bradley, 'Medieval boroughs', p. 129. **63** Ibid., pp 136–7.

century would have encouraged the crown to offer some inducement for settling on the manors, or at least on the outermost, exposed manors.

Though Wolffe established that the royal demesne was relatively unimportant as a source of revenue, the same could not be said of it as a source of patronage. The crown could farm out these lands for a set number of years without alienating them completely. It was not necessary to keep these lands directly in the king's hands because, unlike the Capetian kings of France, for example, kingly power in England was based on political rights, not land ownership. The kingdom was ruled through common law, through a complex judicial system and an administrative apparatus that helped control the population through various obligations, particularly military service and taxation. The royal servants, who were fundamental to administrating the kingdom, were rewarded with grants of lands, offices and annuities from the royal demesne. According to Wolffe, all the king's lands had 'an inescapable political role to play.'[64]

THE OTHER ROYAL LANDS OF CO. DUBLIN

Clearly, as outlined above, the four royal manors in this study were distinct and separate from the rest of the king's lands in Ireland.[65] Other crown lands situated close to those included in this study were Chapelizod, Leixlip, Oughterard, Castlewarden and Okelly. There were also royal lands in modern Co. Wicklow including Bray, Newcastle McKynegan, Othee and Obrun. Though all these manors are dealt with in a peripheral way in this book, for various reasons, they are not the main focus of it. The Knights Hospitallers usually held the manors of Chapelizod and Leixlip and both were only ever in royal hands intermittently and usually lay outside the jurisdiction of the king's officials.[66] Oughterard and Castlewarden only became crown acquisitions in the fourteenth century and, though the king used these lands to reward his servants and officials for a period of time, they ultimately ended up in the possession of the Butlers of Ormond.[67] Despite the fact that the royal lands of Othee and Obrun in the mountains were never alienated from the crown, they were eventually lost to the Irish. Okelly disappeared forever from the sources in the mid-thirteenth century, but at least some parts of this manor were incorporated into the manor of Saggart. Moreover, separate constables were always appointed for Newcastle McKynegan

---

64 Wolffe, *Royal demesne*, pp 34–6.   65 It has also been decided to leave aside royal manors that were more transitory in nature, even if the seneschal of the demesne was responsible for their administration. For example, though Castlewarden and Oughterard were in royal hands from the early fourteenth century, they were quickly granted away to Eustace le Paor and eventually ended up in the hands of the Butlers of Ormond: see D.N. Hall, M. Hennessy, T. O'Keeffe, 'Medieval agriculture and settlement in Oughterard and Castlewarden, Co. Kildare', *Irish Geography*, 18 (1985), 17.   66 Lyons, 'Manorial administration', pp 33–4.   67 Peter Crooks, 'Factionalism and noble power in English Ireland, *c.*1361–1423' (PhD, TCD, 2007), pp 99–100, n. 134.

and Bray and, obviously, they were not under the jurisdiction of the seneschal of the demesne.

The four royal manors in the Vale of Dublin have received a good deal of attention from historians, though perhaps not as much as that given to the church lands around the city of Dublin.[68] These royal manors have been particularly well served in the related fields of settlement and archaeological studies. The secondary material is investigated here to establish what aspects of the history of the royal manors have interested previous researchers and which have to date been neglected.

At the end of the nineteenth century, James Mills, the deputy keeper of the Public Records Office, published a pioneering article on the division of land and settlement in the Dublin region in the aftermath of the invasion. Published in 1894, this article plotted the initial settlement of the lands that constitute modern south Co. Dublin before the formation of the royal manors. He also looked at where the crown lands fitted into the larger scheme of English colonization within this locality.[69] More than a hundred years after its publication, it remains an indispensable work.[70] Mills concluded that in spite of the colonization of the area by a substantial group of settlers there was a sense of continuity too. On the manor of Lucan, for example, the bulk of the revenue came from the rents of betaghs, the native Irish who remained in the locality.[71] As well as preserving the greater part of the pre-invasion population, he argued that the land on which the newcomers settled also retained their old boundaries.

---

68 There is a significant body of work relating to church lands around Dublin, and particularly useful in regard to identifying lands owned by the archbishop of Dublin and the various religious houses is A.J. Otway-Ruthven's 'The mediaeval church lands of Co. Dublin' in J.A. Watt, J.B. Morrall and F.X. Martin (eds), *Medieval studies presented to Aubrey Gwynn SJ* (Dublin, 1961), pp 54–73. Other important articles include: Henry F. Berry, 'History of the religious gild of St Anne in St Audoen's Church, Dublin, 1430–1740, taken from its records in the Haliday Collection, RIA', *PRIA*, 25C (1904–5), 21–106; idem, 'Some ancient deeds of the parish of St Werburgh, Dublin, 1243–1676', *JRSAI*, 45 (1915), 32–44; G.H. Orpen, 'Castrum Keyvini: Castlekevin', *JRSAI*, 38 (1908), 17–27; Liam Ua Broin, 'Rathcoole, Co. Dublin, and its neighbourhood', *JRSAI*, 73 (1943), 79–97; idem, 'Clondalkin, Co. Dublin, and its neighbourhood', *JRSAI*, 74 (1944), 191–218; Bradley, 'Medieval boroughs'; Cathal Duddy, 'The role of St Thomas' Abbey in the early development of Dublin's western suburb' in Seán Duffy (ed.), *Medieval Dublin*, 4 (Dublin, 2003), pp 79–97. 69 James Mills, 'The Norman settlement in Leinster: the cantreds near Dublin', *JRSAI*, 24 (1894), 160–75; see also idem, 'Tenants and agriculture near Dublin in the fourteenth century', *JRSAI*, 21 (1890), 54–63. 70 See Margaret Murphy and Michael Potterton, *The Dublin region in the Middle Ages: settlement, land-use and economy* (Dublin, 2010), passim, for an in depth exploration of the settlement history of medieval Co. Dublin. 71 Mills, 'Norman settlement', 174.

The divisions of land described in charters appear to have pre-dated the English invasion and old place-names were retained too.

Co. Dublin is well served in the field of local studies and John D'Alton's *A history of the county of Dublin*, first published in 1838, contains a substantial amount of material relevant to the medieval county. It is particularly useful because many of the sources he used have been lost since the book's publication. Francis Elrington Ball felt that D'Alton's book could not be improved upon, but considered that the quantity of material that had become available in the period since it was written justified a six volume history of Dublin, which was also called *A history of the county of Dublin*.[72] These six books, which were also published before the destruction of the Public Records Office, offer a broad historical overview of most of south Co. Dublin, including all four manors in this study, and parts of north Dublin, including substantial sections on the medieval period.

A selection of articles written by Liam Price during the middle years of the twentieth century also address the royal manors, though his principal interest was in the king's manors established in the mountains south of Dublin. The manors in the Liffey valley are occasionally dealt with, albeit in a rather peripheral way. An article published in 1954 on the lands granted to Walter Ridelesford that would later be incorporated into the royal demesne serves as a useful addition to Eric St John Brooks' articles on the family and is particularly relevant to this study. The focus in Price's article is on Ridelesford's lands close to Bray on the coast.[73] His article on Dublin place-names ventures into the Liffey valley and the evidence appears to confirm that many place-names in the area of this study pre-date the English invasion.[74] For example, the Lyons – or more correctly Liamhain – element of Newcastle Lyons long pre-dated the English conquest and can be found in a poem in the Book of Rights dating to the tenth or eleventh century.[75] This supports Mills' contention that the new settlers were moving into pre-existing settlements with long-established boundaries. His thorough knowledge of the topography of modern day south Co. Dublin and north Co. Wicklow helped with the identification of lands that Mills did not recognize. His research on the manor of Bothercolyn is particularly relevant to this study, as he identified the lands there as being an external rent of the royal manor of Saggart in 1337–8.[76] It is surprising that he did not connect these lands with the royal manor of Okelly, which was undoubtedly in the same vicinity.[77] After the formation of the royal demesne during King John's reign, a part of the

72 F.E. Ball, *A history of the county of Dublin* (6 vols, Dublin, 1902–20). For comments on D'Alton, see preface of first volume.   73 Liam Price, 'The grant to Walter de Ridelesford of Brien and the land of the sons of Turchil', *JRSAI*, 84 (1954), 72–7; Eric St John Brooks, 'The de Ridelesfords', *JRSAI*, 81 (1951), 115–38; 82 (1952), 45–61.   74 Liam Price, 'The antiquities and place-names of south County Dublin', *DHR*, 2:4 (1940), 121–33.   75 Ibid., 128.   76 Liam Price, 'The manor of Bothercolyn', *JRSAI*, 74 (1944), 115.   77 *RDKPRI*, 35, p. 39.

manor of Okelly dissected the archbishop of Dublin's manor of Tallaght. A parcel of land here, named Kingswood in the sixteenth century, is evidence that this land had belonged to the king, even if the place-name Okelly was no longer in use.[78] In an inquisition from Henry VIII's reign, it was described as being near Saggart and it was probably a part of this manor. Similarly, outlying parcels of land like Bothercolyn and Ballinteer that were once situated within the manor of Okelly were later incorporated into the royal manor of Saggart. Though Price did not make the link between Okelly and Bothercolyn, it is thanks to his research that these connections can be made. His careful investigation of place-names assists greatly in plotting out lands that belonged to the crown.

Though much work has been done in the field of local history, it is in the discipline of settlement studies that most of the research on the royal manors has been carried out. Some of the most noteworthy work carried out in this area is by the historical geographer Anngret Simms. In the early 1980s, she wrote a number of articles on the royal manor of Newcastle Lyons.[79] Both documentary and cartographic resources were used to build up a picture of rural settlement in Dublin in the Middle Ages. Simms' research on this manorial settlement was the impetus behind the production of a book titled *Newcastle Lyons: a parish of the Pale*. Peter O'Sullivan, who also wrote a chapter investigating the place-names found within this parish, edited this volume.[80] Other chapters relevant to the Middle Ages include Leo Swan's exploration of the pre-invasion settlement and Tadhg O'Keeffe's examination of the surviving archaeology to be found on the manor.[81]

Some of the most recent scholarship has shifted from the manors in the Vale of Dublin to the royal lands situated in the mountains and along the coast of modern Co. Wicklow.[82] In an article published in *Wicklow: history and society*, Linzi Simpson focuses on the archaeological sites associated with these manors situated in the mountains and fits them into their historical context.[83] This article offers a rare discussion on the royal demesne as an entity, something that has not been addressed in a meaningful way in the other secondary sources where the manors are usually considered separately. The substantial defensive earthworks found on these royal manors in modern-day Co. Wicklow contrast greatly with the archaeological evidence to be found on those royal manors located in the Liffey valley.[84] It is clear that these manors in the mountains had

78 *CICD*, pp 13, 148.   79 Simms, 'Newcastle as a medieval settlement', 11–23; idem, 'Rural settlement in medieval Ireland', pp 133–52; Anngret Simms, K.J. Edwards and F.W. Hamond, 'The medieval settlement of Newcastle Lyons, Co. Dublin: an interdisciplinary approach', *PRIA*, 83C (1983), 351–76.   80 Peter O'Sullivan, 'Place-names, fieldnames and folklore' in O'Sullivan (ed.), *Newcastle Lyons*, pp 25–43.   81 Leo Swan, 'Newcastle Lyons: the prehistoric and early Christian periods' in O'Sullivan (ed.), *Newcastle Lyons*, pp 1–10; Tadhg O'Keeffe, 'Medieval architecture and the village of Newcastle Lyons' in O'Sullivan (ed.), *Newcastle Lyons*, pp 45–61. 82 Linzi Simpson, 'Anglo-Norman settlement in Uí Briúin Cualann' in Ken Hannigan and William Nolan (eds), *Wicklow, history and society* (Dublin, 1994), pp 191–235.   83 Ibid., p. 191. 84 Ibid., p. 197.

a military function that was absent from the manors in the Liffey valley, at least in the thirteenth century. The lesser density of mottes in south Co. Dublin – and those that do survive like at Newcastle Lyons are fairly unimpressive – suggest the initial settlement of this area was much more peaceful. The large ringwork at Newcastle McKynegan would indicate that it played an important part in the defence of the locality.[85] The appointment of a constable for this manor while a seneschal was appointed for the other royal manors also emphasizes the differences between both groups of manors.

Mary Lyons' PhD completed in 1984 explored manorial economy and administration in medieval Ireland.[86] Her thesis included a chapter devoted to the royal manors and this encompassed not only the four manors in this study but also the manors in modern day Wicklow and Kildare.[87] Unlike most of the previous work cited this chapter dealt with the royal manors as a group. The aim of the thesis was to plot the emergence and subsequent decline of manorial economy in Ireland and the royal manors were one of four case studies. The military position of these crown lands is explored, but this is in relation to how the increased raids from the Irish affected their economic value rather than the consequences on society.[88] Nonetheless, the economic conditions of the royal manors obviously affected society there at its deepest level and, undoubtedly, this work is very important from a social perspective too.

Other historians have taken a more a direct interest in the social history of the royal manors, but, this has been primarily examined through the sixteenth century court rolls, and the rich vein of records that exist from the Middle Ages have not yet been exploited to their fullest potential. Edmund Curtis' translation of the court book of the royal manors of Esker and Crumlin, mentioned at the opening of the introduction is, however, a very important source despite its late provenance. He used the information gleaned therein to help build up a picture of manorial administration and society dating back to a much earlier period.[89] Though it is an early modern source, it essentially deals with a medieval institution and is useful as a means of reconstructing how these manors were once administered. It also provides a great deal of information about the social structure of the royal manors in the early modern period. By comparing the court rolls to earlier archival evidence Curtis was able to establish that little had changed over the preceding centuries. The translation of the court book was accompanied by a very useful discussion on the tenurial obligations of the king's tenants throughout the medieval period. More recently in Anngret Simms' festschrift, Raymond Gillespie has also utilized the court book of Esker and Crumlin to reconstruct settlement and society on the royal manors in the early

85 Ibid., p. 201. 86 Lyons, 'Manorial administration', pp 12–52. 87 These included the royal manors of Bray, Newcastle McKynegan, Obrun, Othee, Chapelizod, Leixlip and Castlewarden: ibid., pp 22–33. 88 Ibid., p. 13. 89 Curtis, 'Court book' (vol. 59), 45–64, 128–48; (vol. 60), 38–51, 137–49.

modern period. The social trends, forms of tenure and settlement patterns that he has identified in this excellent article can be pushed back several centuries, though it was not the purpose of this article to identify this continuity. One of the aims of this book is to identify these same patterns for an earlier period and trace them back to their origins. Like, for example, the propensity for merchants to acquire landholdings here.[90]

The considerable amount of material written about the lands belonging to the king in the Dublin region highlights that there was a great deal of variation among them. The four royal manors in this study, for example, were administered in a radically different way from the royal lands located in modern Wicklow. With this is mind it might be constructive to examine how typical these four manors were when compared to manors elsewhere in Ireland, as well as in England.

MANOR, PARISH AND COMMUNITY

In assessing how typical the four royal manors were in relation to other manors one first has to define 'typical'. In England, the traditional view of the typical or 'classic' manor was that it was conterminous with village and parish.[91] Similarly, in Ireland, Otway-Ruthven believed that the manor and parish were usually coincident.[92] The 'classic' manor was normally held by an aristocrat, had a large demesne and was populated with servile tenants.[93] This begs the question: how 'typical' was the typical manor? In his study of medieval Suffolk Mark Bailey established that the majority of manors in this county did not fit into this neat category. Here manors had a significant proportion of free tenants, few servile ones and, in general, small demesnes. Moreover, lesser lay lords usually held them.[94] The conclusion from this and other English regional studies is that manors varied considerably in their morphology. Location, how they were administered and custom were some of the factors that dictated the form a manor could take.[95]

In Ireland too, the notion that there was such thing as a typical manor is somewhat misleading. Manors generally tended to be larger in Ireland with an average size of about two thousand acres as opposed to six hundred acres in England at the time of the Domesday Book.[96] The royal manor of Esker was closest to the average size at one thousand eight hundred acres and Crumlin was

90 Gillespie, 'Small worlds', pp 197–216.   91 Mark Bailey, *Medieval Suffolk: an economic and social history, 1200–1500* (Woodbridge, 2007), p. 27.   92 A.J. Otway-Ruthven, 'The character of Norman settlement in Ireland' in Crooks (ed.), *Government, war and society* (2008), pp 263–74 at p. 265.   93 Bailey, *Medieval Suffolk*, p. 27.   94 Ibid., p. 31.   95 Robert Bartlett, *England under the Norman and Angevin kings, 1075–1225* (Oxford, 2000), pp 315–16.   96 Frank Mitchell and Michael Ryan, *Reading the Irish landscape* (Dublin, 2001), p. 309; Bailey, *Medieval Suffolk*, p. 27.

slightly larger at two thousand five hundred acres. Compared to these two manors Newcastle Lyons and Saggart were very substantial, and each was over four thousand acres in size.[97] Even within these four manors, there was a great deal of variation, as has been explored above in the first section. The areas of Ireland heavily settled by the English tended to have smaller manors but even here, they were generally much larger than most found in England. Some of the manors located where English settlement was thinnest tended to be very large and were in fact more comparable to small lordships rather than actual manors. The manor of Cloncurry, Co. Kildare, for example was very substantial, containing the parishes of Cloncurry, Scullogestown, Dummurraghill and Donadea, as well as lands in Meath, and it was worth four knight's fees.[98] Large manors were found in Tipperary too. The manor of Moyaliff, for example, was approximately sixteen thousand acres in size. On the other hand, some of the manors in the same locality, like Synone, were much smaller.[99] The point here is that even within one region a great deal of variety could occur.

There were, on the other hand, some characteristics that all manors shared. To quote Brian Graham, it was 'simultaneously a form of settlement, a social system, a place and a legal institution'.[1] Manors were agricultural units containing a population of tenants who owed money rents or services, and often a combination of both, to their overlord. The manor often had its own court from where the tenants' lives could be controlled and regulated either by their lord or the wealthier, free tenants.[2] It was perhaps the most important institution in the Middle Ages and the lives of most people living in rural areas, which at the time were the vast majority of the population, revolved around it. To quote Bailey it was 'central to the organisation of agrarian life'.[3] Some tenants were more independent than others were. The tenants who held the farm of their manor had in essence bought the right to govern themselves independently of their lord. Susan Reynolds defined a local community as a group with 'the right and duty to participate in its own government'.[4] In the late thirteenth century, the tenants of Crumlin claimed to have held the farm of that manor since the reign of King John.[5] By holding the farm of the king for a yearly fee, the tenants had purchased their autonomy, and by Reynolds' definition, they were a community. Another indicator of community was groups forming for the purpose of negotiating with their overlords about issues that affected them all.[6] Evidence of

97 Gillespie, 'Small worlds', p. 198. 98 Otway-Ruthven, 'Norman settlement', p. 270. 99 Mark Hennessy, 'Manorial agriculture and settlement in early fourteenth-century Co. Tipperary', *Surveying Ireland's past: multidisciplinary essays in honour of Anngret Simms* (Dublin, 2004), p. 99. 1 Brian Graham, 'Foreword' in James Lyttleton and Tadhg O'Keeffe (eds), *The manor in medieval and early modern Ireland* (Dublin, 2005), p. 11. 2 Mark Bailey, *The English manor, c.1200–c.1500* (Manchester, 2002), pp 167–78. 3 Ibid., p. 2. 4 Susan Reynolds, *Kingdoms and communities in Western Europe, 900–1300* (2nd ed., Oxford, 1997), p. 102. 5 *CDI, 1285–92*, §855. 6 Reynolds, *Kingdoms and communities*, p. 110.

tenants on the royal manors in this study negotiating with the king as a group can be found in the petitions they sent to the crown.

The parish, along with the manor, was the most important unit of local juris-diction during the medieval period. Reynolds portrays the parish as a place where a concept of community developed, but it was just one of many layers of community.[7] The parish with its church did indeed promote a strong sense of community solidarity, but tenants of the manor were obliged to attend its court and it too played an important part in developing a sense of unity. This was particularly the case when the tenants held the pleas and perquisites of the court and could, more or less, run it autonomously. There are some problems with identifying the manor with the parish: for example, as already mentioned above, the manor of Cloncurry contained no less than four parishes. In the case of the royal manors under review, Newcastle Lyons contained two parishes: Newcastle itself and Kilmactalway. Clearly, in both these cases the manor and parish are not conterminous.

On the other hand, the other three manors in this study do appear to share the same boundaries as their respective parishes and the importance of the parish cannot be underestimated. The church in Newcastle Lyons, which is the best preserved of any that remain on the royal manors, is clear proof of how powerful a hold the church had on medieval society.[8] It was probably constructed at the beginning of the fifteenth century and was part of a religious building boom that gripped the whole of Europe in the aftermath of the Black Death. Like commu-nities elsewhere, the inhabitants of Newcastle Lyons were trying to appease a wrathful God and perhaps prevent further outbreaks of the plague.[9] The communities that built these churches and who were affected by calamitous events like the Black Death feature in many and varied records from the Middle Ages. The preceding paragraphs have identified the manorial community as a valid concept, and the sources that can help develop this idea of community in the royal manors are outlined below.

THE PRIMARY MATERIAL

As they were crown lands the manors in this study feature prominently in records emanating from the central administration. The fire that destroyed the Public Record Office of Ireland in 1922 took with it a significant portion of the state's medieval records. Undoubtedly, much of the original material relating to the royal manors was lost at this time. This fire was, however, just the latest

7 Ibid., p. 97. 8 O'Keeffe, 'Medieval architecture and the village of Newcastle Lyons', pp 45–61; Simms, 'Newcastle as a medieval settlement', pp 11–23; H.G. Leask, *Irish churches and monastic buildings*, 3 (Dundalk, 1960), pp 18–19. 9 Ole J. Benedictow, *The Black Death, 1346–1353: the complete history* (Woodbridge, 2004), p. 4.

episode in several centuries of neglect and loss of our archival heritage.[10] Fortunately, because the manors belonged to the crown, many records concerning them survive in the records of the administration based at Westminster. Some of these are published in calendar form including H.S. Sweetman's *Calendar of documents relating to Ireland*, which was translated and published between the years 1875–86. These five volumes contain most of the records relating to Ireland stored in the National Archives in Kew (TNA) dating from the invasion period up to 1307.[11] Additionally, material from the English chancery, like the patent and close rolls, has been published in calendar form by the former Public Records Office of London. Here too, material relating to the royal manors can be found and they are particularly useful with regard to grants made to individuals who were mainly based in England. It is the fine rolls, however, that are most relevant to this book as the appointment of royal officers associated with the royal manors, like the seneschal of the demesne, is frequently recorded in this source.

A substantial amount of unpublished material relating to these manors is found in TNA. For example, from the late thirteenth century up until the middle of the fifteenth century the rolls of the Irish exchequer were sent to London for audit and can be consulted in Kew. Though there are significant gaps in these rolls, particularly for the later period, much information on the royal manors is contained within them.[12] The Special Collections (SC) were put together in the late nineteenth century, in what was then the Public Records Office, and the material they contain mostly originate from the chancery and the exchequer.[13] SC 8 (Ancient Petitions) is particularly useful to the royal manors as it contains several petitions that either emanated from the manors or from individuals associated with the manors. These petitions often involved tenants asking for relief of their rent and were usually sent by the entire community. These documents are immensely valuable; nevertheless, they can also be problematic. The tenants of the royal manors sent these petitions during turbulent times and, consequently, they cannot be truly representative of their normal day-to-day lives. Moreover, it is also possible that the petitioners were sometimes exaggerating the severity of their situation, and as a result, these petitions must surely be treated with a healthy dose of scepticism.[14]

Records emanating from the chancery can be found in C 47 (Chancery Miscellanea) which contains, among other items, extents of land. It is a very

---

10 Philomena Connolly, *Medieval record sources* (Dublin, 2002), pp 9–10.   11 The National Archives at Kew (former PRO) will henceforth be called TNA.   12 *Admin. Ire.*, pp 52–7; idem, 'Irish revenue, 1278–1384', *PRIA*, 52C (1961–3), 87–100.   13 *SCSMI*, p. 229.   14 Philomena Connolly, 'Irish materials in the series of ancient petitions (SC8) in the Public Record Office, London', *Anal. Hib.*, 34 (1987), 1–106; www.nationalarchives.gov.uk/documentsonline/petitions.asp accessed 25 August 2010; W.M. Ormrod, Gwilym Dodd and Anthony Musson (eds), *Medieval petitions, grace and grievance* (Woodbridge, 2009), passim.

profitable source for records relating to the royal manors. The C 143 series are also chancery records, they mostly contain inquisitions, and they too are a useful source of information on the royal manors and their tenants. The exchequer records stored in the National Archives in Kew are another invaluable resource on the royal manors, particularly the E 101 series.[15] These rolls record revenues that flowed both in and out of the exchequer. The names of individual tenants on the royal manors who paid their rent into the exchequer are recorded in these rolls, and therefore they are immensely valuable in terms of establishing continuity of tenure – or lack thereof.

Aside from the original records located in the National Archives in Kew, some of the records that had been contained in the Public Records Office in Dublin at the time of its destruction were calendared.[16] Between 1810 and 1830, the Irish Record Commission undertook this calendaring of official records.[17] In 1828, *Rotulorum patentium et clausorum cancellariæ Hiberniæ calendarium*, a calendar of the Irish chancery rolls edited by Edward Tresham, was published.[18] This commission also calendared the memoranda rolls of the exchequer and plea rolls of the justiciar's court and common bench, which are now stored in the National Archives.[19] The Public Record office also published the pipe rolls in the yearly *Deputy keeper's reports* until 1922, and this source is particularly useful for evidence of the mounting debts of the royal manors in the early fourteenth century. The *Calendar of justiciary rolls* edited by James Mills is another valuable source and though these volumes mainly deal with criminal activity, they can be much more informative about society in the medieval period than some of the other material available.[20]

Other key printed sources that pre-date the destruction of the Four Courts in 1922 include J.T. Gilbert's *Historic and municipal documents of Ireland, 1172–1320* and his *Calendar of ancient records of Dublin*. These records, though primarily dealing with the city of Dublin, are extremely useful sources for the social history of the county as well. Chapter five will illustrate the close relationship between city and county and these municipal records help identify property in the city held by landholders on the manors, as well as providing information about civic offices held by royal tenants.

Ecclesiastical records can also prove useful. Many of the tenants on the royal manors often held lands from the archbishop of Dublin and other religious institutions. Sources like *Archbishop Alen's register* and *Christ Church deeds* can be used to identify where else royal tenants held land in Co. Dublin, as well as in the

15 TNA, E101/230/1–248/23 all originate from the Irish exchequer.   16 Now the National Archives of Ireland [NAI].   17 Margaret Griffith, 'The Irish record commission, 1810–30', *IHS*, 7 (1950), 17–38.   18 Tresham will undoubtedly be superseded by *CIRCLE*, which provides a reconstruction of letters issued by the Irish chancery throughout the later Middle Ages, http://chancery.tcd.ie/.   19 Connolly, *Medieval record sources*, pp 53–4.   20 *CJR*, passim.

city.[21] Though the bulk of the records used in this monograph address the manors and their respective tenants these people were parishioners too. The parish churches as 'records in stone', in Rodney Hilton's phrase, are the clearest evidence of a parochial community, and it is unfortunate that parish records for Newcastle Lyons, Kilmactalway, Saggart, Crumlin and Esker do not survive for the period of this study.[22] This is not to say that there is no evidence of parochial life though. Both parishes within the manor of Newcastle Lyons were prebends of St Patrick's, as were the churches of Crumlin and Saggart. Nonetheless, though these prebends belonged to St Patrick's Cathedral, the crown retained the right to bestow them on whomsoever it chose.[23] Those clerics working in the royal administration were most likely to benefit from these grants and this highlights the close relationship between the crown and clerical class, which is explored in this book.

The earliest extant parish records date to the late fifteenth century, and even those that do survive from the end of the Middle Ages do not concern the lands in this study.[24] Nonetheless, there is plentiful evidence of the spiritual lives of the inhabitants of the royal manors. Many, for example, donated to religious houses like the hospital of St John the Baptist.[25] Their wills also confirm that they were concerned with the wellbeing of their souls and honouring their dead. It is quite true that the best evidence we have of their piety are the parish churches and though this monograph depends mostly on the archival records to build up a picture of society on the royal manors the value of the material remains in the form of these monuments, tower-houses as well as churches, cannot be dismissed.

---

21 *CCD* are particularly useful as they include secular deeds found in the collections of the cathedral.   22 R.H. Hilton, *A medieval society: the West Midlands at the end of the thirteenth century* (Cambridge, 1983), p. 149; articles written about parish churches in the region include Máirín Ní Mharcaigh, 'The medieval parish churches of south-west County Dublin', *PRIA*, 97C (1997), 245–96; Valerie Twomey, 'St Mary's Church of Ireland parish church, Leixlip, Co. Kildare' in Linda Curran, Valerie Twomey, Patricia Donohoe and Suzanne Pegley (eds), *Aspects of Leixlip: four historical essays* (Dublin, 2001); E. Rynne, 'Excavation of a church site at Clondalkin, Co. Dublin', *JRSAI*, 97 (1967), 29–37.   23 Howard B. Clarke, 'External influences and relations, *c.*1220 to *c.*1500' in John Crawford and Raymond Gillespie (eds), *St Patrick's Cathedral, Dublin: a history* (Dublin, 2009), pp 88–9; Cotton, *Fasti ecclesiae Hibernicae*, pp 2–6, 133, 161, 188, 191.   24 Elizabeth FitzPatrick and Raymond Gillespie, 'Preface' in idem (eds), *The parish in medieval and early modern Ireland: community, territory and building* (Dublin, 2006), p. 16.   25 See, for example, *RHSJ*, pp 204–5.

2

The hinterland of Dublin: from Dyflinnarskíri to royal demesne, continuity and change

INTRODUCTION

This chapter examines the pre-invasion history of the lands dealt with in this study, to investigate their significance before they became English crown lands. The Meic Gilla Mo-Cholmóc family controlled this area before the invasion and after the coming of the English. The lands they held here were subsequently incorporated into the royal manor of Newcastle Lyons.[1] It is likely that these lands were just a small part of their former demesne. It was perhaps this earlier association with a royal dynasty that provided the impetus for the English crown to take control of these lands. The symbolic significance of the English king taking possession of the lands associated with the kingdom of Dublin should not be underestimated, and was undoubtedly patently obvious to the Irish and Ostmen communities who had previously controlled the area. Essentially, by staking his claim to Dublin, Henry II was establishing his right to rule the colony at large. Secondly, to understand fully the significance of the four royal manors comprising this study and establish why they were a distinct and separate entity within the greater royal demesne, it is important to examine this larger area and establish why King Henry II of England took these lands near Dublin into his own hands. The putative pre-invasion royal status of these lands was not the only reason Henry took a personal interest in them; it was also an extension of his policy of retaining and expanding his royal demesne in England.

The royal demesne that Henry took possession of in 1171 incorporated significantly more lands than the area encompassing the four royal manors of the Vale of Dublin formed during the reign of his son John. As well as the non-ecclesiastical lands in south Dublin, it also included much of north Co. Dublin and a significant proportion of modern-day Cos Wicklow and Kildare. Hence, the demesne as a whole, rather than just the royal manors of this study, is dealt with initially. The economic potential of the city situated in the heart of this newly acquired royal demesne indubitably influenced the crown's decision to retain a hinterland around it. Therefore, the relationship between the city and the royal demesne is examined in this chapter. Certainly, the larger towns and

1 MacCotter, *Medieval Ireland*, p. 163.

cities of England were generating a considerable amount of revenue for the crown by the thirteenth century and the king was well aware of the economic potential of his new Irish cities. The fortunes of the royal demesne were intimately tied up with the fortunes of the nearby city of Dublin and it is possible that many of the privileges associated with the city were eventually extended to the lands belonging to the crown in its hinterland.

THE HINTERLAND OF DUBLIN IN THE PRE-INVASION PERIOD

In the centuries prior to the invasion, Irish kings had come to recognize the growing importance of Dublin. From the tenth century onwards, anyone who had aspirations towards the high-kingship also had to be master of Dublin for his claims to be taken seriously. Moreover, it was important to control not only the Hiberno-Scandinavian (or Ostman) town, but the area surrounding it too. The influence of the Ostmen who held the city of Dublin before the invasion extended far into the hinterland. The Mac Torcaill rulers of Dublin held lands as far south as Clonkeen and granted them to Christ Church.[2] When provincial kings controlled Dublin, they controlled the hinterland too. For example, Diarmait Mac Murchada bestowed Baldoyle on All Hallows sometime between 1162 and 1166 and he did so because of the influence he had over Dublin at this time.[3] Both of these grants to the church suggest that the authority of the rulers of Dublin permeated deep into the settlement's hinterland. Thus, when, in the winter of 1171–2, Henry II took possession of not only the city of Dublin but also the area surrounding it as well, he was upholding a long tradition and delivering a clear message that he was now in control.

The rulers of the Dublin region had owned the territory that was later transformed into royal demesne for centuries. After the Vikings had settled in Dublin, the area in the immediate vicinity of the settlement became known as Dyflinnarskíri, which encroached on the ancestral lands of the Uí Dúnchada. This family was the final dynasty to rule what is now south-west Co. Dublin before the invasion.[4] They were lineal descendants of the Uí Dúnlainge, who were the most powerful dynasty in Leinster from the seventh to the eleventh century.[5] They were based at Liamain, which was near the border of Co. Kildare close to where the royal manor of Newcastle Lyons would later be located, and their influence seems to have stretched from here eastwards to the River Dodder.[6] The area under their control encompassed all of the lands that would later be formed into royal manors.

2 *CCD*, p. 43, §44.   3 Marie Therese Flanagan, *Irish royal charters: texts and contexts* (Oxford, 2005), pp 64–85.   4 Bradley, 'The interpretation of Scandinavian settlement', p. 56; Smyth, *Celtic Leinster*, p. 44; MacCotter, *Medieval Ireland*, pp 162–4.   5 Smyth, *Celtic Leinster*, p. 39.
6 Ibid., p. 43.

The territory of the Uí Chellaig Chualann was later formed into Okelly, one of the royal manors in the mountains near Dublin and the one that was closest to the four royal manors in this study. The Uí Dúnchada were probably overlords of this area at the time of the English invasion, but remnants of the Uí Chellaig Chualann dynasty still existed in the form of the Uí Amalgada. The Uí Chellaig Chualann were probably originally settled on the lands of the Uí Dúnchada, but were forced southwards towards the mountains when this dynasty pushed into south Dublin from their ancestral home in what is now Co. Kildare. James Mills assumed that Uí Chellaig Chualann was situated south of Tallaght, but, based on place-name and documentary evidence, Kenneth Nicholls established that this territory not only took in these lands but stretched further east as far as Ballinteer and Balally.[7] A Hamon Hohauelgan held land in Okelly in 1225 and his name would suggest that he was a descendant of the Uí Amalgada. Balally, or Ballyhawyl as it was known in governmental records of the post-invasion period, was called after this family, and Hamon himself seems to have given Edmondstown its name.[8] Just like the Meic Gilla Mo-Cholmóc family, the Uí Amalgada adapted to each subsequent wave of settlement and remained landowners in the area, at least until the late thirteenth century. When the royal manor of Okelly vanished from the records, much of its territory was lost to the Irish, but some areas, like Ballinteer, became outer granges of the manor of Saggart.[9]

In the aftermath of the arrival and settlement of the Vikings, these Irish septs were compelled to pay rent – or tribute – to the new Scandinavian kings of Dublin. A text, possibly of the eleventh century, preserved in the Book of Leinster, refers to a tribute that was imposed on the Uí Dúnchada.[10] It describes how the kings of Dublin imposed arbitrary tributes and rents upon the people and church of Fir Chualann. Nicholls believes that this tract indicates that this area was comprised of Uí Briúin, Uí Chellaig and Uí Théig and that it belonged to the Uí Dunchada, as did Uí Gabla and their own ancestral lands. Much of this substantial area must have been absorbed into Dyflinnarskíri, catastrophically affecting the fortunes of this dynasty. The tract preserved in the Book of Leinster informs us that the cows, boats and other stipends that had previously been paid to the provincial kings and lords of the district were now being paid to the king of Dublin.[11]

From at least the mid-eleventh century, Dublin came to the attention of

7 Mills, 'Norman settlement', 170; K.W. Nicholls, 'Three topographical notes', *Peritia*, 5 (1986), 411; Ballinteer was an outer grange of the royal manor of Saggart in the fourteenth century: *RDKPRI*, 45, p. 56. 8 Nicholls, 'Topographical notes', 412. 9 See introduction for further discussion. 10 Perhaps most conveniently consulted in John Gilbert, *A history of the city of Dublin*, 1, appendix 1 (Dublin, 1854), p. 407; but, for the authoritative edition, see R.I. Best, Osborn Bergin, M.A. O' Brien and Anne O'Sullivan (eds), *The Book of Leinster* (Dublin, 1954–83). 11 K.W. Nicholls, 'The land of the Leinstermen', *Peritia*, 3 (1984), 538; Gilbert, *History of Dublin*, p. 407.

powerful Irish kings who aspired to the high kingship. From this point on, more often than not the king, or 'overking', of Dublin was the son of whichever Irish king was in the ascendant at the time, rather than a local Ostman ruler. Even when the city did have a Norse king, he usually ruled under the protection of an Irish magnate, and thus it is possible that Norse influence in the hinterland was curtailed. This process probably started during the reign of Diarmait mac Máel na mBó, king of Leinster. In 1052, he attacked Dublin, and when the Ostman king fled, he took the kingship himself.[12] The political landscape of the area changed once he established himself in Dublin, as the Ostmen were henceforth no longer just dealing with the local dynasties.

Over the next century, the kingship of Dublin passed between the kings of Leinster, Munster and Connacht.[13] By the time of the invasion, Dublin was intrinsically tied to the concept of high-kingship, as in effect no king could claim the role unless he controlled this area. There were also more mundane reasons why Dublin was a valuable asset to any ruler and, in this regard, in terms of economic value, the hinterland was as important as the town itself. Though the town, with its warriors and its fleet, was what interested the Irish kings, without the hinterland to supply it, the settlement could not have existed. Additionally, many of those whom we would regard as the Ostmen of Dublin must have lived, not in the town but in the hinterland, and supported themselves through farming and related activities: hence, even though most of the evidence refers to Dublin as if to the town alone, this should not negate the importance of Dyflinnarskíri.

FROM DYFLINNARSKÍRI TO ROYAL DEMESNE: CONTINUITY AND CHANGE

By taking possession of the lands around Dublin, the king of England was demonstrating continuity. This was not only because, by this time, precedent had established that whoever ruled Dublin was frequently acknowledged as the most powerful ruler in Ireland, but because this was also the practice in England. In the aftermath of the Conquest, William I took over the *terra regis* of Edward the Confessor, as well as the territories of King Harold;[14] this was not because he needed to hold these lands personally (he had, after all, just gained a kingdom), but it conveyed the message that they were his by right.

In Dublin, continuity can be discerned in the patterns of settlement, which

12 Duffy, 'Irishmen and Islesmen', 94; Donnchadh Ó Corráin, 'The career of Diarmait mac Mael na mBó', *Journal of the Old Wexford Society*, 3 (1970–1), 22–5; 4 (1972–3), 17–24; James Lydon, *The lordship of Ireland in the Middle Ages* (Dublin, 1972; 2nd ed., Dublin, 2003), p. 17. 13 See Duffy, 'Irishmen and Islesmen', passim, for a full account of these events. 14 Wolffe, *Royal demesne*, p. 34.

in many cases appear to have existed before the invasion. At this time, the archbishop of Dublin was already in possession of Clondalkin, Rathcoole and Tallaght,[15] which represents a large portion of modern-day south Co. Dublin; the majority of the remaining lands here were later formed into the royal manors. The fact that the aforementioned manors already seemed to be defined units of land leaves one with the impression that a system at least akin to the manorial system was already in place. It could be argued that, by the early twelfth century, an embryonic form of the structure traditionally, and nowadays controversially, referred to as the 'feudal' system existed in Ireland, or at least in the parts of the country most exposed to outside influence.[16] These areas appear to have been developing along the lines of the rest of Western Europe, both in social structure and in land tenure.[17] In other words, the inhabitants of Ireland did not live in isolation and they were not impervious to outside influences.

The secular lands in south Dublin, which seem to have been in the hands of the Meic Gilla Mo-Cholmóc family and the Meic Turcaill, the latter being the last Ostman rulers of Dublin, were probably formed into units similar to those that belonged to the archbishop. Certainly, those who were granted lands after the invasion seem to have gained possession of pre-existing divisions of land. Their units of landholding already had names, which would imply that they were not moving into virgin territory. When the Normans moved into England, it was already organized into shires and boroughs, and they felt no need to change this structure significantly.[18] Hence, it is more than likely that they respected the land divisions they found in Ireland as well; after all, they had no reason to change a system and structure that was presumably working effectively.

At the time of the English invasion of Ireland, the administrative system in England was still in its developmental phase. England's new Norman rulers had adopted some elements of the Anglo-Saxon administrative system, but the organization of government was still somewhat fluid. It was also quite small when compared to subsequent centuries. It is likely that they did not arrive in Ireland with a ready-made system of administration to impose on the native population. Rather than it being simply a case of imposing a system of their own on their new acquisitions, they probably made use of the structures that were already in place. Generally, manors in Ireland were much larger than those found in England,[19] but the fact that those in the vicinity of Dublin were smaller and closer in size to English manors surely is an indication that this area was much more heavily settled with English colonists than any other part of the country.

---

15 Otway-Ruthven, 'The mediaeval church lands of Co. Dublin', p. 57. 16 For the debate on feudalism, see Susan Reynolds, *Fiefs and vassals* (Oxford, 1994), pp 1–16. 17 Kevin Down, 'Colonial society and economy' in *NHI*, ii, p. 441. 18 W.L. Warren, *The governance of Norman and Angevin England, 1086–1272* (London, 1987), p. 25. 19 Edmund Curtis, 'Rental of the manor of Lisronagh, 1333, and notes on "betagh" tenure in medieval Ireland', *PRIA*, 43C (1936), 63.

Their organization and management, however, were influenced by the conditions with which their new owners were faced. Mills believed that the new owners of the land did not have to clear and lay out their property like colonists, but that it was already settled and occupied.[20] Therefore, on a day-to-day level, in some senses at least, things simply carried on as they always had.

Another indication of continuity is that the betagh class did not disappear after the invasion. Many historians from the first half of the twentieth century, like Edmund Curtis and A.J. Otway-Ruthven, made parallels between the betagh class to be found in Ireland and the villein class that existed in England. When the Normans invaded England in the eleventh century, much of the native population was repressed into this servile class, and a sharp distinction developed between the villeins, who were tied to the land, and freemen.[21] The question is whether the betagh class in Ireland was inspired by the villeinage system in England, or did they develop independently of each other?

The conditions of servitude for the betaghs may well have been similar to those of villeins across the Irish Sea,[22] but this does not mean that they shared a common origin. Curtis certainly believed that the betagh class existed before 1170 and Mac Niocaill and others have further advanced our understanding of what was meant by the term betagh in pre-invasion Ireland.[23] Nonetheless, the betagh class of the post-conquest period bears little similarity to its pre-invasion counterparts. This word appears to have been used very loosely by the English colonists and it is likely that it meant little more to them than 'tenant' or 'client'. Gradually, the term betagh became associated with the Irish who had remained in the conquered areas after the invasion, and this group, by and large, was comprised of the native peasantry. The betaghs on the royal manor of Okelly, as well as the royal manors of Othee and Obrun in modern-day Co. Wicklow, are mentioned in the pipe roll of 1228:[24] they paid £8 10s. 4d. in rent and also gave food at Christmas. Continuity in how the land was organized and the continuous existence of a native Irish peasantry on the royal demesne of Dublin suggest that the changes were not totally unsettling. Moreover, the fact that the Meic Gilla Mo-Cholmóc family was not immediately moved off its landholdings around Newcastle would have made the transition from one rule to another after the invasion less tumultuous than it otherwise could have been.

---

20 Mills, 'Norman settlement', 174.   **21** Gearóid Mac Niocaill, 'The origins of the betagh', *Irish Jurist*, new ser., 1 (1966), 298.   **22** Liam Price, 'The origin of the word betagius', *Ériu*, 20 (1966), 185.   **23** Curtis, 'Rental of the manor of Lisronagh', 64; the betagh class are explored further in ch. 6, below.   **24** *RDKPRI*, 35, p. 21.

HENRY II AND STRONGBOW

When Henry II arrived in Ireland on 17 October 1171,[25] his immediate concern was to curb the growing power of his vassal Richard de Clare, better known to history as Strongbow. Retaining the city of Dublin and its hinterland was one of the methods used to rein in Strongbow, to prevent him from using it to enhance his own power and stop him growing too independent of the crown. Henry II was undoubtedly concerned when Strongbow went over to Ireland at the request of Diarmait Mac Murchada. His marriage to Diarmait's daughter Aoife and the promise of Leinster along with its growing Ostman towns of Dublin, Wexford and, indeed, Waterford in adjacent Munster, made him a formidable threat.[26] Additionally, Henry mistrusted Strongbow because he had sided with King Stephen in the English Civil War. It was almost certainly for this reason that Henry did not recognize his title of earl of Pembroke; during the reign of King Stephen, for instance, Strongbow was referred to as *comes de Pembroc* in official sources, but this title was not used at all during the first half of Henry's reign.[27]

Thus, it would appear that Strongbow was an ineffectual player on the political scene for much of Henry's reign. Very little is known about his career in the two decades between the death of his father Gilbert Fitz Gilbert and his meeting with Mac Murchada, though he did possess substantial landholdings in England, as well as the Welsh marcher lordship of Strigoil.[28] According to Giraldus Cambrensis, 'he had a great name rather than great prospects'.[29] He had obviously gained very little from the English king and consequently he had very little to lose by trying his luck in Ireland. Henry must have realized that he had given him very few reasons to remain loyal if he did succeed in establishing himself in Leinster. In fact, on the death of Diarmait Mac Murchada in May 1171, Strongbow seemed willing to hold Leinster under the high-king Ruaidrí Ua Conchobair, but he failed to gain formal recognition from the high-king for his Irish lands.[30] Ua Conchobair was only prepared to allow him to hold the Ostman towns of Dublin, Wexford and Waterford.[31] Of course, it was easy for Ruaidrí to offer what was never his to give in the first place, but that is not to say that he did not recognize the strategic importance of these settlements. He did lay siege to Dublin after the death of Diarmait Mac Murchada, though he was not successful in dislodging the English. The importance of these towns was not lost on Henry II either, though he perhaps showed more wisdom than the high-

---

25 G.H. Orpen, *Ireland under the Normans* (4 vols, Oxford, 1911–20), 1, p. 255; Curtis, *Medieval Ireland*, p. 57. **26** Lydon, *Lordship*, pp 31, 41. **27** Orpen, *Normans*, 1, p. 89; Robin Frame, *Colonial Ireland* (Dublin, 1981), p. 7; Lydon, *Lordship*, p. 34; Mary Therese Flanagan, *Irish society, Anglo-Norman settlers, Angevin kingship* (Oxford, 1989), p. 114. **28** Orpen, *Normans*, 1, p. 88; Davies, *Domination and conquest*, p. 33. **29** Giraldus, *Expugnatio*, p. 55. **30** Flanagan, *Irish society*, p. 119. **31** Ibid., p. 168; see also Frame, *Colonial Ireland*, p. 10; Lydon, *Lordship*, p. 39; Davies, *Domination and conquest*, p. 36.

king in his decision to retain them. In fact, he and Ruaidrí had a similar problem insofar as neither of them could fully contain Strongbow's Irish ambitions. Henry undoubtedly realized that, given the opportunity, it was not entirely beyond the realms of possibility that Strongbow could use the Ostman fleets to try to recover Pembroke, a lordship to which he had a claim since 1154.[32]

The English king wasted no time in coming to Ireland and the day after his arrival Strongbow submitted to him and in return for surrendering his acquisitions to the king the lordship of Leinster was granted to him for the service of one hundred knights.[33] In an attempt to limit Strongbow's power, Henry retained Dublin and its adjacent territories, as well as Wexford and Waterford. He also confiscated his castles.[34] By taking control of the castles of Leinster himself, Henry indicated how little he trusted Strongbow. This was no more than a short-term solution, however, and eventually Strongbow did regain control of these castles. Henry granted the lordship of Meath to Hugh de Lacy and, while it is possible that this grant was implemented to provide a counterbalance to Strongbow, and limit the extent of his authority in Ireland, it is more likely that it was done to protect Dublin against attacks from Irish kings.[35] Bearing in mind how important the possession of Dublin had become to the concept of high-kingship, the English king must have anticipated that the Irish would try to take it back. In addition, though Tigernán Ua Ruairc had submitted to Henry during his visit to Ireland, his proximity to Dublin meant that he still posed a very real threat to the security of the king's demesne. Clearly, by installing de Lacy in this area, Henry was defraying the cost of maintaining an army to protect the settlement onto his vassal.[36]

Time was to prove that Henry had as much cause to mistrust Hugh de Lacy as Strongbow, especially after he married Ruaidrí Ua Conchobair's daughter. Indeed, it is possible that the king suspected de Lacy of aiming for the high-kingship.[37] Both Leinster and Meath were immediately adjacent to the royal demesne surrounding Dublin, however, and the king needed these lords to help defend his lands. Before he left Ireland, Henry made Hugh de Lacy *custos* of Dublin and, to enable him to carry out the functions of this office, he was granted fees within the royal demesne.[38] De Lacy, therefore, was arguably the

32 Flanagan, *Irish society*, p. 121.   33 Orpen, *Normans*, 1, p. 259; Curtis, *Medieval Ireland*, p. 57; Lydon, *Lordship*, pp 62, 64.   34 Giraldus, *Expugnatio*, p. 89.   35 A.J. Otway-Ruthven, *A history of medieval Ireland, with an introduction by Kathleen Hughes* (Dublin, 1968; repr. corr. London, 1980), pp 52–5; Michael Dolley, *Anglo-Norman Ireland, c.1100–1318* (Dublin, 1972), p. 70; Lydon, *Lordship*, p. 47; Frame, *Colonial Ireland*, p. 15; Flanagan, *Irish society*, p. 224. For two recent opposing views on Henry's 'divide and conquer' policy, see Peter Crooks '"Divide and rule": factionalism as royal policy in the lordship of Ireland, 1171–1265', *Peritia*, 19 (2005), 263–307; C.T. Veach, 'Henry II's grant of Meath to Hugh de Lacy in 1172: a reassessment', *Ríocht na Mídhe*, 18 (2007), 67–94.   36 Veach, 'Henry II's grant of Meath', 74–5.   37 Lydon, *Lordship*, p. 55; Davies, *Domination and conquest*, p. 30; Crooks '"Divide and rule"', 276; C.T. Veach, 'A question of timing: Walter de Lacy's seisin of Meath, 1189–94', *PRIA*, 106C (2009), 166.   38 *Gormanston reg.*, pp 6, 177.

first recipient of royal patronage from the king's demesne lands in Dublin. Marie Therese Flanagan speculates that when Strongbow later became justiciar of Ireland, he too was most likely assigned the same fees.[39] Subsequently, the lands within the royal demesne, excluding the later royal manors, were divided into small knight's fees and, in return, the holders of these lands were expected to muster when needed to defend the city of Dublin against attack.[40] Undoubtedly, this military obligation was quickly transmuted into a financial payment.

The most powerful landowner in Dublin, aside from the crown, was the archbishop of Dublin and, after the death of Laurence O'Toole, this office was usually held by one of the king's loyal servants. Since he owed his office to the king, he did not present the same threat as a secular lord. In theory – though not always in practice – as long as the king gave the archbishopric to one of his own followers, he could depend on his absolute loyalty. Moreover, because the position of archbishop was not hereditary, its holder had little to gain by not remaining faithful.[41] Although Henry had a volatile relationship with the church, he would have considered it as his duty to protect church lands. By establishing a presence in Dublin, the crown would have been in a position to help uphold the archbishop's rights as well as protect his lands. Indeed, it was probably of benefit to both of them, because the king would have the archbishop at hand to help administer or at least keep a watchful eye on his lands. Up to the end of the twelfth century, the only appointments of non-Irish bishops to positions in the Irish church occurred at Dublin, Glendalough and Meath; one diocese was located in the heart of the royal demesne and the other two flanked it. This is surely an indication of the strategic importance of this area to the crown.[42]

COLONIZING DUBLIN

Introduction
By retaining a royal demesne in Ireland, the king was providing land for some of the lesser men – including churchmen, merchants and government officials – who came over in the aftermath of the invasion. In order for the colonization process to be a success, loyal English subjects were needed to settle there. The potential benefits and privileges attached to being a royal tenant must have

---

39 Flanagan, *Irish society*, p. 294. 40 Mary Bateson, 'Irish exchequer memoranda of the Reign of Edward I', *EHR*, 18 (1903), 501–7. 41 Though the archbishops were dependent on the king's favour, they did occasionally defy his authority. For example, the first English archbishop of Dublin, John Cumin, went into exile because of a dispute over royal forest rights on his lands: Aubrey Gwynn, 'Archbishop John Cumin', *Reportorium Novum*, 1 (1955–6), 285–310. 42 Dolley, *Anglo-Norman Ireland*, p. 88.

attracted many colonists to Dublin. Henry II could not really afford to give Ireland the same level of attention that William the Conqueror gave to England in the aftermath of the conquest, and this is probably why he did not retain a larger area than a handful of urban settlements and their hinterlands. These, however, were the areas where colonists were most likely to settle. The English king was never likely to be a regular presence in Ireland, and therefore its conquest was always going to be different from that of England in the previous century. William I of England was also duke of Normandy, but he was able to divide his time between both his dominions. Henry, as head of the Angevin Empire, did not have this luxury. His lands in Ireland undoubtedly featured low in his list of priorities and, at best, he viewed it as an inheritance for a younger son. It was not until the reign of his son John, who succeeded in losing most of the English crown's French territories, that Ireland suddenly took on a new-found importance. It was also at this time that the royal manors in the Liffey valley came into being.

Although Henry was at the head of a large empire, he lived in an age when direct personal supervision was still an essential element of monarchical rule. It was for this reason that medieval kings constantly travelled around their lands, as their authority could only be enforced through their personal presence.[43] By taking control of Dublin and its hinterland, Henry could at least place his royal agents in Ireland to collect revenues, and administer authority and justice over the colonists. It would also ensure that his enemies could not use it as a place of refuge, or as a back door to an invasion of England.

The English king was keenly aware that whoever had control of the hinterland of Dublin would ultimately be master of the city as well. Another way of ensuring royal influence over the city was the introduction of a sympathetic population, and Henry achieved this by giving the city of Dublin to his men of Bristol.[44] Yet, they were not left completely to their own devices because, by appointing Hugh de Lacy bailiff, the king clearly intended to keep a close eye on the city. Later, in 1215, King John sold the farm of Dublin to its citizens but, undoubtedly, the lord of Ireland was receiving revenues from the city long before this date. Just because the king granted the farm to the citizens did not mean that he completely gave up his interests in the town; for example, the crown retained jurisdiction of the River Liffey, even though it ran through the bounds of the city. Moreover, the king could still technically intervene in the business of the

---

43 For discussion on the level of intervention by the Angevin kings in Ireland, Scotland and Wales, see Davies, *Domination and conquest*, pp 66–87; for England itself, see Judith A. Green, *The government of England under Henry I* (Cambridge, 1986), p. 5. 44 *CARD*, 1, frontispiece; *HMDI*, p. 1; Gearóid Mac Niocaill, *Na Buirgéisí, XII–XV aois* (Dublin, 1964), pp 75–6; Howard B. Clarke, 'The 1192 charter of liberties and the beginnings of Dublin's municipal life', *DHR*, 46:1 (1993), 6–7; James Lydon, 'Dublin in transition: from Ostman town to English borough' in Seán Duffy (ed.), *Medieval Dublin*, 2 (Dublin, 2001), p. 128; see also Otway-Ruthven, *Medieval Ireland*, p. 50.

city; for instance, the four pleas of the crown had to be heard by a royal justice, and he retained such local entitlements as the right to requisition two butts of wine from each ship that docked in the city.[45] As was the case in London throughout most of the twelfth century, the royal administration could choose the reeve of the city. Even when the reeve was elected by the citizens of the town, he was still expected to carry out the king's orders.[46] It may well be that, prior to the invasion, the Meic Turcaill performed a function not dissimilar to that of a reeve. In the 1140s, Ragnall mac Turcaill was the head of the family, but while several annals describe him as *rí Gall Átha Cliath* (king of the foreigners of Dublin), the *Annals of the Four Masters* called him *mór mhaor*, which translates as 'great steward'. At the time of Ragnall's death, Ottar was king of Dublin, and therefore Ragnall clearly held some lesser position to him. The office of steward is mentioned in the annals from the ninth century onwards. It began as an ecclesiastical office, but eventually became a secular one too. One of the main functions of this office was to collect tax.[47] During the twelfth century, this office grew to such an extent that the steward became a powerful lord in his own right, often in charge of a fortress. His responsibilities appear to have been quite similar to those of a reeve.

The sheriff and the county
As an aid to colonization and enforcing the king's rule, the hinterland of Dublin was formed into a shire that inevitably gained its own sheriff. Therefore, even though the city itself was not directly in royal hands, the crown's representative was always near at hand, ready to uphold and defend the king's rights.[48] Though sheriffs had existed in England during the Anglo-Saxon period, they became much more powerful and influential in the aftermath of the conquest.[49] They were responsible for collecting the king's revenue, and were also in charge of the judicial and military activities within their respective counties; hence these men were substantially responsible for the financial wellbeing of the crown. The existence of a county court in Dublin in the 1190s suggests that there was certainly a sheriff there by this date, as one institution was synonymous with the other.[50] Many of the sheriffs in England were significant landowners, and this was often the case in Dublin as well. For example, admittedly at a much later

45 Seán Duffy, 'Town and crown: the kings of England and their city of Dublin' in Michael Prestwich, Richard Britnell and Robin Frame (eds), *Thirteenth century England, X: proceedings of the Durham conference, 2003* (Woodbridge, 2005), pp 99, 113. 46 Susan Reynolds, *An introduction to the history of English medieval towns* (Oxford, 1977), p. 103; Duffy, 'Town and crown', p. 97. 47 Duffy, 'Irishmen and Islesmen', 122. 48 Duffy, 'Town and crown', p. 113; see also Dolley, *Anglo-Norman Ireland*, p. 70; Lydon, *Lordship*, p. 48. 49 Astin Lane Poole, *Domesday to Magna Carta* (Oxford, 1951), pp 387–8. 50 *CDI, 1171–1251*, §116; Gerard McGrath, 'The shiring of Ireland and the 1297 parliament' in James Lydon (ed.), *Law and disorder in thirteenth-century Ireland: the Dublin parliament of 1297* (Dublin, 1997), p. 109; Green, *Government of England*, p. 119.

date, Wolfran Barnwell had possession of Drimnagh and Terenure,[51] and he was both sheriff and escheator of Co. Dublin at different times throughout his career, and in 1333–4 was made *custos pacis* of Dublin.[52] The fact that the office of sheriff was almost always granted to an important landowner from the locality suggests that the crown was willing to accommodate local interests and local men.

The emerging merchant class in Dublin

Retaining a royal demesne around the city also served as a means of protecting the citizens from both hostile Gaelic Irish and overbearing Anglo-Irish lords, as well as providing them with much-needed land. There was quite possibly a large contingent of English merchants resident in Dublin prior to the invasion,[53] and Henry knew that it was worth his while to protect these men and those that would come over in the aftermath of the invasion. This mercantile class ensured the economic viability of the colony, but they could prove to be very influential politically too. Certainly, in London by the mid-twelfth century, the merchant class were becoming increasingly wealthy and they had a fleet of ships at their disposal. This gave them political power that was reflected in the privileges and concessions granted to them by the crown. Stephen, who was helped by the Londoners in his bid to secure the crown, was particularly generous to them.[54]

Though the establishment and maintenance of a merchant class was vital to the economic success of Dublin, as well as being an important factor in the colonization of the city, their importance went far beyond this, and, just like their counterparts in London, they proved important to the crown on other levels too. Obviously, their fleets provided a link between Ireland and England, and the officials who came over to administer the colony probably travelled on merchant ships. Many merchants appear to have been very wealthy individuals and their usefulness to the crown as a source of revenue surely explains some of the early grants of lands on the royal demesne in the hinterland of the city to men with mercantile interests.The guild merchant roll provides evidence of a steady influx of merchants into Dublin in the aftermath of the invasion.[55] Some had a close association with the crown. For example, Robert Ruffus, who was responsible for procuring supplies for John's first expedition to Ireland, was granted the manor of Ballymadun in north Dublin.[56] Ruffus was one of John's serjeants, but it is also possible that he had mercantile interests and the evidence would seem to indicate that Elias Cordewener and his son Roger, to whom the manor descended, were also merchants.[57]

A merchant who may have been among this first wave of post-conquest

51 *CDI, 1171–1251*, §680.   52 James Mills (ed.), *Account roll of the priory of Holy Trinity, Dublin, 1337–1346* (Dublin, 1996), p. 176.   53 Lydon, 'Dublin in transition', p. 140. 54 Reynolds, *English towns*, p. 104.   55 *DGMR*, passim.   56 *CDI, 1171–1251*, §§73, 939. 57 *IEMI*, p. 5; Roger served as the first mayor of Bristol in 1215.

settlers was a beneficiary of land on the royal manors and is illustrative of the power and influence held by this class. William Fitz John of Harptree, who held Crumlin in 1216 – and indeed it is likely that he or perhaps his father held lands on this manor since the time of the invasion or shortly after – appears to have been a descendant of the owners of Richmont Castle in Harptree Coombe.[58] During the Civil War, King Stephen captured this castle from its owner, whose name also happened to be William Fitz John. William, son of William Fitz John, made the church of East Harptree in Somerset a prebendary in June 1174.[59] At the time of the conquest of Ireland, William Harptree, son of William and grandson of John granted the church of Crumlin to his clerk Robert.[60] He may be the same man who owned the grant of the prebend of East Harptree. Harptree lies just fifteen miles (24km) south of Bristol, and it is possible that William had mercantile interests here. This is supported by the enrolment of William Harptree in the Dublin guild merchant roll at some point before 1222.[61] In 1213, he offered to pay the enormous sum of four hundred marks and four palfreys to hold William Carew's Irish and English lands, presumably until his heir came of age.[62] As well as holding lands in Berkshire, Carew inherited the manor of Odrone in Carlow from his uncle Raymond le Gros, who was a key figure in the invasion half a century earlier.[63] Fitz John was in arrears of £177 12*d.* of this sum five years later and had not delivered the horses he owed either.[64]

The mote of Castlemore near Tullow built by Gros is likely to have been held by Fitz John, but it is not clear if this was the same castle of which he was dispossessed of in 1224.[65] In this year, William Marshal took a castle belonging to him along with several castles belonging to Hugh de Lacy.[66] This suggests that Fitz John was one of de Lacy's associates and held lands of him, though the exact nature of the connection, if it existed at all, is unclear. Like many barons, de Lacy, the dispossessed earl of Ulster, had fallen foul of King John, but naturally assumed that his lands would be restored after the king's death.[67] When this did not happen, de Lacy grew impatient and spent 1223 ravaging Meath, intent on having his lands restored.[68] The Earl Marshal was appointed justiciar and was dispatched to Ireland to deal with the troublesome baron. If Fitz John was an associate of de Lacy, it would have put him in an uncomfortable position, as William Marshal was his overlord for the lands that had previously belonged to William Carew.[69] Fitz John's betrayal would have been considered serious and

58 *CDI, 1171–1251*, §703. **59** 'Prebendaries: East Harptree', *Fasti ecclesiae Anglicanae, 1066–1300*, 7 (Bath and Wells, 2001), pp 52–3. **60** *Alen's reg.*, p. 37; John D'Alton, *A history of the county of Dublin* (Dublin, 1838), p. 695. **61** *DGMR*, p. 47. **62** *CDI, 1171–1251*, §484: Sweetman uses a variation of spellings for this individual including Carr', Carrio and Karrio, but he is undoubtedly William Carew who died in 1213. **63** Orpen, *Normans*, 1, p. 387. **64** *CDI, 1171–1251*, §864. **65** G.H. Orpen, 'The castle of Raymond Le Gros at Fodredunolan', *JRSAI*, 36 (1906), 368–82. **66** *CDI, 1171–1251*, §1204. **67** See Orpen, *Normans*, 2, pp 251–6. **68** For a detailed account of these events, see Orpen, *Normans*, 3, pp 37–48. **69** Ibid., p. 148.

not one that the Earl Marshal could easily overlook. The confiscated castle was not identified, but Orpen believes that the group of castles taken by Marshal – of which Fitz John's was one – was in Meath and hence it is possible that he held lands here too.[70] William Fitz John of Harptree is absent from the records after this date, but Richard Harptree who was enrolled in Dublin's guild merchant roll in 1241–2 may have been his heir.[71]

Early patronage

When Strongbow gained possession of Dublin, he granted lands in its vicinity to some of the men who had accompanied him. Many of those who came over with Strongbow came from relatively humble or obscure origins. He granted to Walter Ridelesford substantial lands in south Co. Dublin and, though he was acting on behalf of the crown, it is not implausible that he was merely re-granting lands he had already given him before Henry's arrival.[72] Ridelesford was such an obscure character that Orpen could not trace his origins; Brooks was more successful, but his investigations established that the family was better known, and altogether more successful, in Ireland than England.[73] Rewarding men like Ridelesford would have meant they were tremendously beholden to the king; certainly to a much greater extent than men who already had substantial landholdings and needed patronage less than these 'made men'. Since Ridelesford held the lands of Henry rather than Strongbow, it was less likely that he would support the earl if he had any designs on setting up an independent lordship in Ireland.

Henry and future English kings would use lands in the royal demesne to reward followers and gain support. One of the earliest grants in south Dublin was to Mac Gilla Mo-Cholmóc,[74] at Newcastle Lyons. He had been lord there before the invasion and, as son-in-law of Diarmait Mac Murchada and brother-in-law of Strongbow, was well connected. He had already attacked the settlement at Dublin before Henry's arrival; therefore, the king may have thought it wise to keep him on his side. The land around Newcastle Lyons given to Mac Gilla Mo-Cholmóc became part of the royal manor during the reign of John.[75] By this time, the family had inevitably become more anglicized and, as is well known, appear to have abandoned their Gaelic surname for the less cumbersome *filius Dermoti* (Fitz Dermot), and they remained prominent in Dublin for several generations.

---

70 Ibid., p. 44.   71 *DGMR*, p. 78.   72 Brooks, 'The de Ridelesfords', 116.   73 Ibid., 115–16.
74 Orpen, *Normans*, 1, p. 368.   75 *CDI, 1171–1251*, §569.

THE INTRODUCTION OF MANORS AND ROYAL ADMINISTRATION

The standard unit of land management in the parts of Ireland occupied by the English was the manor, and they were often situated on the site of an old settlement centre.[76] The king and his subjects used this manorial organization as a means of establishing English administrative, economic and agricultural practices in Ireland. Organizing the royal demesne into manors meant the introduction of officials like reeves and bailiffs, who would have been responsible for managing the farms and collecting the rents. As mentioned above, Henry made Hugh de Lacy bailiff of Dublin after his visit there,[77] though it is unknown if his power extended beyond the city.[78] These officials were also responsible for running the manorial courts. In England, the administration of justice was the second most lucrative source of income for the crown, after land.[79] Henry undoubtedly saw the establishment of courts and English justice in Ireland as a very valuable source of revenue. Though no records of court proceedings for any of the royal manors survive for the period before 1590, there is plenty of evidence to suggest that these courts existed from a much earlier period. There are several mentions of tenants of the royal manors having to pay fines; for example, on 26 April 1286, Thomas Crumlin was fined ten marks for trespass,[80] and, though no more details are given, it is likely that he received this fine at the manor court of Crumlin. In 1281, Hugh Crus paid 7s. for the pleas and perquisites of the court of Saggart;[81] this and other similar examples illustrate that these manorial courts had the capacity to generate revenue for the crown.

Giraldus described Ireland as being more pastoral than arable at the time of the invasion, but he also acknowledged that it was fertile, with the prospect of yielding rich crops.[82] Arable farming had certainly been carried out extensively in the centuries before the arrival of the English, and this was particularly true of the Dublin hinterland,[83] which had to cater for a substantial urban population. Logically, this population could be sustained more easily if cereal growing was the main occupation rather than animal husbandry. It is estimated that late Viking Age Dublin needed at least 10,000 acres of grain just to make enough bread for the settlement.[84] Not even the area that comprised the later royal demesne could have supplied the town, and therefore the importance of arable farming should not be underestimated. Here, too, there seems to be continuity rather than radical change.

Thus, it would appear that the arrival of the English did not trigger an

---

76 Down, 'Colonial society', p. 453; see MacCotter, *Medieval Ireland*, p. 48 for a discussion on the relationship between the indigenous *túath* and the manor. 77 Orpen, *Normans*, I, p. 368. 78 Flanagan, *Irish society*, p. 286. 79 Green, *The government of England*, p. 6. 80 *CDI, 1285–92*, §217. 81 *CDI, 1252–84*, §1814. 82 Giraldus, *Topographia*, pp 34–5. 83 Down, 'Colonial society', p. 440. 84 Mary Valante, 'Dublin's economic relations with hinterland and periphery in the later Viking Age' in Sean Duffy (ed.), *Medieval Dublin*, I (Dublin, 2000), p. 74.

agricultural revolution, at least around Dublin. The crown probably managed the land in a similar way to its previous owners. Growing cereal in his demesne certainly proved profitable for the king. In 1227, Richard de Burgh purchased £62 16s. 8d. worth of grain from the manors of Esker, Crumlin and Saggart.[85] This was clearly a substantial amount of grain, suggesting that the manors were farmed for profit rather than solely supporting those living on the land. In 1224–5, the mayor of London purchased one thousand crannocks of wheat from William Marshal;[86] if he was producing enough of a surplus to export to England, it is likely that the same was true of the royal demesne.

Another reason for the retention by the king of the shire of Dublin for his own use was that the land was more valuable than that found elsewhere in Ireland. Under the 'feudal' system, land was divided into a unit known as a knight's fee. In theory, this was the amount of land required to support a knight. In Dublin, the amount of land needed was ten ploughlands; in the lordship of Meath this rose to twenty, while in more unsettled areas of this lordship the number of ploughlands required rose to thirty.[87] Initially, it would seem that the crown intended to retain most of the land around Dublin, but in 1235, Henry III decided to let most of the royal demesne out to farm, keeping just Crumlin, Newcastle Lyons, Esker and Saggart in his own hands.[88] The sheriff of Dublin was ultimately responsible for all aspects of the running of these manors, including financial, judicial and administrative organization. He was also responsible for the defence of the manors. These duties became the responsibility of the seneschal of the royal demesne from the beginning of the fourteenth century at the latest.

As time went on, the need to defend the mountainous area to the south of Dublin probably became a major factor in the king's decision to retain these manors. Esker and Crumlin were both close to the city, and further from the mountains, and were relatively safe, but Newcastle Lyons and Saggart were close to the march for much of the medieval period. This threat is clearly illustrated in Robert Owen's petition to the king in the 1270s, where he offered to exchange lands in Newcastle Lyons, which was in the 'land of peace', with lands in Saggart, which was located next to the 'land of war'.[89] Both these manors were located close to the mountains and were strategically important. Saggart was located at the main inland pass from the Leinster Mountains (when, for example, Ruaidrí Ua Conchobair lay in wait in Clondalkin for Diarmait Mac Murchada in 1170 he had expected the Leinster king to come this way and not take the more hazardous approach over the mountains).[90] The defence of the manors in the later medieval period is examined more closely in the concluding chapter of this book.

85 *RDKPRI*, 35, p. 30. 86 *CDI, 1171–1251*, §1285. 87 Down, 'Colonial society', p. 443.
88 *CDI, 1171–1251*, §2254. 89 *CDI, 1252–84*, §930. 90 Orpen, *Normans*, 1, p. 209.

Henry had come to Ireland in 1171 to control his over-mighty liegemen. He perhaps knew even then that he could not achieve an overall conquest of Ireland. He needed to establish a foothold, however, and this was most easily done by making the Ostman towns and their hinterlands his own. By introducing his royal officials into his demesne, he was ensuring that there were men there loyal to him. Because of this, the seeds of English administration were sown here, and this was best seen in the establishment of manors. Nevertheless, it is most likely that the origins of these manors go back to earlier times, and the newcomers improved what they found and introduced a more sophisticated model. Establishing a demesne and eventually transforming the secular lands of south Co. Dublin into royal manors was not Henry's purpose when he came to Ireland; rather, it was a consequence of the English settling here.

CONCLUSION

In 1177, Henry II made his youngest son, John, lord of Ireland.[91] It is possible that if John had not become king of England, he could have ended up taking a more hands-on approach to governing Ireland. If Henry's plans to grant the land of Ireland to his youngest son had materialized, the royal demesne surrounding the city of Dublin would have become its new lord's personal demesne. The royal manors did not come into being until John was king and this suggests that these lands were earmarked for him if subsequent events had not led him to the English throne. When the possibility of him being in Ireland for any extended period became remote, it was no longer necessary to retain a substantial royal demesne in Ireland. The fact that most of the royal demesne was farmed out to lesser tenants during the reign of Henry III would support this argument. John Gillingham argues that Henry II did not perceive his lands as being one single unit, but rather as a divisible family estate. Since Ireland was one of his acquisitions, he was not obligated to pass it on to his heir.[92] By the time Henry III became king of England, Ireland *was* part of the royal inheritance and, after this point, it was less likely to be separated from the crown.

A significant proportion of the Angevin Empire having been lost during the reign of King John, Ireland became much more significant to the crown. The loss of most of the crown's substantial landholdings in France would have served as a serious blow to both prestige and revenue. The title of lord of Ireland and the revenues that it brought with it gained new importance for the English king. In his attempt to hang on to his territories across the English Channel, John spent at least £30,000 between 1201 and 1203, and some of this money certainly

91 F.X. Martin, 'Overlord becomes feudal lord' in *NHI*, ii, p. 112; Flanagan, *Irish society*, p. 131; John Gillingham, *The Angevin Empire* (London, 2001), pp 29, 32. 92 Gillingham, *Angevin Empire*, p. 121.

came from his Irish lands. It is unknown how much he was getting from Ireland between these dates, but from October 1203 until October 1204, he received at least £1,700,[93] and much of this must have come from his royal demesne. The revenues of Ireland and particularly those of the royal manors would become increasingly important to the crown and would make a significant contribution to the Welsh and Scottish campaigns of Edward I later in the thirteenth century. By the first few decades of the fourteenth century, however, the manors no longer yielded a profit and they probably become more beneficial for those living on them, because of the privileges associated with them, than they were for royal government.

The introduction to Dublin of a royal demesne, and later the concept of the ancient demesne, played a key part in forming the identity of the colonists. The privileges of being a tenant of the king may have been an inducement to settle in Ireland, and it was a position that many Dubliners sought out throughout the medieval period. Certainly, in the first century of the colony's existence, the crown could expect to receive some profit from its lands here, but once the attacks in the mountains intensified from the end of the thirteenth century, the manors ceased to be a significant source of revenue. The manors, however, did not cease to be of use to the crown, as they became important as a means of bestowing patronage in the form of both lands and office to royal servants and locals alike. This importance is investigated in the following chapter.

93 Ibid., pp 93, 97.

3

Patronage and the royal manors

INTRODUCTION

Throughout the later Middle Ages, the crown used patronage in the form of land grants, wardship and marriage as a means of garnering the support of its subjects.[1] In England, this system of patronage can be traced back to the reign of Henry I and it served as 'a means of consolidating the position of that class of society later known as the gentry'.[2] When the crown acquired land around Dublin in the aftermath of the invasion in 1169, this system of royal benefaction was introduced to Ireland. The four royal manors in this study were an important source of patronage, which the English king, or his representative in Ireland, could use as a means of rewarding servants and favourites.[3]

The use of the crown lands in Ireland as an instrument of patronage has not received the same attention as the exploitation of crown lands for this purpose elsewhere within the British archipelago.[4] Nevertheless, members of the king's household in England, as well as administrators based in Ireland, actively sought out grants of these manors, which belies their relative neglect in the secondary sources. 'English politics was court politics' and the lion's share of patronage that was the king's to bestow was divided among this small and exclusive group who lived in the king's household or who could be counted among his favourites.[5] As is demonstrated below, this group were also the main recipients of grants of land belonging to the crown in Ireland.

To maintain and retain any sort of influence in Ireland, the king had to strike a balance between rewarding men in the locality and those close to the centre of power. It was vital that he kept his followers in court happy, while ensuring that those living in Dublin, who provided the military and administrative backbone of the locality, were not deprived of royal largesse. While it may appear that those courtiers who received grants of land or annuities on the royal manors had

---

1 J.A. Tuck, 'Richard II's system of patronage' in F.R.H. du Boulay and Caroline M. Barron (eds), *The reign of Richard II: essays in honour of May McKisack* (London, 1971), p. 3; R.A. Griffiths, *King and country: England and Wales in the fifteenth century* (London, 1991), p. 161. 2 R.W. Southern, 'The place of the reign of Henry I in English history', *PBA*, 48 (1962), 132. 3 Lyons, 'Manorial administration', pp 41–2. 4 In his investigation of patronage during the reign of Edward I, Michael Prestwich refers to Ireland briefly but focuses on the king's other dominions: see idem, 'Royal patronage under Edward I' in P.R. Coss and S.D. Lloyd (eds), *Thirteenth century England, I* (Woodbridge, 1986), pp 46–7. 5 Bartlett, *Norman and Angevin kings*, pp 28–35 (quote at p. 28).

no real effect on the locality, aside from extracting its revenues, this was not necessarily the case. Rather than viewing them as parasites that sucked the profits out of the area, it might be more productive to regard them as invaluable conduits between core and periphery. Even those who never set foot in Ireland had to nominate attorneys to look after their Irish affairs, and this process created a bond between the king's subjects of Ireland and England. A by-product of these beneficiaries of the king's favour nominating locals to act on their behalf in Dublin was that some of the rewards of patronage filtered back into the locality. Patronage not only reinforced the relationship between subject and crown, but, by extension, it also reinforced the Englishness of the English of Ireland.

Profit does not appear to have been paramount in the crown's decision to retain lands surrounding the city of Dublin. Even in the prosperous thirteenth century, when these lands had the potential of yielding a profit, they were farmed out at a fixed rent that did not reflect their true monetary value.[6] Similarly, across the Irish Sea, there was little evidence of any kind of effort being made to make royal estate management yield an income on a scale comparable to the kind of revenue that could be derived from taxation.[7] In other words, the English king was never dependent on the crown lands in any of his dominions as a source of cash income. Towards the end of the thirteenth century, when the manors in Dublin began to fall into arrears, any hope of operating them as a profitable concern – if such hopes were ever entertained – was abandoned. The main value of the royal manors, apart from their strategic importance, was as a means of rewarding royal servants and local administrators. This system of patronage worked on two levels. Those granted direct leases of land on the royal manors exploited the land for revenues, which in turn paid the pensions and annuities of other officials, who had no direct interests in the manors. Members of the king's household normally received an annuity or pension as they were based in England, and direct grants of land were usually reserved for those working in the Dublin administration. The experience in Ireland was identical to that in England, in that government servants often received grants of land in lieu of a regular salary.[8] By granting out royal manors for a term of years, or duration of office, the crown had the means to pay officials for services rendered at a time when the concept of a regular salary was unheard of.

It appears that the crown normally left to the justiciar (the king's representative in Ireland) the decision of who to grant these lands to. As has been noted in the previous chapter, during Hugh de Lacy's period in office as *custos* of Dublin and Strongbow's time as justiciar, both men granted lands that were originally

6 This rent was fixed in the 1260s but, due to the debts that mounted during the fourteenth century, the administration of the manors was carried out by reeves elected by the tenants and answerable to the exchequer: see Lyons, 'Manorial administration', pp 21, 296 and ch. 4, below. 7 Wolffe, *Royal demesne*, p. 30.   8 Ibid., p. 37.

part of the royal demesne to friends and followers. Occasionally, patents for grants of the royal manors were made from both Dublin and London to different individuals. This was clearly due to miscommunication between the crown and the justiciar. Many members of the king's household, who had no obvious connections with Ireland, actively lobbied for grants of the royal manors. This is indicative of the importance of these four manors. These grants were not necessarily sought for profit, and it would appear that they bestowed a certain status on the grantee. There were times when the king took a more direct interest in regard to who was being given these lands. When the crown was experiencing a time of crisis and needed to garner support, it was much more likely that the king would grant the manors to allies or potential allies. It was at these times that men of significance on a wider political scale received grants of the royal manors.

THE KING'S FAVOURITES AND ROYAL OFFICIALS

Patronage in the twelfth and thirteenth centuries

Though patronage was important on every level of society and touched even the most humble peasant, the first section of this chapter will mainly focus on the beneficiaries of royal largesse who were granted entire manors or received substantial annuities. These included men who were part of the king's household, as well as those at the topmost layer of administration within the colony. Some of these men made a significant impact on Irish affairs, while others may have never visited Ireland. Certainly, very few of them, even those who dwelt in the nearby city, would have actively involved themselves in any of the practicalities of manorial administration, and their interest went no further than receiving their profits, as well as the prestige of being a crown tenant.

Among the earliest recipients of royal patronage in Dublin after the invasion were the original inhabitants of the area – the Meic Gilla Mo-Cholmóc family, who rapidly anglicized their name to FitzDermot. In 1207, King John granted the 'cantred of Lynhim' to Diarmait Mac Gilla Mo-Cholmóc.[9] This was presumably a confirmation of an earlier grant and represented the lands of Newcastle Lyons in south-west Dublin. Nevertheless, the use of the word cantred implies a larger geographical area than that of the manor of Newcastle Lyons and may have incorporated the lands of some of the other royal manors, particularly nearby Saggart. Certainly, the Meic Gilla Mo-Cholmóc held Kilmactalway, which lies just north of Newcastle Lyons.[10] These lands remained in their possession until 1215, when King John resumed custody and the lands of Kilmactalway were incorporated into the royal manor of Newcastle Lyons.

9 MacCotter, *Medieval Ireland*, p. 163.   10 Ball, *Dublin*, 4, pp 63–4.

Not only were they in possession of this manor up to 1215, it is also likely that these lands belonged to them before the invasion. The pipe roll for 1262 reveals that John FitzDermot held lands in Rowlagh in Clondalkin, as well as in Lucan and Palmerstown.[11] An ancestor of his, who was also called John, held lands on the royal manor of Esker, for which he paid rent of two otter skins in 1227.[12] There is also evidence of their descendants living on this royal manor.[13] Moreover, it has been suggested that this family held Ballyfermot.[14]

This bestowal of patronage probably served as an aid in the introduction of the new order into the locality and it may well have ensured that the colonization of the area by the English was a less unsettling process than it otherwise could have been. This was important, as there was probably only a limited displacement of the greater part of the local population, particularly those at the lower end of the social scale. Certainly, the evidence from the manors belonging to the archbishop of Dublin suggests that many of the native Irish remained in this area even in the fourteenth century.[15] By the time of the resumption of the lands by the crown in the early thirteenth century, the local population, both native and colonist, would have grown accustomed to each other and this change would have been less disruptive.

The Meic Gilla Mo-Cholmóc did not retain all the lands that had once belonged to them in the hinterland of Dublin, and the extensive grants made to men like Walter de Ridelesford after the invasion are early examples of royal patronage in Ireland. Even if Strongbow or de Lacy had granted lands in this locality to their own followers, once it had been taken into the king's hands he became their immediate overlord, regardless of their previous associations. Other families, including the Crumlins/Russells and the Tyrells, benefited from the king's generosity, but the king gained too, because now he had a group of men who owed their advancement to him.

While evidence of patronage on the royal manors can be found as soon as Dublin came into royal hands, substantial proof exists from the early fourteenth century onwards, when the amount of surviving primary sources increases significantly. Leasing out the manors became increasingly rare as the fourteenth

11 *RDKPRI*, 35, p. 44.   12 Gilbert, *History of Dublin*, p. 233.   13 *CDI, 1293–1301*, §§132, 289. 14 The evidence that this family owned this manor is based on the erroneous assumption that Ballyfermot means 'Dermot's town': see Ball, *Dublin*, 4, p. 101. Indeed, in some documents dating from the late thirteenth century, it is called Ballydermot, but it is more commonly styled Balitormod (see, for example, *CDI, 1293–1301*, §§280, 587). –ormundr (Thormod) is an Old Norse personal name, but the *baile* component is entirely Irish: see Magne Oftedal, 'Scandinavian place-names in Ireland' in Bo Almqvist and David Greene (eds), *Proceedings of the Seventh Viking Congress* (Dublin, 1976), p. 127. The name Ballyfermot probably dates to no earlier than the middle of the twelfth century, as there is scant evidence that *baile* was used before this date: Liam Price, 'A note on the use of the word *baile* in place-names', *Celtica*, 6 (1963), 119–26. Therefore, though it is conceivable that the FitzDermots were the owners of these lands at the time of the invasion, it is more likely that their owner was an Ostman.   15 Otway-Ruthven, 'Norman settlement', p. 271.

century progressed and, eventually, such leases became almost exclusively associated with royal patronage.[16] It is true that the manors became increasingly unprofitable at this time, and the crown may have decided that, instead of trying to yield revenue directly, the best alternative was to use them as a means of rewarding royal servants. Judging by petitions for grants of lands, their potential profitability did not appear to be of the utmost importance. In fact, Prestwich observed that people sought out grants even though they must have been well aware that there was no guarantee they would be profitable.[17] A royal official who was an early recipient of lands on the royal manors was Henry Compton, who was granted the manor of Crumlin in 1292. His grant of this manor has received a lot of attention in the sources, thanks in no small part to the resistance this grant received from Thomas Crumlin and his fellow tenants on that manor.

Henry Compton

Henry Compton's origins are obscure, and the fact that his surname is also a common place-name makes it difficult to establish if he is related to other people of the same name, or even if the sources are dealing with one man or several individuals who happen to share the same surname. Considering all this, there are some scraps of evidence that may yield clues as to his lineage and possibly where he originated. In an English letter patent of 9 June 1293, Henry is described as being the son of Richard Compton.[18] An examination of earlier Irish administrative records does not reveal any evidence of this man, but a search of the English patent rolls for the third quarter of the thirteenth century reveals a Richard Compton, who may be Henry's father. He appears in the rolls between 1263 and 1268 before completely disappearing from the records.[19] He is the only Richard Compton found in the records in the second half of the thirteenth century and he served the bishop of Worcester. It is feasible that he is related to Henry, though this connection cannot be proven definitively.

Henry Compton had a long association with a William Calne, whose surname may serve as a clue to his place of origin. His association with Calne dates from 1291 at the latest and continues up until at least 1310.[20] During these two decades, Compton served as Calne's attorney in Ireland, while Calne remained in England. He is probably the William Calne who served as escheator of Wiltshire in 1263.[21] There was a manor in this county called Calne, which is probably where William originated, but, more significantly, there was another manor adjacent to Calne called Compton Bassett.[22] This could be where Henry Compton was born, and William Calne could have been his patron. It is possible that his career in Ireland is connected to Calne's Irish interests.

William Calne's wife, Roesia Longespee, had previously been married to

16 Lyons, 'Manorial administration', p. 42.   17 Prestwich, 'Royal patronage', p. 50.   18 *CPR, 1292–1301*, p. 21.   19 *CPR, 1258–66*, pp 275, 553, 570, 607.   20 *CPR, 1281–92*, p. 461; *CPR, 1307–13*, p. 278.   21 *CPR, 1258–66*, p. 291.   22 *VCH, Wiltshire, 17* (London, 2002), pp 3–8.

William Dene, who had at one point served as sheriff of Cork and was justiciar of Ireland at the time of his death in 1261.[23] William Dene held substantial lands in Cos Wexford and Kilkenny.[24] Nevertheless, William Calne did not appear to spend much time in Ireland after he married Roesia. In 1283, they were given protection here for two years while remaining in England.[25] Both husband and wife were involved in a judicial case in Wexford in 1286;[26] thus, it would seem that Roesia still had an interest in her previous husband's lands in the barony of Keir in Wexford. The majority of references to William Calne in the Irish administrative records deal with him giving others power of attorney in Ireland rather than coming here himself, and the name that comes up the most frequently is that of Henry Compton.[27]

Henry Compton's activities in Ireland were not devoted exclusively to serving as an attorney to the Calnes; he was also a royal official. Indeed, his grants of the royal manor of Crumlin would suggest strong associations with the crown. In fact, the earliest reference to Compton was from a patent letter of 1286, where it was recorded that he was going with the king beyond seas.[28] In May of that year, Edward I was in Paris, where he did homage to Philip IV, the new king of France, for his lands in Aquitaine. He remained on the Continent, involved in various diplomatic negotiations until August 1289.[29] A large entourage would have accompanied the king as he travelled around Europe and it is conceivable that Henry Compton was a part of it and that he came to the king's attention at this time.

Alternatively, Henry may have owed his advancement to one of the king's representatives in Dublin. Certainly, in England, the endowment of royal office and lands was in the control of the great officers of the state, predominantly the treasurer.[30] In Ireland, it was often the case that the king's representative, the justiciar, was responsible for making grants of land on the royal manors rather than the impetus coming from England. In any case, by 1290 Henry Compton was already well established in Ireland and working in the chancery. He would go on to play an active part in Irish administration throughout the 1290s and beyond. For example, on 3 April 1292, Compton and the mayor of Dublin were given custody of the seal and counter-seal of the merchants of that city, and a few days later, on 8 April, Henry received the seal for merchants for all fairs of cities and market towns in Ireland. The possession of these seals indicates that Compton was an important cog in the wheel of the Irish administration, and this importance is made evident in the favour being bestowed on him by the crown.[31]

---

23 He died from injuries sustained at the battle of Callan: *CJR, 1295–1303*, p. 402; Orpen, *Normans*, 3, p. 142; Otway-Ruthven, *Medieval Ireland*, p. 195. 24 *Inquis. Lagenie* (Kilkenny), §20, Jac. I. 25 *CPR, 1281–92*, p. 75. 26 *CDI, 1285–92*, §215. 27 *CPR, 1281–92*, pp 461, 468; *CPR, 1292–1301*, pp 21, 190, 328, 332, 393, 561; *CPR, 1301–7*, pp 106, 328; *CPR, 1307–13*, p. 278. 28 *CPR, 1281–92*, pp 245–7. 29 Maurice Powicke, *The thirteenth century, 1216–1307* (Oxford, 1962), pp 251, 255, 261. 30 Anthony Tuck, *Richard II and the English nobility* (London, 1973), p. 4. 31 *CPR, 1281–92*, pp 482, 483.

Henry Compton also appears to have had close ties with the merchants of the city of Dublin. In 1297, he abused his power by allowing the ex-mayor (Robert Wyleby), the current mayor (Thomas Colys) and Geoffrey Morton[32] (a future mayor) use the seal that was in his keeping in his absence without the approval of the Irish council.[33] He argued that he could not be present when these merchants used the seal, because he was serving as the receiver for the liberty of Kildare, but even his actions here were suspect. Instead of rendering his account for the liberty, he tried to flee Dublin by sea. Escape proved futile, as his boat was driven back to shore and he was committed to gaol. He did not remain here long, however, and he had certainly gained his freedom by early 1298, because at this time he was granted the office of keeper of the rolls and the writs of the common bench. He remained in this office up until at least Michaelmas term 1300.[34] Henry Compton's grant of Crumlin is early evidence of the crown attempting to use the revenues of the royal manors as a means of rewarding men in the Irish administration. On this occasion, the administration was unsuccessful in making good on the grant, but many future administrators held lands or annuities on the royal manors.

The fourteenth century

As the fourteenth century progressed, the problem of absenteeism, which had been an issue even in the previous century, was becoming acute. In many cases, the ownership of Irish lands was transferred across the Irish Sea with its heiresses, as the main lines of some of the most important English families died out.[35] That, however, did not mean that these families disappeared off the Irish scene completely; many survived through cadet lines. These men were not likely to inherit much of the family property, and many ended up serving the crown or some other great lord. One of those men was Nicholas Verdon, who was granted one hundred marks from the royal manor of Newcastle Lyons in 1337, and, in the following year, he received a grant of the entire manor.[36] Nicholas was the brother of Theobald Verdon, who was a substantial landowner in both Ireland and England but who had no sons to carry on the family name. Theobald was clearly anxious to provide for other members of his family, and he alienated some of his lands in Louth to Nicholas, who had already inherited property in the same county from his father.[37] Nicholas augmented these bequests with the grant of Newcastle Lyons. He received this grant because of 'the great place which he will hold and holds in Ireland'; he may have been a younger son, but

32 For an account of his career, see Philomena Connolly, 'The rise and fall of Geoffrey de Morton, mayor of Dublin, 1303–4' in Seán Duffy (ed.), *Medieval Dublin*, 2 (Dublin, 2001), pp 233–51. 33 *CJR, 1295–1303*, p. 123. 34 *CPR, 1292–1301*, p. 331; Connolly, *Exchequer payments*, p. 589. 35 Beth Hartland, 'Reasons for leaving: the effect of conflict on English landholding in late thirteenth-century Leinster', *JMH*, 32:1 (2006), 18–26. 36 NAI, RC 8/21, 189–91; *CFR, 1337–47*, p. 94. 37 A.J. Otway-Ruthven, 'The partition of the de Verdon lands in Ireland in 1332', *PRIA*, 66C (1968), 409.

his brother's early death made him a much more important figure than he
perhaps otherwise would have been. One of the most significant grants he
received from the king, jointly with his younger brother Miles in 1316, was the
wardship of Theobald's lands while his nieces were underage and unmarried.[38]
These grants were possibly used as a means of ensuring Nicholas' good behaviour, because he often found himself on the wrong side of the law.[39] He was
responsible for many robberies and at least one murder, for which his older
brother in his capacity as justiciar obtained a pardon.[40] Yet, in spite of this behaviour, he could not be dispensed with.

During the Bruce invasion, he proved to be an active and aggressive opponent
of both the Scottish invaders and the native Irish. Clearly, the grant of the royal
manor of Newcastle Lyons was in response to the positive and energetic role he
played in defending the colony.[41] Without a doubt, men like Nicholas Verdon
were vitally important to the survival of the lordship, and the crown's recognized
this importance through its generous grants and its willingness to overlook past
transgressions. The statutes concerning absenteeism and degeneracy reflected
how concerned the crown was with its increasingly tenuous hold over the
lordship.[42] The English king was, of course, the most important absentee lord in
the country; therefore, having able men in the locality protecting his interests
was imperative. The crown was well aware that it could easily lose the loyalty of
men like Verdon, who had already displayed a tendency towards lawless behaviour, and patronage was an important means of guaranteeing their allegiance.
Aside from the financial benefits of these royal grants, which may have been
negligible by this time, they also offered the grantee the prestige of being associated with the king, which must have enhanced his reputation in his own locality.
Being a royal servant also meant having the king's protection in the law courts,
so men like Verdon could have viewed these grants as protection against crimes
not yet committed.

The king also used his property in Ireland as a means of paying debts. Edward
III granted Robert Clinton, one of his yeomen, extensive lands in Ireland in
recompense for four hundred marks of £1,000 owed to him when the king
bought a fourth part of the ransom of the archbishop of Le Mans, who was
taken prisoner during the Battle of Poitiers.[43] These lands included the manors
of Celbridge and Kilmacridok in Co. Kildare, the manor of Lucan and the mill
of Lutterellstown in Co. Dublin. The grant stipulated that if for some reason
some part of these lands was taken from Clinton, the king would make good his
losses out of the manors of Newcastle Lyons or Crumlin. In 1358, Robert

38 Ibid., p. 401.   39 Brendan Smith, *Colonisation and conquest in medieval Ireland: the English in
Louth, 1170–1330* (Cambridge, 1999), p. 133.   40 Ibid., p. 104.   41 NAI, RC 8/21, pp 189–91;
Smith, *Colonisation and conquest*, pp 111–12.   42 *Stat. Ire., John–Hen. V*, pp 470–1.   43 *CPR,
1358–61*, p. 63; Michael Prestwich, *Plantagenet England, 1225–1360* (Oxford, 2005), p. 345; K.B.
McFarlane, *The nobility of later medieval England* (Oxford, 1997), p. 30.

Clinton was retained as a king's yeoman and granted an annuity of £20 per annum for life. About two-thirds of this sum was derived from the farm paid yearly by Thomas Dent for the manor of Esker, the remainder came from the issues of the manor of Newcastle Lyons.[44] Thomas Dent had served as seneschal of the royal manors in the 1330s, and later he was granted the office of justice of the common bench and ultimately became chief justice of the bench.[45] He also had the farm of the manor of Esker for life because in the grant made to Robert Clinton it was promised that he would receive this manor after Dent's death. It seems that, though the king would often grant annuities from his lands in Ireland to his followers and members of his household, the actual farm of the manors was normally granted to men who served in the Irish administration. Robert Clinton may not have spent any time in Ireland; indeed, it is very unlikely that he did, as his grant stipulated that he be retained to stay with the king. Therefore, his only interest in Esker was the annuity he received from it, and Thomas Dent was responsible for the practical administration of the manor, which included providing this annuity. Thus, the royal manors provided revenues to reward men of the king's household and at the same time endowed local men with land and offices.

Towards the end of Edward III's reign, Esker was granted to Reginald Lovel, and in 1378, Richard II confirmed this grant.[46] Lovel had some previous experience in Ireland. He visited the country at least twice during the 1360s, the first visit being with Lionel, duke of Clarence, in 1361. He returned in the latter half of the decade with William Windsor.[47] In spite of his Irish experience, Lovel had no direct involvement in the affairs of the manor, apart from ensuring he received his annuity.[48] He clearly made some personal connections with tenants on the royal manors during his time in Ireland, however, because in 1375–6 Robert Kissock of Esker and John Beg of Saggart were serving as his attorneys.[49] Being granted an annuity was no guarantee that it would be paid promptly, and in Lovel's case, he was owed over £11 during the first year of Richard's reign.[50] Similarly to Clinton, Lovel was granted Esker on the condition that he remained with the king.[51] It is perhaps surprising that there are not more examples of non-payment of annuities from the royal manors, and it may be the case that most grantees, unlike Lovel, did not push the matter because they did not expect to be able to collect the revenues. This would support the idea that the prestige of being the holder of a grant from the king was just as important as any financial rewards they might expect, if not more so.

---

44 *CPR, 1358–61*, p. 213. 45 NAI, RC 8/16, pp 134–5; RC 8/25, pp 134–5; Lyons, 'Manorial administration', p. 50; *Admin. Ire.*, pp 122–3. 46 *CIRCLE*, CR 1 Ric. II, §47. 47 Transcript by Philomena Connolly among the papers of the Irish Chancery Project; *CPR, 1361–4*, p. 46; *CPR, 1367–70*, p. 185. 48 Connolly, *Exchequer payments*, p. 542. 49 *CIRCLE*, PR 49 Edw. III, §156. 50 TNA, E101/246/5, §44. 51 *CPR, 1377–81*, pp 295–6.

Cornelius Clone, Gaelic knight

Cornelius Clone was granted a yearly annuity of forty marks from the manor of Crumlin around the same time Lovel was granted his annuity from Esker.[52] What marks Clone out from other recipients of royal favour in this study is that he was Gaelic Irish in origin. Yet it would be a mistake to put too much emphasis on his racial origins, because, like other recipients of annuities on the royal manors, Clone was a member of the king's household. He had served as an esquire to Edward III and, during Richard II's reign, he had worked his way up to the rank of knight. Unfortunately, his origins are obscure and it is difficult to deduce how he made his way into royal service. His family bore the cognomen 'of Fynatha', but the name he was known by – Clone – denotes where he came from;[53] some possibilities are Cloyne and Clonmacnoise, but the 'Clon' prefix to a place-name is so common in Ireland that it is not really possible to pin down his place of origin with any degree of certainty.

In 1383, Cornelius Clone's family in Ireland was granted the use of English law, indisputably demonstrating his influence in court. Three years previously, he had been granted the manor of Crumlin for life.[54] There is no evidence that he spent a substantial amount of time in Ireland, however. In 1382, he was granted protection for one year while he travelled to Ireland on the king's service,[55] but in the following year he was granted the profits of the manor though he was an absentee and serving abroad with the king's brother, John Holland.[56] He may have accompanied Holland on the bishop of Norwich's 'crusade' in Flanders.[57] The responsibility placed on him is clear evidence that he was a highly trusted royal servant. For example, in 1384 he represented the marshal of England in a court case.[58] Moreover, in the previous decade he travelled to Ireland in the company of Roger Mortimer on the king's service.[59] He was well rewarded for his efforts: not only did he receive an annuity from Crumlin but he also received additional lands in Meath, including the manors of Belgard and Fore in 1383. He was given permission to negotiate with the king's enemies – both English and Irish – in order to bring about a truce. He was also granted judicial powers in the locality of Belgard and Fore, which would have made him very powerful within that region. He could not have lived long enough to enjoy these grants because, sometime before 8 July 1384, the king's butler, John Slegh, was granted the manor of Crumlin for life; since Clone had been granted the same manor on the same terms, he almost certainly was deceased.[60]

Anne, wife of Philip Courtenay, lord lieutenant of Ireland, was granted custody of Crumlin at the time that Clone was granted an annuity from this royal manor.[61] Philip Courtenay was the son of Hugh Courtenay, tenth earl of

52 Ibid., p. 481; *CIRCLE*, CR 4 Ric. II, §§13–14.   53 *CPR, 1381–5*, p. 226.   54 *CPR, 1377–81*, p. 481; *CIRCLE*, PR 9 Ric. II, §248.   55 *CPR, 1381–5*, p. 121.   56 Ibid., p. 316.   57 Gerald Harris, *Shaping the nation: England, 1360–1461* (Oxford, 2005), p. 450.   58 Ibid., pp 430–1.   59 *CPR, 1377–81*, p. 409.   60 *CPR, 1381–5*, p. 442.   61 *CIRCLE*, PR 8 Ric. II, §26.

Devon, and through him was a direct descendant of Edward I.[62] Therefore, when the king granted Courtenay's wife one of his royal manors, he was patronizing not just a royal servant but a family member – albeit a distant one. The Thomas Mareward, who served as seneschal of the king's demesne in Dublin in 1360, or perhaps a son of the same name, became seneschal of Crumlin in 1385, but Philip Courtenay and the new grantee of the manor, John Slegh, continued to reap the dividends.[63] It was Mareward's responsibility to make sure these annuities continued to be paid.

The king's butler
Cornelius Clone's successor to Crumlin, John Slegh, was appointed chief butler of the king's household on 12 October 1382.[64] When he was granted Crumlin two years later, it was on the condition that the king's lieutenant in Ireland, Philip Courtenay, would continue to receive the revenues and profits pertaining to the king of that manor.[65] Again, this demonstrates the dual purpose of the royal manors in rewarding members of the king's household in England and paying the fees of those working within the Irish administration. Slegh was a much-favoured royal servant who received many offices and grants of land throughout his career. Granting out these offices and lands cost the king nothing and, in return, it gained him service and loyalty.[66] It also meant he did not have to put any effort into obtaining the revenues of these grants, putting the onus on those on whom they were bestowed to collect what they were owed. Slegh was also created purveyor of many English ports and he normally granted these offices to a deputy. Therefore, not only could the king reward his clients through patronage, but they in turn could become patrons and build up their own circle of men beholden to them.

Slegh was also granted the office of collector of customs in the ports of Dublin, Cork, Waterford, Limerick and Drogheda, and he appointed Robert Halum as deputy in his place.[67] His nomination of attorneys and deputies to look after his affairs in Ireland is clear evidence that he did not personally administer the offices he received. It is likely that Slegh used the services of individuals in Ireland to represent him here, and a local could have benefited from Slegh's patronage by acting as his attorney. Slegh received multiple grants from the crown, and deputies filled many of his offices. He was in a position to offer employment to many individuals in Ireland and, obviously, he would have established many contacts here. Moreover, these individuals now had a close

---

62 G.E. Cockayne, *Complete peerage of Great Britain and Ireland*, 3 (London, 1937), p. 329.
63 *CIRCLE*, PR 9 Ric. II, §219; NAI, RC 8/27, pp 578–9; it is likely that there were two Thomas Marewards, because his death was recorded in 1421 (TNA, E28/36/39; *SCSMI*, p. 181). Therefore, it is probable that they were father and son, but it is not clear if the seneschal of demesne and the seneschal of Crumlin are the same man. 64 *CPR, 1381–5*, p. 176. 65 Ibid., p. 442; *CIRCLE*, PR 9 Ric. II, §248. 66 T.F. Tout, *Chapters in administrative history*, 2 (Manchester, 1920), pp 333–4. 67 *CPR, 1389–92*, p. 467.

connection to the crown and the centre of power. When John Slegh made plans in 1394 to visit Ireland, it was not so he could pursue his own interests here, he was in fact going as part of King Richard's retinue. That is not to say that he did not use this trip to deal with some of his own affairs, which were then in difficulties. By the summer of 1394, he was in arrears because the deputies he had nominated to collect the customs of the Irish ports had failed to pass on to Slegh the money that had been paid to them. This reveals one of the potential problems of making grants to absentees. Due to his close proximity to the king, the offices and lands that he had already been granted, and the grants he hoped to receive in the future, Slegh would certainly have endeavoured to make sure that these debts were paid. As events transpired, he died within twelve months, still heavily indebted to the king, but in its determination to seize its pound of flesh, the crown took his goods and retained them until his debt was satisfied. He did leave a widow who served as executrix of his will, and presumably what was left was turned over to her. Slegh may even have died in Ireland; the last reference to him alive is in a patent letter dating to May 1395, when the king was still in Ireland, and in subsequent letters, he is recorded as being deceased.[68]

Crisis of 1399: continuity and change

Slegh's death meant that he avoided the crisis of Richard II's deposition, but it certainly affected the career of the next holder of the manor of Crumlin, John Lufwyk. He was an esquire of the king's chamber and someone who clearly had a close relationship with Richard, as he served as an executor of his will.[69] While patronage could be used as a political tool to gain support, it was also used to reward those with whom the king was particularly intimate. In the 1390s, Richard II had many lucrative posts, lands and wardships in his gift, but he granted them to a very small group of men with whom he was close.[70] This policy must have contributed greatly to the general acceptance of Henry Bolingbroke's usurpation of the throne.

In the summer of 1395, Lufwyk, who already held the office of yeoman of the robes, was granted Crumlin, as well as the office of collector of the customs of the Irish ports, as Slegh had held them. After Slegh's mishandling of this office, the administration were not willing to allow the customs to sink into arrears again and Lufwyk was ordered to account for the issues and profits at the Irish exchequer personally, even if he did grant the office out to a deputy. In 1396, Lufwyk became the first layperson to hold the office of keeper of the privy wardrobe,[71] one of the four main spending departments of the king's household. Located in the Tower of London, the privy wardrobe served as a storehouse for weapons and armour.[72] The armourers and tentmakers, which had been

68 *CPR, 1391–6*, pp 5, 53, 305, 483, 519, 564, 652, 667. **69** Chris Given-Wilson, *The royal household and the king's affinity* (London, 1986), p. 181. **70** Ibid., pp 166–7. **71** Tout, *Chapters*, 4, p. 462; *CPR, 1391–6*, p. 667. **72** Given-Wilson, *Royal household*, p. 84.

attached to the great wardrobe up to the reign of Edward III, were now associated with the privy wardrobe.[73] Lufwyk's account from 1399 provides an inventory of weaponry for Richard II's final, ill-fated, trip to Ireland, as well as the expense involved.[74] Lufwyk accompanied Richard to Ireland and remained loyal to the king even after his deposition, taking part in the earls' rebellion in January 1400.[75] As a result, he lost his place in the household and all the grants Richard made to him. By the end of 1399, the keepership of the privy wardrobe and the manor of Crumlin were in the hands of John Norbury.

Lufwyk's fate was the exception rather than the rule, and the cause of it was probably his exceptionally close relationship with the old king. The transition between reigns was a relatively smooth one, and was marked as a period of continuity rather than change. The volume of grants renewed in the first year of Henry IV's reign bears this out. Evidence of this continuity can be found on the royal manors. At the end of 1399, Henry granted 12*d.* a day from the issues or fee-farm of Esker to John Humbleton.[76] This was not a new grant, but rather a confirmation of a grant made during Richard's reign. Likewise, in 1400 Laurence Newton, one of the king's serjeants in Ireland, had a grant of 12*d.* daily from the manors of Esker and Newcastle Lyons confirmed by the new king.[77] Prominent among the group of Richard's adherents who quickly became loyal subjects of the new regime was Janico Dartasso, who became the recipient of the 12*d.* a day annuity from Esker when Humbleton surrendered his grant.[78] Dartasso stood by Richard to the very end, and he aroused the wrath of Henry by refusing to take off the old king's livery badge. He was imprisoned in Chester Castle.[79] From such an unpromising start, Dartasso won the new king over with remarkable speed and profited well from this new association. By the second year of the reign, he was granted the office of constable of Dublin Castle and he continued to be a recipient of royal patronage during the reign of Henry V.[80] It was during this period that he received the manors of Esker, Newcastle Lyons and Saggart. Unlike many of the other recipients of royal patronage who did not originate from Ireland, Dartasso seems to have spent a substantial amount of time here. Henry IV was clearly tolerant of those who had supported the old regime, as long as they were loyal to him now that he was king.

Henry had no choice but to be tolerant, his position on the throne being anything but secure. Obviously, he could not afford to antagonize any but the most rebellious of Richard's supporters. On the other hand, neither could he afford to neglect his own followers. One of the most prominent of these to have

73 Tout, *Chapters*, 4, p. 475.   74 T.F. Tout, 'Firearms in England in the fourteenth century', *EHR*, 26 (1911), 678, 701.   75 Tout, *Chapters*, 4, p. 466; Given-Wilson, *Royal household*, p. 181. 76 *CPR, 1399–1401*, p. 35.   77 Ibid., p. 198.   78 *CPR, 1408–15*, p. 422.   79 Edmund Curtis, 'Janico Dartasso, Richard the Second's "Gascon esquire": his career in Ireland', *JRSAI*, 63 (1933), 182–205; S. Walker, 'Janico Dartasso: chivalry, nationality and the man-at-arms', *History*, 84 (1999), 31–51; Given-Wilson, *Royal household*, p. 174.   80 *CPR, 1399–1401*, p. 35.

profited from lands on the royal manors was John Norbury. As early as 31 July 1399, Henry had promised Norbury John Lufwyk's goods and property if they were to become forfeit, including the royal manor of Crumlin.[81] Henry clearly used the threat of forfeiture in an attempt to get Lufwyk to change his allegiances and, indeed, it was perhaps a ploy that worked on most occasions.

By the time Henry IV ascended the throne, John Norbury had been in his service for at least a decade. In the summer of 1390, he had travelled with him to Lithuania to take part in a crusade with the Teutonic knights.[82] By early 1399, he was an esquire of John of Gaunt, duke of Lancaster, and his daughter was married to Nicholas Usk, the treasurer of the duke's household. He was made treasurer of the exchequer on 23 September 1399, even before Henry officially became king, clearly a sign that his patron held him in high regard.[83] Norbury's relationship with Henry was evidently as close as the one between Lufwyk and Richard II. This is reflected in the speed with which he attained the rewards for his loyalty. As soon as Henry was in a position to reward Norbury, he did so and he gave him the promised grants of lands and offices that had once belonged to Lufwyk, including the office of keeper of the king's privy wardrobe and the manor of Crumlin.[84] Norbury enjoyed the advantages of royal favour, but the crown also gained from his skills as a soldier and administrator, experience that served him well in the household office that supplied and manufactured military equipment. Men like Norbury would prove indispensable to Henry when it came to dealing with the resistance that would inevitably follow his usurpation of the throne. Trust was just as important as experience, and the king demonstrated the level of faith he had in Norbury by making him one of his councillors in 1404.[85] In 1406, his presence was considered so essential for the 'good counsel and advice' he provided, that he was required to stay and attend the king rather than carry out a previous order to guard the castle at Guînes.[86] With so many adapting so easily to whatever regime was in power at the time, the personal loyalty of men like Lufwyk and Norbury to their respective monarchs must have been particularly valued, and the reward of royal patronage is surely proof of this gratitude.

Problems could arise when men received patronage from more than one lord, and this had the potential of leading to divided loyalties. John Norbury was not only a recipient of the king's patronage; he had previously been in the service of his father, John of Gaunt. He also received gifts and patronage from Henry's queen, for whom he served as a squire.[87] In 1408, he was one of Thomas of Lancaster's attorneys in England while the king's son was in Ireland serving as lord lieutenant.[88] Obviously, since this patronage was received from other

---

81 Michael Bennett, *Richard II and the revolution of 1399* (Stroud, 1999), p. 161.   82 Madeline Barber, 'John Norbury (c. 1350–1414): an esquire of Henry IV', *EHR*, 68 (1953), 67.   83 *CPR, 1396–9*, p. 595.   84 *CPR, 1399–1401*, p. 122.   85 *CPR, 1401–5*, p. 412.   86 *CPR, 1405–8*, p. 203.   87 Barber, 'John Norbury', 72.   88 *CPR, 1405–8*, p. 439.

members of the house of Lancaster, it is unlikely that Norbury's loyalties were divided, but because men were free to seek out patronage wherever they could find it, it does at least suggest that even the bestowal of royal favour could not guarantee complete loyalty to the crown.

Henry's insistence that Norbury stay by his side and evidence in the patent rolls of Norbury nominating attorneys in Ireland imply that he spent little, if any, time here.[89] Conversely, the next recipient of the manor of Crumlin must have spent much of his time in Ireland, because he played an important role in the Irish administration. In 1400, Laurence Merbury became treasurer of Ireland and the grant of this office was renewed in the first year of Henry V's reign.[90] In 1406, he was appointed chancellor of Ireland and served in this office on three subsequent occasions.[91] In 1415, he was granted the manor of Crumlin for life.[92] Norbury had also held the same manor for life – clear evidence of how highly he was regarded by the king – but he died shortly after the royal patron to whom he owed so much.[93] Merbury was given permission to receive the issues and profits of the manor, even when absent from Ireland, but it was not until 1420 that he was ordered to find a deputy to occupy the office of chancellor when the king commanded him to come to England.[94] In the following year, he was back in Ireland, serving as an attorney for Beatrice, widow of Gilbert, lord of Talbot.[95]

Magnate power

Laurence Merbury owed his advancement in Ireland not only to the king but also to Gilbert Talbot's younger brother, John, Lord Furnival, who later became first earl of Shrewsbury and first earl of Waterford. John's family were kinsmen of the Talbots of Malahide in north Dublin and he had a claim to the lordship of Wexford too; therefore, John Talbot had links to Ireland even before his appointment as lieutenant in 1414. Talbot most probably organized the grant of Crumlin manor to Merbury in the following year. Once the period of crisis marking the end of Richard II's and much of Henry IV's reigns had abated, the impetus for granting out the royal manors usually came from the justiciar in Dublin. Certainly, the powerful magnates that dominated the Irish scene throughout the fifteenth century – namely the Talbots, Butlers and Fitzgeralds – all had an influence in dividing the patronage pie, and the grants at their disposal included the four royal manors in this study.[96] Additionally, when the

89 Ibid., p. 440. **90** *CPR, 1399–1401*, p. 387; *CPR, 1413–16*, p. 20. **91** Paul Brand, 'Chancellors and keepers of the great seal, (A) 1232–1534' in *NHI*, ix, pp 504–5. **92** *CPR, 1413–16*, p. 326; *CIRCLE*, PR 2 Hen. V, §125. **93** *CPR, 1399–1401*, p. 122. **94** *CPR, 1416–22*, p. 300. **95** Ibid., p. 375. **96** For magnate power and conflict in fifteenth century Ireland, see, for example, D.B. Queen, 'Aristocratic autonomy, 1460–94' in *NHI*, ii, pp 591–618; Crooks, 'Factionalism and noble power', passim; Elizabeth Matthew, 'The governing of the Lancastrian lordship of Ireland in the time of James Butler, fourth earl of Ormond, *c.*1420–52' (PhD, University of Durham, 1984), passim; Margaret Griffith, 'The Talbot–Ormond struggle for

Fitzgeralds were in the ascendant in the second half of the century, they constructed castles on the royal manors of Newcastle Lyons and Crumlin, which gave them a physical presence in the locality.[97]

Before the end of Henry IV's reign, the manors of Esker, Newcastle Lyons and Saggart were in the hands of John Dabrichcourt.[98] He, like Norbury, received lands forfeited during the usurpation, gaining property in Kent and Rutland,[99] but he had also received grants from the previous king. In April 1399, Richard II confirmed two grants that had previously been made to Dabrichcourt by John of Gaunt, granting him fifty marks from the manor of Duffeld on the condition that he would serve only the king.[1] Dabrichcourt had been John of Gaunt's steward and his close ties with the house of Lancaster certainly suggest that he could not be easily bought, though in early 1399, when nothing seemed certain, he might have thought it wise to hedge his bets. Nonetheless, Richard's insistence that he take an oath promising only to serve him suggests that his loyalties lay elsewhere. The rewards he subsequently received confirm that he was held high in the estimation of the new king and that of his son, to whom he subsequently served as keeper of the Tower of London.[2]

When Dabrichcourt was granted the royal manors of Esker, Newcastle Lyons and Saggart, in addition to the granges of Milltown and Kilmactalway, in Newcastle Lyons, and Ballinteer, which was an outlying grange of Saggart, at least four other men were receiving annuities from the revenues of these lands.[3] John Humbleton received 12*d*. a day from the fee-farm of Esker,[4] Laurence Newton collected 12*d*. daily from the issues of Esker and Newcastle Lyons[5] and Thomas Brayles and Thomas Dounes received annuities of 40*s*. apiece, which were derived from the revenues of all three manors. All, apart from Thomas Dounes, were granted these annuities for life, with the promise that they would revert to Dabrichcourt on their demise. Naturally, there was no guarantee that he would outlive these men and these annuities would have put a significant dent into the potential profits he otherwise could have expected from the manors.

PATRONAGE AND THE KING'S TENANTS

Introduction
As has been demonstrated above, many members of the king's household, as well as administrators within the Irish colony, benefited from grants of lands and annuities on the royal manors. Patronage, however, filtered down though all levels of society, and a significant number of the king's tenants were beneficiaries

control of the Anglo-Irish government', *IHS*, 2 (1940–1), 376–97.   **97** *CICD*, p. 43.   **98** *CPR*, *1413–16*, p. 55.   **99** Given-Wilson, *Royal household*, p. 234.   **1** *CPR, 1396–9*, p. 534.   **2** *CPR*, *1413–16*, p. 103.   **3** Ibid., 55; *CIRCLE*, PR 9 Hen. IV, §34.   **4** *CPR, 1399–1401*, p. 35.   **5** Ibid., p. 198.

of royal largesse. This patronage usually came in the form of administrative office, either within central government, or at county and local level. Wolffe believed that the royal demesne in England did not serve as 'a nursery of royal administration and justice'.[6] He also dismissed the importance of the revenues of the royal demesne in England as a means of rewarding officers and servants, declaring that they made only an 'intermittent, fluctuating and normally rather insignificant contribution to the expenses of government'.[7] This writer does not believe that this reflects the experience in Dublin, where the royal manors played a significant part in providing officials for both central and local government. Moreover, it provided the means for paying the salaries of at least some of these individuals. The locality benefited too, as its inhabitants were drawn into the sphere of royal government. This in turn strengthened the link between core and periphery. Involvement in government at all levels also helped shape the identity of the king's tenants and was a vital factor in the development of a gentry class.[8] This investigation of the administrators associated with the royal manors begins with central government, followed by an examination of county administrators. Local manorial officers are dealt with in the following chapter, as are the office of the seneschal of the royal demesne, a position that was usually filled by an outsider who rarely had any interests on the royal manors aside from this office. The focus here is on known tenants of the manors who held government, civic and county office.

The social structure of the royal manors – and by extension Co. Dublin – was multi-layered, and power was distributed more widely than has hitherto been fully appreciated. Indubitably, those who appear most prominently in the sources in the thirteenth and fourteenth centuries – though they may not necessarily have held entire manors – had multiple parcels of land that combined to create substantial landholdings. These large landowners were undoubtedly members of the gentry rather than belonging lower down the social scale. Furthermore, many individuals and families who had lands on these manors became full-time administrators. For example, at least two generations of the Russell/Crumlin family were involved in county administration and they may have supplemented their revenues with the salary of administrative office. In contrast, though some of the earliest tenants on the royal manors can be identified as having important roles in the administration of the lordship, there were many layers of administration, and the upper strata of the peasant class could potentially have filled many offices within the manors.

6 Wolffe, *Royal demesne*, p. 30.   7 Ibid., p. 65.   8 The gentry class in England has received more attention than their counterparts in Ireland: see, for example, Peter Coss, *The origins of the English gentry* (Cambridge, 2003); Bennett, *Community, class and careerism*; Hugh Thomas, *Vassals, heiresses, crusaders and thugs: the gentry of Angevin Yorkshire, 1154–1216* (Philadelphia, 1993); Raluca Radulescu and Alison Truelove (eds), *Gentry culture in late medieval England* (Manchester, 2005); E. Acheson, *A gentry community: Leicestershire in the fifteenth century, c.1422–c.1485* (Cambridge, 1992).

The officers of the exchequer, chancery and judiciary

In Dublin, the revenues of the royal manors were used as a means of rewarding individuals involved in central government. The advantage of using these lands is clear, since the four manors were in such close proximity to the city of Dublin. In 1216–17, Bartholomew de Camera held the royal manor of Esker, and – as his name would suggest – he worked in the exchequer of Dublin, holding the office of chamberlain in the early years of the thirteenth century.[9] He first appeared in the records in 1206–7.[10] Aside from Esker, he also received the church of Dungarvan and a prebend in the diocese of Ossory.[11] Simon de Camera, who was a tenant on the manor of Saggart, and appeared on several jury lists in the last quarter of the thirteenth century, may have been related to him or, alternatively, he too may have been employed in the exchequer.[12] It is likely that Bartholomew received the grant of Esker because of his connections within the exchequer. He, in turn, may have been in a position to grant smaller parcels of lands on the royal manors to other family members. Simon may be a descendant of one of these relatives. As is illustrated below, many tenants on the royal manors shared surnames with clerics who had originally come to Dublin to work in the administration, which would suggest that they settled on these lands thanks to the influence of these men.

By 1229, William Fitz Wido of London, the first dean of the chapter of St Patrick's Cathedral, had succeeded Camera to the manor of Esker.[13] There is evidence of a manor house here during Fitz Wido's tenure, because he was granted the manor for life on the condition that the houses there would revert to the king on Fitz Wido's death. The chapter of St Patrick was permanently granted two acres in Liscaillah in Esker. This land was used to build dykes and fish ponds and it was adjacent to both the manor house and the church, thus providing some clues as to the form of the settlement.[14] Fitz Wido also appears in the records as William de London, and he was the nephew of Henry de London, archbishop of Dublin.[15] Since Henry established the chapter of St Patrick's Cathedral, it is clear that he was instrumental in the nomination of William as its first dean. Henry also provided another of his nephews, Simon Blund, with the position of precentor of the same cathedral, demonstrating that nepotism was alive and well in thirteenth-century Dublin.[16] Walter de London and Robert Blund, who were canons of St Patrick's during the 1220s, may also have been related to the archbishop.[17] Another Robert Blund, who held the prebend of Swords and died in 1277, was possibly a member of this family too.[18]

---

9 *CDI, 1171–1251*, §740; *Admin. Ire.*, p. 118.   10 *CDI, 1171–1251*, §321.   11 Ibid., §§518, 984.
12 *CDI, 1285–92*, §953; *CDI, 1293–1301*, §§106, 264; *CJR, 1305–7*, p. 235; *RHSJ*, pp 204–5.
13 Cotton, *Fasti ecclesiae Hibernicae*, p. 91.   14 *CDI, 1171–1251*, §§1752, 1762, 1763.
15 *Alen's reg.*, pp 47–8; *CDI, 1171–1251*, §1731.   16 Cotton, *Fasti ecclesiae Hibernicae*, p. 109;
Eric St John Brooks, 'Archbishop Henry of London and his Irish connections', *JRSAI*, 60
(1930), 5.   17 Cotton, *Fasti ecclesiae Hibernicae*, p. 192.   18 Ibid., p. 135.

Archbishop Henry also helped advance other members of his family with lands rather than offices. Andrew Blund, another nephew of the archbishop, was granted lands in Kinsaley in north Dublin.[19] Though he eventually sold all his Irish property, the surname Blund was a common one on the royal manors, and some of them may have been members of this family.[20]

H.G. Richardson and G.O. Sayles observed how vital the chapter of St Patrick's was in providing officials for the Irish administration in the immediate aftermath of the invasion and in subsequent centuries.[21] Many members of this cathedral community participated in royal service throughout the medieval period, and it is therefore not surprising to see a significant number of them holding lands on, or offices associated with, the royal manors.[22] Though arguably the same could be said of other religious establishments in Ireland at the time, the career of Thomas Snitterby, who held lands on the manor of Newcastle Lyons, demonstrates the importance of this particular institution. He first came to Ireland in 1285 and eventually became a prebendary of St Patrick's Cathedral. By the end of the century, he was serving as a justice of the bench.[23] He later held Waspailstown in the vicinity of Newcastle Lyons.[24] Thomas' patronymic indicates that he came from Snitterby in Lincolnshire, and he returned there at the end of his life. His Irish career undoubtedly provided a window of opportunity for relatives like Nicholas Snitterby, who, in 1337, held the post of baron of the exchequer.[25] Like his relative, he subsequently became a justice of the bench. Though he was superseded as a baron of the exchequer in 1342, he was reappointed again in 1352 and 1354.[26] In 1351, he was granted papal permission to choose a confessor. This indult specified that he was a layman; therefore, though he had an administrative career like Thomas Snitterby, he did not follow him into the church.[27] There is really no evidence linking Nicholas Snitterby to the royal manors, but on St Patrick's Day in 1370 another Thomas Snitterby, who may well be his son, captured two Irishmen in Newcastle.[28] It is possible that this second Thomas was a tenant on this manor and the family may have owed their establishment here to the first Thomas.

The Brun family
The importance of the church as a means of supplying the administration in Dublin – and consequently providing tenants for manors in its vicinity – is borne out by the Brun family. Judging by the multiple examples of people sharing this, albeit not uncommon, surname in the south Dublin area, this was a family that,

19 Brooks, 'Archbishop Henry of London', 5.   20 For examples of Blunds living in Newcastle Lyons, see *CDI, 1252–84*, §§1170, 1814, 1834; *CDI, 1285–92*, §§309, 330, 341, 371, 501; *CDI, 1293–1301*, §§41, 139, 206, 226, 264, 279, 363, 408, 550, 587, 613, 637, 748, 825; *CDI, 1302–7*, §§4, 72.   21 *Admin. Ire.*, p. 2; see also Clarke, 'External influences', p. 81.   22 Clarke, 'External influences', p. 89.   23 F.E. Ball, *The judges in Ireland* (2 vols, New York, 1927), i, pp 57–8. 24 NAI, RC 8/8, pp 664–5.   25 *Admin. Ire.*, p. 109.   26 Ball, *Judges*, i, p. 76.   27 *CPL, 1342–62*, p. 455.   28 *CCM, 1515–74*, 5 [Book of Howth], p. 169.

having initially arrived to serve in the administration, deeply permeated local society. Brownstown, just to the north of Newcastle, was almost certainly named after this family, as Fromund Brun held lands there.[29] Moreover, the Brun family also held a substantial amount of land elsewhere in Dublin. It would perhaps be useful to use the Brun family as an illustration of royal tenants who were also major landowners across Co. Dublin. With this purpose in mind, their associations with other royal tenants, as well as their landholdings elsewhere in Dublin, are investigated below.

The Brun family owed their initial advancement in Ireland to their association with the priory of Holy Trinity. At some point before the death of the archbishop of Dublin, Laurence O'Toole, in 1180, William Brun was granted lands in Killester in north Co. Dublin.[30] One of the witnesses on a couple of the deeds relating to this transaction was Osbert Trussell, who can perhaps be identified as Osbert Russell, whose descendants would become very prominent tenants on the manor of Crumlin. Indeed, they became associated with this manor to such an extent that they eventually adopted the surname Crumlin. Undoubtedly, the tenants on the royal manors had close ties with each other that are only hinted at within the sources, but it is likely that the Russells and the Bruns were close associates if they are appearing on each other's charters. Like the Russells, the Brun family held lands on the archbishop's manor of Swords.[31] William Brun's son, Owen – who held the office of chamberlain of the exchequer before 1222 – was granted the tithes of David Latimer's lands in Artane.[32] Thomas Crumlin later acquired these lands through marriage.

The Bruns also had associations with other tenants on the royal manors. In 1207, Owen Brun and Bartholomew Camera of Esker were responsible for bringing 1,500 marks of the issues of Ireland over to England.[33] Clearly, both men held positions of great trust and the grants of land made to them exemplify their importance to local administration. Moreover, not only were these men acquiring land, they were also in a position to grant lands to others. It was in this way that patronage percolated down through the different layers of manorial society. Owen Brun assigned lands that had previously belonged to his father to the hospital of St John of Jerusalem at Kilmainham. Additionally, lands here that Owen Brun granted to the citizens of the city of Dublin also eventually passed into the hands of the Hospitallers.[34] In 1205, he paid thirty marks for the custody of the land and heir of David Bas.[35] As well as receiving the profits of this land until his ward came of age, he had the right to bestow the marriage of the heir on whomsoever he chose. He could have sold this marriage to someone else, thereby making a profit from the transaction, or married the heir off to one of his own relatives or associates. Accumulating land and wealth through

29 *CDI, 1252–84*, §1740.   30 *CCD*, pp 123–4, §468.   31 *Alen's reg.*, p. 17.   32 Ibid., p. 33.
33 *CDI, 1171–1251*, §357.   34 *CARD*, 1, p. 163.   35 *CDI, 1171–1251*, §274.

marriage was a sure way of enhancing the family's prestige and standing in the community.

In 1273, Fromund Brun, who was almost certainly related to Owen Brun, paid the enormous sum of £1,243 5*s.* 1/2*d.* of the rent and arrears of Newcastle Lyons into the exchequer.[36] The family was in possession of Brownstown, a grange within this manor. In the mid-thirteenth century, Brun served as chancellor.[37] The preponderance of chancellors of Ireland holding lands on the royal manors in the fourteenth century is discussed below. Coincidently, many of these individuals were dignitaries of St Patrick's, again emphasizing the importance of this institution to the administration of the colony.[38] Fromund Brun's acquisition of the chancellor's office appears to have been the pinnacle of a long career in the Dublin administration. He served as clerk of the justiciar John fitz Geoffrey in 1248 and he was also at this time described as the pope's chaplain.[39]

Other individuals with this surname were involved in the running of the Irish administration. In 1251, for example, William Brun served as a baron of the exchequer, and in 1255 he was responsible for making an extent of Balscadden – near Balbriggan in north Dublin – which was then part of the king's demesne.[40] Towards the end of the century, Geoffrey Brun (like Owen before him) held the office of chamberlain of the exchequer.[41] He was also clerk of the king's works in Ireland and was responsible for the construction and upkeep of the king's castles here.[42] He held the manor of Lucan and he may have been related to Maurice Brun, a contemporary of his living on the nearby manor of Ballyfermot.[43] This might suggest that individuals who held large grants of land on the royal manors were able to secure land for their relatives and followers on other surrounding manors. While the royal manors were often viewed as a unit – for example, the seneschal of demesne often had jurisdiction over these four manors or they were sometimes all granted to the same individual – they were not divorced from the rest of the locality. Many of the more substantial tenants on the royal manors owned lands elsewhere and they probably used all the property at their disposal to provide for other family members or associates.

Several other Bruns also held other property on the royal manors. Nigel

---

36 *RDKPRI*, 36, p. 50.   37 *CDI, 1171–1251*, §1840; this royal letter mentioning Brun as chancellor is dated by Sweetman to 1230, but it is undoubtedly of a later date, as the subject of the letter – Hugh de Coolock – appears in sources dating to the 1270s.   38 Clarke, 'External influences', p. 85.   39 *CDI, 1171–1251*, §2966; Fromund Brun was elected to the office of archbishop of Dublin in 1271 by the dean and convent of the Holy Trinity at Christ Church, but the dean and chapter of St Patrick's chose William de Corner as their candidate (*CPL, 1198–1304*, p. 457; *CDI, 1252–84*, §913). This double election led to a stalemate, and the archbishopric remained vacant for eight years until John de Derlington's investiture (*CDI, 1252–84*, §1545). Perhaps in an attempt to assuage the loss of this office, the king ordered the justiciar in 1282 to grant Fromund a prebend or other benefice in his gift (*CDI, 1293–1301*, §1987).   40 *CDI, 1171–1251*, §3128; *CDI, 1252–84*, §482.   41 *Admin. Ire.*, pp 118–19; *CDI, 1285–92*, §750; *CDI, 1293–1301*, §98.   42 *CDI, 1285–92*, §558.   43 *CDI, 1293–1301*, §264; NAI, EX 2/1, p. 10.

Brun, a knight described as the king's valet in the sources, held the manor of Chapelizod in 1290 and became escheator of Ireland in 1308.[44] He had previously held the position of seneschal of the liberty of Kildare.[45] He also had possession of Balyhaueny, which appears to be Owenstown near modern-day Mount Merrion, and these lands were part of the royal demesne at this time.[46] This property, which was also known as Rabo, corresponds to modern-day Roebuck, close to Dundrum. These lands would later pass into the hands of his son, Fromund.[47] This Brun was clearly named after the older Fromund, which strongly implies a familial connection. In 1281–2, Nigel received Fromund's fee for his position as chancellor, confirming this association.[48] When Nigel was granted 160 acres in Balyhaueny in 1306, it was because he did not hold any other lands in the king's demesne at that time.[49] Nigel was subsequently granted extensive royal lands in the Dublin Mountains, including Glencree, in 1308.[50] By 1309–10, he was paying rent of Finnstown and Kissoge on the royal manor of Esker.[51] At around this time, William Brun held lands in Ballydowd, also on the manor of Esker, and it is possible that he was related to Nigel.[52] Even though Nigel already held substantial lands, it is clear that these royal acquisitions enhanced his social standing within the local community. The status attached to possessing property on the royal demesne cannot be overestimated.

Nevertheless, though he would have actively sought out the grant of these lands, they would not have been given to him unless it was also beneficial to the crown. The king rewarded him because he depended on him not only within the lordship itself, but also in his other dominions. In 1301–2, Nigel received a royal letter requesting aid in the Scottish wars, and his enrolment of receipts regarding his pay while in Scotland into the exchequer in 1303–4 confirms that he answered this summons.[53] He had previously spent time in the service of Richard de Burgh, earl of Ulster, emphasizing the fact that even those who had long careers in royal service did not depend on rewards and preferment from the king alone, but often served more than one master.[54]

Other Bruns were either tenants on the royal manors or were closely associated with other known tenants, and they may have acquired these lands because of their family connections. For example, Richard Brun was certainly a tenant in Saggart, as he paid the farm of this manor in 1301.[55] He also served as a pledge to Richard Beg, provost of Saggart, in 1306.[56] Though it cannot be said with any certainty that these lands were on one of the royal manors, Simon Brun held a messuage in Dublin from the king's escheator in 1281.[57] When Walter Brun was killed in suspicious circumstances in 1272–3, the inhabitants of Esker,

44 *CDI, 1285–92*, §665; *Admin. Ire.*, p. 126.   45 *CDI, 1293–1301*, §391.   46 *CJR, 1305–7*, p. 69.   47 *CDI, 1302–7*, §319; Ball, *Dublin*, 2, p. 77.   48 *Exchequer payments*, p. 66.   49 *CJR, 1305–7*, pp 213–14.   50 NAI, EX 2/1, p. 295.   51 *RDKPRI*, 39, p. 28.   52 *CJR, 1305–7*, p. 282.   53 *CDI, 1302–7*, §§47, 295.   54 *CDI, 1285–92*, §910.   55 *CDI, 1293–1301*, §825. 56 NAI, EX 2/1, p. 159.   57 *CDI, 1293–1301*, §1780.

Ballyfermot, Lucan and Palmerstown were fined because they buried him without summoning the coroner or raising the hue.[58] Unfortunately, there is no solid evidence that Walter was local to the area, though it is likely that he was and he may even have been a member of this family. John Owen of Saggart was a tenant of Nigel Brun's son Fromund.[59] The location of these lands is not identified, but Nigel was also a tenant of the king. In 1319, he requested relief of crown rent due to losses incurred from the Bruce invasion, and, therefore, it is possible that his lands were in Saggart and that John Owen was renting lands from him there.[60] Like other members of his family, the younger Fromund was employed in public service and – like the elder Fromund – he held the office of chancellor of Ireland. Once again, the holding of the chancellor's office is linked with the possession of royal lands. Moreover, he had interests in Dublin city because he quitclaimed Buttevant Tower – one of the towers on the city walls – to the mayor and commonalty in 1327.[61] Twenty years later, he, or perhaps his son, served as sheriff of Dublin; thus marking more than a century and a half of service by this family to the king in city and county.[62] He was certainly one of the more important people in the county at the time, because an entry in the papal register for 1354 describes him as being a knight.[63] The Brun family continued as owners of Roebuck in south Dublin until the mid-fifteenth century, when this manor passed into the hands of the Barnewall family through an heiress. According to F.E. Ball, the Bruns also owned much of what is now Clonskeagh until they died out in the male line.[64] This family was involved in the administration of the colony almost from its inception, and many of them benefited from grants of land on the royal manors. The first of them to arrive here were clerics, but members of their retinue and relatives who joined them in the colony undoubtedly benefited too. These clerics had the power to acquire lands on the royal manors for family members and associates, and the proliferation of Bruns on the royal manors for the rest of the medieval period suggests that they made good use of their influence.

Royal servants and local patronage

Although the church performed a vital role in attracting colonists to settle on the royal manors, some families owed their position to royal favour and beneficial marriage alliances rather than their association with churchmen. The experience in Ireland was similar to that in England, where royal lands and offices were used to reward those involved in royal service. For example, the recipients of grants of land on the royal manor of Havering in Essex were usually royal servants and, like their English counterparts, it is likely that the beneficiaries of royal grants on the Dublin manors leased their lands to locals.[65] Yet many left an indelible

58 *RDKPRI*, 36, p. 25. 59 NAI, RC 8/4, p. 491. 60 *CARD*, 1, pp 149–51. 61 Ibid., pp 115–16. 62 *Exchequer payments*, p. 422; *CPR, 1348–50*, p. 22. 63 *CPL, 1342–62*, p. 526. 64 Ball, *Dublin*, 2, p. 77. 65 McIntosh, *Autonomy and community*, p. 19.

mark on the locality, like the Waspails, who were an important family both in Dublin and in the rest of the lordship throughout the thirteenth century. They owed this importance to royal service and the holding of public office. It is likely that Roger Waspail visited Ireland with John, future king of England, on his first expedition here as lord of Ireland. Yet there is no evidence of him being in the country until 1204, by which time he was married to Margery the daughter of Thomas Fleming, who had been granted substantial lands in Kildare by Strongbow.[66] It seems likely that the marriage was contracted during his visit here with the future king. He continued to be the recipient of royal favour after he settled in Ireland, and in 1224, he became seneschal of Ulster.[67] On 22 April 1225, Earl William Marshal, then justiciar, was ordered to grant Roger £20 worth of land out of the escheats of Ireland.[68] Clearly, the purpose of this grant was to support him while in the king's service. Waspail died shortly after this grant was made and his son Henry succeeded him. He subsequently died without issue and was succeeded by his brother, Roger. We know that this Roger possessed lands near the king's demesne of Newcastle Lyons by 1230, because in that year Henry of Tallaght was granted lands in the vicinity between the king's lands and Roger's lands.[69] It is unknown when these lands were acquired and thus it is entirely possible that they were in the family's possession since his father's time. The presence of this family in the area is still felt through the place-name Waspaillstown. There is another Waispaillstown – now known as Westmanstown – near Clonsilla in north Dublin, and it is possible that it was named after the same family. The holder paid the service of half a knight for this land.[70] Adam Roche held this military tenure during the reign of Edward I, but if Roger held it earlier in the century, the reason for his presence in Co. Dublin is abundantly clear.[71] Not only were administrators and farmers needed to maintain the colony, but also fighting men were essential to protect it.

In 1265, in the midst of the Barons' War, Roger Waspaill became justiciar of Ireland on the instigation of Simon Montfort, though it appears unlikely that he ever assumed office.[72] There is no evidence of Waspail suffering any reversal of fortune due to his support of Montfort. Nonetheless, it does indicate that grants of lands, offices and the other benefits of royal patronage could not guarantee complete and undivided loyalty to the crown. The Waspails also owned substantial lands in Limerick, and, in 1280, another Roger, probably the previous Roger's son, exchanged these lands for lands in Dorset.[73] It is clear that this Roger spent most of his time in England from at least 1277, because from this time on he was nominating attorneys in Ireland to look after his interests.[74] It

66 *Knights fees*, p. 85.   67 *CDI, 1171–1251*, §1158.   68 Ibid., §1272.   69 *Alen's reg.*, pp 64–5.
70 A.J. Otway-Ruthven, 'Knight service in Ireland' in Crooks (ed.), *Government, war and society*, p. 157.   71 Bateson, 'Irish exchequer memoranda', 502.   72 *CDI, 1252–84*, §727; see Robin Frame, *Ireland and Britain, 1170–1450* (London, 1998), pp 59–69, for an account of the effects of the Barons' War on Ireland.   73 *Knights fees*, p. 86.   74 *CDI, 1252–84*, §§1354, 1817, 2185.

appears that the main branch of the family moved away from Ireland around this time, though there is still evidence of Waspails in Ireland. In the 1280s, a William Waspail served as a juror and, sometime before 1284, the justiciar knighted him. He was also one of the executors of the will of Adam St John.[75] It is likely that he was Roger's brother or son. In January 1299, another Roger Waspail was in possession of a freehold in Lucan; this included fishery rights as well as shares in two mills and, while it is possible that he is the aforementioned Roger, it seems more likely that this tenement belonged to another member of the family.[76] They no longer had any claim on Waspaillstown by the early fourteenth century, as Thomas Snitterby had possession of these lands in 1313.[77] The Waspails endured into the latter half of the fourteenth century and another William Waspail is mentioned as a juror in the city of Dublin in 1371–2.[78] The family is clearly not as prominent in Ireland in the fourteenth century as it once had been, and, certainly, no member held any important administrative position. It is likely that the main branch of the family decided to move its interests back to England, where they had maintained lands throughout the thirteenth century. The Waspails were the beneficiaries of royal patronage, but they were much more than that. The fact that a townland in Newcastle Lyons still bears their name and that at least three generations of their family lived in Ireland implies that they left their mark on the locality, even if the sources do not fully bear out the extent of this impact. They clearly were an integral part of local society throughout the thirteenth century.

Local patronage as an aid to colonization

Some major families who came over to Ireland in the aftermath of the invasion did not receive lands on the royal manors, but many were nonetheless involved in some capacity in the administration of these manors. Additionally, individuals sharing the same surname as some of these prominent families became minor tenants and it is possible that they also shared kinship ties with them. For example, the Luttrell family first became associated with Ireland when Geoffrey Luttrell, a close companion of King John, came to Ireland in 1204 to serve as a mediator between the justiciar and magnates of Ireland. A decade later, he served as sheriff of Dublin and was responsible for rendering the accounts of the royal manors.[79] There is no evidence that he was granted Luttrellstown in Co. Dublin and the infiltration by this family into Dublin society may in fact be thanks to Robert Luttrell, who was another canon of St Patrick's.[80] It appears that Robert owed his initial advancement to Geoffrey's close links with the crown and, as well as serving as treasurer of St Patrick's, he also held the posts of chancellor and treasurer of Ireland.[81] The Luttrells permeated Dublin society

75 Ibid., §§1666, 2361. 76 *CJR, 1295–1303*, pp 222–3. 77 NAI, RC 8/8, pp 664–5.
78 *CARD*, 1, p. 138. 79 PR 14 John, 7. 80 F.E. Ball identifies him as a kinsman of Sir Geoffrey Luttrell in: *Judges*, 1, p. 46. 81 *Alen's reg.*, pp 47–8; *Admin. Ire.*, pp 92, 98.

and, although they are mainly associated with Luttrellstown in Clonsilla, some members of this family also held lands on the royal manors. For example, in 1319, William Luttrell owed the king 60s. of the rent of Esker.[82] During the first quarter of the fourteenth century, another Geoffrey Luttrell appeared on several Dublin jury lists, including one case involving tenants from the royal manor of Saggart.[83]

Several other families and individuals could be cited as examples of tenants on the royal manors who also served as vital cogs in the wheel of the local and state administration. The Owen family, however, are particularly prominent in the records of the time, and they held lands on all four royal manors.[84] Roger Owen served as the king's pleader in the second half of the thirteenth century.[85] He was responsible for representing the king's interests in judicial proceedings within the colony. The position was an important one and the king's pleader was considered to be of a higher status than a king's attorney was, and often attained judicial office.[86] Roger Owen's experience as king's pleader does not appear to have been a particularly happy one. He sent a petition to England complaining that even though he had carried out these duties for a long period, he had yet to be remunerated for his services. He pointedly added that, had he been working for one of the Irish magnates instead of the king, he would have earned a large salary.[87] In the same petition, Roger requested an exchange with the king of land in Newcastle Lyons for land in Saggart. He claimed that the king's lands in Saggart were close to the lands of war and declared that it would be to the crown's benefit to exchange these for lands belonging to him in Newcastle. Sweetman dated this document to 1272 and hence, even at this relatively early date, it would appear that the locality was under pressure from the Irish in the nearby mountains. Of course, Roger could have been exaggerating the severity of the situation in the hope that this seemingly altruistic act would either encourage the payment of his salary or help him get a larger parcel of land in Saggart than the one he was giving up in Newcastle Lyons. It appears that his request was granted, as there is evidence of him paying arrears of the rent of Saggart in 1288.[88]

Richardson and Sayles estimate that he was in the king's service for fourteen years.[89] Individuals who refused to take up public office could be fined or suffer the confiscation of their property. Nonetheless, though participation in local and central government was compulsory, the careers of men like Roger Owen reveal that some freely chose to become administrators and could remain in service for a significant length of time. Roger and his descendants owned parcels of land on the royal manors, and elsewhere in Dublin and Kildare, but participation in public office appears to have been at least as important an indicator of Roger's

82 NAI, RC 8/12, p. 476.   83 *CJR, 1305–7*, pp 480–1.   84 *Alen's reg.*, pp 185–9. The Owen family is examined in detail in ch. 4, below.   85 *Admin. Ire.*, p. 174.   86 Ibid., pp 41–2. 87 TNA C 47/10/13/6; *CDI, 1252–84*, §930.   88 *CDI, 1285–92*, §371.   89 *Admin. Ire.*, p. 40.

position in society as the ownership of land. The prestige of being in service to the king was clearly important to Roger; otherwise, he would not have spent over a decade as a royal servant, particularly as financial reward often appeared to be unforthcoming. In fact, the parcels of royal land granted to Roger may have been a way of compensating him for wages unpaid.

Roger already held lands in Ballymadun by 1249–50, part of the dower of his wife Aufrica.[90] Roger held one third of two mills on this manor in north Dublin, while the king held the other two thirds. Roger held one third of the entire manor through his wife and, as Roger Cordewener had enfeoffed all the other tenants of their lands, it indicates that he was a previous holder of the manor.[91] Aufrica had previously been married to John Cordewener and it is likely that Roger was his father.[92] A Roger Cordewener, who later held the office of mayor of Bristol, had served as King John's messenger in Ireland at the turn of the thirteenth century. His name and place of origin indicate that he was a merchant and, as someone who travelled extensively, he was well suited to the role of messenger. His father, Elias, had originally held the manor of Ballymadun from Robert Ruffus, who had attended the future King John on his first expedition to Ireland.[93] It was Ruffus' responsibility to procure supplies for the earl while on expedition and, therefore, he, like Cordewener, may have been a merchant.[94]

County administrators

Most of the administrators dealt with thus far were associated with central government in offices within the exchequer, the chancery or the courts. Many tenants, however, were also involved in local administration at both county and manorial level. The Russell/Crumlin family are a case in point. They served in county administration for at least two generations, and multiple generations of the family served in manorial administration. In terms of county administration, the most successful member of the family was Adam Crumlin, who served as sheriff at the end of the thirteenth century.[95] This family was probably typical of many Dublin families who were involved in county administration in this period; with this in mind, it might be useful to examine their background to establish the calibre and social status of the men who were granted these offices.

The Crumlins appear prominently in the sources throughout the thirteenth and fourteenth centuries and, like many of their fellow tenants, they seem to have had an association with a canon of the cathedral of St Patrick. Patrick Russell, parson of the church of Balrothery in north Dublin, may have been a member of the Russell family of Crumlin, and his presence there could have been the impetus for their move to Ireland.[96] Though the Russells are more closely associated with Crumlin, they did possess lands in north Dublin. Osbert

90 *CDI, 1171–1251*, §3035. 91 *IEMI*, p. 5. 92 *CDI, 1171–1251*, §§1830, 1842, 1865. 93 Ibid., §939. 94 Ibid., §73. 95 NAI, EX 2/1, p. 71; *CDI, 1293–1301*, §§658, 825; *CJR, 1295–1303*, pp 261, 264. 96 *Alen's reg.*, pp 34–5.

Trussell, who held lands in Wimbletown in Lusk in the early thirteenth century, was possibly a relative of the Russells of Crumlin.[97] The fact that he lived in Dublin about a generation before Osbert Crumlin suggests a family association, as the personal name Osbert was relatively rare in Ireland.[98] At around the same time that Osbert Trussell held lands in north Dublin, William Crumlin was paying the yearly rent of a pound of pepper for land in Crumlin.[99] Future members of the same family would pay a pound of pepper annually for a messuage on this manor and it is almost certainly the same holding. William paid £16 in pepper for this property in 1212, which would suggest that he was several years in arrears by this date. It appears that the family had been living on this manor since the end of the twelfth century at the latest. They also continued to maintain interests in north Dublin. During the middle of the thirteenth century, John Crumlin granted thirty-seven acres of land in Swords to Margery Crumlin – who was probably his daughter – and her new husband, Richard Killeich.[1]

Osbert Crumlin appears to have succeeded William to the lands in Crumlin and he was probably his son. An interesting entry appears in the English patent rolls for the year 1257, when an Osbert Cromelin of Worcester was granted a respite from knighthood because he was old and feeble.[2] Osbert Crumlin of Dublin had possessed lands in Tallaght in the mid-thirteenth century, which made him a contemporary of Osbert of Worcester.[3] This appears to be more than a coincidence. Not only did they share the same name, but the Cromelins in Worcester appear to have had kinship ties with the Russells of that same county. In the reign of Henry II, lands in Huddington in Worcestershire came into the hands of Simon son of Adam Croome. Simon held these lands from Roger St John, who in turn held them of the bishop of Worcester. By the end of the thirteenth century, Richard Hodington was in possession of this estate. He may have been the same Richard Cromelyn who held the vill of Huddington in 1298. Alternatively, Richard Hodington may have married Richard Cromelyn's daughter, Lucy; it is unclear if there were one or two Richards. The Cromelyns of Worcester may not have had any landed interests in Dublin for some time and, therefore, it is plausible that the family decided to adopt the name of the place where all their interests now lay. In any event, the lands descended through the Hodington family until the fifteenth century, when they died out in the direct male line.[4] One of the heiresses married a William Russell and it is possible that the Cromelyns were a cadet branch of the Russell family. It was often the case that when one branch of a family died out in the male line, the heiress married into another branch to ensure the retention of their ancestral lands. In 1397, John Russell of Strensham inherited Earl's Croome and Baughton – also in Worcestershire – which had also belonged to Adam Croome two centuries

---

97 Ibid., p. 66. 98 Ibid., pp 64–5. 99 PR 14 John, 11. 1 *Alen's reg.*, p. 116. 2 *CPR, 1247–58*, p. 522. 3 *Alen's reg.*, pp 120–3. 4 *VCH, Worcestershire*, 2 (London, 1906), p. 409.

earlier.[5] There is a further interesting link between the Cromelyns and the Russells of Worcester. A tomb in the church of the manor of Strensham in the same county contains a panelled altar tomb, with a marble slab – built for Sir John Russell, who died in 1556 – bearing the arms of not only the Russell family but also of the Hodington and Cromlyn families.[6]

If Osbert Crumlin and his namesake in Worcester were the same man – which appears likely – it offers some clue as to the Crumlins' social status. Osbert Cromelin of Worcester was offered respite of knighthood, which meant that the family could at least claim to be among the ranks of the lesser nobility at this time. In fact, Osbert lived during a period in which inclusion in the knightly class was becoming more exclusive.[7] A century earlier, membership of this class was based on military service, but it was gradually developing into an elite class where wealth and ancestry superseded the importance of possessing military skills. Osbert was excused, not because he could not bear the financial responsibility of being a knight, but because of his advanced age. This confirms that they were people of consequence in their localities on both sides of the Irish Sea.

Roger Crumlin may have succeeded Osbert to his lands in Crumlin. This individual appears in the plea rolls of 1277, where he is accused of raping Sara Norreys.[8] The sources are certainly patchy for the first half of the thirteenth century, and this seems to be the only reference to Roger Crumlin, but it is likely that he was the same individual as Roger Russell, who appears occasionally in the witness lists of Dublin charters from the third quarter of the thirteenth century. He witnessed a charter relating to the church of St Audoen in 1258–9, and a couple of years later he appeared in Reginald of Gloucester's charter granting lands to the hospital of St John the Baptist.[9] Since both of these, as well as other charters featuring Roger, deal with land and people in the vicinity of south Dublin, and as witnesses for charters were usually drawn from the immediate locality, it is plausible that he is Osbert Crumlin's son. From the 1280s onwards, the administrative records improve considerably, and it becomes easier to trace this family.

Throughout the 1280s, either Thomas Russell or Thomas Crumlin regularly paid the rent and farm of the manor of Crumlin.[10] The evidence would suggest that this was the same individual and that he was Adam's father. It was not unusual in this period for the same person to be known by two or even three different surnames. An exchequer receipt of Easter 1289 states that Thomas Russell of Crumlin – and it is important to note that both forms of his surname are given here – was fined five marks for trespass, and a receipt from Michaelmas term 1288 records that Thomas Crumlin had previously been fined five marks.[11]

5 *VCH, Worcestershire*, 3 (London, 1913), pp 316–22. 6 *VCH, Worcestershire*, 4 (London, 1924), pp 206–7. 7 Coss, *English gentry*, p. 69. 8 NAI, RC 8/1, p. 602. 9 *RHSJ*, pp 33, 88–9. 10 *CDI, 1252–84*, §1780; *CDI, 1285–92*, §§309, 341, 371, 466, 475, 780. 11 *CDI, 1285–92*, §§434, 475.

There are no other examples of tenants in Crumlin being fined in this period, and hence it is likely to be the same fine, or a different fine given for a similar offence. The only other person paying rent on this land at this time was Thomas the clerk. He was occasionally called Thomas the clerk of Crumlin, though it is not clear if this is the same Thomas. He may have simply been described as a clerk because he could read.

The earliest reference to Thomas Crumlin in administrative sources dates to 1276, when Ralph Sauser accused him of 'violently' depriving him of the custody of his ward, the unnamed – and underage – daughter and heir of Adam Latimer, and then marrying her.[12] In the following year, Ralph went to court, looking for over £35 owed to him by the king for the custody of Adam Latimer's lands.[13] This would imply that Latimer's daughter was quite a substantial heiress. Thomas Crumlin's lands and chattels – as well as those of his wife – were confiscated until he agreed to appear in court. The outcome of the case is unknown, but in the long term, it could not have been detrimental to Crumlin, as his property was eventually returned to him. It must have been back in his possession by 1284 when he was included on a jury of the leading knights and free tenants of Dublin.[14] This was not the only occasion that Thomas Crumlin found himself on the wrong side of the law. In 1286, during Easter term, he was fined ten marks for trespass. Unfortunately, it does not specify the nature of the misdemeanour, but for such a large amount of money it must have been a relatively serious transgression. In the same term, he was fined a mark for contempt, and again the reference is vague but it may have been an attempt to avoid public office or jury service.[15] Thomas was fined on several different occasions but, unfortunately, the records never specify exactly why. Nevertheless, the fact that he was capable of paying those fines would certainly suggest that he was a person of substantial means.

Thomas' brushes with the law should not obscure the fact that he was also a trusted member of the community who served in the administration as both a juror and a tax collector.[16] He was responsible for collecting the fifteenth; this was a tax, which was assessed on a fraction of the value of an individual's movable goods. In England, this fraction often varied, but after 1334 it became standardized to one fifteenth of the value of a taxpayer's movable property.[17] The fifteenth appears to have been the norm in Dublin at least half a century before this date. In the 1290s, Thomas Crumlin and Geoffrey Harold collected this tax in the Vale of Dublin on several occasions.[18] The late thirteenth century marked the apex of Ireland as a source of revenue for the English crown. Edward I put extreme financial pressure on the colony as a means to fund his wars, and men like Thomas Crumlin facilitated this operation. His value as a royal servant

---

12 *CDI, 1252–84*, §1313.   13 Ibid., §1341.   14 Ibid., §2344.   15 *CDI, 1285–92*, §215.
16 *CDI, 1293–1301*, §§332, 443, 475, 528, 549, 586, 612.   17 *VCH, Essex*, 4 (London, 1956), pp 296–302.   18 *CDI, 1293–1301*, §§48, 90, 130.

explains why he was granted the farm of the king's demesne in Crumlin. The pitfalls of public service are revealed by a memoranda roll entry from 1310–11, wherein, two decades after their time as tax collectors, Geoffrey Harold and Thomas – or rather his heir, John Crumlin – still owed the considerable sum of £103 18s. 4d.[19]

As well as the money rents he paid for the manor of Crumlin, Thomas also paid one pound of pepper per year for the plot of land that had once belonged to Osbert Crumlin.[20] This is certainly the same plot of land that William Crumlin owned in 1212.[21] This parcel of land in Crumlin is separate and distinct from the one carucate and eight acres of land that belonged to the king's royal demesne.[22] A memoranda roll entry for 1309–10 states that the property for which the Crumlin family paid a pound of pepper consisted of two messuages and twenty-nine acres of land.[23] John Russell was paying the rent for this land into the exchequer by this time, which supports the theory that the Crumlins and the Russells were the same family.[24] Moreover, he is a contemporary of John Crumlin, who is described as the son and heir of Thomas Crumlin, who had previously paid the rent of this tenement.[25]

In fact, Crumlin manor was much larger than the parcel of land belonging to the Crumlins and the 128 acres that was granted to Henry Compton; it was estimated as being about 2,500 acres.[26] At the time, Compton held the 128 acres of demesne land in Crumlin, Thomas Crumlin continued to pay rent for lands on this manor into the exchequer and thus he must have had other holdings here aside from lands on the demesne and the messuage that had once belonged to Osbert Crumlin.[27] His son, Adam, had almost seventy acres sown with wheat and oats in Crumlin in 1304 and, even without taking into consideration any land that would have lain fallow, this holding is larger than the one that belonged to Osbert.[28]

It is unlikely that the Crumlin family held as much property as families like the Bruns and the Deveneys, but their interests extended far beyond the manor of Crumlin. The parcels of land they owned all over Dublin added up to a substantial landholding. The previously mentioned lands they possessed in north Dublin, as well as their property in Tallaght, do not cover the extent of their holdings. In the 1220s, a Robert Crumlin had lands near Donore in the Liberties.[29] This place survives as a street name and this property probably corresponds with lands owned by Adam Crumlin in the Coombe in the following century.[30] In 1296–7, Adam held a messuage with an orchard in Coolock. He also had thirty-six acres, three acres of meadow and two acres of pasture on the same

19 NAI, RC 8/5, pp 308, 323, 337, 339. 20 *CDI, 1285–92*, §§149, 271, 434. 21 PR 14 John, 11. 22 *CDI, 1285–92*, §855; *CDI, 1293–1301*, §264. 23 NAI, RC 8/4, p. 468; RC 8/5, p. 308. 24 NAI, EX 2/1, p. 169. 25 NAI, RC 8/4, p. 886. 26 Gillespie, 'Small worlds', p. 198. 27 *CDI, 1285–92*, §965. 28 NAI, EX 2/1, p. 174. 29 *Alen's reg.*, p. 62. 30 NAI, EX 2/1, p. 174.

manor.[31] Adam's grandfather, Adam Latimer, held lands in Artane, which is adjacent to Coolock, and consequently these lands may have originally belonged to the Latimers. The family had held lands in this area since the late twelfth century, and Adam Latimer, son of Adam, held Artane in 1337.[32] If he was underage in 1296, Adam Crumlin may have held these lands in wardship. William Russell granted half a carucate of land in Ballymakelly near Newcastle Lyons to Adam when he was sheriff of Dublin.[33] It is likely that they were related to each other, and the family may have held these lands of the archbishop of Dublin in the thirteenth century. This transaction is recorded in Archbishop Alen's register, and the lands were within the archbishop's manor of Rathcoole. Adam's son, Richard, later granted this parcel of land to John Fox, but Russells continued to hold land in the manor of Newcastle Lyons as late as the mid-sixteenth century and, therefore, they may have owned other property in the area.[34] John Crumlin, son of Thomas and brother of Adam, owned lands in Stratbaly in Co. Dublin in 1306.[35] There is a Stratbaly close to Kilsallaghan in north Co. Dublin, which is close to other places mentioned in the same source. John Crumlin had been accused of stealing cattle from Ratoath and bringing them to Stratbaly. Ratoath is in south-east Meath, not far from the border with north Dublin and close to Swords, where the Crumlin family held lands. The Russells also held property in the city of Dublin.

Adam Crumlin, sheriff of Dublin

Many men would have become full-time administrators because they were younger sons who could not expect a large inheritance from their fathers and therefore had to make their own way in the world. Adam Crumlin may fit into this category. John Crumlin inherited the parcel of land in Crumlin that had previously belonged to Thomas Crumlin; therefore, it is likely he was Adam's older brother. Adam also held land in Crumlin, but the division of land among heirs would have naturally meant that he did not hold as much land as his father held and, therefore, he may have needed to find an alternative source of income to maintain his status.

The sheriff was the most important royal official in the county and he served as a conduit between crown and community. This office was the reserve of members of the local elite and its holders came from the most politically prominent families. Adam Crumlin's qualifications for this office are clear. His family was established in the locality for at least a century and their parcels of lands scattered across the county added up to a substantial landholding. Moreover, they already had a history of being involved in county administration. The duties of the sheriff of Dublin included collecting amercements and other fines

---

31 TNA SC 12/18/18; *SCSMI*, p. 266.   32 *Alen's reg.*, p. 33; *RDKPRI*, 45, p. 25.   33 *Alen's reg.*, pp 200–1.   34 Gearóid Mac Niocaill, *Crown surveys of lands, 1540–1: with the Kildare rental begun in 1518* (Dublin, 1992), p. 84.   35 *CJR, 1295–1303*, p. 253.

imposed by the royal courts. Additionally, it was his duty to collect other revenues owed to the crown.[36] One of his most important roles was the administration of the county court. The first reference to a county court in Dublin appears in 1200; consequently, the office of sheriff was already established by this date and indeed had probably been in existence for quite some time.[37] The sheriff was also in charge of maintaining castles and gaols in his county and, by extension, he was accountable for prisoners until they were summoned to court.[38]

The office of sheriff would have enabled Adam to carve a place for himself in local society as well as providing him with a means of living. His involvement with the office of sheriff of Dublin dated back to at least 1290, when he served as clerk to the sheriff.[39] In this period, whoever served as sheriff of Dublin was often also sheriff of Meath.[40] For example, Adam appeared as sheriff in judicial cases held in Meath while he served as sheriff of Dublin.[41] In 1304, a memoranda roll entry records that he was appointed sheriff of Meath again, though on this occasion he held this office for only a month.[42]

Clearly, the sheriff's resources were stretched to the limit. Adam's stint as sheriff of Dublin suggests that an administrative career could prove not only time-consuming but also very expensive. Robert Blund of Tallaght took Adam to court on at least two occasions, seeking money owed to him, but each time the then sheriff claimed that Adam did not have the means to pay him back because all his goods had been taken to pay debts owed to the king.[43] In 1304, 38½ acres of wheat and twenty-nine acres of oats at Crumlin were taken from Adam to satisfy debts owed to the king.[44] The court, however, did not accept that Adam could not pay Robert Blund, and pressure was put on the sheriff to make Adam satisfy this debt. It established that, though all of Adam's lands in Crumlin were indeed in the king's hand, he also had rents from property in the city and on the archiepiscopal manor of St Sepulchre. It was ordered that Robert Blund was to be paid from these rents.[45] It is clear that the sheriff was reluctant to extract this money from Adam. He was undoubtedly keenly aware that a year or two down the road another sheriff might have the awkward duty of confiscating his property in order to pay debts acquired while on the job. There are multiple examples of ex-sheriffs owing arrears on their accounts. Some of these debts were still outstanding long after their deaths, which meant that the duty fell on their descendants to pay these arrears. Adam Crumlin still owed money three decades after his term as sheriff – and long after his death – underlining the

---

36 A.J. Otway-Ruthven, 'Anglo-Irish shire government in the thirteenth century' in Crooks (ed.), *Government, war and society*, p. 130; McGrath, 'Shiring of Ireland', pp 107–38.   37 *CDI, 1171–1251*, §116.   38 Otway-Ruthven, 'Anglo-Irish shire government', p. 130.   39 *CDI, 1285–92*, §598.   40 Otway-Ruthven, 'Anglo-Irish shire government', p. 124.   41 *CJR, 1295–1303*, p. 283.   42 NAI, EX 2/1, p. 109; *CJR, 1305–7*, p. 1.   43 *CJR, 1305–7*, p. 22.   44 NAI, EX 2/1, p. 174.   45 *CJR, 1305–7*, p. 199.

pitfalls of this office.[46] Alternatively, this could be a result of the reluctance of subsequent sheriffs to call in these debts.

Adam appears to have been the last person in his family to serve as an administrator at county level, though his brother John did serve as provost of Crumlin, just as his father had done before him.[47] John, who is usually referred to as John Russell, though he is occasionally called Crumlin, first appears in the records in 1301 and he frequently pays the rent of Crumlin manor in the early years of the fourteenth century.[48] He was dead by 1317, when his lands in Crumlin passed into the hands of his son, Ralph.[49]

Serjeants and sub-serjeants

A sheriff like Adam Crumlin needed several subordinates to assist him in carrying out his many duties. Aside from clerical staff, a group of serjeants assisted the sheriff.[50] Indeed, Adam himself may have been a serjeant, which may have served as an apprenticeship for his later career as sheriff. Within this group, there was a wide social gradation, as a substantial landowner normally filled the office of chief serjeant, with sub-serjeants usually plucked from a lower rung on the social ladder. Richard Blund of Tallaght served as the king's serjeant pleader and may well have been related to William and Thomas Blund of Newcastle Lyons, who were his contemporaries.[51] Richard and William Blund were both responsible for paying the issues of the archbishopric of Dublin into the exchequer in 1299–1300, and hence there might have been some kinship association between them.[52] Unfortunately, the surname Blund is relatively common in Dublin – and indeed elsewhere – at this time, and thus more evidence is needed before a tie can be firmly established between them.

From 1275 until 1284, Hugh Cruys served as king's serjeant for Co. Dublin.[53] This office became a hereditary one within the family and they were occasionally described as the chief serjeants of Leinster. The Cruys family continued to hold this office until the early years of the seventeenth century. Moreover, they also served as chief serjeants of Louth for much of the medieval period.[54] Between 21 December 1276 and 2 February 1277, Hugh Cruys was paid twenty marks for the custody of Saggart.[55] On other occasions, he was paid a fee for guarding the Vale of Dublin.[56] The office seems to have been a profitable one, and there are multiple examples of Cruys being rewarded for services rendered. Additionally, because the serjeant performed the sheriff's routine duties and was more closely involved in the practical aspects of administration, he was better

46 *RDKPRI*, 45, p. 24; NAI, EX 8/4, 999; Richard Crumlin is named as Adam's heir in the memoranda rolls for 1309–10, so he may have been deceased by this time. **47** *RDKPRI*, 39, p. 38. **48** *CDI, 1293–1301*, §825. **49** *RDKPRI*, 42, p. 18. **50** Otway-Ruthven, 'Anglo-Irish shire government', p. 135. **51** *CJR, 1305–7*, p. 12; they paid the rent of the manor of Newcastle Lyons several times towards the end of the thirteenth century: *CDI, 1293–1301*, §§587, 637, 748, passim. **52** *CDI, 1293–1301*, §§658, 735. **53** *Exchequer payments*, p. 104. **54** Otway-Ruthven, 'Anglo-Irish shire government', p. 136. **55** *CDI, 1252–84*, §1389. **56** Ibid., §1294.

placed to accept bribes. He also had more opportunities to resort to extortion than his superior did.[57] The records do not reveal if Hugh Cruys used his office in this manner, but he certainly enjoyed its legitimate rewards. On 6 February 1279, he was granted the manors of Newcastle Lyons, Saggart and Crumlin for twelve years.[58] The 1270s had been a particularly tumultuous decade for those living in this locality. It was at this time that the English started to lead expeditions into the Dublin and Wicklow mountains in order to subdue the Irish. The focus of these expeditions was Glenmalure, which was held by the O'Tooles.[59] It is clear, however, that the threat was also felt much closer to Dublin. In 1272, Roger Owen described Saggart as being in the land of war, and by the mid-1270s, several men were paid to guard this manor.[60] Therefore, the decision to grant Saggart along with Newcastle and Crumlin to Hugh Cruys was an eminently sensible one. As king's serjeant, he was well suited to maintain the defence of this manor against the marauding Irish and perhaps it was even hoped that he could turn the fortunes of this manor around and make a profit. Moreover, even if generating some sort of income from Saggart proved unfeasible, he still had the potential profits of the other manors upon which to rely.

Some individuals with links to the royal manors served as serjeants in other parts of the country. Geoffrey Brun served as deputy of the sheriff of Waterford in 1290. Furthermore, it would appear that he used the office for his own personal benefit. Adam Brun – who was the king's coroner in Waterford – complained that Geoffrey had confiscated a horse and five other beasts on account of money owed, but sold them before Adam had time to pay back the whole debt. Adam dryly observed that, as a consequence, Geoffrey had become rich and within a very short time.[61] In the same year, Philip Brun – also of Waterford – accused Geoffrey of unjustly taking 3½ marks worth of his chattels for debts owed by Reginald Brun.[62] Geoffrey does not appear to have been disciplined for these offences, highlighting the potential for extortion attached to this office.

It is even possible to establish the social standing of some of the holders of this office, as there were different ranks within the serjeantcy. In 1306, Richard Pudding accused the king's serjeant Henry Kissok and his sub-serjeant John Lung of injuring his horse while it was in their custody.[63] All three were tenants of various royal manors. Richard Pudding was an Irishman living on the manor of Saggart who had been granted the right to use English law in 1285.[64] The

57 Otway-Ruthven, 'Anglo-Irish shire government', p. 137. 58 *CDI, 1252–84*, §1528. 59 *CSMA*, 2, p. 318 refers to an expedition which occurred in 1274 and *CDI, 1252–84*, §1389 mentions another expedition that took place two years later; see also James Lydon, 'Medieval Wicklow: "a land of war"' in Ken Hannigan and William Nolan (eds), *Wicklow, history and society: interdisciplinary essays on the history of an Irish county* (Dublin, 1994), pp 151–89. 60 *CDI, 1252–84*, §§930, 1294, 1389, 1496; *Exchequer payments*, pp 12, 17, 18, 22. 61 *CDI, 1285–92*, §770. 62 Ibid., §818. 63 *CJR, 1305–7*, p. 251. 64 *CDI, 1285–92*, §1108; TNA, SC 8/331/15677; Philomena Connolly, 'Irish material in the class of ancient petitions (SC 8) in the

serjeant Henry Kissok was a major tenant on the manor of Esker.[65] He also held
the manor of Bothercolyn – which was situated in the mountains south of
Tallaght and probably formed part of the royal manor of Okelly – in 1296.[66] The
sub-serjeant John Lung was probably the son of Martin, who paid the pleas and
perquisites of the manor of Newcastle Lyons into the exchequer in 1298 and
who was a tenant on the manor of Saggart as well.[67] He does not feature as
prominently in the sources as Kissok, and this suggests that he was positioned
lower down the social scale. There is no evidence that his father Martin was ever
responsible for paying the rent of the farm of Saggart into the exchequer –
though he is identified in the justiciary rolls as coming from this manor – and
this suggests that he possessed a comparatively small holding. The delivery of
rents to the exchequer appears to have been mainly the responsibility of those
who possessed relatively substantial landholdings. In 1307, John Lung was
promoted to the office of serjeant of the king and it therefore seems possible that
minor tenants could use public office to improve their social standing.[68]

The coroner
Tenants on the royal manors also held other important posts in county administration, including that of coroner. Unlike the office of sheriff, the position of
coroner appears to have been an unattractive one and, as a result, the sheriff was
occasionally ordered to compel a potential coroner to take his oath of office by
threatening to distrain his property.[69] An examination of the career of Thomas
Kent, the coroner for Fingal in north Co. Dublin who also served as seneschal of
the king's manors of Dublin and Kildare, yields some clues as to why this office
was unpopular.[70] On at least two occasions while Kent was in office, the rights of
jurisdiction of the coroner of Co. Dublin were challenged. In 1320, Kent was
called to view bodies in St Mary's and St Thomas' abbeys. As a result, the right
of the county coroner to hold inquests within the jurisdiction of these abbeys
was questioned by city bailiffs Richard of Swords and John Crok.[71] Kent argued
that both abbeys were outside the jurisdiction of the city and within the king's
land. The jury decided against him, but he managed to avoid going to gaol
because they were of the opinion that he had acted out of ignorance rather than
malice.[72]

Some years later, in 1344, John Mareshal of Marshallsrath in Newcastle
Lyons was charged with the same offence of infringing on the rights of the city
bailiffs during his tenure as coroner for Leinster. The verdict of the justiciar's
court was the same as in the proceedings against Kent, and the bailiffs estimated
that, because of Mareshal's intrusion, the king and city had been damaged to the

Public Record Office', *Anal. Hib.*, 24 (1987), 103. **65** *CDI, 1293–1301*, §§550, 587, 613.
66 Ibid., §329. **67** Ibid., §550; *CJR, 1305–7*, p. 235. **68** *CJR, 1305–7*, p. 447. **69** *CJR,
1295–1303*, pp 60, 411. **70** *HMDI*, pp 533–4. **71** *CSMA*, i, pp 6–10. **72** *CARD*, i, pp
154–6.

sum of one thousand pounds. Mareshal did not appear and the sheriff distrained his property.[73] If he was punished for his actions, he was quickly pardoned because he was serving as constable of the castle at Balytenyth by 1346.[74]

Other individuals who appear to have come from the royal manors served in the office of coroner. Some even held this office in other jurisdictions. John of Tassagard (Saggart) was one of two coroners in Drogheda in 1311. He was committed to gaol for not recording the judgment of a murder into the coroner's rolls, but was out again shortly afterwards when he was charged with being an accomplice in a murder.[75] Around the same time that John of Tassagard was coroner for Drogheda, Richard Kissok of Esker served as coroner for Dublin. An inquisition recorded in the justiciary rolls yields up some information concerning his duties as coroner. Kissok gave evidence in the justiciar's court that John Lumbard, who had been charged with the murder of John Harold, had no free land.[76] Since Lumbard was hanged for the murder, the coroner was also expected to hold an inquisition to establish what was to be done with his property. It appears that Lumbard had some association with the royal manors, as Thomas Kent, the seneschal of the king's lands there, gave evidence that he held chattels worth 24s. Though the office of coroner was an unpopular one, the men who held it must have been significant figures in their locality. At any rate, they must have been landowners or otherwise the sheriff's threat to confiscate their property would have been meaningless.

CONCLUSION

From the time of Henry II, English kings were aware of how valuable the lands around Dublin could be as a means of bestowing patronage on their followers and officials. Throughout the later medieval period, the primary function of the royal manors was two-fold. Firstly, it served as a reward or incentive to those who had been, or could be, of some use to the king, who usually happened to be members of the royal household. Secondly, it played a part in paying the expenses and wages of those involved in the governing of the colony.

In the fourteenth century, several of those receiving annuities from the royal manors were key members of the king's household. Many, if not most, of those individuals probably never came to Ireland. Even though the impetus for granting these pensions often came from London, these grantees needed representatives here to ensure that their annuities were paid. Local men within the locality often served as their attorneys. Logically, this provided a link between Dublin and the king's household in England. These locals benefited from these

---

73 Ibid., pp 145–7.   74 *Exchequer payments*, p. 416. Ballytenyth is now Powerscourt in County Wicklow.   75 *CJR, 1308–14*, pp 166–7, 168, 223.   76 Ibid., p. 237.

interactions because they could use their contacts in the royal court to gain the king's attention.

Wolffe highlights the importance of the crown's English and Welsh lands as a source of patronage dating from the reign of Henry III. The dissolution of the Angevin Empire gave these lands a newfound importance. The crown's Irish holdings were, of course, another important source of patronage that, depending on the ability of the king, 'provided a cement or a solvent of political unity and effective government'.[77] The evidence would suggest that English kings took more interest in their Irish lands during periods of crisis. For example, during the end of Richard II's and, later, Henry VI's difficult reigns, the crown took a more direct interest in their Irish manors.[78] It is at these times that men like Norbury, whose loyalties were suspect and whose interests were not necessarily within the lordship of Ireland, acquired the royal manors. On the other hand, this was not usually the case, and the English king was generally content to leave the job of granting these lands out to his justiciar in Ireland.

While the royal manors were a significant source of patronage for the royal household in England, they were even more important as a means of rewarding local administrators in Ireland. Moreover, these individuals, particularly those clerics working in the chancery and exchequer, played an important part in the initial colonization of the lordship. Many were granted lands on the royal manors or acquired smaller parcels of land there for associates and relatives, resulting in many families with origins that could be traced back to clerics living on these manors for generations. By these means, the hinterland around the city of Dublin, of which the royal manors were an important component, acquired enough settlers to transform the conquered territory into a colony.

Whether the grants were of land or annuities, it is obvious that the grantees sought out these endowments. It is clear that they perceived the manors as being attractive acquisitions, even when the evidence suggests that there was little profit to be made. Certainly, this implies that these grants were primarily sought for the prestige of being associated with the crown. It was during the fifteenth century that the manors became particularly associated with the office of chancellor, but other chancery officials were supported by the rents drawn from here as well. For example, in 1471, Thomas Dowdall, the keeper of the rolls of chancery, was paid £20 from the rents of the royal manor of Esker.[79]

The use of royal manors of Co. Dublin as a means of bestowing patronage has many parallels with what was going on with the royal manors in England. Just like in England, the king's Irish manors were used to supplement the salaries of crown officials.[80] Lands on the royal manor of Havering, close to London,

77 Wolffe, *Royal demesne*, p. 227.   78 See Áine Foley, 'The king's favourites and royal officials: patronage and the royal manors' in Seán Duffy and Susan Foran (eds), *The English Isles: cultural transmission and political conflict in Britain and Ireland, 1100–1500* (forthcoming), for an account of the crisis that marked Henry VI's reign.   79 Gillespie, 'Small worlds', p. 203.   80 Wolffe,

were used as a means of rewarding royal servants throughout the medieval period.[81] Its proximity to the city would have made property here a very desirable acquisition for a royal official based there, and such was also the case in Ireland. All of the royal manors in this study were close to the city of Dublin, which must have made them attractive to officials working there. There is no doubt that this is the reason officials, like the chancellor, received substantial grants on the royal manors.

The impetus for these local appointments would have come from within the Dublin administration. The justiciar, in particular, used patronage for his own benefit as well as that of the crown. It is likely that most beneficiaries of royal lands in Dublin, like Thomas Dent, who served as seneschal of the royal demesne, owed their lands and offices within the royal manors to local affiliations rather than any lobbying done at the court in England. That is not to say that some did not travel to England to secure their grants of land on these royal manors in Dublin. It is probable that Thomas Fitzgerald, prior of the hospital of St John of Jerusalem at Kilmainham, did just that in the early fifteenth century in the hopes that it would supersede a grant made at the same time by the chief governor, John Talbot, with whom he was not on good terms.[82]

Undeniably, the crown did not possess the means to support a bureaucracy with paid servants on a local level and the administration of the locality could not function without the voluntary service of the leading tenants of the royal manors. These tenants not only served in their own locality, but also in the administration of the colony at large. While participation in administrative office could be financially worthwhile, it was perhaps more important that it gave an individual social standing within the community and it helped define those who belonged to the local elite. While Peter Coss believes that, in England, the holding of office alone was not enough to indicate gentry status, it still must be considered one of the key factors that defined this class.[83] The royal manors could serve as 'a nursery of royal administration and justice' and there are many examples of the kinsmen and followers of clerics and other royal servants following them into royal service.[84] The tenants played an important role not only in the offices outlined above, but also as jurors, seneschals, reeves and other more minor offices. These offices helped distinguish men like Adam Crumlin as members of the gentry. This was particularly important for those who – though they were members of the leading families in the county – were not likely to inherit much land. It is possible that Adam used the office of sheriff to acquire property or he may have used the office for financial gain of a less legitimate sort. In any case, these offices gave many royal tenants careers in local government and supplemented the incomes generated from their landholdings.

Royal demesne, p. 37.   **81** McIntosh, *Autonomy and community*, p. 19.   **82** *CPR, 1446–52*, p. 56.
83 Coss, *English gentry*, p. 10.   **84** Wolffe, *Royal demesne*, p. 30.

4

Manorial administration in the fourteenth century

INTRODUCTION

The various administrative offices associated with the royal manors are examined in this chapter. Many of those who served in the lesser offices, including that of reeve and provost, came from the immediate locality and were often tenants on the royal manors. These locals, however, did not monopolize all offices associated with these manors. The most prominent office – that of seneschal of demesne – was often held by a man who did not have any previous associations with the royal manors and who was of a higher social rank than the king's tenants. Despite the fact that, technically at least, all manorial officials served the king, those that came from the locality were more concerned with protecting the rights of their fellow tenants. The men who served as seneschal usually did not have this conflict of interest. This individual was usually an outsider who owed his office to the crown. It was only in his best interests to uphold the tenants' wishes when they coincided with those of the king. There is evidence that the tenants, with the assistance of their provost, vigorously upheld their rights, and this is seen clearly through the petitions emanating from the royal manors that survive. It can also be found in a case involving the 'poor men of Crumlin' and Henry Compton, which is explored below.

LOCAL MANORIAL OFFICIALS

Introduction
The first section focuses on the local officials who were responsible for the administration of individual royal manors. Naturally, administrators were essential for the maintenance of these manors, including their defence and smooth running, and ensuring that revenues continued to flow into the exchequer to pay the annuities of royal servants and favourites. These local officials had the most effect on the daily lives of the royal tenants. Certainly, these men – particularly those who served as reeves and bailiffs – permeated deeper down through the social ranks than the royal servants discussed in the previous chapter. Though all were certainly freemen, some may have been well-to-do peasants rather than men who belonged securely to the gentry class. In fact, social distinctions were

probably blurred and relatively non–defined among this group, where kinship ties and shared experience were more important than social rank.

Unlike many of the manorial offices on the royal demesne in England, there was usually a practical dimension to the offices dealt with here. Even the seneschal of the royal demesne, who was often a clerk of the exchequer, was expected to carry out the functions of his office or find a responsible deputy to take his place. This is in direct contrast to what was happening in England. For example, on the royal manor of Havering, in Essex, many of the offices associated with the manor were largely honorific.[1] If these offices did have a practical aspect to them, they were usually granted to a poorly paid deputy. The grantees were frequently only interested in the revenues they could generate from these grants. In Dublin, even when the seneschal was compelled to use a deputy, he was still responsible for the actions of this individual. This may explain why at least one seneschal, William Epworth, decided to relinquish the office entirely rather than entrust it to someone else. Occasionally, the functions of the office were neglected to the point where it lapsed into a sinecure. Nonetheless, for the most part – and particularly during the fourteenth century – the administration chose men who could carry out the functions of seneschal, and on at least one occasion a statute was enacted to ensure that this office was held only by those who were qualified for the job.[2]

Manorial seneschals

As well as a seneschal overlooking the royal manors as a group, individual manors had their own seneschals. During Henry del Nasshe's term as seneschal of the royal demesne in the mid-1320s, Haket de la Sale was seneschal for the manor of Newcastle Lyons. Since one of their main functions was the defence of the manors, the appointment of a similar officer to individual manors was probably undertaken at times when extra defence was required. It does seem that the terms 'seneschal' and 'reeve' were used interchangeably. The offices were clearly separate, however, and the reeves were subordinate to the seneschal. That the offices were separate from each other is clear because often seneschals and reeves served on the same manors at the same time. When Haket de la Sale was seneschal of Newcastle Lyons, for example, John Schynnagh and John son of Richard served as its reeves.[3] In 1378, John Beg was serving as seneschal of Newcastle Lyons.[4] It is likely that he was related to the Beg family who were prominent tenants on the manor of Saggart and who held administrative posts on this manor over the previous two centuries.[5] Unlike the seneschals of

---

1 McIntosh, *Autonomy and community*, pp 20–1. 2 *Stat. Ire., John–Hen. V*, p. 425. The office of seneschal of demesne is explored more fully below. 3 *RDKPRI*, 42, pp 54–5; Schynnagh may be derived from Sionnach, the Irish word for fox, and there was a family of this name living on the royal manors during the medieval period. 4 D'Alton, *History of Dublin*, p. 681; it is possible that Beg came from the Irish word beag. 5 This family are discussed below.

demesne, the seneschals of individual manors were usually from the locality or had previous associations with the royal manors.

Reeves and receivers
Though the office of reeve is not specifically named in the sources until 1307, it is clear that it existed long before this date.[6] In the court case between Henry Compton and the tenants of Crumlin in the early 1290s, a Richard the provost was summoned to answer why the tenants of Crumlin impeded Compton in holding his grant of the manor.[7] He is probably the same person as Richard le Reve, who was responsible for paying part of the rent of the manor of Crumlin in the same decade.[8] Thomas le Reves served as one of Richard's pledges and he may have been reeve of Crumlin at about this time.[9] Since the receiver served as a check and balance to the reeve, it is clear that this office must have been in existence by this time.[10] In 1309, the provosts and receivers of the king's demesne lands were summoned to the exchequer to account for money owed to the king. The implication here is that the terms 'reeve' and 'provost' were used interchangeably for what was, in fact, the same office. During the 1280s, Reginald le Reve was one of many men responsible for paying the rent for Crumlin, and in the following decade, Cokinus Reve paid the rent of the same manor.[11] It is possible that these were not their surnames, but rather an indicator of their occupation as manorial reeves. In 1278–9, Richard son of Robert, John le Lung, Reginald Beg and John Cusyn accounted in the exchequer for the farm of Saggart for the previous seven years. Richard Gerveys and the executors of Laurence Cusyn also paid sums into the exchequer in this period.[12] It is possible that they were reeves rather than farmers, as those granted the farm of manors usually held them during the king's pleasure or for a set number of years.[13] It is likely that the tenants of Saggart collectively held the farm of the manor, which would have been paid into the exchequer by their representative, the reeve. As six of them were responsible for paying the farm within a period of seven years, it is more likely that they were reeves, as this office was normally held for a shorter period, usually a year.

The main function of the reeve was to collect the rents from the other tenants and deliver them into the exchequer, but he could also be responsible for summoning jurors and taking extents of the manors. In 1309, John Lympit was accused of not summoning eleven jurors – he was meant to serve as the twelfth juror himself – to extend lands in Newcastle; instead, he decided to take it upon

6 NAI, EX 2/1, p. 181.   7 *CDI, 1285–92*, §855. This case is explored more fully below.
8 *RDKPRI*, 37, pp 26, 32; though Sweetman describes him as Richard the provost, in *IEMI*, §80, pp 42–3, he is called Richard the reeve.   9 *CDI, 1285–92*, §855.   10 *RDKPRI*, 38, p. 86.
11 *CDI, 1285–92*, §§215, 271; *CDI, 1293–1301*, §264.   12 *RDKPRI*, 36, p. 42.   13 For example, in 1293 William de Estdene held all the king's demesne lands of Chapelizod during the king's pleasure (*CDI, 1293–1301*, §69) and in 1305 John de Seleby was granted the same manor for a term of six years (*CDI, 1302–7*, §401).

himself to conduct the extent.[14] The reeve could also be responsible for paying other officials out of the issues of the manor. In 1307, the reeve of Saggart was ordered to pay Thomas Kent 50s. for defending this manor in times of war.[15]

It was the responsibility of the reeve or bailiff to account for the farm of the manor.[16] This would suggest that the individuals named in the exchequer receipts who paid in the farm of the manor were serving in this capacity, though the sources rarely specify their role. In 1306, Richard Beg was provost of Saggart and his family already had a long history on this manor.[17] John Beg may have also served as provost of Saggart, because in 1281 he, along with Robert Deveneys, John Reynald, Simon Camera, Richard Gerveys and William Comyn, paid the farm of Saggart for the previous three years into the exchequer.[18] In Easter term 1286 and on several subsequent occasions, John paid the farm of the same manor.[19] Sometime before 1328, another John Beg served as provost of Esker and he may have been the older John's son.[20] From 1296, Richard Beg was paying rent for lands in Saggart.[21] John Beg was still occasionally paying rent on this manor and it is likely that Richard was his son.[22] Richard appears to have been an important individual within his community and he served as provost on more than one occasion.[23] He also served as a juror on inquisitions.[24] The family's interests extended beyond Saggart; they also held lands in Clondalkin at the end of the thirteenth century, and they may have had property in Esker, as Thomas Beg served as a pledge for William Kissok of Esker in 1306.[25] He also stood in as a pledge for Henry Kissok, who was serjeant of Saggart in the same year.[26] Sometime before 1318, he was provost of the manor of Crumlin and subsequently he held the office of provost of Esker.[27] Additionally, at some point before 1313, Nicholas Beg served as provost of Crumlin.[28] In the 1350s, Adam Beg was paid £1 for capturing John O'Toole and bringing his head before the king's council, and he received £1 13s. 4d. for burning the dwellings of the O'Tooles and the O'Byrnes.[29] Nevertheless, even though the Beg family seem to have had interests on several royal manors and appear to have continued to reside in the vicinity well into the middle of the fourteenth century, there is no evidence that they were major landholders. No member of the family appears to have held any administrative office above manorial level. Consequently, it is likely that this family were peasants, albeit very prosperous ones.

In 1321, Warin Owen was the receiver of the manor of Newcastle Lyons.[30] In

14 NAI, EX 2/1, pp 475–8.   15 Ibid., p. 238.   16 McIntosh, *Autonomy and community*, p. 24. 17 NAI, EX 2/1, p. 159.   18 *RDKPRI*, 36, p. 67.   19 *CDI, 1285–92*, §§215, 271, 1078, 1148; *CDI, 1293–1301*, §§4, 21, 41.   20 *RDKPRI*, 43, p. 29.   21 *CDI, 1293–1301*, §§329, 363, 408, 550; *CDI, 1302–7*, §72.   22 *CDI, 1293–1301*, §§363, 587.   23 *RDKPRI*, 39, p. 56. He was provost of Saggart again in 1313–14.   24 NAI, EX 2/1, pp 258–9; *IEMI*, §160, p. 87.   25 An inquisition from 1293 names Robert Beg as coming from Clondalkin (*CDI, 1293–1301*, §106). He was responsible for paying the issues of the see of Dublin into the exchequer at the end of the thirteenth century (ibid., §658).   26 NAI, EX 2/1, p. 153.   27 *RDKPRI*, 42, pp 27, 30. 28 *RDKPRI*, 39, p. 50.   29 *Exchequer payments*, p. 483.   30 *RDKPRI*, 42, p. 32.

the previous century, Roger Owen had held the highly prestigious job of king's pleader and, in comparison, the office of receiver, as held by Warin Owen, was a humble one, which may suggest a decline in his family's fortunes. Yet, this is more likely to indicate that Warin was a younger son who had to find his own way in the world. He had a brother called John who may have inherited the bulk of his father's property.[31] Warin continued to serve the king and later became a collector of the king's subsidy for the war in Scotland, and thus the office of receiver was just one stage in an administrative career and not the whole, as seems to be the case with many members of the Beg family.[32] Other individuals who can be placed firmly within the gentry served as manorial officials. Thomas Crumlin and his son, John Crumlin, were provosts of that manor, but Thomas also served as a tax collector, and his younger son, Adam, was sheriff.[33] Clearly, their interests – unlike the Begs' – extended beyond the royal manors.

Lesser members of prominent families may also have filled manorial offices. Richard Brun, who was provost of Saggart in 1313, may have been related to the Brun family.[34] Robert Brun was provost of the same manor in 1339–40, and he may have been his son.[35] The Kissok family were important tenants on the manor of Esker, and some members of this family were involved in manorial administration. In 1324–5, William Kissok was provost of this manor.[36] Nicholas Callan served as provost of Saggart in the same year, and his family had property on this manor, though their main interests were within the nearby city, where they were prominent merchants.[37] Robert Aylmer, who was provost of Newcastle Lyons at this time, also came from a family with a significant presence in the locality throughout the late medieval period.[38] It would appear that individuals from widely diverse social groups could fulfil the functions of this office.

By the 1320s, Newcastle Lyons and Saggart, the largest of the four royal manors, had more than one reeve apiece. In 1321–2, Newcastle had at least two. Warin Oweyn was reeve for the main settlement at Newcastle and John Aylmer was reeve for Colmanstown, a subordinate grange on the same manor.[39] Later that same year, Roger Warin was reeve for Newcastle Lyons but, in addition, the manor now had two external reeves: Adam Aylmer for Colmanstown and Reginald Heyne for Athgoe.[40] In 1324, Nicholas Callan and Henry White of Ballinteer were provosts of Saggart.[41] The pipe roll does not specify if one of these men was an external reeve; the manor of Saggart, however, was large and had some outlying granges not connected to the rest of the manor, and, therefore, additional reeves were needed. This manor certainly had an external reeve by 1332–3, when William le Dyer was responsible for all its outlying areas, while

31 NAI, EX 2/1, p. 340.   32 *RDKPRI*, 45, pp 52–3.   33 *RDKPRI*, 39, pp 37–8.   34 Ibid., p. 50. The Brun family are examined in ch. 5.   35 *RDKPRI*, 47, p. 38.   36 *RDKPRI*, 42, p. 54. 37 He was provost again in 1337–8, *RDKPRI*, 45, pp 55–6.   38 *RDKPRI*, 42, p. 55.   39 Ibid., p. 32.   40 Ibid., p. 34.   41 Ibid., p. 54.

Thomas Bretnagh was responsible for the central caput.[42] In 1337–8, Simon de la Sale was the external provost for Saggart, and he may have been related to Haket de la Sale who served as seneschal of demesne two decades before.[43] It is possible that Esker sometimes had more than one reeve, because, like Newcastle Lyons, it consisted of several granges rather than being composed of one central caput. In 1328–9, the reeves John Beg and John Francis accounted for the arrears of this manor.[44] Since Crumlin was a smaller, more compact, manor and, like Saggart, was centralized rather than dispersed, it is likely that it never had more than one reeve at any one time.[45] Additionally, many of the reeves and provosts serving on the royal manors may have been Irish. Names like Kissok, Beg, Heyne and Bretnagh at least suggest the possibility that the native population played a part in the administration of the manors. Alternatively, they could have been nicknames adopted by English settlers that eventually developed into surnames.

As was the case with so many other administrative offices, those elected reeves on the royal manors were occasionally unable or unwilling to fulfil the duties of the office, or found it financially prohibitive. For example, in 1303, Peter Alwyne and John Montaygne, the provosts of Crumlin, were in mercy for not coming to account.[46] In the following year, Alice, the widow of Hugh Godman, who had previously served as provost of Newcastle Lyons, promised to pay the arrears owed to the crown by her husband before his death.[47] Also in 1304, John Lympit and William le Blund – then reeves of Newcastle – were committed to Dublin Castle for not paying the arrears of their account.[48] In 1307, when John Cook did not pay the rent of the lands he held in Saggart, it was the reeves who became responsible for paying it.[49] Clearly, those assuming the responsibilities of this office could find themselves out of pocket, and, considering this, it is surprising that there is so little evidence of administrative corruption.

John Lympit was one of the very few reeves for whom there is evidence of dubious behaviour while in office.[50] In 1309, he was accused by his fellow tenants of Newcastle Lyons of taking their rent for the previous five years, but instead of paying the money into the exchequer, he used it for his own personal benefit to purchase lands and livestock. They also accused him of allowing some of the tenants to not pay their rents, in exchange for gifts. These tenants complained that, although they previously could have paid their rent, they were no longer able to do so because the Irish had subsequently robbed them. John was found guilty and sent to prison, but he clearly still had friends on the manor, because local men Thomas le Blund and Walter Fox later secured his release.[51] John Lympit appears to be the exception rather than the rule, but, in spite of the lack

---

42 *RDKPRI*, 43, p. 61. 43 *RDKPRI*, 45, pp 55–6. 44 *RDKPRI*, 43, p. 29. 45 Ibid., p. 30. Both John Montayngne and Maurice Colman are mentioned as being reeves of Crumlin in this pipe roll entry, but it is clear that they served in different years. 46 NAI, EX 2/1, p. 54. 47 Ibid., p. 65. 48 Ibid., p. 95. 49 Ibid., p. 297. 50 Ibid., pp 475–8. 51 Walter Fox may be related to John Schynnagh: see above, n. 3.

of evidence for corruption among the reeves and receivers, the men that held this office in the mid-fourteenth century were obviously found wanting. A statute that in 1360 reformed the election of senior officials also took measures to make sure that those officers who belonged at a lower level in the manorial hierarchy, including the receivers, were also appropriate candidates.[52]

LOCAL OFFICIALS AND THE COMMUNITY OF THE ROYAL MANORS

Introduction

Though technically the reeves and provosts on the royal manors served the king, they were also expected to uphold the rights of the royal tenants, at least by the tenants themselves. The previous chapter explored the value of these four royal manors as instruments of royal patronage. Often, those granted lands on the royal manors left when they retired from the administration or gained similar employment in England. How the long-term tenants on the royal manors reacted to these transitory occupants of their land will be explored in this section. Occasionally, the king was the defendant in cases against tenants who may have resented the crown's policy of using the royal manors as an instrument of patronage for royal servants and favourites. Just like their counterparts living on royal lands in England, it appears that the tenants residing on the royal manors in this study took great exception to undue interference from the crown and its representatives. They wanted as much autonomy from the king as they could get, and this was usually achieved by purchasing the farm of the manor for a set fee that was paid into the exchequer annually.[53] Once they had acquired the privilege, any change in the status quo normally met with opposition (though, on the royal manors of Dublin, this resistance appears to have been rather moderate). When Thomas Crumlin was deprived of the farm of the demesne of Crumlin, for example, he and his fellow tenants on the manor of Crumlin took recourse to law, though they employed other methods to demonstrate their opposition to this grant to an outsider as well.

The poor men of Crumlin

A court case dealing with the royal manor of Crumlin dating from the early 1290s sheds some light on tenants' attitudes towards outside beneficiaries of royal patronage and how they dealt with the issue of property passing to someone from outside their locality. It reveals a community who, though loyal to the king, were prepared to establish and defend their own rights. They did use official channels, but, on occasion, they were also prepared to take matters into their own hands. Though 'the men of Crumlin' or 'the poor tenants of the vill

---

52 *Stat. Ire., John–Hen. V*, p. 425.   53 Hilton, *Medieval society*, p. 219.

of Crumlin' are named throughout these judicial proceedings, two men stood out from the rest of the community: Henry Compton and Thomas Crumlin.[54] This is because they had most to gain or lose depending on the outcome of the court case. The support given to Thomas Crumlin by the rest of the tenants on this manor is clear evidence of solidarity among this group. By standing together, they succeeded in having Henry Compton's grant of the demesne lands on this manor cancelled.

When the crown granted Henry Compton one carucate and eight acres of land in Crumlin, as well as awarding him the pleas and perquisites of Newcastle Lyons and Saggart, they must have anticipated the opposition mounted by the communities of these three manors. As tenants of ancient demesne, the residents of Crumlin had special privileges attached to their tenure, which they would not have relinquished easily. There are other instances of local men putting up resistance to outsiders who were granted land on the royal manors. In 1340, John Fontaynes, king's yeoman, was granted forty marks a year from the farm of Crumlin for services to the king in Ireland and elsewhere,[55] but the manor had already been granted to John Jordan, who is likely to have been a member of the Jordan family of Newcastle Lyons. In spite of the fact that the king had already revoked this grant, Jordan persisted in harassing Fontaynes with 'divers writs of the king' until the crown was forced to annul his letters patent.[56] Jordan appears to have been acting alone, however, and there is very little evidence of any other beneficiary of royal patronage being met by such intense local opposition. Nevertheless, this is not to say that this was the only occasion that they defended their interests as a community against an outsider. Raymond Gillespie described the tenants on the royal manors in the sixteenth century as being a 'community of interest';[57] this appears to be an accurate description of the community in the late thirteenth century as well. This unique group of inquisitions dating from the end of the thirteenth century reveals brief but clear glimpses of a community looking out for its own and safeguarding each other's interests.

The inquisitions set up to establish if Henry Compton should be granted lands on the royal manor of Crumlin revealed that one man certainly stood out prominently from the rest of the tenants. Moreover, the man in question, Thomas Crumlin, featured significantly in contemporary sources. Throughout the 1280s, either Thomas Russell or Thomas Crumlin, who appear to be the same individual, was mainly responsible for paying the rent and farm of the manor. There was clearly more than one tenant on the manor, because the inquisitions taken in 1290 and 1291 refer to the tenants of Crumlin as a group and not to one individual person.[58] Thomas Crumlin was probably responsible for collecting the rents and delivering them to the exchequer. When Henry Compton was granted the manor, he was ordered to make restitution to Thomas

54 Henry Compton's career and the Crumlin family are investigated in ch. 3.   55 *CPR, 1340–5*, p. 74.   56 Ibid., pp 461–2.   57 Gillespie, 'Small worlds', p. 201.   58 *CDI, 1285–92*, §855.

for the fruits sown on the land prior to the time that it came into his hands on 6 April 1292. The same fine roll entry signifies that the king's demesne in Crumlin had previously been committed to Thomas,[59] so even though there was a community living on this land rather than one individual or family, it is clear that there was a hierarchy – or that, at the very least, Thomas was first among equals – and he had the most to lose from Henry Compton's intrusion. Evidence can be found in England of men acquiring leases of manors with the assistance of their fellow tenants. In 1374, an unnamed local man, with the support of the king's tenants, acquired a nine-year lease on the royal manor of Eastwood in Essex.[60] The fact that the 'poor men of Crumlin' were so central in the case between Henry Compton and Thomas Crumlin would suggest that, although they held the farm, Thomas was their chief representative and perhaps the reeve of the manor. These tenants probably would not have been inconvenienced by the grant made to Compton; the only difference was that they would now have to pay their rent to him instead of to Thomas Crumlin.

The Crumlin inquisitions

Edward I granted the lands of Crumlin and the pleas and perquisites of that manor, along with the pleas and perquisites of Newcastle Lyons and Saggart, to Henry Compton in 1290. The profits of the court of Newcastle Lyons were worth five marks and those of Saggart were worth 50s., compared to 20s. for Crumlin. Nonetheless, for the next two years, the crown would go back and forth in the decision as to who actually should have possession of the manor. After Henry's initial grant, there was some doubt as to whether he should hold the lands, as it was claimed that the ancestors of the current tenants had possession of the manor since the time of King John. The crown hesitated for two years before finally officially granting the demesne lands on Crumlin to Henry on 28 March 1292,[61] though ultimately he would only have possession of these lands for a few months.

Many of the most important men of Dublin appeared on the juries of both inquisitions held to establish the legitimacy of Compton's grant. The first inquisition was held in the exchequer of Dublin on 27 July 1290 to establish if it would be in the king's interest to grant one carucate and eight acres of demesne land in Crumlin to Henry or whether it should be left in the hands of the men of Crumlin. Many of the jurors listed had lands in nearby manors and some had close ties with the other royal manors. For example, John Beg paid the farm of Saggart in 1292–3,[62] as did Simon de Camera in 1295,[63] and Walter White paid rent in Newcastle Lyons.[64] It must have been of some concern for those among the jurors who were tenants of Newcastle Lyons and Saggart to see the profits emanating from their courts being granted to Henry and, undoubtedly, they

---

59 Ibid., §1073. 60 Wolffe, *Royal demesne*, p. 63. 61 *CDI, 1285–92*, §1073. 62 *CDI, 1293–1301*, §4. 63 Ibid., §264. 64 *CDI, 1285–92*, §341.

would have wanted to support their fellow tenants in Crumlin. Peter Russell may well have been a relative of Thomas Crumlin, and John Stede – like Thomas – was responsible for collecting tax in the Vale of Dublin.[65] In addition, many of the men who served as jurors in these inquisitions also served with Thomas Crumlin as a juror in other cases, including Luke Chamberlain, Simon Camera, Reginald Bernard, William White, John Cosyn and Wolfran Barnewall;[66] thus, he was one of their own. As a result, it was hardly surprising when they decided that it would be more to the king's advantage to allow the men of Crumlin to continue to hold this land, rather than grant it away to Henry Compton. They were compelled to admit, however, that they could not foresee any loss to the king if he did grant the land to Henry, which may have been a determining factor in the decision to grant him Crumlin on 15 September 1290.

The matter did not end there, and another inquisition was held on 20 December 1291. The jurors of this inquisition confirmed that it would not be to the king's loss if Henry Compton was granted these 128 acres, provided that the tenants currently there were not disturbed. The one tenant who was inconvenienced was Thomas Crumlin, and the king ordered Henry Compton to reimburse him for crops grown on the land before it came into his possession.[67] A glance at the jurors of this inquisition reveals that Luke Chamberlain was the only one who had sat on the jury for the previous inquisition. This time, the jurors looked more favourably on Henry Compton, and perhaps this was because they did not have as close connections with the men of Crumlin as those who took part in the previous inquisition. None of the jurors appear to have been major tenants on the royal manors, though Wolfran Barnewall, sometime sheriff of Dublin, owned extensive lands in south Dublin, including the manors of Drimnagh, Terenure and Ballyfermot, as well as Balrothery in north Dublin. Some of the other jurors, like Adam of Howth and Richard of Naul, appear to have been landowners in north Dublin. It could be argued that they did not feel a particularly strong sense of loyalty towards men of whom they were not close neighbours. In addition, they would have nothing to lose if Henry Compton was granted the pleas and perquisites of Saggart and Newcastle Lyons, unlike the jurors listed in the inquisition of the previous year.

Solidarity within the community
Henry Compton must have initially received his grant shortly before the first inquisition took place, because the tenants of the three manors involved were summoned to come before John, archbishop of Dublin and justiciar of Ireland, at Waterford on 17 July 1290. They were ordered to answer accusations of impeding Henry 'in holding and having the king's demesne lands and meadows of Crumlin, and the pleas and profits of these vills'.[68] It would appear that the

---

65 *CDI, 1293–1301*, §475.   66 *CDI, 1252–84*, §2344.   67 *CDI, 1285–92*, §1073.

tenants of the manors had decided to take matters into their own hands and attempted physically to prevent Compton from taking up his grant. Thomas Crumlin, Richard the provost and Philip the clerk represented Crumlin; Richard Gerveys and Robert Londhary represented Saggart, and Master Maurice of Newcastle and Hugh Godinan represented Newcastle Lyons. Richard the provost was obviously a local official, and the other men who organized this resistance to Compton probably were too. There is no evidence that violence was used, and they may have employed the same style of gentle resistance that was used by the tenants of the royal manor of Havering in Essex in the mid-thirteenth century.[69] When the crown attempted to foist a full-time official named Thomas le Rus on Havering, the tenants 'engaged in quiet obstruction of the bailiffs' work' and, though their actions were not violent, they eventually won the day and no further attempts were made to install a representative of the crown on this manor.

Even though there were further attempts to install Compton in Crumlin, in the long term the tenants and local officials – like their counterparts in Havering – were ultimately successful. After two years of going back and forth, the decision was made that the 128 acres of demesne should remain in the hands of the men of Crumlin, so ultimately the judicial process did work in their favour. On 6 April 1292, the king ordered the chancellor of Ireland to grant to Henry Compton the first church in the king's gift worth £20 or forty marks that fell vacant. The timing of this would suggest that this grant was made as a consolation for the loss of Crumlin.[70] Though in the previous month the king had committed these lands in Crumlin to Henry, by 23 November of that year, the land, as well as the pleas and perquisites of the manor, were back in the hands of the men of Crumlin.[71] The only evidence of Henry Compton paying farm of the manor is from a single exchequer receipt from Easter term 1293 and the amount paid probably covered the few months he had possession of the land in the previous year.[72] He may have been compensated for the loss of the demesne with land in Newcastle Lyons, because he was paying farm of this manor in Trinity term 1297 and Hilary term 1298–9.[73]

It is difficult to ascertain why exactly the tenants ultimately won out and managed to retain the royal demesne lands of Crumlin for themselves. The fact that their ancestors allegedly had possession of this land since the time of King John could have gone in their favour, or perhaps the king felt that there was no reason to significantly change a situation that had worked for almost a century. Alternatively, if tradition alone was not a persuasive enough reason to leave the tenants where they were, maybe they had other methods to make sure they were not moved. The sources suggest that they used some degree of resistance against

68 Ibid., §855.   69 McIntosh, *Autonomy and community*, pp 41–2.   70 *CPR, 1281–92*, p. 482.
71 *CDI, 1285–92*, §1073.   72 *CDI, 1293–1301*, §21.   73 Ibid., §§408, 587.

this move; they had after all 'impeded' Henry Compton from gaining possession of Crumlin;[74] though how exactly they went about this is not made clear. They obviously worked as a community to force Compton out, as no one tenant is singled out as stopping him from taking up his grant. If the king decided it was not worth the trouble of forcing the communities of Crumlin, Newcastle Lyons and Saggart to accept the grant, it may imply that the movement against him was significant. It is also worth noting that 1293, the year after the matter had been resolved, was the first time since 1286 that Crumlin had paid arrears on the manor into the exchequer.[75] They paid over £7, and it is possible that the tenants held back from paying their rent while the situation was in limbo, or they could even have withheld their rent as a form of protest. This is a method of resistance used with great effect in England, and there is evidence on the royal manor of Havering of tenants refusing to make payments of rent or, alternatively, being very slow in paying them when confronted with unreasonable demands.[76] Unfortunately, there is a gap in the Irish pipe rolls between 1292 and 1300, which could have given more evidence to support this argument. No more arrears are recorded in the exchequer receipts until 1298, and even then the sum is not particularly significant, being only 40*d*.[77] It is only from 1301 onwards that larger amounts of arrears of rent begin to accumulate in Crumlin.

Even though the tenants regained the farm of Crumlin, there does seem to be a subtle power shift within the community. Up to this point, at least throughout the 1280s when the records begin to become relatively abundant, almost exclusively Thomas Crumlin was paying the rent. After 1292, however, we find several different tenants paying the rent into the exchequer, including Roger Monte, Alexander Deveneys,[78] John Fonte[79] and John Attewelle.[80] Perhaps the tenants who had found themselves capable of standing up to Henry Compton were now also able to stand up to Thomas Crumlin. Alternatively, he may have felt disillusioned by his recent treatment, and this might have influenced his decision to step back from public duty. In Michaelmas term 1292, he was fined half a mark because he did not 'come when summoned'.[81] This could mean he ignored a summons for jury duty or failed to take up some administrative office, which might suggest bitterness due to previous experience with the administration. On the other hand, it may have had nothing to do with the case and he may have reduced his administrative duties simply because he was getting older. Thomas occasionally paid the rent of the manor throughout the 1290s, but usually in conjunction with his son Adam.

Henry Compton's tenure on the manor of Crumlin was short-lived, as the sitting tenants proved impossible to dislodge. A family with as long a history in the area as the Russell/Crumlin family had a strong advantage over Henry

74 *CDI, 1285–92*, §855.   75 *CDI, 1293–1301*, §21.   76 McIntosh, *Autonomy and community*, p. 50.   77 *CDI, 1293–1301*, §550.   78 Ibid., §41.   79 Ibid., §§206, 226, 264.   80 Ibid., §264. 81 *CDI, 1285–92*, §1148.

Compton, as they would have built up a complex network of connections among other important tenants in south Dublin through family alliances and a sense of common cause. Compton could not compete against this and, as a clerk, he could not have taken the route other men would have taken by marrying into this close-knit society. He remained an outsider.

SENESCHAL OF THE ROYAL DEMESNE

Introduction

Though manorial officers could come from widely diverse social backgrounds, there was one official who, more often than not, was a member of the gentry: the seneschal of the royal demesne. This office was remarkable in the fact that it did not have an exact equivalent on the royal demesne in England. Yet the office of seneschal probably owed its creation to administrative innovations that occurred on the king's demesne in England. A significant proportion of the holders of this office were exchequer officials, and this mirrored the trend in England, where the exchequer was closely involved in the administration of the royal demesne. For example, this institution exercised direct supervision of assessment of tallage and was involved in the settlement of disputes that occurred within the crown lands of England.[82]

In May 1236, Walter Burgo and Warner Engayn became keepers of the entire ancient demesne in England, apart from the crown lands in Yorkshire, Northumberland, Cumberland and Lancaster, of which Robert Crepping became keeper. This transfer of royal lands from the control of the sheriff resulted in the decline of this office in England.[83] The king was concerned that sheriffs were getting too powerful and, for that reason, the impetus behind creating these keepers was undoubtedly to diminish some of the power associated with this office.[84] This reorganization of the royal demesne was a resounding failure. Debts started to mount up in the exchequer almost immediately, and in 1240, after a series of inquests, many keepers and bailiffs were dismissed. In some cases, new keepers replaced them, but, generally, the crown preferred farming the manors out to a third party for a fixed sum.[85] After the term of office of Burgo, Engayn and Crepping, the office of keeper of the ancient demesne appears to have been abandoned and there is no evidence that anyone succeeded them. There was another attempt to create an office to oversee the administration of the king's demesne in England in 1275. At this time, three stewards were appointed and their remit covered the whole of the country apart

---

82 See Appendix 1, below, for list of seneschals of royal demesne. The list includes a description of other offices held by these manorial officials; Hoyt, *Royal demesne*, p. 122. 83 Ibid., pp 156–7. 84 Prestwich, *Plantagenet England*, p. 88. 85 Wolffe, *Royal demesne*, p. 66; Hoyt, *Royal demesne*, p. 158.

from Durham, Lancaster and Cornwall. Again, this office was abandoned after a single term of office.[86] William Gernet had custody of the king's manors in Ireland in 1278, and it is possible that he was a keeper, though the sources do not specify this, and that the creation of his office was inspired by the recent innovations on the royal demesne in England. Gernet may not have held the office of seneschal, but he was certainly a predecessor of this officer and it is likely that he performed similar functions, even if the sources are silent on this point. Attempts to establish an officer to administer the royal demesne in England were quickly aborted on at least two occasions, but in Ireland the office of seneschal of demesne, once it was established in the early fourteenth century, survived into the nineteenth century. It is likely that this office did not succeed in England because the royal demesne there was much larger and the area that crown officials were expected to administer was very fragmented. In Ireland, the four manors that the seneschal was responsible for were relatively close to each other in south Co. Dublin.

The first known seneschal of the royal demesne in Dublin, Thomas Kent, was not only responsible for Crumlin, Newcastle Lyons and Saggart, but he was also accountable for the royal manors in Kildare, namely Leixlip, Ballysax and Okethy, as well as Baliogary in north Dublin.[87] The custody of these manors was granted to him in 1307 but, though he was never previously explicitly called the seneschal of demesne, he may in fact have already held this office for quite some time.[88] He paid the pleas and perquisites of the courts of Newcastle Lyons and Saggart in 1301, and the perquisites for the court at Crumlin in 1301–2.[89] In 1304, the castle at Leixlip was committed to Kent, and, in 1305, he owed the pleas and perquisites of the court of Saggart to the king.[90] Similarly, he owed part of the profits of the manor court of Newcastle Lyons in the same year.[91] When the mayor and bailiffs of the city of Dublin seized the millstones belonging to the merchants of the society of the Friscobaldi of Florence, they delivered one of them to Kent for use at the mill in Leixlip.[92] He acquired eighty acres, as well as the king's garden, in Leixlip to hold for five years in 1307.[93] In the same year, he was given the responsibility of holding a court at Ballysax and Baliogary, as well as the power to grant lands to farm and repairing houses on the manor of the former manor.[94] Consequently, though the first extant evidence of Kent holding the office of seneschal comes from the end of 1307, it is clear that he was already actively involved in the administration of most of the king's manors for many years.

---

86 Wolffe, *Royal demesne*, pp 66–7. 87 Now Garristown. 88 NAI, EX 2/2, p. 248. 89 *CDI, 1293–1301*, §4. 90 NAI, EX 2/1, pp 118, 131. 91 Ibid., p. 132. 92 Ibid., p. 147. 93 Ibid., p. 201. 94 Ibid., pp 203, 210. Moreover, the receiver of Baliogary was ordered to pay de Kent one mark for his fee of having the custody of this manor from Easter to Michaelmas of that year: ibid., p. 239.

Structural reform and the creation of the office of seneschal

The impetus of Thomas Kent's appointment as seneschal of demesne may have been the acquisition by the crown of the Pippard lands in 1302.[95] In addition to lands in Co.Louth, the Pippard manors of Leixlip, Castlewarden and Oughterard came into royal hands at this time. Mary Lyons believes that these new acquisitions provided a stimulus for structural reform of the king's lands in Dublin and Kildare.[96] Thomas Kent's appointment as seneschal may have pre-dated the Pippard acquisitions, however. As has already been demonstrated, he was certainly seneschal for Newcastle Lyons, Crumlin and Saggart by 1301. Therefore, it appears more plausible that the creation of this office was inspired by the structural reform of Co. Dublin after the 1297 parliament, particularly when one takes into account that there is no evidence that the seneschal was ever responsible for Castlewarden and Oughterard. After the establishment of Kildare as a county at this time, it was given its own sheriff and thereafter it fell outside the jurisdiction of the sheriff of Dublin. Dublin itself was considerably larger at the end of the thirteenth century, as it included much of modern-day Wicklow. In addition, the sheriff was responsible for the administration of the Verdun lands of Meath, as well as the church crosslands.

Functions of seneschal of demesne

The duties of both the sheriff and the seneschal of demesne overlapped in many key areas in relation to the royal manors. It is possible that this office was created to alleviate some of the pressure on the sheriff, or it may have been done to remove some of his powers. If this was the case, it was comparable to the policy implemented in England almost a century before, where the office of sheriff was stripped of much of its authority. In Ireland, both offices had military functions and, considering the strategic importance of the royal manors to the overall defence of Dublin, it made sense to create an officer with similar powers to the sheriff whose duties would be specifically focused in this area. In 1307, the reeve of Saggart was ordered to deliver 50s. from the issues of the same manor to the then seneschal, Thomas Kent, for his efforts in aiding in its defence.[97] Aside from their military responsibilities, both these officers were agents of the exchequer. In this respect, the financial and judicial duties of the seneschal of demesne mirrored those of the sheriff. In 1305, Thomas Kent was responsible for paying the pleas and perquisites of the manor court of Saggart to the crown.[98] It was also his responsibility to choose jurors to serve in this court. When he became seneschal of all the king's demesne lands, he was ordered to hold courts on these manors and take the fealties of the king's tenants there.[99] In his capacity as seneschal, he also had the power to summon reeves and receivers to come to the exchequer and satisfy debts owed to the king.[1]

---

95 *CDI, 1302–7*, §149.   96 Lyons, 'Manorial administration', p. 39.   97 NAI, EX 2/1, p. 238.
98 Ibid., p. 131.   99 Ibid., p. 248.   1 Ibid., p. 636.

An examination of some of the duties undertaken by Walter Burgo, when he served as keeper of the royal demesne in England in the 1230s, might be useful in illuminating some of the duties attached to the office of the later seneschal of royal demesne in Ireland. Just like the Irish seneschal, Burgo was expected to officiate over judicial cases held on the lands belonging to the royal demesne. In addition, he held inquests and made extents of the king's lands; functions that would be part of the later Irish seneschal's duties as well. The keeper of the royal demesne in England was also expected to maintain any buildings belonging to the king on his lands. Though we do not have any evidence for this in Ireland, it is likely that the seneschal was granted the sub-manor of Milltown on the understanding that he would maintain the mill there. Walter Burgo also served as a liaison officer between the local officials working on the various manors under his jurisdiction and central administration.[2] Though all manorial officials working on the royal manors were – technically at least – royal officers, the tenants of the manors chose the reeves and bailiffs. Naturally, their loyalties tended to be with their neighbours, not their distant employer in England. The seneschal of the royal demesne, on the other hand, was rarely a local. Clearly, his primary role was to serve as the king's representative within the locality.

The records of the manorial courts, which would have shed much valuable light over the duties of the seneschal of demesne, do not survive for the royal manors of Dublin for the Middle Ages. The earliest court rolls originating from these four manors to survive come from the end of the sixteenth century. Nevertheless, the court book for the royal manors of Crumlin and Esker must be utilized, even though it is a late source. Despite the fact that this court book lies outside the scope of the study, the operations of the manorial court in Esker and Crumlin had probably changed little over the preceding centuries. Furthermore, court rolls survive from the nearby manors of Lucan and Maynooth from the 1440s and 1450s, and the seneschal of the earl of Ormond, who held both Lucan and Maynooth at this time, was responsible for the operation of his courts here. The earl's seneschal in 1443 was John Martyne, and his expenses at the manor court of Lucan were recorded at the end of each day, though the sums involved were relatively small amounts.[3] On 2 May 1443, the court roll records the services of a judge and, two weeks later, Richard Barby is paid expenses. Barby may have been the aforesaid judge, but normally only the expenses of the seneschal are recorded. In 1453, Remund Roche, who was then serving as seneschal for the earl of Ormond, was allowed expenses of between 12*d.* and 20*d.* per day. The court book for Esker and Crumlin confirms that in the late sixteenth century the seneschal did not always preside over the court, but instead nominated a deputy to carry out his duties.[4] Since keepers of individual manors

---

2 Hoyt, *Royal demesne*, p. 158.   3 *SCSMI*, pp 230–8.   4 Curtis, 'Court book' (vol. 59), 46, 52; (vol. 60), 38, 46.

often served alongside the seneschal in the fourteenth and fifteenth centuries, it is possible that the proceedings of the manorial court were often devolved onto them. The seneschal of demesne did not decide the outcome of court cases; it was the tenants on the royal manors, serving as jurors, who adjudicated these cases.[5]

Statute of labourers

The fifteenth-century court rolls can offer some clues as to the extent of a seneschal's power. For example, he had the authority to make tenants fulfil any services attached to their tenure or comply with statutes enforced by parliament. The king's tenants must have occasionally greeted this authority with resentment. When Walter Burgo was keeper of the royal demesne in England in the thirteenth century, the tenants of the manors of Feckenham, Lugwardine and Marden complained that he demanded customs and dues above and beyond what they were accustomed to render.[6] In the later fifteenth-century court rolls for the manor of Lucan, many incidences of tenants breaking the statute of labourers are recorded.[7] The fact that the earl of Ormond had to put pressure on his tenants to work on the manor suggests that the population was relatively small and the demand for workers was high. Certainly, the reports of wastelands on the royal manors in the fourteenth and fifteenth centuries suggests that there were not enough tenants to farm the lands. If court rolls survived for the royal manors, it is likely that evidence of tenants breaking the statute of labourers would be found there too. Though the late medieval period can sometimes be perceived as being bleak, it was also a time when tenants – particularly the peasant class – had more options open to them than in previous centuries. The tenants on the manor of Lucan were obviously able to find better paid employment elsewhere, if they were neglecting their manorial duties. The seneschal of demesne may have had to compel tenants to fulfil these duties. There is no mention of the statutes of labourers in the sixteenth-century court book, which would suggest that there was not quite the same demand for workers at this time or that services were commuted to cash payments. In any case, services owed by tenants living on the king's lands were always less than those demanded from other lords.[8] This is why tenure of royal lands was so eagerly sought.

The keeper of the royal demesne: the seneschal's predecessor

Though the term 'seneschal of demesne' does not appear until the early fourteenth century, it is possible that some individuals had already undertaken some of the functions that would later be associated with this office by the latter half of the thirteenth century. Indeed, the job may have preceded this title by several decades. In 1278, William Gernet was paid 50s. for custody of the king's

5 Curtis, 'Court book' (vol. 60), 141.   6 Hoyt, *Royal demesne*, p. 158.   7 *SCSMI*, p. 235.
8 Wolffe, *Royal demesne*, p. 25.

manors in the Vale of Dublin and it is possible he was one of the earliest keepers of the royal demesne.[9] There appear to be no other references to this individual in the sources and, therefore, his identity cannot be established. In 1281, William Deveneys was keeper of the king's demesne lands in Ireland, which would have involved him closely in the administration of the king's manors.[10] He expended a great deal of energy in reclaiming lands that had been previously lost to the Irish, and his duties were comparable to those of the fourteenth-century seneschals. For that reason, it might be more accurate to view the role of seneschal of demesne as an office that already existed in some form, but also one that had been expanded and changed by the structural reforms of the counties of Dublin and Kildare. Deveneys held many important offices in Ireland in the late thirteenth and early fourteenth century. Like many of the later seneschals, he was an officer of the exchequer, though he is also often described as a knight in various sources.[11] He is possibly related to William Deveneys of Hartland, who is listed in the Dublin guild merchant roll for 1257–8.[12] Entering the church would have been an obvious career choice for the son of a prosperous merchant. Henry de London, the archbishop of Dublin, had, after all, come from a mercantile background.[13] In the 1280s, Deveneys was engrosser of the great rolls of the exchequer and was paid 5*d.* a day for this work.[14] He also held the post of remembrancer of the exchequer, but was removed from this office by Stephen de Fulbourne, bishop of Waterford, when he refused to sell land he owned in Dunbro to the bishop, who wanted to consolidate his property in that area.[15] This proved to be just a minor setback in a successful administrative career, for as soon as he capitulated and sold his land to Fulbourne, he acquired the posts of marshal, prothonotary and keeper of the *Originalia*. Deveneys was granted these exchequer offices even though, strictly speaking, the same person should not have held them at the same time.[16] In 1300, his long career in the exchequer culminated with the post of baron.[17] He also undertook judicial work, serving as both a justice itinerant and a judge of the common bench.[18]

His position as keeper of the king's demesne lands would have involved him in the day-to-day administration of the royal manors of Dublin and undoubtedly served as a means for him to acquire lands on these manors. In 1283, three carucates and forty-five acres of land were granted to him in the tenement of Brownstown for the rent of seven pounds of silver.[19] This can be identified with Brownstown, a sub-manor within Newcastle Lyons. He was also granted

---

9 *CDI, 1252–84*, §1496.   10 Ibid., §1835; *Exchequer payments*, pp 69, 71, 75, 79.   11 Ball, *Judges*, 1, p. 60; for example, in a petition dated to 1290 he is described as a clerk, *CDI, 1285–92*, §622; likewise, in the fine rolls for 1299 he is described as a clerk: *CDI, 1293–1301*, §683.   12 *DGMR*, p. 98.   13 Brooks, 'Archbishop Henry of London', 5.   14 *CDI, 1252–84*, §2034; *Exchequer payments*, p. 87.   15 *CDI, 1252–84*, §§1781, 2332. This is situated in the parish of St Margaret in north Dublin.   16 *CDI, 1285–92*, §2.   17 *Admin. Ire.*, p. 106.   18 Ibid., pp 26, 143, 151; NAI, RC 8/4, p. 71.   19 *CDI, 1252–84*, §2070; *CIRCLE, Antiquissime roll*, §1.

Ballycolman, another parcel of land within the same manor. In times of peace, the lands granted to Deveneys were worth £51 13d. to the crown, but in 1284 he paid the much reduced sum of 10½ marks a year because much of the land remained waste due to war with the Irish.[20] Some of the other lands granted to him were in the mountains, including Balitened, which is modern-day Powerscourt in Wicklow.[21] The proximity of these lands to the Irish explains why he received them so cheaply. William stressed in a petition dated to 1290 that he had restored these lands to peace. In return, he requested a charter of warren, which was duly granted to him. This gave him the right to hunt and kill small game on his own lands, a privilege usually reserved to the monarch. He also petitioned for the right to erect a gallows and the power to judge the Irish, the king's rebels and traitors who broke the peace on his land. This privilege was denied. The same petition informs us that the king had enfeoffed him of lands in the mountainous parts of Ireland.[22] This was almost certainly a portion of the crown lands located in the Dublin Mountains, including the aforesaid Balitened. The petition states that the betaghs who had previously occupied these lands had fled when they were in a state of war.[23] He sought permission to recover his tenants and, evidently, he thought the gallows would serve as a deterrent if they considered absconding again. He was given permission to seek out and recover his betaghs with one stipulation; if they were living elsewhere on the king's demesne, they were to be left unmolested. William Deveneys also held lands in Saggart. This is confirmed by the pipe roll for 1281–2, which records that he paid part of the rent of this manor. He also had close associations with some of the known tenants of this manor. In 1305, when Walter Schyreburn paid 6s. arrears of the rent of Saggart, Deveneys served as his pledge.[24] Martin Deveneys – whose association with Saggart dates back to 1290–1, when he served as a pledge for two tenants on this manor, and who subsequently turns up as a tenant in his own right on the same manor – may well have been a relative of William's.[25]

William Deveneys was a substantial landowner who held lands elsewhere in Dublin. He is mentioned in relation to Rathcoole in a memoranda roll entry for 1312. This manor belonged to the archbishop of Dublin and is adjacent to both Newcastle and Saggart. It is possible that, as well as being a royal tenant, William also held lands of the archbishop.[26] He also held half a carucate of land on the royal manor of Bray.[27] In 1293, he paid the rent of the farm of the royal manor of Chapelizod, previously held by William Pren, the king's carpenter.[28] By the early fourteenth century, he was in possession of 1½ carucates of land in Thorncastle and Donnybrook, which included fishery rights at Thorncastle.[29] In 1324, he owed one-tenth of a knight's service for the land of Thorncastle.[30]

20 CDI, 1252–84, §2329. 21 CDI, 1285–92, §§271, 309. 22 Ibid., §622. 23 Sweetman has Petagii, but this must be Betagii. 24 NAI, EX 2/1, p. 132. 25 CDI, 1285–92, §855. 26 NAI, RC 8/6, p. 224. 27 CDI, 1252–84, §2340. 28 CDI, 1293–1301, §41. 29 NAI, RC 8/2, pp

He also held a part of one carucate of land in Ballybother and Balimony.[31] According to G.T. Stokes, Ballybother was an older name for Booterstown; this seems entirely plausible, as Deveneys also held lands in nearby Thorncastle.[32] Balimony is unidentified, but it is likely to have been close to Ballybother.

William may have acquired land for some of his relatives in his capacity as keeper of the king's demesne. Though there is evidence of Deveneys in this area before his period in office, none of them were associated specifically with the royal manors. A Robert Deveneys is mentioned in the pipe roll of 1281–2, and it is possible that he was related to William, who, incidentally, appears in the same pipe roll entry.[33] Robert's father was another William, who passed away before 1277, by which time Robert was 14 years of age. William had held one carucate of land in the vill of Robert of Lyons. This was the inheritance of William's wife, Emma. She was presumably Robert of Lyons' daughter, and it is likely that the lands in question lay within the manor of Lyons, adjacent to Newcastle Lyons.[34] Though kinship ties with the administrator William cannot be established with any degree of certainty, the fact that they held lands close to each other might suggest that they came from the same family group. It is surely no coincidence that, after he became keeper of the royal demesne, individuals who shared the same surname began to feature as tenants on some of the royal manors. In 1292, Alexander Deveneys paid rent for land on the manor of Crumlin, and he continued to do so until at least 1295.[35] During the 1290s, Walter Deveneys and Alexander Deveneys paid rent on the manor of Saggart.[36] It is likely that men like William Deveneys may have had only a transitory association with these royal manors. Their offices were usually for a set number of years and if they did receive lands on the manors, these grants lasted for their lifetime at most, though probably just for the duration of their office. Eventually, they would come back into royal hands to be granted out again to whomsoever the crown chose. Yet, these men could – and did – provide for their families, associates and servants with smaller parcels of lands within these manors. Tenants were less likely to be removed from these smaller portions of land because, regardless of whoever possessed the manor, men and women were needed to work the lands.

In 1285, John Kent paid the arrears of his account of the king's manors.[37] Though this exchequer receipt does not specify exactly the extent of John Kent's responsibilities, it is clear that he was accountable in some way for the manors as a group. It is certainly plausible that he too was a precursor of the seneschal of demesne. Since both he and Thomas Kent were associated with the royal

66–7; 8/9, pp 806–7; *CDI, 1293–1301*, §618. **30** *RDKPRI*, 42, p. 53. **31** *CDI, 1285–92*, §§47, 50. **32** G.T. Stokes, 'The antiquities from Kingstown to Dublin', *JRSAI*, 25 (1895), 13. **33** *RDKPRI*, 36, p. 67. **34** *CDI, 1171–1251*, §1405. **35** *CDI, 1285–92*, §1148; *CDI, 1293–1301*, §§21, 41, 264. **36** Ibid., §§139, 206, 226, 264, 279, 329, 363, 587. **37** *CDI, 1285–92*, §149.

manors, it is feasible that they came from the same family, though it is true that
Kent is a common enough surname during this period. He may be the same John
Kent who served as a baron of the exchequer and was deceased by 1293.[38] This
would have meant that he was active a generation before Thomas, which means
that it is entirely possible that he was Thomas' father or uncle. In 1299–1300,
Thomas Kent served as an attorney in England for another John Kent while he
was in Ireland, and this might be the same individual as the John Kent who was
pardoned in 1297 for burning down the church at Stacumny, which lies between
Celbridge and Leixlip not far north of Newcastle Lyons.[39] Thomas held land in
nearby Leixlip in the first decade of the fourteenth century, and it is plausible
that he and John were related. In fact, Ralph Pippard, for whom Thomas may
have worked and who held Leixlip in the 1290s, granted the manor of Dysart in
Co. Meath to an individual named John Kent at some point before he gave his
lands up to the crown.[40] Thomas Kent may have come from a family with a
tradition in manorial management. If he was related to the older John Kent, it
means that his links with the royal manors extended back at least one generation.
Alternatively, he may have been in the service of Ralph Pippard, and when
Pippard gave up his lands to the crown, Kent may have gone into royal service.
The Tyrel family were also close associates of the Pippards, and Kent may have
owed his grant of lands near Tyrellstown, in north Co. Dublin, to this family.[41]

Early fourteenth-century seneschals
In 1307–8, Robert Mouncens became seneschal of demesne.[42] His background
is unknown, but he was possibly related to John Mounceaux, a tenant in chief of
the king who died in England sometime before 1316.[43] His commission was
either short-lived or abortive, because Thomas Kent was serving as seneschal by
1 August 1307.[44] Mouncens received the grant of this office directly from the
king at Windsor Castle and it is possible that he had no connection with Ireland,
and that, consequently, the claims of Thomas Kent superseded his.[45] Kent
appears to have been followed in this office by Maurice Tyrel in 1314.[46] Maurice
was probably the son of Gerald Tyrel, sometime sheriff of Roscommon and
owner of the nearby manor of Lyons.[47] Sometime before 1309, Gerald granted
lands in Saggart and Newcastle Lyons to Maurice, and this would suggest that

---

38 *CDI, 1292–1301*, §67.   39 Ibid., §730; *CJR, 1295–1303*, p. 191.   40 *CJR, 1305–7*, p. 353.
41 NAI, EX 2/2, pp 590–1. Thomas was granted the manor of Kilcock in Co. Kildare, and
Belgree, which is near Tyrellstown in north Co. Dublin, in the early fourteenth century. The free
tenants, farmers and betaghs of these manors were ordered to be conscientious with regard
Thomas and the payment of their rents and farms and the fulfilment of their customary services.
42 NAI, EX 2/2, pp 329, 330, 348, 370; *CFR, 1307–19*, pp 20, 23.   43 *CFR, 1307–19*, p. 284.
44 NAI, EX 2/2, p. 248.   45 Ibid., p. 329.   46 NAI, RC 8/9, p. 548.   47 See Áine Foley,
'Violent crime in medieval Dublin: a symptom of degeneracy?' in Seán Duffy (ed.), *Medieval
Dublin*, 10 (Dublin, 2010), pp 220–40, for an account of Gerald's sons, Henry and Thomas, and
ch. 6, below.

there was a close family connection.[48] If he was one of Gerald's sons, he could not have inherited much from his father, as Robert Tyrel had possession of the manor of Lyons after his father's death. It is likely that Maurice was a younger son and therefore would have had to find an alternative source of income. A career in service to the crown would have been a logical choice for the son of a knight.

John Beneger followed Maurice as seneschal of demesne in 1316.[49] He spent time in Scotland in the company of Edward, prince of Wales, in 1301–2, and the exchequer paid his expenses incurred on this expedition, including the wages of men-at-arms as well as the cost of transporting these men and their horses to and from Scotland.[50] Beneger's tenure as seneschal coincided with the great European famine and the Bruce invasion. Someone with military experience in Scotland would have been invaluable at this time, particularly as the Bruce brothers were attacking lands dangerously close to the royal manors including Castleknock and Leixlip, and they may even have passed through the king's lands on their way from Dublin to Leixlip.[51] The Scots were not the only problem, because the Irish of the Wicklow Mountains, namely the O'Byrnes and the O'Tooles, took advantage of the unsettled conditions and started attacking the nearby lowlands of Dublin.[52]

This office must have passed out of his hands sometime before 1320, because by this time Haket de la Sale was serving as seneschal.[53] Haket was probably related to John de la Sale, who was almost certainly a tenant on the manor of Saggart, since, while there is no direct evidence that he owned land here, most of his known associates were tenants or held administrative offices on this manor. In 1294, John, together with Robert and Richard Landhary and John Beg, owed Francis Malesard, a merchant of Lucca, fifteen crannocs of wheat.[54] Two years later, Robert Landhary and John Beg paid the farm of Saggart into the exchequer.[55] John Beg was still paying this farm in 1298–9.[56] In 1290, when the tenants of Crumlin, Newcastle Lyons and Saggart impeded Henry Compton in taking up his grant of Crumlin, as well as the pleas and perquisites of the other two manors, Robert Landhary was summoned to court on behalf of the tenants of Saggart, and John Beg acted as his pledge in this case.[57] Also in 1294, John de la Sale was summoned to an inquisition involving the dean and chapter of St Patrick's and John, the vicar of Tallaght.[58] Tallaght manor was adjacent to Saggart; hence, the signs indicate that John was a local, even though there is no explicit evidence as to where exactly he held lands. John was pardoned for not appearing at the inquisition because he was poor. This might have been no more

48 NAI, RC 8/5, pp 275–7. **49** NAI, RC 8/10, p. 729. **50** *Exchequer payments*, p. 170. **51** Seán Duffy, 'The Bruce invasion of Ireland: a revised itinerary and chronology' in idem (ed.), *Robert the Bruce's Irish wars: the invasions of Ireland, 1306–1329* (Stroud, 2002), pp 35–6. **52** Ibid., pp 31–2. **53** NAI, RC 8/12, p. 259. **54** NAI, EX 2/1, p. 9. **55** *CDI, 1285–92*, §215. **56** *CDI, 1293–1301*, §587. **57** *IEMI*, p. 43, §80. **58** NAI, EX 2/1, p. 20.

than a ploy to avoid attending court, but it could also be the case that John's poverty was genuine. This would imply that he was of low social status. In 1304, he was again involved in judicial proceedings with the vicar of Tallaght, and Haket de la Sale gave security to pay 20s. on John's behalf.[59] Evidence that he did possess lands can be found in a memoranda roll entry for 1305 when he gave security to pay 22s. in arrears of rent. Richard Beg, the reeve of Saggart, was his pledge, and it is likely the land was situated on this manor. These arrears were not paid for several decades, and in 1332 Nicholas Beg, son of Richard, paid 10s. of it and gave security for the balance.[60] Even though there is no conclusive evidence that John de la Sale was a member of the peasantry, the evidence suggests that he was an individual of limited means.

Haket de la Sale may have obtained the important office of seneschal of demesne through ability rather than his connections. Compared with other seneschals, he held this office for a short period. He was granted the office on 5 March 1319, but held it for only two years, while it is likely that his successor held the post for in excess of five years.[61] Haket served as seneschal at a tumultuous time in the aftermath of the great European famine and the Bruce invasion. Judging by the petitions emanating from the tenants of the royal manors, the Scottish invasion had devastating consequences that lasted – if these petitions can be trusted – for decades after the event. Though less is said about the effects the famine had on the population, the increased attacks from the Irish in the mountains meant that these were desperate times. The act of strengthening the defences of Dublin city in 1316 may have had as much to do with the threat of the Irish attacking the settlement from sheer desperation as with the threat posed by the Scottish army.[62]

If this were the situation in the city, the problems facing the tenants on the royal manors – and particularly the outlying ones – would have been much more acute. Yet, even a manor so close to the city as Crumlin was suffering badly. In 1319, the smallholders of Crumlin were in arrears to the tune of 69s. 2d. As a consequence, the sheriff distrained their sheep and confiscated 171 animals to cover their debts to the king.[63] The seneschal of demesne was the individual usually responsible for collecting rents and arrears and, therefore, his job would have been especially difficult in times of war and famine. This must have created some resentment towards the holder of this office, and he may have been unpopular during times of crisis, which would have added to the difficulties of performing this job. This would have been particularly true if the seneschal was a local, like Haket de la Sale, as he would still have to live among the tenants once his term in office was completed, which might at least partly explain why an

59 Ibid., p. 92. 60 NAI, EX 2/1, p. 132. 61 CCR, 1318–23, p. 60; NAI, RC 8/12, p. 741; he is still referred to as the seneschal of the demesne in the pipe roll for 1321–2: RDKPRI, 42, pp 54–5. After he stepped down, Henry del Nasshe served as seneschal of demesne until 1327: RDKPRI, 43, p. 66. 62 Exchequer payments, p. 234. 63 NAI, RC 8/12, pp 94–5.

outsider was usually chosen. What is more, administrative posts could be a financial liability at the best of times and, consequently, in the aftermath of famine and war, men may have been less than eager to take on responsibilities that could put them out of pocket. Indeed, the financial pressures of the job may have been the reason that Haket served for such a short period.

Locals and clerics

It would appear that Thomas Kent and at least two of his successors, Maurice Tyrel and Haket de la Sale, were local to the area and, though they served in the office of seneschal, none of them seem to have been associated with the central administration or its various departments. Little is known of Henry Nasshe, but he may be the individual of the same name from Tipperary who appears in the justiciary rolls in 1305.[64] This Henry was fined for not serving as a juror at an assize and, therefore, he was probably an individual of reasonably high status. It is possible that, like John Beneger, he had experience in Scotland. Between 31 August and 29 September 1301, a Henry del Nasshe, the ship's master of the *Godale* of Rye, was paid £20 wages for himself, two constables and forty-eight sailors going from the port of Dublin to Scotland in aid of the king's war there.[65] Like Beneger, he could be expected to play an active part in the defence of the crown lands. He too disappears from the records once his term in office was complete. As the son of a knight, Maurice Tyrel was clearly a member of the burgeoning gentry class, and it is likely that Thomas Kent was of similar social status. Henry Nasshe, as the owner of a ship, was likely to have been involved in trade. Haket de la Sale's origins, on the other hand, are unclear, and it is quite possible that he was a member of the peasantry. None of these men appear to have progressed into other administrative roles once their term as seneschal was complete. Therefore, in its first few decades of existence, the office of seneschal did not serve as a stepping-stone for professional administrators, but rather it was a duty usually undertaken by a local.

From the second quarter of the fourteenth century, the trend was to give the office of seneschal to clerics, and there was a particular emphasis on exchequer officials receiving grants of this office. This development began in 1327, with Thomas Warilowe's appointment as seneschal.[66] He was already engrosser of the exchequer and, in the same year as he was granted the office of seneschal, he became clerk of wages.[67] Thomas must have proved an effective seneschal, because three years later, in 1330, he was made constable of Leixlip Castle and he held both posts concurrently.[68] Though Warilowe was a cleric, he took on all the practical responsibilities of defending the royal manors. In 1331–2, he was paid £20 from the exchequer in compensation for expenses incurred while he

---

64 *CJR, 1305–7*, p. 25. 65 *Exchequer payments*, p. 162. 66 NAI, RC 8/16, p. 411.
67 *Exchequer payments*, pp 280, 286, 334, 343. 68 *RDKPRI*, 43, p. 39; *Exchequer payments*, p. 325.

was in the king's service and to recoup the ransom he had to pay when the O'Tooles captured him.[69] It is likely that Warilowe was leading an expedition against the Irish in the Wicklow Mountains when he got captured, and this brief entry in the exchequer rolls hints at the militaristic aspects of the office of seneschal of demesne that must have increased in importance as the fourteenth century progressed. During his time as seneschal of the royal demesne, Warilowe was responsible for paying the wages of the men going in the company of Roger Outlawe, deputy justiciar, to Munster to subdue the O'Briens and other enemies of the king. Outlawe was prior of Kilmainham, and it is possible that Warilowe was one of his fellow Hospitallers who may have accompanied him on this expedition.[70] It is perhaps surprising that the majority of men chosen for this office during the first half of the fourteenth century were churchmen, since the holder was expected to play an active part in defending the manors. What is more astonishing is the ardency with which many of them carried out their duties.

It is also possible that John Baddeby, a previous constable of Leixlip Castle, had served as seneschal of the royal demesne before Warilowe's term of office, because in the pipe rolls of 1324–5 he is described as seneschal.[71] Unfortunately, the source is not specific in regard to where he served as seneschal, but it is unlikely that it is referring to Leixlip, since the custodian of the castle was always described as 'constable'. Since other seneschals of royal demesne served as constable for Leixlip, it is certainly possible that Baddeby was among their number.

Like Thomas Warilowe, Thomas Dent may have used the office of seneschal as a stepping-stone to further advancement within the administration.[72] He came from Dent in Yorkshire and, just a year before he became seneschal in 1332, he, along with many others, was charged with stealing forty horses and three hundred sheep from John Mowbray of Ingelton in the same county.[73] Dent was also accused of breaking into Mowbray's chaces and warrens and stealing deer, hares, rabbits and pheasants, in addition to assaulting his servants. From such an unpromising start, this clerk went on to enjoy a highly successful career in the Irish judiciary. He would subsequently become a justice of the common bench before progressing to the position of chief justice of the bench.[74] In 1359, he held the farm of the manor of Esker, paying the annual sum of £15 13s. 4d. into the exchequer.[75] This sum was granted as an annuity to the king's yeoman, Robert Clinton, with the promise that he would receive a grant of the manor after Dent's death. Dent played a central role in the Irish administration for two decades, but he never lost his links with England. In 1343, he served on a commission in Westmoreland, and from at least 1361, he must have been living

69 *Exchequer payments*, p. 342.   70 Ibid., p. 334.   71 *RDKPRI*, 42, p. 52.   72 NAI, RC 8/16, pp 134–5.   73 *CPR, 1330–4*, p. 59.   74 *Admin. Ire.*, pp 122–3; *CPR, 1334–8*, p. 477; *CPR, 1340–3*, p. 252; *CPR, 1343–5*, p. 316.   75 *CPR, 1358–61*, p. 213.

back in England permanently, because from that time on, he nominated attorneys in Ireland to handle his affairs here.[76] One of his attorneys was John Dent, a merchant and a native of Yorkshire who was probably a kinsman. John was pardoned in 1364 for non-payment of a debt and, in the following year, he transported two hundred quarters of peas from Kingston upon Hull to Gascony.[77] The family does not appear to have settled in Ireland, as they do not turn up in the Irish sources after this date.

Thomas Dent's successors also used the office of seneschal of the king's lands to help advance their administrative careers. Walter Bardelby, who became seneschal in 1333, shortly went on to become keeper of the rolls.[78] At the time he was granted the office of seneschal in 1334, Walter Coumbe was a king's clerk serving as chamberlain of the exchequer.[79] According to D'Alton, Thomas Smithe became seneschal of the manors of Newcastle Lyons, Saggart and Crumlin in 1336.[80] Smithe or Smothe first appears in the records in 1326–7, when he was clerk of the stores of Dublin Castle.[81] He continued in this office for some years and it would have been his responsibility to ensure that the castle was properly armed and garrisoned. Between 1339 and 1341, Thomas Smothe and the previous seneschal, Walter Coumbe, were granted £10 for their good service and their labours and expenses in the king's service in various parts of Ireland.[82] Smothe, like many of his predecessors, was an officer of the exchequer; in 1341, he served as remembrancer and still held this office in 1347.[83] It was the duty of this officer to compile the memoranda rolls to 'remind' the barons of any business pertaining to the exchequer. Thomas had a wife named Alice, and on 16 August 1344, they received papal permission to choose a confessor.[84] In 1322, Henry Moreville granted Thomas Smothe land in Donnybrook.[85] These lands had originally belonged to Walter Ridelisford, but had passed through the Frambald family before they were granted to Smothe by Richard Frambald.[86] Frambald had taken these lands back, but Thomas' son, another Thomas, who would serve as seneschal in 1360, eventually succeeded in regaining the property.[87] William Epworth followed the elder Thomas in the office of seneschal in 1343. William also served in the exchequer as a baron but, because he found his other duties very demanding, he was forced to give up the post a couple of years later and was succeeded by Thomas Pipard.[88]

Thomas Pippard, unlike his predecessors, appears to have had no obvious connection with the exchequer, though he was a royal official who went to Calais

76 *CPR, 1343–5*, p. 93; *CPR, 1361–4*, p. 130.   77 *CPR, 1364–7*, pp 34, 50.   78 Ball, *Judges*, 1, p. 36. According to D'Alton, *History of Dublin*, p. 696, William de Barthelby was made seneschal of the manors of Newcastle Lyons, Saggart and Crumlin in 1333.   79 *CPR, 1330–4*, p. 546; *Admin. Ire.*, pp 122–3; *IEMI*, p. 178, §290. 80 D'Alton, *History of Dublin*, p. 696. 81 *Exchequer payments*, pp 325, 329, 334, 337.   82 Ibid., p. 398.   83 Ibid., pp 409, 423. 84 *CPL, 1342–62*, p. 157. 85 *CCD*, 142, §560; later known as Simmonscourt. 86 Ibid., p. 128, §490.   87 Ibid., p. 157, §642.   88 NAI, RC 8/22, p. 649; *Admin. Ire.*, pp 110–11; *CPR, 1343–5*, p. 562.

on urgent business concerning the king between 10 April and 23 August 1347.[89] This happened to be in the middle of his term as seneschal of the royal demesne and, though he was originally granted the office on the stipulation that he would personally perform the duties of seneschal, he was clearly allowed to nominate a deputy while he was away on the king's business in France.[90] The Black Death occurred during Pippard's tenure in office, though it is not known if his duties continued to be performed by a deputy once he had completed his royal errand overseas. William Botte (or Butler) succeeded him in 1352. This may be the exchequer clerk who accompanied Thomas Mynot, baron of the exchequer, to Munster in 1356–8 on the king's business.[91]

William Barton became seneschal in 1353, and, like many of his precursors, he was attached to the exchequer. By the time he obtained this post, he was already a tenant on the manor of Crumlin, and, in 1352–3, he was granted lands in Kilmactalway, Milltown and Rancailagh.[92] According to D'Alton, Barton was granted the custody of a mill, as well as one carucate and fifty acres in Saggart, Milltown, Rancailagh, Angerston and Kilmactalway for seven years.[93] Angerston survives under the modern place-name Aungierstown, and is situated just north of Kilmactalway and to the east of Milltown. For that reason, it is likely that Rancailage was in the same vicinity.[94] These grants would have given him a personal stake concerning the defence of this group of manors. The granges of Kilmactalway and Milltown contained mills and, even in difficult times, these lands were much sought after for the potential revenue that could be drawn from the mills. Two years after he came to office, Barton was responsible for purveying food to feed the justiciar's forces going to subdue the Irish, as well as paying the wages of the men-at-arms going on these expeditions.[95] Though Barton clearly expended a considerable amount of energy in assisting with the defence of the locality, he also used the office to advance his own interests. He served as a senior clerk in the chancery as well as the chief engrosser of the exchequer, before becoming a chamberlain.[96]

Thomas Smothe, whose father had previously served as seneschal, and who, like Barton, happened to be a cleric, followed him in the office of seneschal in 1360. There is, however, no evidence that he was associated with the exchequer.[97] A deed from 1362 reveals that Smothe's property in the vicinity of Donnybrook consisted of ten messuages and a carucate, as well as rents of 43s. 4d. It is confirmed that this land had previously belonged to Smothe's father, but that he

89 *Exchequer payments*, p. 420.   90 NAI, RC 8/23, p. 449.   91 *Exchequer payments*, p. 485. 92 *CIRCLE*, CR 18 Edw. III, §111; TNA, C 47/10/22/7.   93 D'Alton, *History of Dublin*, p. 685.   94 Though Rancailage sounds very similar to Ranelagh they are not the same. Ranelagh did not attain its name until the eighteenth century. A house in the locality that was modelled on Ranelagh Gardens in London gave its name to the area. During the medieval period, this place was variously known as Colonia and Cullenswood and belonged to the archbishop of Dublin: see Ball, *Dublin*, 2, pp 108–10, for a brief history of the area.   95 *Exchequer payments*, pp 464, 468, 472.   96 *Admin. Ire.*, pp 18, 123.   97 NAI, RC 8/27, p. 579.

had held them without licence. Nonetheless, the younger Thomas was allowed to continue in possession of this property.[98] Though this area had passed through many hands, it would become so intrinsically associated with this family that it later became known as Smotescourt.[99] Smothe augmented his holding in Donnybrook by leasing lands there called Caldecot of Sir Elias Ashbourne, knight, in 1336.[1] He also received lands in nearby Merrion from John Cruys.[2] The Smothe family also had interests in the city and in north Dublin at Kinsaley.[3] As the younger Thomas was a cleric, he left no children, which may explain why he granted some of his lands in Donnybrook to other churchmen.[4] He granted an acre of meadow, a dovecote and a small park to the chaplain, John Mynagh.[5]

The Black Death

The plague that devastated most of Europe in the mid-fourteenth century must have had dreadful consequences for those living and working on the royal manors. Even so, it appears to have had no immediate effect on the type of men granted the office of royal seneschal, who continued to be mainly exchequer officials. This only changed in 1360, when a statute was passed ordering that seneschals and receivers of the king's demesne lands had to be henceforth appointed on the advice and ordinance of the chancellor, treasurer and the council. The implication is that there was some dissatisfaction with the men who had previously held these offices. The statute also stipulated that if any of the current seneschals and receivers were not fit to undertake the office they were to be immediately removed.[6] It may be no more than a coincidence, but the type of man chosen as seneschal of demesne for the rest of the fourteenth century usually possessed a great deal of military experience and was a laymen rather than a cleric. Certainly, while some of the exchequer officials and clerics who had previously served as seneschal were prepared to take an active part in defending the royal manors, others were unable or unwilling to deal with the increasing attacks of the Irish from the mountains. The statute also reveals that, though some seneschals did not satisfactorily fulfil the duties of the office, this position was not a sinecure. Unlike the experience on the royal demesne in England, the offices associated with the royal demesne in Ireland were not honorific. On the royal manor of Havering in Essex, for example, offices were granted to royal officials from nearby London on the understanding that they did not have to fulfil personally the duties associated with these offices.[7] Plainly, this would not do in Dublin, and the administration there knew that the office of seneschal would be better served if it was filled by a layman with military experience who

98 *CCD*, p. 164, §689. 99 Smothescourt is now known as Simmonscourt. 1 *CCD*, p. 150, §605. 2 Ibid., p. 171, §741. 3 Ibid., p. 125, §475; p. 143, §570. 4 Ibid., p. 170, §736; p. 171, §745. 5 Ibid., p. 174, §767. 6 *Stat. Ire., John–Hen. V*, p. 425. 7 McIntosh, *Autonomy and community*, pp 20–1.

would be active in performing the duties pertaining to it. Additionally, it was at this time that the administration moved itself to Carlow, and this might explain the disconnection between the exchequer and those serving as seneschal.[8]

In 1360, Thomas Mareward was the first of these laymen to serve as seneschal of the royal demesne.[9] In 1389–90, Mareward – or possibly a son – was the mayor of the city of Dublin and, a decade later, he served as sheriff of Co. Dublin on at least two occasions. Additionally, he was seneschal for Crumlin in 1385, and this would suggest that he had the military experience required to assist in the defence of the royal manors.[10] In 1374, Richard Cardiff granted a messuage in Picot's Lane in the parish of St Michael to Thomas Mareward, and, in 1390, the mayor and community of Dublin city granted him land at St Patrick's Gate just outside the walls of the city for a rent of 12*d*.[11] The grant of lands in such a strategic position may have had some association with the defence of the city. Thomas was not only a beneficiary of lands within the city, but a benefactor too. In 1379, he and his wife Cecelia granted a messuage in High Street to Adam Piers and Roger Foul, and, in 1392, they granted a messuage in Rochelle Street – now known as Back Lane – to the former.[12] The bulk of Mareward's property was in Skreen, Co. Meath, however. At the time of his death, sometime before 5 December 1421,[13] his substantial property came into the king's hands, because his son and heir, Thomas – a minor – was also deceased by this time.[14] The lands were granted to John Charneles, but they eventually came back into the family's possession. We know this because Richard Mareward was baron of Skreen in the mid-fifteenth century. Richard also served as sheriff of Dublin in 1459, and John Mareward, who was mayor of Dublin in 1392–3, may have been his father.[15] Since Thomas senior's heir was underage at the time of his death, it is possible that John was either his brother or an older son who had died before his father. Walter Somery succeeded Mareward, and his term in office coincided with the second major visitation of the plague.[16] On this occasion, the effects of the pestilence on the royal manors are discernible in the sources. In the summer of 1362, many of the tenants on the manors of Newcastle Lyons, Crumlin and Saggart had succumbed to the disease, and it was Somery's grim duty to find new tenants to replace them.

In 1388, Geoffrey de Vale became seneschal of Esker, Newcastle Lyons and Saggart. In the following year, he was granted these manors for life, as well as sixty acres in Kilmactalway and a mill at Milltown.[17] William Barton had previously held lands in Kilmactalway and Milltown during his term as seneschal of

---

8 Thanks to Peter Crooks for this observation.   9 NAI, RC 8/27, pp 578–9.   10 D'Alton, *History of Dublin*, pp 200, 681.   11 *CCD*, p. 84, §255; p. 169, §730.   12 Ibid., p. 170, §735; p. 174, §775.   13 Unless Thomas was very young when he served as seneschal, this is likely to be his son. The sources do not clearly differentiate between them.   14 TNA, E 28/36/39; *SCSMI*, p. 181.   15 *Stat. Ire., Hen. VI*, p. 605.   16 NAI, RC 8/28, p. 91.   17 *CPR, 1385–9*, p. 533; D'Alton, *History of Dublin*, pp 649, 681.

demesne, and it is likely that these are the same lands and that they had become associated with this office by this time. Like his predecessor, Vale was granted the custody of a mill and, though the location of the mill granted to Barton is not specified, it was probably in Milltown. It appears that seneschals, like other government servants, did not always receive regular salaries. This appears to have been the experience in England too, where crown officials were often granted lands on the royal manors instead of financial remuneration.[18] It is possible that land on the royal manor of Newcastle Lyons was granted to the seneschals in lieu of a salary. There is only one example in the roll of exchequer payments of the seneschal of the royal demesne in Dublin receiving a fee, which would suggest that this was not the norm.[19]

The Vale family had been in Ireland since at least the mid-thirteenth century, when Richard Vale held lands in Decies, Waterford.[20] William Vale and Geoffrey Vale, who appear in the Christ Church deeds for the years 1218 and 1260 respectively, may have been among of the first members of this family to come to Ireland.[21] Also during the thirteenth century, Adam Vale served as attorney for Thomas de Clare, lord of Thomond.[22] Both Adam and his brother Stephen fought in the battle of Lewes on the king's side against Simon Montfort, and this loyalty would be rewarded by a grant of the custody of Rindoon Castle (in modern Co. Roscommon) to Adam in 1280.[23] In the following year, he was paying the farm of the royal manor of Newcastle McKynegan.[24] Richard Vale, who was possibly a descendant of his namesake from Decies, served as sheriff of Waterford at the beginning of the fourteenth century and he may be the Richard Waleys who attended the parliament in Kilkenny in 1310.[25] This was the beginning of a long tradition of royal service within this family. The main branch of the Vale family was based in Johnstown, Co. Carlow, and many members of the family – including Geoffrey – served as sheriffs of this county.[26] In 1359, William Vale was sheriff and he was granted £10 in part payment of £20 in recompense for the goods and chattels lost by members of his retinue while fighting against the O'Nolans and the O'Byrnes.[27] Geoffrey Vale was sheriff of Carlow in 1375, and his fee for holding this office was £20.[28] He was sheriff once again three years later and was granted a fee of twenty marks.[29] Simon Vale was sheriff of the same county in 1389, and it would appear that this family controlled the office of sheriff of Carlow for much of the fourteenth century.

---

18 Wolffe, *Royal demesne*, p. 37. 19 *Exchequer payments*, p. 428: between 9 December 1346 and 9 June 1348 Thomas Pippard was paid £7 10s. for his office as seneschal at the exchequer. His fee was £5 per annum. 20 *CDI, 1252–84*, §234. 21 *CCD*, p. 40, §25; p. 51, §90. 22 *CDI, 1252–84*, §§1342, 1348. 23 Ibid., §1427. 24 Ibid., §§1780, 1814. 25 TNA, E 101/233/16; *SCSMI*, p. 71; *Stat. Ire., John–Hen. V*, p. 259. 26 NAI, 999/217/1i. 27 *Exchequer payments*, p. 493. In NAI, 999/217/1ii, it says that Thomas Wale [*sic*] of Johnstown, sheriff of Carlow, was granted £20 for killing the O'Nolans. Both documents say that Donald Tagsone O'Nolan and Philip O'Byrne were killed by the sheriff and, consequently, this must be the same individual. 28 NAI, 999/217/1iii. 29 NAI, 999/217/1iv.

Later, in the 1430s, Henry Vale was parson of Carlow, but also combined this ecclesiastical office with the much less spiritual office of constable of the castle there.[30]

It is clear that Geoffrey Vale came from a family experienced in county administration. Defending Co. Carlow against the rebellious Irish would have given him the skills necessary to defend the royal manors now under serious threat from the Irish in the Dublin Mountains. The state of these manors in the second half of the fourteenth century is clearly reflected in the appointments of both Thomas Mareward and Geoffrey Vale as their seneschals. The desperate need for men with military experience to defend the royal manors was now unmistakably evident. While some of the ecclesiastics who had held this office fulfilled it with great energy, others were content to let deputies carry out their duties. This state of affairs was not to last. Even though the Irish in the mountains had been a threat almost since the colony was established, and the first half of the fourteenth century had been fraught with difficulties, events like the Black Death and subsequent plagues as the century progressed, undoubtedly exacerbated the existing problems in this frontier zone.

During his tenure as sheriff of Carlow, Geoffrey Vale had proved to be more than capable of maintaining a defence against both the Irish and the English rebels. He was granted the enormous sum of £100 to retain men in his company, buy horses and armour, and spy on the Irish. He also succeeded in killing Domhnall Cáomhánach Mac Murchadha who – it was said – attempted daily to destroy and devastate Leinster.[31] Undoubtedly, it was hoped that he would have the same success in Dublin. Moreover, he may have been accompanied by a retinue similar to that which he had as sheriff of Carlow. His predecessor, William, also had a company of men to help in the defence of Carlow. A small standing army would have been a crucial aid in Geoffrey's ability to defend the royal manors against attacks. His efforts were appreciated, and evidence of this can be found in the grant for life of unidentified manors in Ireland to the value of £23 in 1399.[32] This grant was made to him in consideration of the expenses he bore in the wars against the king's enemies and because his demesne lands – presumably his property in Carlow – had been destroyed by the Irish.

CONCLUSION

One of the primary functions of the royal manors was as a means of rewarding men who could be usefully employed at all levels in the administration of the

---

30 *Exchequer payments*, pp 574, 578.   31 Ibid., pp 535–6; Robin Frame, 'Two kings in Leinster: the crown and the MicMhurchadha in the fourteenth century' in Robin Frame, T.B. Barry and K. Simms (eds), *Colony and frontier in medieval Ireland: essays presented to J.F. Lydon* (London, 1995), pp 155–75.   32 *CPR, 1399–1401*, p. 146.

colony – not only with lands, but, as this chapter demonstrates, also with manorial office. An examination of tenants and officials on the royal manors in the thirteenth and fourteenth centuries gives the impression that they were aware of their rights and fought to uphold them. The case involving Henry Compton and the tenants of Crumlin indicates a sense of solidarity among this group, and one that extended beyond this manor to the royal manors of Newcastle Lyons and Saggart. Certainly, the sources indicate that the tenants of the royal manors looked after their own.

The evidence reveals that, throughout much of the late medieval period, exchequer officials were frequently granted the office of seneschal, and it is possible that they viewed this office as a useful supplement to their income. Nonetheless, at least during the thirteenth century, it was not considered a sinecure, and they were expected to fulfil the duties associated with this office. Most of those granted the office of seneschal, aside from a brief period during the first half of the fourteenth century, were outsiders, and they were usually members of the gentry. On the other hand, those who served as reeves and bailiffs came from a much more socially diverse group, so that although some were certainly members of the gentry, it was common to find prosperous peasants filling these positions as well. The seneschal must have worked closely with the reeves and other manorial officers of the royal manors, and probably delegated much of his responsibility onto them. Even though the seneschal, for example, was in charge of taking extents and making sure rents were collected, there is plenty of evidence of lesser manorial officials carrying out these and other similar tasks. Many of those who served as seneschals used their privileged position to establish family members and associates on small parcels of land within the royal demesne. Consequently, after their term of office ended, the smaller tenants they had established on the manors remained. The same family often held these modest holdings for several generations and, consequently, they became an integral part of the social fabric of the locality. It appears that the bailiffs, reeves and receivers of the royal manors were mainly derived from this group.

The office of seneschal of the royal demesne may have been born out of the administrative innovations that followed the parliament of 1297, when new counties were created and power was devolved from the sheriff of Dublin. The creation of Co. Kildare, with its own sheriff, and the removal of the sheriffdom of Meath from the authority of the Dublin sheriff, might imply that the area he controlled was too large for one man to administer. The office of seneschal is noteworthy, because it did not have an exact equivalent in England. Despite the fact that attempts were made to create a similar office across the Irish Sea, they ultimately failed.

Why did this office endure in Ireland? It may have succeeded for the simple fact that it was needed here. A unique set of conditions existed in south Dublin that, for the most part, did not exist in England. From the late thirteenth century onwards, the Irish began to threaten the manors near the mountains, and it was essential to have officials who were capable of defending the area. This need became more acute with the arrival of the Bruce brothers, which coincided with the great European famine. The men employed as seneschal at this time had experience fighting against the Scots, and this suggests that at times there was a deliberate policy to employ men with the skills needed to defend the area from outside threats. Seneschals like John Beneger, who spent time fighting in Scotland, understood their enemy and, arguably, had the expertise required to deal with them.

The ebb and flow of the fortunes of the royal manors can be discerned through the kind of men chosen for the offices of keeper and seneschal of demesne. The appointment of William Deveneys as keeper of the king's demesne lands in 1281 may have been a response to the rise of the O'Tooles and the O'Byrnes in the Dublin Mountains. Orpen observed that the temporalities of the see of Dublin were in the king's hands during the 1270s and he hypothe-sized that the harsher rule of the king's officials caused disturbances among the Irish.[33] Even at this early date, there were tensions between the Irish and the tenants on the manors of south Dublin. The creation of the office of keeper of the royal demesne may have come about in response to these tensions. Even though Deveneys was a cleric, he proved very effective in restoring order to the area. Moreover, he may have granted parcels of land to his kinsmen to help bolster the defence of the locality. The practicality of using locals who had a stake in defending the manors was not lost on the administration.

Certainly, men like Haket de la Sale and Thomas Kent appear to have had close links with the local community; yet, later in the fourteenth century, an outsider usually held this post and occasionally it appears to have been little more than a sinecure. At this time, it was normally granted to an individual associated with the exchequer, and occasionally the chancery, who may or may not have had any practical involvement in the day-to-day administration of this office. Logically, it would be in the best interests of a local to put a concerted effort into the defence of the royal manors, if only for the selfish motive of self-preservation. There was no guarantee that someone who held this office just for the fee it provided would put any effort into adequately fulfilling his duties or ensuring that a suitable deputy was found. This meant that the men carrying out the practical aspects of the office may or may not have had the skills or means to fulfil their functions properly. Paradoxically, most of the exchequer clerks who were granted this office in the first half of the fourteenth century happened to be capable men, and many of them had practical military experience. This was

33 Orpen, *Normans*, 4, p. 15, Orpen uses the term seneschal, even though it is not found in the administrative sources until the beginning of the fourteenth century; see also Lydon, 'Medieval Wicklow', pp 151–89.

fortunate, as there was always the risk that their neglect could seriously compromise the defence of the manors, which in turn threatened the safety of the entire county. It appears that this did become a problem as the century progressed, and, in 1360, a statute was passed to ensure that those who held this office were capable of fulfilling the duties connected to the job.[34] In the aftermath of the Black Death, men with military experience were selected for this office, which suggests that this was a particularly difficult period for the locality.

34 *Stat. Ire., John–Hen. V*, p. 425.

5

The royal manors and the city of Dublin

INTRODUCTION

The retention by Henry II of Dublin and the other Ostman towns as crown property meant that control of the most economically viable areas of the island came into royal hands. He immediately ensured the future economic development and prosperity of the city of Dublin when he granted it to the men of Bristol. The motivation behind issuing this charter was not only to attract merchants and craftsmen to Dublin, but also to officially acknowledge the trading links that had already existed between both settlements.[1] The king used these pre-existing economic links between Ireland and England to control his newly acquired territory. The retention of a hinterland around the city, including the lands that would subsequently become the royal manors of Newcastle Lyons, Saggart, Esker and Crumlin, was as vital to this economic prosperity as the acquisition of the city itself.

The advantages of controlling the hinterland around the city for the crown increased in the thirteenth century when the citizens were granted the fee-farm of the city because, though royal officials were no longer directly involved in its administration, their continued interests within the royal demesne meant that they were always close at hand. Additionally, its uses in rewarding royal servants and favourites based both within the locality and across the sea in England have already been investigated. Another important reason for retaining this hinterland was to supply the city with resources, and merchants were needed to exploit these resources. The value of this mercantile group based within the city, who virtually dominated city government throughout the medieval period, is best demonstrated through the grants of land they received on the royal manors as well as elsewhere on the king's demesne.[2] Just like the clerics who formed the nucleus of government within the colony, these men were the recipients of royal patronage. Though Gillespie has explored the importance of the royal manors to the merchant class of Dublin for the early modern period, the evidence establishes that the incidences of merchants holding lands on the manors can be

---

1 Aubrey Gwynn, 'Medieval Bristol and Dublin', *IHS*, 5 (1946–7), 275–86; Howard B. Clarke, '*Angliores ipsis Anglis:* the place of medieval Dubliners in English history' in Howard B. Clarke, Jacinta Prunty and Mark Hennessy (eds), *Surveying Ireland's past: multidisciplinary essays in honour of Anngret Simms* (Dublin, 2004), p. 47. 2 Duffy, 'Town and crown', p. 108.

traced back to an earlier period.[3] The four royal manors were intrinsically linked to the city of Dublin from their foundation, and their fortunes invariably rose and fell with those of the city.

The political importance of merchants during the initial invasion period was investigated in chapter two. Clearly, members of the mercantile class, like William Fitz John of Harptree, who held Crumlin in 1216, were significant figures who played a vital part in the transformation of colonial Ireland from a speculative military conquest into a settlement with definite administrative and economic structures. These trends in Ireland reflected trends found elsewhere in Europe at this time, particularly in the areas that had remained outside the sphere of Roman influence in the previous millennium. Merchants always played a key part in the colonization process, but this importance intensified from the tenth century onwards, when populations grew and began to push outwards to the fringes of Europe. This process was accelerated by the crusading movement, which got underway in the following century. In the aftermath of the First Crusade, the rulers of the newly established Crusader States founded towns on their lands to attract colonists, particularly the artisans and craftsmen necessary to exploit the natural resources of the region. Italian merchants were drawn here to develop the economic potential of the conquered territory. Moreover, the Crusader States became dependant on the fleets of these merchants in order to ferry men and goods to and from newly conquered territories.[4] Elsewhere in Europe, similar patterns can be detected: for instance, when German traders pushed eastwards, they established seasonal trading outposts that were eventually transformed into permanent settlements. In 1200, Riga, a trading outpost on the Baltic Sea, was moved to a new site by Bishop Albert of Livonia and, in order to encourage merchants to settle there on a more permanent basis, he granted them special privileges. These incentives were successful and eventually the new settlers acquired a town council and their own seal. Some of their privileges were remarkably similar to those enjoyed by their contemporaries in Dublin; for example, they had freedom from toll and from trial by ordeal.[5] The rulers of newly conquered lands encouraged merchants to come and settle by founding towns or giving already established settlements a corporate identity.

The Irish experience in the aftermath of the English invasion was replicated all over Europe, but evidence of merchants being an important factor in colonization can be found closer to home. In Scotland, the earliest burghs were located on lands belonging to the crown, which strongly suggests that they were founded by kings.[6] The customs governing Scottish towns, known as the 'Laws

3 Gillespie, 'Small worlds', pp 202–3. 4 Robert Bartlett, *The making of the Middle Ages: conquest, colonisation and cultural change, 950–1350* (London, 1993), p. 183; Andrew Jotischky, *Crusading and the crusader states* (Harlow, 2004), p. 151. 5 Jotischky, *Crusading*, pp 194–5. 6 G.W.S. Barrow, *Kingship and unity: Scotland, 1000–1306* (London, 1981), p. 87.

of the Four Burghs', were partially based on the customs of Newcastle upon Tyne – which probably date to the reign of Henry I of England – and contained many mercantile privileges. These were designed to promote colonization and no doubt were influential in drawing settlers from as far afield as Flanders, the Rhineland and France, as well as England.[7]

From at least the eleventh century, Dublin was a significant trading centre that dominated the Irish Sea region and provided a link between Ireland and the world beyond. Though the number of merchants in Dublin may have increased in the aftermath of the English conquest, they already had a history of trading and settling here.[8] In fact, it is possible that merchants provided some of the impetus for this invasion. John Bradley suggested that this group may have funded Strongbow's expedition to Ireland in 1170 as a means of protecting their pre-existing trading rights in the city.[9]

The merchants were not only interested in the city but also in the surrounding hinterland, which was vital to its existence. Food and raw material was produced here to both feed the city and provide resources for its markets. The benefits flowed in both directions since the producers of these goods also required the city as a market to sell their surplus produce. In the thirteenth century, Ireland became an important source of cereal for the overseas market. In 1224, William Marshal sold one thousand crannocks of wheat from his lands in Ireland to the mayor of London.[10] The king was using his own lands for the same purpose. In 1228, the justiciar, Richard de Burgh, paid the substantial sum of £62 16s. 8d. for corn to the tenants of Esker, Crumlin and Saggart. This money generated by the sale of the corn was used to pay the fees of the previous justiciar, Geoffrey Marisco.[11] Moreover, later in the thirteenth century, there is evidence from tenants from the royal manors paying their rent in corn rather than cash. Walter and Robert Deveneys paid their share of the rent of Saggart in corn in 1298. In the same year, Thomas Blunt, Yerward Adgo and William Blund paid the arrears of the manor of Newcastle Lyons by the same method.[12] This cereal could have been used to sustain the royal administration in Dublin or pay administrators' wages, but by this date it is much more likely that it was used to help support Edward I's war effort in Scotland.[13] Merchants who held lands on the royal manors and elsewhere in the county may have used at least a portion of their lands to grow crops or rear animals to sell at market. The hides sold by members of the Callan family, who are examined below, may have come from the cattle reared on their lands in Saggart. Likewise, the wool sold by William Douce, a member of another mercantile family discussed later in this chapter, may have come from sheep he kept in Newcastle Lyons.

7 Ibid., pp 93, 97–9.   8 Clarke, '*Angliores ipsis Anglis*', p. 46.   9 John Bradley, 'A tale of three cities: Bristol, Chester and Dublin and "the coming of the Normans"' in Howard B. Clarke and J.R.S. Phillips (eds), *Ireland, England and the Continent in the Middle Ages and beyond* (Dublin, 2006), pp 51, 60.   10 Down, 'Colonial society', pp 484–5.   11 *RDKPRI*, 35, p. 30.   12 *CDI, 1293–1301*, §587.   13 Lydon, *Lordship*, p. 103.

The evidence indicates that the trend of merchants holding lands on the royal manors dates back to the thirteenth century and, indeed, may have begun very shortly after the conquest. Many of the merchants awarded lands on these manors filled important civic offices within the city. There are several examples of mayors or bailiffs benefiting from royal patronage in the form of property on the royal manors. Subsequently, the descendants of many of these men settled in the countryside around Dublin and some eventually left their mercantile roots behind, choosing to concentrate all their interests in the hinterland. Yet, many men whose main interests were firmly in the county retained or acquired interests in the city and some held civic office too. Prominent members of the merchant class who held land on the royal manors are examined below. The focus is on the careers of four families, namely the Marshals who held lands in Newcastle Lyons, the Douces who held lands in Saggart and Newcastle Lyons, the Callans who held lands in Crumlin and Saggart, and the Owens who held lands in Esker, Newcastle Lyons and Saggart. Between them, these four families held lands on all four royal manors and at least one member of each family held the office of mayor. The Marshals and Owens were prominent members of civic society as early as the first half of the thirteenth century. The Douce and Callan families did not achieve prominence in the city until the latter half of the same century, by which time the Owens had transferred their interests from the city to the county. By the end of the fourteenth century, the main branches of the Marshal and Douce families appear to have died out, or at least they were no longer prominent families in Dublin, but the Callans continued to prosper in Dublin for at least another century and the Owens were still important landowners in Co. Dublin in the sixteenth century. The presence of these mercantile families on the royal manors was important because they ensured that revenues flowed from the countryside into the city.

This group of individuals bear striking similarities to the urban gentry identified by Rosemary Horrox in England during the late medieval period. She argues that merchants who bought their way into county society were not trying to leave their mercantile roots behind and, in fact, considered the holding of high civic office to be as much an indicator of gentility as the ownership of land.[14] It was to their advantage to maintain their links with the town. This was particularly true if they held a burgage or were members of a guild, with all the privileges that these entailed.[15] Like many members of the urban gentry in England, their counterparts in Ireland tended to possess scattered estates rather than whole manors, and this is certainly true of many of the more prominent families with holdings on the royal manors.[16] These estates, augmented with lands from other lords, both lay and ecclesiastical, could add up to very substantial landholdings,

14 Rosemary Horrox, 'The urban gentry in the fifteenth century' in John A.F. Thomson (ed.), *Towns and townspeople in the fifteenth century* (Gloucester, 1988), pp 22, 32. 15 Reynolds, *English towns*, p. 102. 16 Horrox, 'Urban gentry', p. 26.

but because of their piecemeal acquisition, they did not always have an obvious administrative base. It is therefore possible, indeed probable, that many Dubliners continued to be based within the city even after they acquired property on the royal manors and elsewhere.

CITY AND CROWN

The king's men of Bristol

When the city of Dublin was granted to the men of Bristol in the aftermath of the invasion, merchants proved to be a vital factor in the colonization process, not only of the city but of its surrounding hinterland as well.[17] There is evidence of the importance of merchants in attracting settlers later in the medieval period too. In 1455, a statute of the Irish parliament claimed that merchants drew other people to the city, thus bringing benefits to the crown through greater profits from customs.[18] Though many of the merchants enrolled into the Dublin guild merchant prior to 1223–4 originated from Bristol, the men who settled in Dublin were drawn from all over England and beyond. These men were not only an important element of civic society, but they helped shape how society developed in its hinterland too.[19] Throughout the medieval period, the merchants, as much as the royal officials that moved between London and Dublin, would serve as a conduit between core and periphery.

The citizens of Dublin were keenly aware that if they were to have any semblance of independence from the king's more important tenants-in-chief – especially the lords of nearby Meath and Leinster – they would have to make sure their city was not entirely dependent on them for resources. Likewise, Henry II must have appreciated the value of bequeathing his city on a community who would be completely dependent on his goodwill rather than an individual tenant-in-chief who could perhaps prove more difficult to control. Certainly, one reason that he retained a demesne around the city was as a means of ensuring that this community could be maintained. The evidence suggests a very close relationship between the city and adjacent hinterland. Many of the most important tenants on the royal manors were prominent merchants in the city. Moreover, they were often substantial landowners elsewhere in Dublin and further afield. Occasionally, some of the higher-ranking royal tenants were granted lands elsewhere in Dublin in knights' fees. Those who held these small knights' fees were obliged to protect the city and muster at its gates if there was a threat of attack.[20]

---

17 *CARD*, 1, p. 1.   18 *Stat. Ire., Hen. VI*, p. 337.   19 *DGMR*, pp 3, 5, 9.   20 Otway-Ruthven, 'Knight service in Ireland', pp 157, 161–2; Bateson, 'Irish exchequer memoranda', 508.

Merchants and favourites

It is clear from charters that the crown protected the interests of merchants. This is reflected in a charter from 1192 in which foreign merchants were prohibited from buying goods from anyone except local merchants. In addition, they were not allowed to sell goods retail, or remain in the city for longer than forty days.[21] This indicates the importance of the local merchant class to the prosperity of a city. The crown showed favour not only through economic privileges, but through the granting of land as well. Many of those individuals granted knights' fees close to Dublin were of a mercantile background. The English king obviously granted these parcels of land to merchants to induce them to set themselves up in business in the city and help develop and maintain its commercial importance. There is evidence, however, that King John used lands in Dublin to reward merchants who may have served him in other capacities too. In 1184–5, Robert Ruffus was employed to procure supplies for the bake-house and kitchen of Prince John's court and convey them from Gloucester to Bristol.[22] It is likely that these supplies were earmarked for John's expedition to Ireland. What is more, Ruffus, who was one of John's serjeants, was responsible for bringing one thousand marks from London to Bristol to fund the expedition.[23] While John was still count of Mortain, he granted the manor of Ballymadun in north Dublin to Ruffus.[24] It is likely that he received this manor during John's first visit to Ireland and, though he was employed as a serjeant, his involvement with procuring supplies for John may imply that he had a mercantile background. It would at least suggest he had close connections within the mercantile class. The manor of Ballymadun would later pass to Elias Cordwaner,[25] whose name indicates that he too was of a mercantile or artisan background. There was a Roger Cordwaner – who later became the first mayor of Bristol – serving as the king's messenger in Ireland in 1204.[26] Employing merchants as messengers was eminently sensible, as these men were always on the move. Roger could have potentially used his trips to and from Ireland to conduct his own business as well as fulfilling his role as the king's messenger.

Defending Dublin

Horrox identifies the urban gentry of England as a group that played an important peacekeeping role, just like their rural counterparts.[27] Many merchants in Dublin served a similar, and very important, role in the vicinity of the royal manors, as this locality formed part of the defensive buffer between the city and

---

21 *CARD*, 1, p. 4. **22** *CDI*, *1171–1251*, §73. **23** Clarke, '*Angliores ipsis Anglis*', p. 48. **24** *CDI*, *1171–1251*, §939; *Gormanston reg.*, pp 129–30. **25** *CDI*, *1171–1251*, §1611; a cordwainer made or sold leather goods. **26** Ibid., §§119, 240; there is also a Roger Cordwaner from Hereford listed in the *DGMR* (p. 3), who would appear to be this Roger. In 1216, he served as the first mayor of Bristol: *RAST*, §§10, 17–18; Thomas Duffus Hardy (ed.), *Rotuli Litterarum Clausarum* (2 vols, London, 1833), 1, p. 283. **27** Horrox, 'Urban gentry', p. 22.

the Irish in the mountains. The continued residence of merchants with a stake in the locality went some way towards guaranteeing its stability. Though the county community was primarily responsible for its defence, it was in the interests of the inhabitants of the city to help protect this area, especially since the upper echelons of the county community and the city elite were often the same. Even though evidence of the need for this line of defence exists from the thirteenth century, it was especially acute from the mid-fourteenth century onwards. The efforts of individuals like William Douce, who built a stone fortalice in Saggart in the early fourteenth century, and John Owen, who was responsible for mustering a force of men to defend the marches of Dublin a century later, is testament to how important these families were to the defence of the area.[28]

The citizens of the city were well aware of their importance in the continued survival of the colony and clearly took advantage of this situation. In 1358, Edward III granted the merchants of Dublin permission to land merchandise in Dalkey because the port of Dublin was silted up and was too shallow for large ships.[29] In the petition, the merchants threatened to move their trade elsewhere and the king was conscious that their departure would be detrimental to the fortunes of the city and, by extension, to the surrounding countryside. The petition stated that their withdrawal would lead to the destruction of the city and, to drive their point home, it was followed by an ominous and – by this late date – somewhat jaded warning that the city stood on the frontier near the Irish enemies. The message is clear: without the lifeblood provided by the merchants, the colony would collapse. While some allowance must be made for exaggeration, the merchants and other townsmen played a vital role in the continued survival of English Ireland. Statutes of the Irish parliament passed to protect the rights of merchants are a clear indication of the importance of this social group to the crown.[30] Conversely, it was in their best interests to maintain the security of the city, which was most effectively achieved through the defence of its hinterland. In 1475, a statute recounts how the mayor and citizens would venture out of the city when needed to help defend it against the Irish and English rebels.[31] During the reigns of Henry VI and Edward IV, the citizens of Dublin were granted sums varying from £6 to £30 from the fee-farm of the city to aid in its defence.[32] Part of this money was invested in purchasing harness, which demonstrates that their responsibility for the defence of the city did not stop at its walls. They were expected to pursue the enemy if the need arose.

---

28 *IEMI*, §175; *CIRCLE*, PR 3 Hen., IV, §227. 29 *CARD*, 1, pp 19–20. 30 *Stat. Ire., John–Hen.*, *V*, pp 265–7, 319–21. 31 *Stat. Ire., 12–22 Edw. IV*, pp 449–53. 32 *CARD*, 1, p. 31.

THE MARSHALS

THE MARSHALS

The origins of the Marshals

The Marshals were among the earliest, most prominent families granted lands on the royal manors, and they had ecclesiastical as well as mercantile interests. Arnulph Marshal, who held property in Dublin in New Street near St Patrick's in the first quarter of the thirteenth century, appears to have been an early representative of this family in Ireland.[33] Arnulph Bruning, marshal, who appears in the witness list of a charter relating to the hospital of St John the Baptist from the middle of the thirteenth century, may be the same individual.[34] It is possible that he was the marshal of the exchequer, and if this was the case, Bruning may have been this family's original surname. Alternatively, early examples of this family in Dublin are found in the pages of the Dublin guild merchant roll. At some point before 1222, a Godfrey Marshal was enrolled as a member of this guild. By the end of the 1220s, Roland and Philip Marshal joined him. A Robert Marshal appears in the roll for 1240–1 and he may be related to the previously mentioned Roland, as a Robert, son of Roland Marshal, appears in the same roll for the year 1255–6.

Henry Marshal, royal tenant

It is not until 1260–1 that a Marshal with a definite association with the royal manors can be identified. In this year, Henry Marshal was enrolled as one of the Dublin guild merchants.[35] Twenty years later, he had attained the office of mayor of the city.[36] By 1284, he held eighty-five acres known as le Rath on the royal manor of Newcastle Lyons.[37] In addition, he held a plot of land just outside the Newgate of the city next to the king's highway. Furthermore, Andrew Pollard and his wife, Lettice, granted him lands in Terenure at about the same time he was granted land on the royal manor. This property had previously belonged to Lettice's father, and Henry's son, Thomas, would subsequently make a grant of it to the Hospital of St John the Baptist. Thomas' lord, Reginald Barnewall, issued a charter giving Thomas permission to make this grant to the hospital.[38] Like many of the major tenants on the royal manors, the Marshals had more than one overlord. This family not only held lands from the king and the Barnewall family, but also from that other great landowner, the archbishop of Dublin. Evidence of families holding land from both the king and the archbishop is relatively easy to identify, because of the type of records that have survived; it is more difficult to establish if many of these tenants held lands from other major landowners in Dublin. The only evidence that the Marshals held

33 *Alen's reg.*, p. 83; *RHSJ*, §§149, 150.   34 *RHSJ*, §148.   35 *DGMR*, pp 11, 57, 77, 82, 96, 102.   36 Berry, 'Mayors', p. 157.   37 *CDI, 1252–84*, §2344.   38 *Alen's reg.*, pp 295–6; *CARD*, I, p. 107; *RHSJ*, §§342–4.

lands from the Barnewall family is the charter preserved in the register of the Hospital of St John the Baptist.

Within the city, Henry owned a house close to the church of the Holy Trinity at Christ Church.[39] This appears to be the same property as the stone house on the north side of this church that he granted to the Hospitallers in 1283–4 and which was granted back to him in 1290.[40] Another son of Henry's, named William, possessed property next to St Thomas' Abbey and it is possible that this land had previously belonged to his father.[41] Incidentally, at around this time, one John Marshal held property in St Thomas' Street as well, which he rented out to a certain Richard and Agnes French.[42] Though he was a prominent merchant, Henry evidently did not make all his money in the city; he invested in land in the surrounding countryside too. He probably owned other property aside from that already listed, because when he was enfeoffed of the lands of le Rath in Newcastle Lyons, the inquisition states that the value of other lands he possessed greatly exceeded the value of lands he was being granted on this manor.[43]

Why was this family so important that at least two of them were rewarded with substantial parcels of land on the royal demesne? Henry was certainly a person of note, since a sizeable portion of land was alienated from the royal manor of Newcastle Lyons, and consequently awarded to him at fee farm. He held land here from at least 1284, and it is likely that he had already held these lands for some time.[44] In 1291, this tenement was granted to Henry in fee farm for the rent of £4 3s.[45] This meant that these eighty-five acres were permanently alienated from the rest of the royal manor. This, in essence, made his tenure to the lands more secure and enabled him to pass this property, which he had already held at the king's pleasure, to his heirs.[46] The lands eventually became known as Marshallsrath and kept this name even after the family no longer held this property. Henry was undoubtedly rewarded with crown lands because of his usefulness as a merchant. The sources confirm that he conducted a considerable amount of business with the king and his representative in Ireland, the justiciar. As well as supplying the chequered cloth for the exchequer on more than one occasion, he also supplied four millstones – two for the royal castle at Athlone and two for Dublin Castle – for the considerable sum of twenty-eight marks.[47] Additionally, throughout the 1280s, the justiciar, Geoffrey Geneville, purchased several expensive pieces of cloth from Marshal.[48]

39 *CARD*, 1, p. 109.   40 *CDI, 1285–92*, §703; *CARD*, 1, pp 163–4.   41 *CARD*, 1, pp 114, 122–3.   42 *RHSJ*, §19.   43 *IEMI*, §82.   44 *CDI, 1252–84*, §2344.   45 *CDI, 1285–92*, §953. 46 Ibid., §996.   47 Connolly, *Exchequer payments*, pp 54, 117; *CDI, 1252–84*, §1892.   48 *CDI, 1285–92*, §169.

Henry Marshal, merchant

The evidence from exchequer receipts and the amount of prisage he paid reveals that Henry was heavily involved in the wine trade.[49] In 1287, he paid ten marks for prisage of wines and, in the following year, he was paying £19 11s. ¼d. In 1293, he paid into the exchequer 110s. for prisage, and later that same year he was £25 18s. 11¾d. in arrears of his account.[50] It is clear that Henry was importing a large amount of wine into Dublin.[51] The volume of trade being carried out by Henry Marshal is a clear indication that he was a wealthy individual. The sort of goods Henry traded in is informative concerning his social standing within his community. He seemingly traded in high-status items. Very few people would have been wealthy enough to purchase millstones, and the transactions conducted with Geoffrey Geneville, who on one occasion bought cloth valued at £40, suggests that he sold luxury goods.[52] Joan, the wife of Sir Theobald Butler, owed Marshal money for wine in 1287, so his customers included the highest nobility of the colony.[53] The crown's favouritism towards Henry is further demonstrated by a grant in 1292 allowing Henry and fellow merchant Robert Wyleby, who would later become mayor, export two hundred crannocks of corn to England.[54] This must have been a rare and unusual concession, because the royal bailiffs were ordered not to impede the merchants in exporting this corn.

Henry's involvement in the wine trade would indicate that his interests extended beyond Ireland, particularly to France. In 1280, when he was mayor of the city, Henry obtained letters of protection that covered a period of five years.[55] It seems that he intended to go overseas once his term as mayor was complete, and it is likely that, as a wine merchant, he made several trips to the Continent throughout his career. Therefore, though Henry held lands on the royal manor of Newcastle Lyons, he may have not spent much time there. It is likely that he rented out his lands to smaller tenants and his interests there extended no further than the gathering of rents. In 1296, over £35 belonging to William Contino, who was the valet of Warin Meys of Picardy, was found hidden in Henry's house. This was presumably within the city, and it is likely that Henry resided there to protect his mercantile interests rather than on his property in Newcastle. The money that belonged to William Contino was sown into a corset, which indicates that he attempted to keep the money hidden. Three hides belonging to Giles Courtray were found in Henry's house as well.[56] In the previous year, England had gone to war with France and, based on the evidence of an Irish exchequer receipt roll, French merchants in Dublin were suffering the consequences of this conflict.[57] The property of at least two French

---

49 A prisage, in this case, was the right of the English crown to take two tuns of wine from every ship importing twenty tuns or more.   **50** *CDI, 1285–92*, §§341, 371; *CDI, 1293–1301*, §§21, 41.   **51** *HMDI*, p. xxxiv.   **52** *CDI, 1285–92*, §169.   **53** *Ormond deeds, 1172–1350*, §279.   **54** *CDI, 1285–92*, §1097.   **55** *CDI, 1252–84*, §1705.   **56** *CDI, 1293–1301*, §260.   **57** Prestwich,

merchants was discovered in Henry Marshal's home, and it raises the tantalizing possibility that he was concealing the money on their behalf. The exchequer roll clearly indicates that the money and merchandise were found in his house; nowhere does it say that he had willingly surrendered this property. At the very least, the fact that these items were left on his property and that he was in debt to a Roger Bongre, a merchant of Bruges, is an indicator of his international trading interests.[58] He probably formed long-term professional, and perhaps personal, relationships with Continental merchants. If he had close connections with the men whose goods were in his home, then it is certainly plausible that he attempted to protect their property. Henry's international connections belie the generally perceived notion of the tenants on the royal manors and on other manors around Dublin as a prosperous peasant class.[59] While this was possibly true of the men to whom Henry rented his land, he himself belonged to the ruling elite of the city and county.

Henry Marshal, mayor of Dublin

The evidence demonstrates that Henry was one of the wealthiest members of the merchant class based in Dublin. His attainment of the mayoralty further confirms that he was a part of that small and exclusive group that controlled the city throughout the medieval period. His rise to this office was quite spectacular, as there is no evidence of Henry serving as a provost, unlike most of his fellow mayors. By the time Marshal attained this office in 1279, he may have already held land on the royal manor of Newcastle Lyons – it is evident from an extent taken in 1284 that his tenure of this property pre-dated it.[60] If he was already a tenant of the king when he held the office of mayor, not only did he have to serve the needs of the city, but he had to balance these interests with those of the king as well. It was vital that his actions did not negatively influence his relationship with the crown, and his trading interests with the Irish administration doubly reinforced this obligation. It was also in the best interests of this administration to keep Henry on its side. One of the reasons he was granted the lands in Newcastle Lyons was that the administration feared that this land would become waste and uncultivated if it passed into the wrong hands. It seems that their fears were justified, because lands belonging to the king elsewhere in Dublin had been abandoned and left unprotected.[61] The Irish administration was aware that the security and continued profitability of the city of Dublin was entirely dependent on maintaining control of the lands that lay between it and the mountains. Even before Henry was granted lands in Newcastle Lyons, the nearby manor of Saggart was described as being in the land of war. The grant in fee farm of lands

---

Plantagenet England, p. 165; *CDI, 1293–1301*, §260. **58** He owed Roger Bongre, a merchant of Bruges, £10, *CDI, 1293–1301*, §260. **59** Richard Britnell describes the colonists who settled in Ireland as a privileged peasant class: idem, *Britain and Ireland, 1050–1530: economy and society* (Oxford, 2004), p. 174. **60** *CDI, 1252–84*, §2344. **61** *CDI, 1285–92*, §953.

he already held ensured his continued presence in an area that could so easily become absorbed into the land of war.

The plot of land Henry was granted outside the walls of Dublin in 1282 had previously belonged to Richard Chalk, who was a watchman of the city, and it is possible that the duties of watchman were the responsibility of whosoever held this land. It is therefore possible that Henry had undertaken to defend this area, which lay next to the Newgate.[62] As mayor of the city, its defence would have been of paramount importance to Henry, and this concern may have extended beyond his time in office.[63] This is seen most clearly in his taking the responsibility of collecting the murage of the city. Evidence that Henry collected this murage is found in a memoranda roll entry from 1309, when the mayor and bailiffs of the city were ordered to summon those who had collected this murage since 1283–4 and to have them account for the sums collected. Henry was dead by this time, but Robert Wyleby, who was collector of the murage with Henry, appeared and accounted for their time in this office.[64] In fact, Henry's interest in the city's security may have been the primary motive behind his grant of lands on one of the royal manors. Nonetheless, it is likely that there were other reasons for granting these lands to him. One of these advantages is addressed in the inquisition of 1291. It establishes that when Henry was given lands directly from the king it meant that the crown would have ward and marriage of all of Henry's other lands as well. Moreover, since the value of his other lands greatly exceeded the value of his property in Newcastle Lyons, it could only be to the crown's benefit to bestow these lands on him.[65] Another benefit of rewarding merchants like Marshal with lands and office was that the king could look to them for loans when the need arose. Though there is no direct evidence of Henry Marshal giving the king money, it is likely that he was granted land and received concessions in exporting corn because he had previously made financial loans to the crown.

Henry Marshal, royal servant

Henry served the crown more directly as a royal servant too, and this reflected trends in England. Sylvia Thrupp observed how some of the leading merchants of London held key royal posts in the fourteenth century; an examination of the careers of merchants in Dublin like Henry Marshal would suggest that the experience here was similar.[66] In 1305, he, together with John Decer, who had previously served as mayor, was a collector of the new custom of wine. Edward I nominated his cupbearer, William Trente, to audit the accounts, and he was ultimately responsible for collecting this custom. Obviously, Trente could not have taken on all the responsibilities of this office himself and deputies were

62 *CARD*, 1, p. 107.   63 Berry, 'Mayors', p. 157.   64 NAI, EX 2/2, p. 536.   65 *CDI, 1285–92*, §953.   66 Sylvia Thrupp, *The merchant class of medieval London, 1300–1500* (Chicago, 1962), pp 53–4.

needed in the localities to ensure that this collection could be carried out efficiently. Marshal and Decer were responsible for auditing the accounts of the collectors and receivers of the custom in Ireland. As merchants, they were well placed to carry out the financial aspects of this office and, indeed, to transport the revenues collected to England.[67] By nominating men in the localities, Trente served as a conduit between core and periphery. Not only were Marshal and John Decer representing Trente in the localities, but he in turn served as their direct link to the English crown. One of the principal motivations in seeking out these customs was to pay back loans received from merchants. Certainly, in England, as the thirteenth century progressed, the crown increasingly recognized how useful the merchant class was to them financially. It was in this period that a proper taxation system developed, particularly with the introduction of a permanent customs system in 1275. In this year, Edward I summoned men from the merchant class to attend parliament, and this was an acknowledgment of their long-standing importance as a political group. Furthermore, it was recognition of the fact that, without their approval, these customs would not or could not be granted.[68] This desire by the crown to ingratiate itself with the merchant class in England is reflected in Ireland in the positive treatment received by merchants like Henry Marshal.

Thomas and William Marshal

Henry Marshal had at least two sons: Thomas and William. In 1305, the Dublin chain book mentions that Thomas had a house within the city.[69] A memoranda roll entry from 1309 describes Thomas as being Henry's heir and this is confirmed by Thomas' possession of Henry's property in Newcastle Lyons after his death.[70] Thomas appears to have also had some interests in the royal manor of Crumlin, because in 1322–3 he was answerable for part of the rent of this manor.[71] Thomas and his father Henry had previous associations with tenants on this manor. In 1303, both men stood as security for John Crumlin to pay 100s. that he owed to the king in rent.[72] It is possible that they held land from John in Crumlin. In addition, Thomas inherited lands from Henry in Terenure, close to Crumlin, but subsequently granted them to the hospital of St John the Baptist.[73] Though Thomas inherited his father's property in Co. Dublin, it was another son, William, who followed his father into civic office. As far as can be established, Thomas does not appear to have held civic office, but William served as a bailiff of the city at least three times between 1319–20 and 1324–5, and was mayor of Dublin in 1327–8.[74] In contrast to his brother, all of the property that

67 *CDI, 1302–7*, §428.   68 Prestwich, *Plantagenet England*, p. 495.   69 *CARD*, I, p. 223. A justiciary roll entry from 1306 confirms that Thomas was Henry's son: *CJR, 1305–7*, p. 277. 70 NAI, EX 2/2, pp 536, 640; *RDKPRI*, 39, pp 50, 57, *RDKPRI*, 42, pp 30, 32, 53; *RDKPRI*, 43, pp 31, 33; *RDKPRI*, 47, p. 33.   71 *RDKPRI*, 42, p. 52.   72 NAI, EX 2/1, pp 61, 115. 73 *RHSJ*, §19.   74 Berry, 'Mayors', p. 159.

William owned appears to have been in or near the city. In 1320, he was granted lands between the gate of St Thomas' Abbey and the city cistern. He was granted this property on the condition that he would maintain the city watercourse between the abbey and this cistern.[75]

When Henry acquired parcels of land around Dublin, it was probably as a means of giving one of his sons access to county society while allowing another son the opportunity to continue with his mercantile interests in the city. This trend can be identified in England among the urban gentry and fathers would make provision for younger sons by either accumulating land or finding them suitable positions in church or government.[76] Acquiring land or a career in service did not necessarily signify a desire to leave the town behind, but it did provide for family members who were not expected to go into the family business. Moreover, becoming a landowner and assimilating into local county society or entering a profession could only enhance the family's social standing. In Henry Marshal's case, all his efforts appear ultimately to have been in vain, because his family were no longer prominent within Dublin society after the death of his sons. By 1326, William Douce was in possession of Marshallsrath in Newcastle Lyons, which would suggest that Thomas was either deceased by this date or had granted this property away.[77] In addition, Thomas gave Douce a messuage with a cellar known as the Bakehouse of the Rame in the parish of St Audoen in Dublin city.[78] Significantly, he had given his lands in Terenure to the church some years earlier, which might suggest that he had no direct heirs to whom he could pass his lands. It is unclear why he granted his lands to William Douce, but it is possible that there was some family connection. One possibility is that Douce married into the Marshal family. Thomas' brother William was certainly dead by 1359, when William Walsh surrendered the grant of his property next to St Thomas' Abbey back to the mayor and commonalty of the city.[79] It appears that William left no children either; and this is confirmed by the conspicuous absence of the Marshal family from the list of mayors and bailiffs after William's term as mayor in 1327–8.

Other Marshals

While Henry and John were the most prominent members of the Marshal family, other men who shared the same surname held lands in Dublin. Though it appears that no kinship connection can be established between the two families, there were also Marshals living in Rathcoole who held lands of the archbishop of Dublin. This manor is in close proximity to Newcastle Lyons

75 *CARD*, 1, p. 114.   **76** For example, in Nottingham a merchant named Thomas Thurland put his son into Lincoln's Inn to study law, but his grandson must have eventually inherited his mercantile interests, as he served as mayor of Nottingham in the later fifteenth century: Horrox, 'Urban gentry', pp 22, 29–32.   **77** Ball, *Dublin*, 4, p. 58.   **78** Berry, 'St Anne', §60.   **79** *CARD*, 1, pp 122–3.

where Henry Marshal held lands and it is certainly possible that they are related. Their occupancy of Rathcoole can be dated back to at least the mid-thirteenth century when Simon Marshal held eighty-five acres there.[80] At the end of the century, these lands were held by John Marshal, who was an ecclesiastic, and another John Marshal held them later in the fourteenth century.[81] The younger John was certainly a contemporary of Thomas and William Marshal. Like William, he was actively involved in public office-holding and served as the king's coroner for the parts of Leinster outside the city in 1344.[82]

In 1283, Ralph Marshal was granted one carucate and fifty acres in Ballycorus in Rathmichael in fee farm. It is clear that these lands belonged to the crown, because Marshal was expected to pay suit twice a year at the king's court in Brownstown. The charter was confirmed in Aberconwy in Wales and the witnesses included Edmund, the king's brother and the earls of Suffolk, Lincoln and Carrick.[83] This would strongly suggest that Ralph took part in the successful Welsh campaign of 1282–3. What is more, the calibre of the witnesses in his charter would imply that Ralph's services overseas were particularly valued by the crown. In 1298–9, he was pardoned of all robberies and homicides he committed in Ireland because of the good service he had done to the king in both Scotland and Flanders.[84] If this group of men all shared kinship ties, then this family with interests on the royal manors permeated all aspects of Dublin society, and included individuals who were merchants, clerks, mayors, bailiffs and soldiers.

THE DOUCE FAMILY

William Douce and the royal manors
William Douce, who succeeded Thomas Marshal to his lands on the royal manor of Newcastle Lyons, was another merchant who benefited from royal patronage. Aside from this property, he held several other parcels of land on the same manor. In 1307–8, he obtained all the lands, meadow, pasture, moor, houses, gardens and edifices that had once belonged to William Blund in Athgoe.[85] In 1320, Douce augmented his property here with an additional two messuages and sixty acres with appurtenances.[86] He also held lands on the adjacent royal manor of Saggart. In about 1312, William petitioned the king and council to grant to himself and his heirs a parcel of land called Galleroieslonde on this manor.[87] In

---

80 NAI, EX 2/1, p. 81; *Alen's reg.*, pp 108–10. 81 *Alen's reg.*, pp 183–5. 82 *CARD*, 1, pp 145–7. 83 *CDI, 1252–84*, §2089. Obrun was one of the royal manors in the mountains of Leinster. 84 *CDI, 1293–1301*, §596. 85 Athgoe was a grange on the manor of Newcastle: NAI, EX 2/2, pp 273, 294. 86 *IEMI*, §194. 87 TNA, SC 8/105/5250; C 143/91/8; *CICD*, p. 67. There is evidence of a family called Galroy living in Saggart during the reign of Henry VIII, and it is possible that they derived their name from this place.

this year, an inquisition was held to decide whether he should be granted forty acres in Saggart, though it is not clear if this is the same parcel of land.[88] The inquisition reveals that William already had land bordering this forty acres and that he had built a stone fortalice in order to defend it against the Irish in the Leinster mountains. The jurors agreed that it would be to the king's advantage to make this grant to Douce, and these lands were subsequently bestowed on him in 1315, at an annual rent of 46s. 8d.[89] This grant reveals the dangers of pigeon-holing individuals into certain roles. Even though Douce was a successful merchant, who served as bailiff in 1306 and went on to be mayor on at least three occasions between 1322 and 1331, his interests extended beyond the city. Not only was he interested in acquiring lands in the county, but he was also willing to put the effort into defending this area against the king's enemies.[90]

Douce held land elsewhere, including close to the city just outside the Newgate.[91] Furthermore, evidence from a deed dating to 1342 reveals that he also possessed lands within the city. In this year, he granted two shops on High Street, as well as property on Cook Street, Pycot's Lane and Scarlet Street, to Simon Somirdeby, chaplain. Some of this property in the city was still in the family's hands in 1381 because it is included in Joan Douce's will.[92] Joan Douce was possibly a daughter or granddaughter of William's. There is evidence of a will belonging to William that dated to 1341, and he probably died not long after he granted property in the city to Simon Somirdeby.[93] The property listed in the deed from 1342 does not appear to exhaust the extent of this family's holdings in the city, because Joan's will also lists a messuage in the parish of St John and four shops in Francis Street, as well as five shops in St Thomas Street and two stone houses in Kisher's Lane.[94] Joan was clearly a substantial heiress, but she did not leave any property to family members, or at least not to people who can be identified as being her kin. It is likely that the family had died out in the male line by this time. Apart from the substantial bequests she makes to the church, as well as the sick and needy of the city, the main beneficiary of her will appears to be William Decer. It is possible that William was a relative of Joan's, though this is not specifically identified in the document. In 1305, William Douce and John and William Decer served as pledges for Gerald Jeofne, and three years later both men stood as sureties for Andrew Ashbourne, which indicates that these two families must have known each other well.[95]

Based on the evidence of the surviving sources, William Douce appears to have been primarily involved in the wool trade.[96] The wool merchants in England at this time were a very influential group, because Edward I depended on them to finance his military expeditions.[97] The lands bestowed on Douce

88 *IEMI*, §175. 89 *CFR, 1307–19*, p. 249. 90 Berry, 'Mayors', pp 158–9. 91 *CARD*, I, p. 121. 92 Berry, 'St Anne', §60. 93 Ibid., p. 51; this will was in the collection of St Anne's deeds in 1772 but is no longer extant. 94 Ibid., §20. 95 NAI, EX 2/3, p. 652; *CJR, 1305–7*, pp 463–4; *CJR, 1308–14*, p. 48. 96 See, for example, *CJR, 1305–7*, p. 90. 97 Thrupp,

were indicative of his value to the crown. Merchants like Douce and Henry Marshal were rewarded because they had the ways and means to finance the Edwardian war machine. Furthermore, merchants played a part in military expeditions within the colony; the wealthier merchants would have been in a position to lend their ships to the king. In 1332–3, William Douce, Adam Burnel and Robert Joye were compensated to the sum of £20 for victuals lost in a storm at sea en route to Arklow to maintain the king's army there.[98] Without the help of merchants to supply food, money and other resources, as well as offer the use of their ships, it would not have been possible for these military operations to take place.

THE CALLAN FAMILY

The Callans and Kilkenny
The Sampson family demonstrate how important the merchant class were in terms of aiding military expeditions. They were more usually known by the name Callan, and who held property in both Crumlin and Saggart. They were prominent members of Dublin society throughout the medieval period, and it is likely that during the course of the fourteenth century they had a name-change from Callan to Gallane. Jeffry Callan is recorded as a bailiff in the city of Dublin in 1385–6 and the Geoffrey Gallane who held this office five years later was almost certainly the same person. References to members of the Gallane family in the sources are scarce before this time, but one that does deserve notice is a grant by Robert Clahull to William Galoun of lands in Ballyfermot around the middle of the thirteenth century.[99] This charter appears in the register of St John the Baptist and, since Brooks estimates that this register was compiled in the last quarter of the fourteenth century, it is possible that William Galoun is actually William Callan.[1] If the compiler of the register was aware that this family was now known as Gallane, he may have chosen to use the then current spelling of their name. William's benefactor, Robert Clahull, was a member of a family who held property in Gowran in Co. Kilkenny, which was not far from the market town of Callan, where the family almost certainly originated.[2] Since trade was the raison d'être of this settlement, it is likely that many of the men who came from here were merchants. It would be logical of Clahull to bestow lands on someone with whom he had a previous association, and William Galoun or Callan may have already held lands from the Clahulls in Kilkenny. Gallanstown in Ballyfermot was named after them and they had lands there until the first quarter of the fifteenth century and possibly later.[3]

No one listed in the Dublin guild merchant roll, which continues up to 1295,

Merchant class, p. 52. **98** *Exchequer payments*, p. 353. **99** *RHSJ*, §296. **1** Ibid., p. xi.
2 *Knights fees*, pp 56–9. **3** Berry, 'St Anne', §141.

can be identified as coming from Callan. Nevertheless, it is possible that the Walter Sampson, nephew of Simon, who appears in this roll, is one of their ancestors.[4] Like the Douce family, the Callans only appear to become prominent within Dublin at the end of the thirteenth century. Certainly, the pressure to supply provisions for Edward I's military campaigns opened up tremendous opportunities for ambitious mercantile families at this time, and people like William Douce and William Sampson of Callan built up careers that placed them and their families among the most prominent in the city. When David Sampson of Callan served as mayor in 1277, he had not previously served as bailiff, which was relatively unusual. The first time he appears in the sources is in the early 1270s, probably not long after the family were granted lands in Ballyfermot.[5] Therefore, the transition from small market town to the upper levels of Dublin civic society appears to have been remarkably rapid.

The Callans and the royal manors

The family's association with the royal manors dates to at least 1301, when William Sampson of Callan paid £20 8s. of the arrears of the farm of Crumlin in victuals.[6] Later, during the fourteenth and fifteenth centuries, the Gallanes held lands in Crumlin. Thomas Bodenham granted Hugh Gallane one messuage of land on this manor to hold for fifty years on 11 December 1346. The deed describes how Bodenham bestowed these lands on Hugh because he was in urgent need of money. Bodenham must have been in serious difficulties, because further grants were issued on 22 and 23 December giving Gallane full and permanent possession of these lands.[7] The family may have previously held property here, because in 1418 Thomas Gallane granted Robert Gallane not only this messuage, but also other parcels of land on the same manor.[8] Moreover, the Callans also held property on the royal manor of Saggart. In 1307–8, William Sampson was granted a half share of the king's mills in Saggart because Margery Pudding, who had previously held them, was not able to maintain them in a good state. Margery was the wife of Irishman Richard Pudding of Saggart, who features in the sources in the last quarter of the thirteenth century.[9] Pudding paid the farm for the mills at Saggart in the last years of the thirteenth century, but Margery was paying this rent by 1302 and, therefore, it is likely that he was dead by this date.[10] William Sampson and Margery Pudding did not hold the mills for long, because two years later they were granted to John Butler.[11] In spite of this, the family's interests on this manor did not end there. In 1304, William Sampson junior was fined half a mark for killing Hugh McRegan, an

---

4 *DGMR*, p. 5. 5 *CDI, 1252–84*, §890. 6 *CDI, 1293–1301*, §825; *RDKPRI*, 38, p. 68. 7 Berry, 'St Anne', §§137–40. 8 Ibid., §141. 9 See, for example, *CDI, 1285–92*, §§1108, 1109; *CDI, 1293–1301*, §§41, 139, 264. A petition from about 1285 reveals an Irishman called Richard Pudding who was granted English law at this time: TNA, SC 8/331/15677. 10 *CDI, 1293–1301*, §§550, 587, 637; *CDI, 1302–7*, §72. 11 NAI, EX 2/2, pp 261–2; EX 2/3, p. 505.

'Irishman of the king'.[12] It is possible that this William was a son of William Sampson of Callan. In 1312–13, Nicholas Callan was provost of Saggart and he served as provost on at least two subsequent occasions in 1324–5 and 1337–8.[13]

Property in the city and civic office
The Callans also owned property in the city of Dublin. Like Henry Marshal and William Douce before him, John, son of William Sampson of Callan, possessed a plot outside the Newgate in 1336.[14] In fact, his plot of land lay next to Douce's land. John had served as a bailiff of the city in the previous year, and this may have provided the impetus to grant him these lands. Alternatively, his brother Robert may have influenced the making of this grant, because his seal appears on the charter. In 1343, Thomas Callan was granted land known as Thingmót in the eastern suburbs of the city.[15] This suggests that even after they started acquiring property in Co. Dublin they continued to maintain their interests in the city. Certainly, in the fourteenth and fifteenth centuries, members of the Gallane family, including Hugh Gallane, who inherited the messuage in Crumlin in 1346, and John Gallane, who appeared in the Dublin assembly roll in 1454,[16] were merchants. This John is probably the same individual who was granted a messuage in Crumlin by his father Robert Gallane in 1448, and who owned property in High Street in the same period.[17] Furthermore, members of this family served as mayors and bailiffs of the city. David Sampson of Callan was mayor of Dublin on no fewer than five occasions between 1277–8 and 1282–3. In 1331–2, John Callan served as bailiff, an office he was to hold at least eight more times, though he never became mayor of the city. Geoffrey Gallane was mayor in 1396–7 and he had already served as bailiff three times. Robert Gallane held the office of mayor in 1410–11 after serving twice as bailiff, and he is almost certainly the same individual who held lands in Crumlin in 1418.[18]

William Callan never held the office of mayor or bailiff, but the sources confirm that he was a very important citizen in the city. The length of Callan's career might suggest two separate individuals – perhaps a father and son – instead of one person, and, sure enough, William Callan senior and junior are both referred to occasionally within the same source, which confirms that a distinction had to be made between both men.[19] In 1301, the elder William was responsible for paying the farm of the city.[20] He was responsible for collecting

12 NAI, EX 2/1, p. 90.   13 *RDKPRI*, 39, p. 37; *RDKPRI*, 42, p. 54; *RDKPRI*, 45, pp 55–6. 14 *CARD*, 1, p. 121.   15 Ibid., 165; *CSMA*, 1, pp 15–16; Seán Duffy, 'A reconsideration of the site of Dublin's Viking Thing-mót' in Tom Condit and Christiaan Corlett (eds), *Above and beyond: essays in memory of Leo Swan* (Dublin, 2005), p. 356.   16 Berry, 'St Anne', §140; *CARD*, 1, p. 282.   17 Berry, 'St Anne', §142; Colm Lennon and James Murray, *The Dublin city franchise roll, 1468–1512* (Dublin, 1998), p. 49.   18 Berry, 'Mayors', pp 157–61; idem, 'St Anne', §141. A reference to Robert Gallane and his wife Cecily from 1404 can be found in *CPL, 1396–1404*, p. 626.   19 A William Callan senior is referred to twice in the *CJR, 1305–7*, pp 277, 280, and William Callan junior appears in a memoranda roll from 1304: NAI, EX 2/1, p. 90.

the arrears of the accounts of previous mayors and bailiffs too.[21] More signifi-cantly, he played a key part in providing the crown with supplies for its armies in his capacity as a royal purveyor.[22] On 28 March 1305–6, the treasurer and chamberlains of the Irish exchequer were ordered to supply Thomas Colice and William Callan with £200 to enable them to purchase victuals to send to Scotland. Similar writs for the same amount were issued in April, June and October 1306. Then, on 1 January 1306–7, the exchequer was ordered to grant these men the considerable sum of £700 to supply the English army in Scotland.[23] Aside from these foreign campaigns, provisions had to be found for armies within the colony. In 1321–2, Robert Woder, Robert Thurstayn and William Callan owed £54 7s. 1½d., a sum that they had received from the mayor and bailiffs to buy provisions for the war against the Irish in the Leinster mountains. These men had owed this amount since 1309–10, which demon-strates what huge financial liabilities offices like this could be.[24] It also illustrates that the commonalty of the city was expected to play its part in defending the colony, at least financially.

John Sampson was a contemporary of William Callan, and they are almost certainly related, as there are occasional references to John being from Callan.[25] In 1296, he paid the exchequer five marks for goods of Giles Courtray, a merchant of Flanders.[26] This implies that John, too, was a merchant. Moreover, just like William, he too was responsible for paying the farm of the city.[27] In 1305–6, he was assigned to carry out any building repairs needed on Dublin Castle, as well as the mills near it and the houses of the exchequer. He served as keeper of the works of the castle and king's mills continuously for the next twenty years.[28] Like William, John does not seem to have held the office of either bailiff or mayor; the John Callan who served as bailiff of the city in the 1330s was William's son and is therefore likely to have been a much younger person.[29]

Cattle merchants

The many references to Henry Marshal trading in wine and William Douce in wool suggest that there was a degree of specialization concerning the products sold by merchants. At least two members of the Callan family bought and sold animal hides, and it is possible that they specialized in this. In 1309–10, the sheriff of Dublin was ordered to levy two tuns of tanned hides from the goods of Richard Tanner of Wells and John Sampson.[30] The amount taken by the

20 *CDI, 1293–1301*, §§289, 825. **21** *CDI, 1302–7*, §4. **22** James Lydon, 'The Dublin purveyors and the wars in Scotland, 1296–1324' in Gearóid Mac Niocaill and Patrick Wallace (eds), *Keimelia: studies in medieval archaeology and history in memory of Tom Delaney* (Galway, 1988), pp 436–7, 441. **23** *CDI, 1302–7*, §§500, 548, 552, 580, 602; *CJR, 1305–7*, pp 282, 302. **24** *RDKPRI*, 42, p. 32; *RDKPRI*, 45, p. 41. **25** For example, see NAI, RC 8/11, pp 278–9. **26** *CDI, 1293–1301*, §260. **27** He and John Stakepoll paid £20 in 1296: *CDI, 1293–1301*, §289. **28** *Exchequer payments*, pp 187, 197, 202, 207, 247, 249, 253, 256, 261, 264, 307, 597; *CDI, 1302–7*, §456; NAI, EX 2/1, p. 147. **29** Berry, 'Mayors', p. 159; *CARD*, 1, p. 121.

sheriff was almost certainly just a fraction of their merchandise, and it is likely that they had a substantial number of hides in their possession. The surname of Sampson's associate, Richard Tanner, might also suggest that he specialized in this trade and his place of origin infers that Sampson traded with foreign merchants. In the same year, the sheriff was ordered to apprehend Simon Sutton, who did not pay William Callan for eleven hides he had sold to him.[31] The number of hides involved might suggest that the Callans were wholesalers rather than retailers. Having farmlands near the city meant that the Callans could raise livestock to sell in the city, perhaps to men like Richard Tanner, who would have tanned the hides to manufacture leather products.

THE OWEN FAMILY

Origins

The Owen family appear to have started out as a mercantile family before moving into administration during the mid-thirteenth century. This process may have begun almost as soon as the family settled in Ireland with Roger Owen, who served as both provost and mayor of Dublin city on at least three occasions between 1234 and 1250.[32] He was already a prominent merchant, inducted into the Dublin guild merchant roll in 1224–5.[33] He clearly demonstrates the importance of merchants in the process of colonizing Ireland generally and Dublin specifically. As well as having an obviously important role in the towns, men like Roger Owen also made up a substantial section of the population of the surrounding countryside and they influenced the ways in which society developed here. The next generation produced another Roger Owen who had a long administrative career serving the king, and he was probably a close relative of the elder Roger, perhaps even his son. He attempted to exchange lands in the royal manor of Newcastle for lands in Saggart, and these lands may have been in the family's possession in the elder Roger's time. As mayor of Dublin, Roger senior had the political influence required to acquire these lands. Alternatively, if he obtained these lands before he attained this office, his position as a landowner as well as a merchant would have set him apart as an individual worthy of this office. He possessed a stone house in the city by 1244, which would suggest that he was a man of some means.[34] The younger Roger did not follow his namesake into civic government and is conspicuous by his absence from the lists of mayors and bailiffs of the city. Moreover, he divested himself of at least some of the property the elder Roger had previously held in the city. In 1279, he, along with James Bermingham, granted a plot of land within the city to the Carmelite

30 NAI, EX 2/3, p. 651.   31 NAI, EX 2/2, p. 401.   32 *DGMR*, p. 111; *CSMA*, 1, pp 432, 490; Berry, 'Mayors', p. 157.   33 *DGMR*, p. 51.   34 *CARD*, 1, p. 85.

order.[35] Instead of concentrating his efforts in the town, he focused his energies on county administration, began to accumulate parcels of land in the hinterland of the city, and added to the property his family already possessed there. For example, he acquired a half a carucate of land in Rowlagh, on the royal manor of Esker.[36] It is almost certain that the lands of Ballyowen, which were on the same royal manor and were adjacent to Rowlagh, were named after this family.

Rowlagh

Just like the younger Roger, future generations of the Owen family focused their interests outside the city. Yet the merchant interests of the elder Roger appear to have been the impetus for this family settling in Ireland and their integration into the social fabric of the royal manors. By 1306, Roger the younger's son, John, was in possession of the land of Rowlagh. In 1309, John paid the rent of half a pound of pepper for these lands to the king.[37] The family were still in possession of Rowlagh during the reign of Richard II, and an inquisition from the reign of Henry VIII reveals that this land remained in their possession as late as 1517. It was at this time that it passed into the hands of the Bath family through an heiress, Catherine Owen. It can be established that this is the same plot of land, because they were still paying the customary rent of half a pound of pepper.[38] The jurors valued this land, which constituted half of the lands of Rowlagh, at 24s. per annum. Warin Owen, another son of Roger's, held land in Rowlagh too, and this appears to have been a separate and distinct holding from that of his brother as he paid a money rent rather than the customary rent of pepper. It is possible that one of these parcels of land became known as Ballyowen rather than Rowlagh to differentiate between the properties. Alternatively, Warin may have possessed the lands of Coldcut adjacent to Rowlagh. The family held one messuage and thirty acres here in the sixteenth century.[39]

Saggart and Newcastle Lyons and other lands

The inquisition establishing the property owned by Catherine Owen at the time of her death reveals that the family had property on other royal manors in the sixteenth century. Moreover, it is likely that the majority of this land, like Rowlagh, had been in their possession for the previous two centuries and more. Certainly, the Owen family were paying rent for lands on the manors of Newcastle Lyons and Saggart in the latter half of the thirteenth century.[40] Warin Owen, who held lands in Rowlagh, had lands in Greenoge close to Newcastle Lyons early in the fourteenth century as well.[41] Also at this time, John Owen possessed lands in Wespaillstown in Saggart, though his son Richard would

---

35 *IEMI*, §37. 36 *CJR, 1305–7*, p. 235. 37 NAI, RC 8/4, pp 506–7; RC 8/6, p. 228; EX 2/3, pp 541–2. 38 *CIRCLE*, CR 4 Ric. II, §32; *CICD*, pp 3–4. 39 *CICD*, p. 3. 40 *CDI, 1285–92*, §371. 41 NAI, RC 8/4, p. 785 and EX 2/2, pp 269, 340 identify Warin as John Owen's

relinquish these lands to Walter Fox, a member of a prominent family on this manor.[42] When Walter received these lands, it was agreed that he could pay off £7 worth of arrears at 20s. per annum, which confirms that the Owens had not been making a profit there for quite a while. Later, during the reign of Henry IV, John Owen held one messuage and twelve acres in Rangaillagh, on the manor of Newcastle Lyons.[43]

The Owen family possessed lands in Blundelstown adjacent to Newcastle Lyons in the early thirteenth century, and they continued to hold these lands for the next two centuries. Warin Owen augmented his lands in nearby Greenoge with property here.[44] He acquired two messuages, forty acres and half a carucate in Blundelstown at some point between 1311 and 1314 from Nicholas Eggesfeld.[45] In 1402, another John Owen held land in Blundelstown of the king for the service of 5s.[46] This continuity of the same family in the same locality can be traced through ownership of land, which is particularly useful when dealing with a relatively common surname like Owen. Blundelstown, though adjacent to Newcastle Lyons and now in the parish of Clondalkin, was not among the property of the archbishop of Dublin, but it was not a part of the royal manor of Newcastle either. In 1517, when the property passed out of the family's hands, the service for this land was assessed at 55s., or one foot soldier, which meant it was valued at a portion of a knight's fee.[47] This property, therefore, was one of the small knight's fees in Co. Dublin, created to provide a defence force to protect the city.

The Owens possessed property elsewhere in Dublin. Warin Owen held lands in Swords, which made him a tenant of the archbishop of Dublin.[48] In 1326, he held one carucate worth 60s. in Ballymaguire, which was on the manor of Lusk and, therefore, the archbishop was his overlord there too.[49] Later, in the fifteenth century, as well as the land in Blundelstown and Rangaillagh, John Owen held lands of the crown in Celbridge in Co. Kildare. Furthermore, he held lands at Donaghmore, just north of Celbridge from John FitzGerald, sixth earl of Kildare.[50] This association with Co. Kildare may have gone back quite some time and could have originated with their association with the Kenley family. At the beginning of the fourteenth century, Warin Owen was serving as attorney to both Walter and John Kenley.[51] When John died in 1305, Warin owed him the considerable sum of £40, which may have been connected to his services as attorney, or, alternatively, it may have been rent owed for lands held of Kenley.[52] Walter Kenley had interests in Co. Kildare and served as a juror in a court case

brother.   42 NAI, EX 2/1, p. 174.   43 *CIRCLE*, PR 4 Hen. IV, §304; CR 4 Hen. IV, §15. 44 *CIRCLE*, PR 4 Hen. IV, §304.   45 Nicholas acquired these lands in 1308 from William Bloundel, whose family had given the area its name: *CJR, 1308–14*, p. 30.   46 D'Alton, *History of Dublin*, p. 563.   47 *CICD*, p. 3.   48 NAI, RC 8/6, pp 28–31.   49 *Alen's reg.*, p. 178. 50 *CIRCLE*, PR 4 Hen. IV, §304; CR 4 Hen. IV, §15.   51 *CJR, 1295–1303*, pp 292, 441; *CDI, 1293–1301*, §132.   52 *CJR, 1305–7*, p. 144.

there in 1302.[53] He was probably related to Albert Kenley, who served as sheriff of Kildare in the same year and held the manor of Rathdown.[54] Walter held lands in Nangor and Kilbride as well, close to Newcastle.[55] By 1306, he was serving as a justice of the bench and he held the office of chancellor of the exchequer too.[56] In 1304, both Warin and John Owen served as pledges for Walter, as did many other tenants of the royal manor of Saggart.[57]

The Owens also held lands from the Tyrell family at Blanchardstown.[58] According to D'Alton, a townland here called Owenstown derived its name from this family. Certainly, Owynsmill near the townland of Diswellstowns in the parish of Castleknock belonged to the Owens in the sixteenth century and may be the same place D'Alton was describing.[59] Owynsmill may be the watermill John Owen granted to Cicely Howth along with twenty-one acres of wood and other property in 1381.[60] By the sixteenth century, the Tyrells' interest in Castleknock and Blanchardstown had passed into the hands of the Barnewell and Burnell families. At this time, the Owens held land worth ten marks per year from the Barnewalls in Blanchardstown and land worth 40s. per annum from the Burnells on the manor of Castleknock. The Owens held lands all over Dublin from several landlords, for the whole of the late medieval period and, through continuity of tenure, their on-going presence in the same locality can be traced. They survived the crisis experienced in the fourteenth century probably because not only did they possess lands in vulnerable areas like Saggart but they owned lands in relatively safe areas like Esker too, in addition to extensive lands in north Dublin, from which they could probably draw a profit even in the grimmest of times. By spreading their interests around and ensuring they were not dependent on the goodwill of one overlord, they probably did a good deal to ensure their continued existence in Dublin.

Defending the marches

The sources illuminate why a family like the Owens were granted lands not only from the crown, but also from local magnates, both lay and ecclesiastical. Men like Walter Kenley, who may not have spent all their time in Ireland, used the services of families like the Owens as attorneys or stewards of their lands, for

---

53 *CDI, 1302–7*, §132. **54** *SCSMI*, pp 99, 113, 119; *CDI, 1302–7*, §§25, 37, 40; NAI, EX 2/1, p. 206; Linzi Simpson, 'Dublin's southern frontier under siege: Kindlestown Castle, Delgany, County Wicklow' in Seán Duffy (ed.), *Medieval Dublin*, 4 (Dublin, 2003), p. 296. Kindlestown Castle was named after this family. After the death of Albert Kenley in 1307, Walter claimed that a brass pot and iron cap found among the goods of Albert belonged to him, suggesting a family connection: NAI, EX 2/2, p. 257. **55** NAI, RC 8/1, pp 340–1. This memoranda roll entry states that Nangor and Kilbride were worth one knight's fee and the service of a foot soldier. A pipe roll entry from the eleventh year of Edward III's reign (*RDKPRI*, 45, pp 25–6) specifies that Kilbride was worth one foot soldier. **56** NAI, EX 2/1, p. 186; *CDI, 1302–7*, §498; Ball, *Judges*, 1, p. 60. **57** NAI, EX 2/1, p. 119. **58** D'Alton, *History of Dublin*, p. 563. **59** *CICD*, p. 3. **60** D'Alton, *History of Dublin*, p. 563.

example, while other business took them overseas. Kenley's duties as chancellor of the exchequer would have included travelling to England on occasion and his interests in Ireland needed to be protected while he was away. The Owens proved important to the defence of the area as well. In the thirteenth century, Roger Owen was willing to trade lands in Newcastle Lyons – within the land of peace – for lands in the royal manor of Saggart, which even then was located in the land of war. The implication here is that if he received these lands he would be willing to defend them. Roger did subsequently hold lands in Saggart, though it is unknown if he was successful in reclaiming this property from the land of war. These may be the same lands in Wespaillstown that his grandson Richard eventually relinquished to Walter Fox, which would suggest that ultimately this family was not able to secure this area and return it permanently to the land of peace.[61]

In 1315, Warin Owen and the aforementioned Walter Fox were given the responsibility of picking eighty men from Newcastle, Lucan and Esker to maintain a ward in Saggart that would, along with six men-at-arms, protect the area against the Irish of the Leinster mountains.[62] This coincided with the Bruce invasion and the Dublin administration was undoubtedly concerned that the Irish would take advantage of Edward Bruce's presence in Ireland and attack the city and surrounding countryside. Six years later, Warin was reeve of the manor of Newcastle Lyons and his job may have had a military aspect. As has been explored in the previous chapter, the role of seneschal of demesne was often a military one, but occasionally the office was held in sinecure. When Warin was reeve, Henry del Nasshe was serving as seneschal of demesne but, since little is known of him, it cannot be said with any certainty that he undertook any of the practical aspects of this office.[63] It is possible that as well as the administrative duties that would normally be expected of the reeve, Warin was expected to see to the defence of this manor. His experience in defending Saggart from the Irish in the previous decade would suggest that he was more than capable of fulfilling this function. In 1335, Warin Owen, together with Peter Harold and John Cruys, were responsible for collecting a subsidy granted to Edward III for his war in Scotland.[64] His fellow collectors were, incidentally, members of families who would also play an important part in the defence of the region. By entrusting Warin with this responsibility, the administration probably viewed him as someone with influence in his locality. An individual who could muster his fellow tenants to defend the area against the Irish would naturally be more successful in obtaining this subsidy than someone who had no ties here. His brother John played an even more vital role in the defence of the area, because in 1310–11 he served as sheriff of Dublin.[65]

Later generations of the family would prove important to the defence of the

61 NAI, EX 2/1, p. 174. 62 *HMDI*, p. 372. 63 *RDKPRI*, 43, p. 66. 64 *RDKPRI*, 45, pp 52–3. 65 NAI, RC 8/5, pp 669–70; *RDKPRI*, 39, p. 47.

area as well. In April 1402, under the authority of the then sheriff, Thomas Mareward, John Owen and Robert Tyrel were responsible for assessing the military service of the county, as well as arraying men to come to the marches of Dublin to defend them against attacks.[66] Furthermore, Owen and Tyrel were responsible for levying a tax known as 'smok-silver' to cover the expenses of defending the county. In the following year, John Owen, along with Christopher Hollywood and Henry FitzWilliam, was appointed keepers of the peace for the county. Also at this time, Owen and Hollywood, together with Thomas Serjeant and Thomas Howth, were granted forty marks to aid them in defending the marches.[67]

While the Callans maintained interests in both city and county throughout the medieval period, the Owens' interests were primarily in the county. Yet they did not totally abandon the city. Even though they no longer held civic offices, individuals with the surname Owen continued to work in the city. As late as 1471, William Owen, a girdler, was a citizen of the city. Three years later, John Owen, another girdler, was made a freeman of the city. Denis Owen, a shoemaker, was admitted to the city in 1482 and Margaret Owen, who was described as Denis' apprentice, was given citizenship of the city in 1501.[68] Though there is no way of connecting these individuals with the Owen family of this study, it is possible that they came from the same family group. It is not likely that every member of the family inherited land or was otherwise provided for, and therefore some of them may have maintained a trade.

CONCLUSION

The focus of this chapter has been limited to four families, but this by no means exhausts the examples of families and individuals who had interests that spanned both the city and the royal manors. In fact, the division between city and county is somewhat artificial and may not have been one that contemporaries would have recognized. Although civic authorities jealously guarded the rights of the city against county interference – for example, when John Marshal the coroner for Fingal was reprimanded for viewing bodies within the jurisdiction of the city – most of these families had landed interests in the county.[69] Likewise, some of the prominent members of the county community held property in the city. For instance, in spite of never holding civic office within the city, Adam Crumlin held property there and his contemporary, Adam Russell the goldsmith, may have been a kinsman.[70] Moreover, this family may have had mercantile connections. William Russell, a fisherman who appears in the guild merchant roll, may

66 *CIRCLE*, PR 3 Hen. IV, §227.   67 *CIRCLE*, PR 3 Hen. IV, §249.   68 *Dublin franchise roll*, pp 5, 8, 17, 37.   69 *CARD*, 1, p. 145–7.   70 Adam Crumlin received rents from at least four properties within the city in 1306: *CJR, 1305–7*, pp 198–9. Russell was the proper surname of the

have been a relative too. Certainly, Robert Crumlin, who appears in the same roll – where his occupation of baker is recorded – had a clear link with the family since he held lands that were later held by Adam in the area of the Coombe.[71]

The royal manors served as a means of rewarding merchants of the city. They may also have been used as an inducement to attract merchants there. The presence of merchants on these manors ensured that their resources and the rent they yielded would find their way into the exchequer and help fund military expeditions both home and abroad. Many of them also proved to be capable protectors of the marches, and provided military muscle as well as financing this defence. Possessing lands in the royal manors gave men from the city that extra incentive to protect this area, which, by extension, helped to preserve the colony. Merchants were a key element in populating the county, because not only did they, their kinsmen and their descendants settle on manors outside the city, but other men in turn rented land from them. For example, at the beginning of the fourteenth century, Thomas Marshal may have held land in Crumlin of John Crumlin. Most importantly, the statute of 1455 stresses the importance of merchants, not only in colonizing the locality, but also in replenishing the population of the county throughout the later medieval period.[72]

Crumlin family: *RHSJ*, §55.   **71** *DGMR*, p. 75.   **72** *Stat. Ire., Hen. VI*, p. 337.

6

Living on the edge: outsiders on the royal manors[1]

INTRODUCTION

The English settlers only ever made up a small fraction of the community on the royal manors; the vast majority of those living and working there during the late Middle Ages were Irish and, in a legal sense, they were outsiders.[2] Circumstance made them outsiders; however some of them chose, through the purchase of English law, to acquire the legal rights of an Englishman. In contrast, some of the English chose to put themselves outside the law through their criminal behaviour. In a literal sense, they became outlaws. Both groups are explored here.

The documentary evidence appears to support the view that the majority of the population living in Dublin remained Irish, even after the invasion of Ireland. On the manor of Lucan, for example, the bulk of the revenue came from rents of betaghs – tenants who were Irish in origin.[3] The first section examines the Irish living on the royal manors of Crumlin, Esker, Newcastle Lyons and Saggart, and explores the relationships between them and the English living in this locality. The way in which locals dealt with those who indulged in criminal behaviour can offer a valuable insight into society and this is explored in the second half of the chapter. In some cases, English felons were ostracized, though the majority appear to have been eventually rehabilitated and welcomed back into society. Studying crime can also be revealing regarding the gradations within society as the various social classes usually committed crimes for widely different reasons and the sort of felonies committed were often quite dissimilar. Simply put, the peasantry, who were mostly Irish, were more likely to be involved in petty crime, whereas members of the gentry were often to be found committing more serious offences, if only because they had the means to do so. As was the case in England, some members of the gentry became outlaws and formed gangs, which they used to terrorize and extend their control over the local community. The Tyrel brothers, who originated from the manor of Lyons,

---

1 Earlier versions of this chapter were published in Áine Foley, 'Violent crime in medieval County Dublin: a symptom of degeneracy?' in Seán Duffy (ed.), *Medieval Dublin*, 10 (Dublin, 2010), pp 220–40; idem, 'Chieftains, betaghs and burghers: the Irish on the royal manors of medieval Dublin' in Seán Duffy, *Medieval Dublin*, 11 (Dublin, 2011), pp 202–18. 2 James Mills concluded that in spite of the colonization of the hinterland of Dublin by a substantial group of settlers, the Gaelic Irish still made up a considerable proportion of the population: idem, 'Norman settlement', 174. 3 Ball, *Dublin*, 4, p. 36.

adjacent to the royal manor of Newcastle Lyons, left their mark on the locality. Some tenants on the royal manors sheltered these outlaws, while others became members of their gang.

Introduction
An examination of the petitions that emanated from the beleaguered tenants of the royal manors from the latter part of the thirteenth century onwards may lead us to suppose that the interactions between the English and Irish were predominantly negative and that there was a policy of social exclusion against the Irish. Though it is certainly true that the Irish living in the mountains exacerbated the difficult conditions that defined the fourteenth century, it is also important to bear in mind that, in spite of the influx of English settlers, the bulk of the population living on the royal manors was probably always predominantly Irish. This was particularly true on the outer manors of Saggart and Newcastle Lyons. The relationships that developed between the Irish and English living there will be explored to challenge this supposition. Even though many of the Irish tenants were betaghs who were tied to the land, their rights were often defended, even to the detriment of English tenants. Other tenants of Irish extraction who could buy English law did so. As a result, they became almost indistinguishable from their English counterparts on the manors.

Betaghs
Though betaghs were found on the manors belonging to the archbishop of Dublin during the late sixteenth century, the court rolls for Esker and Crumlin, which date from this period, reveal that betaghs had long since disappeared from here.[4] Nevertheless, they were undoubtedly an important element of society in the period under review. In fact, a family by the name of Betagh lived on the royal manor of Esker in the early modern period, and they may possibly be descendants of Adam and Ralph Betagh featured in the sources three hundred years earlier.[5] Unfortunately, it is unknown where in Dublin Adam and Ralph Betagh had lands.

    In 1307, Henry Kissok acquired forty-five acres in Esker that had previously belonged to Maurice Moleran, a betagh of the king.[6] Henry also held lands in Bothercolyn, a part of the manor of Saggart, at this time and he may have acquired this mountainous property from an Irishman as well.[7] An inquisition established that Moleran had no goods with which to pay the rent of 8½*d.* per

4 Curtis, 'Court book' (vol. 60), 143.   5 Idem, 'Court book' (vol. 59), 48; *CDI, 1285–92*, §§965, 1078, 1148; *CDI, 1293–1301*, §206.   6 NAI, EX 2/1, pp 193–4.   7 *CDI, 1293–1301*, §391.

acre owed for this land. He had also sold his house there and had concealed another five acres he held on this manor to avoid paying rent on it. This confiscation of land clearly had more to do with Moleran's shortcomings as a tenant than his ethnicity. Indeed, the evidence would suggest that removing betaghs from their land and granting them to Englishmen was unusual. This might imply that the Kissok family were Irish. They either took their name from Kissoge in Esker or gave the area this name. They may have been a Gaelic Irish family who had acquired English law. As can be seen below, the royal courts protected the rights of Irish tenants on the king's lands. This was probably because the Irish, the majority of whom were probably unfree tenants, had more tenurial obligations than their English counterparts, and it was to the crown's advantage to protect these rights.

This policy of protecting the rights of the betaghs is illustrated in a case dating from 1310. In this year, David Otrescan complained of being illegally ousted from lands in Saggart that had belonged to his father, Nicholas, a betagh.[8] The new occupant of the lands was John Fangoner, an Englishman, who claimed rights of this land through his wife Ostina. She appears to be Nicholas' granddaughter, as the lands had previously passed from Nicholas to his son John, David's brother. This case shows an example of intermarriage between the Irish and the English, which would have gone unrecorded if not for the dispute over these lands. John Fangoner argued that Ostina held these lands as her inheritance at the time he married her. Even though the court did not dispute this, David the Irishman received seisin of these lands. The court ruled in his favour because he was a 'true betagh of the king', who could pay the rent and services for this land. Though probably in every other respect the courts would uphold the rights of an Englishman against one of the native Irish, they knew that John Fangoner could not be compelled to carry out the customary obligations associated with this holding. Unlike David Otrescan, he could move away at any time and take his goods with him. As a betagh, Otrescan was tied to the lands. David Otrescan's holding was nine acres and, while this is a small plot by modern standards, it was more than enough to sustain a family at that time. In England, large peasant holdings varied between twelve and eighty acres and thus Otrescan's was modest, but bigger than average for a smallholder, which was about five acres.[9] What is more, Otrescan's landholding was probably larger than that of cottagers living on the same manor. It is important to differentiate between cottagers and betaghs, because, though betaghs were tied to the land, they could also sometimes be very substantial landholders.

The amount of property left behind when Clement Ocathyl, one of the king's betaghs, was slain at Cruagh in the Dublin Mountains in 1303 may suggest that he was a substantial landholder.[10] At the time of his death, he possessed four

---

8 NAI, EX 2/3, pp 488–9. 9 Bartlett, *Norman and Angevin kings*, pp 319–20. 10 NAI, EX

cows with calves, one ox and three horses, thirty sheep and a pig. Aside from the livestock, he also had a considerable amount of grain and other foodstuff in his possession and among his personal property was a brass pot worth half a mark, and a chest. John Archer, Richard Rikeman, Augustine Ocolan and Godfrey Brotham stood security to pay his heriot, the death duty owed to the king. These men, both English and Irish in ethnic origin, also undertook to keep these goods in safekeeping until Ocathyl's sons came of age. Though no landholding is mentioned, this memoranda roll entry does specify that these sons would inhabit the demesne lands of the king. Ocathyl probably lived on one of the royal manors, perhaps one of the outer granges of the manor of Saggart. This case confirms that the tenurial rights of the Irish tenants on the royal manors were protected.

Land usage as evidence of social status
In 1306, over eight crannocks of oats belonging to Conor O'Hanley, who was also a betagh of the king, were found in the house of William Fetting in New Street near St Patrick's after Fetting's death.[11] In the same year, Gregory Bree and John Colchester acknowledged that they had goods worth in excess of 10*s.* that had previously belonged to another recently deceased betagh of the king named William Oharchur. What is clear is that both of these men had a reasonably large amount of cereal in their possession at the time of their deaths, and this may indicate that they were involved in arable farming. Land usage is a useful indicator of social status, and the extent of the lands and chattels an individual possessed obviously offered many clues as to his or her place in society. If O'Hanley and Oharchur did grow cereal, they probably held fertile, low-lying lands, and were reasonably prosperous. Wealth was assessed by the amount of land a person possessed. Lyons observed that land usage among the tenants of the royal manors was linked to the size of their holding.[12] The larger the holding, the more likely it was that its owner would be involved in tillage farming. Moreover, it follows that the greater the involvement in tillage farming, the higher up the social scale that person was likely to be, and the less likely he/she was to be Irish.

Those lower down the social scale were more likely to be involved in raising livestock. In 1295, John Ó Tíre, an Irishman who held lands in Ballinteer, which formed part of the manor of Saggart, received hens as rent from the betaghs on his land.[13] When, in 1319, a group of smallholders on the manor of Crumlin – perhaps the descendants of the 'poor men of Crumlin' who resisted Henry Compton's grant of the royal demesne there – went into arrears, the sheriff seized their sheep. This seizure occurred at harvest time, but there is no mention

2/1, p. 60.   11 Ibid., p. 160.   12 Lyons, 'Manorial administration', p. 35.   13 *CDI, 1293–1301*, §259.

of the sheriff taking any crops from them. This is probably because this particular group of tenants did not grow cereal on a significant scale.[14] While these few examples cannot prove that social status was linked to different forms of farming practice, it does seem reasonable that this was the case. This changed somewhat as the fourteenth century progressed, when there was a general shift from tillage to pastoral farming. The unpredictable conditions of the colony were part of the reason for this shift in farming practices. Judging by the rents they paid, the betaghs living on John Ó Tíre's lands probably held small areas of land. Betaghs like Ocathyl, however, owned a substantial amount of goods, indicating that it is not possible to pigeonhole them into a particular class. While some held little more land than a cottager did, others – at the very least – could count themselves among the most prosperous tenants on the manors.

The legal status of the betagh

In terms of legal status, the betaghs of the royal manors appear to have had many similarities with villeins living on the royal demesne in England. Though English villeins could not appeal to royal courts, these courts would often intervene and investigate any infringement of their rights as tenants on the king's lands.[15] This is echoed in Dublin in the case already mentioned involving David Otrescan, whose rights as a king's betagh were upheld against the claims of an Englishman. The crown did this because it simply made more sense to protect the rights of a legally unfree tenant because of the customary obligations they were compelled to perform.[16] Ensuring that tenants were obligated to remain on their lands was even more important in Dublin than in England, because an empty parcel of land made the whole locality vulnerable. Lands that were waste could fall into the hands of the Irish in the nearby mountains, or English outlaws, which resulted in the rents and profits being forever lost to the crown.

Further similarities between English villeins and Irish betaghs are found at the end of the thirteenth century, when William Deveneys, who was granted extensive lands on the royal demesne in Dublin, sought permission to seek out and recover the betaghs attached to this land.[17] He received permission to bring them back on the condition that if these betaghs were residing elsewhere on the king's demesne they would be left unmolested. This was very similar to the legal protection granted to villeins in England, where any found residing on the ancient demesne of the king for more than a year and a day could remain there. Their former lords lost all rights to them.[18] The privileges granted to the king's tenants, even those who were legally unfree, indicate how valuable they were to the crown. Certainly, to maintain the royal lands, workers were needed and the crown ensured that they would continue to constantly replenish their pool of

---

14 NAI, RC 8/12, pp 94–5. 15 Hoyt, *Royal demesne*, p. 196. 16 See Hilton, *Medieval society*, p. 129, for some of the obligations associated with villeinage in England. 17 *CDI, 1252–84*, §2070; *CIRCLE, Antiquissime* roll, §1. 18 Hoyt, *Royal demesne*, p. 187.

tenants by extending this privilege to newcomers, even if it was to the detriment of other lords.

English law granted to Irish living on the royal manors
The Irish living on the royal manors did not have the same recourse to the law as those among their English neighbours, particularly those belonging to the emerging gentry. Nevertheless, they must have had a lot in common with the peasantry of English extraction living on the manors, as they too would not have had the same access to justice as their wealthier neighbours. Some of the petitions discussed below mention both the English and the Irish tenants on the royal manors and, while they are visible as a group, separately they do not feature prominently in the sources. Most of the sources relied on for an assessment of the royal manors are administrative in nature and they tend to offer a distorted view of the social make-up of the locality. The Irish were technically outside the law and did not serve in local administrative office or did not appear in the panels of jurors. Therefore, most are invisible within these sources. Some Irishmen do turn up in these administrative documents, however, particularly those who purchased English law. The Irish often had names that did not appear to be obviously Irish, and sometimes the only evidence that we have of their ethnic origins is the fact that they were granted English law. Consequently, there could be many Irishmen in the sources who are not identified as being Irish. One famous example is Robert Bree, who served as mayor of Dublin between 1292 and 1294, but there is also evidence of ambitious men of his ilk on the royal manors.[19]

In 1292, William, son of Donald Clerk, and his children received a grant of English law.[20] William came from Newcastle Lyons and this patent roll entry is the only indicator of his ethnic origins. Donald is probably an anglicized version of Domhnall, but he gave his son an English name. He may have been descended from a cleric or his name may indicate that he was able to write. If he had an education, he may have been an administrator, which would suggest that not everyone of Irish origin living on the manors was a betagh. It would at least suggest that not all Irishmen worked the land and that they did have other occupations. He may have given his son an English name because he wanted his family to assimilate into English society.

In about 1285, an Irishman from Saggart called Richard Pudding petitioned for and obtained English law.[21] Richard was a burgess, and therefore, even before he applied for English law, he was already enjoying the benefits associated with being a freeman. Saggart was a borough, which meant that it possessed a municipal corporation and special privileges conferred by royal charter. Boroughs were

19 *CDI, 1285–92*, §748; *HMDI*, pp xxx–xxxi; H.F. Berry, 'Catalogue of mayors, provosts and bailiffs of Dublin city, AD1229 to 1447' in Howard Clarke (ed.), *Medieval Dublin: the living city* (Dublin, 1990), p. 158. 20 *CDI, 1285–92*, §1096. 21 TNA, SC 8/331/15677.

towns in the legal sense of the word, but many in Ireland never developed beyond rural settlements. These boroughs were created to attract English colonists.[22] The benefits of creating a borough in Saggart are clear. It was closer to the mountains and more at risk from Irish raids than other areas of Dublin, and therefore its privileges gave potential tenants an incentive to settle there. An Irishman may have been accepted as a burgess because it was difficult to find enough suitable Englishmen to settle in the area. Moreover, Saggart was part of the ancient demesne, with all the privileges that entailed. His status as a tenant living on the king's ancient demesne would have set Richard Pudding apart from other tenants living on the king's lands – Irish or English. It is likely that Richard, though he was not of English extraction, applied for English law in order to continue enjoying the privileges that he already had as a freeman on this manor. In 1292, Pudding was in debt for £8 to the king, possibly connected to his purchase of English law.[23] It is likely that he paid a substantial amount of money to obtain this privilege. Richard was allowed to pay off his debts in instalments of 20s. a year; hence, even though he could not afford to pay off the whole sum at once, he must have been relatively prosperous if he was capable of paying a portion off it each year. Pudding appears to have frequently been in legal difficulties. He was fined 15s. in 1288 and 40d. in 1292 for unspecified trespasses.[24] In 1294, Pudding paid the farm of the royal manor of Saggart into the exchequer and he may have held the office of reeve at this time, as this officer was usually responsible for collecting the rent.[25] Four years later, he was paying the rent on the mills of this manor.[26] The tenement containing the mill was usually the most lucrative holding on the manor, particularly if the other tenants were obliged to grind their corn there as well. Richard Pudding was probably dead by 1302, because by now his wife Margery was responsible for paying the rent on these mills.[27]

English reaction to lawless behaviour by the Irish

It is likely that there were many Irishmen living on the royal manors who purchased English law, or who assimilated themselves into English society to such an extent that no one remembered that they were Irish anymore. Nonetheless, these few examples of Irishmen willing to assume the identity of Englishmen should not be taken as typical. There is evidence that the Irish did see themselves as being separate and distinct from their English neighbours, and it is true in many cases that they were treated differently because of their ethnicity. The clearest proof of this can be found in their treatment by the

22 For medieval rural boroughs, see John Bradley, 'Rural boroughs in medieval Ireland: nucleated or dispersed settlements?' in Jan Klápště (ed.), *Ruralia III* (Prague, 2000), pp 288–93, and for Dublin boroughs, Bradley, 'Medieval boroughs'. 23 *CDI, 1285–92*, §§1108, 1109; *CFR, 1272–1307*, p. 311. 24 *CDI, 1285–92*, §§371, 1148. 25 *CDI, 1293–1301*, §139. 26 Ibid., §§550, 587, 637. 27 *CDI, 1302–7*, §72.

courts. Sources like the justiciary rolls, for example, are very informative as to the kinds of punishments handed out to the various different ethnic groups. Ciaran Parker observed that in Waterford an Irishman was no more likely to be convicted than an Englishman, but if found guilty was more likely to be hanged.[28] This seems to have been the case in Co. Dublin too. It appears that these Irish were often also the poorest members of society. Cormok de Carrickbrenan, who was undoubtedly an Irishman, was hanged for the murder of Jordan Waleys,[29] who was most probably of Welsh extraction. The justiciary roll entry reveals that Cormok had no chattels, and thus perhaps social status, as well as ethnicity, played a part in how some of the Irish were treated by the courts.

An Irishman executed in spite of the fact that he had the ways and means to pay his fine was likely to have been a particularly notorious individual, or a repeat offender. Milo Mcbridyn of Cruagh, for example, hanged in 1305, must have been reasonably well off because his wife Raghenilda paid 60s. for the return of his goods after his execution.[30] Among the men who served as her pledges were Reginald Barnewell, one of the most prominent landowners in Co. Dublin, and William Corbaly, who probably came from Corbally in Saggart. All of the pledges were Englishmen. Incidentally, Reginald Barnewell was also one of the jurors who decided her husband's fate.[31] McBridyn was charged with killing Henry Golygthly, though his body was not found. His son, Luke, assisted him, and it is possible that he was pardoned, though his fate is unknown. Perhaps, if prominent members of the gentry were standing as pledges for Luke's mother, they may have assisted him in gaining a pardon too.

In 1305, the community of the royal manor of Saggart showed a solidarity that transcended ethnic divisions. Kevin of Saggart, likely to have been an Irishman, was charged with receiving his son Martin, a thief. The jury, however, found him not guilty. The same jury found Andrew Deveneys and his wife Grathagh not guilty of receiving Kelt, a man of David McKilecoul O'Toole. Grathagh was an O'Toole herself, but had married an Englishman; it is possible that they were the parents of John Deveneys, who was employed by William Long of Saggart as his squire. Some years later, William and John were charged with stealing a bull belonging to Robert Darditz in the liberty of Trim and driving it into Dublin.[32] William was the son of Martin Long, who served on the jury that acquitted Andrew Deveneys and his Irish wife. As tenants on the same manor, they would have known each other, and, obviously, it would have been difficult to convict someone with whom one was on personal terms. Kevin of Saggart may have even named his son after Martin Long; this Christian name was certainly not common in the locality at this time. Other members of the jury

28 Ciaran Parker, 'The politics and society of County Waterford in the thirteenth and fourteenth centuries' (PhD, TCD, 1992), p. 334.   29 *CJR, 1305–7*, p. 498.   30 Ibid., p. 485.   31 Ibid., pp 478–9.   32 *CJR, 1308–14*, p. 163.

were indubitably locals; Reginald Barnewell, mentioned above, owned the manors of Ballyfermot, Drimnagh and Terenure, while John Owen was a major tenant on the royal manors of Esker and Saggart. The jurors not only acquitted Grathagh, but also described how she often went up into the mountains and assisted in the recovery of cattle stolen by her kinsmen. In later years, Grathagh again got into trouble for her close association with the O'Tooles when she was accused of spying on the men of Saggart on behalf of the Irish in the mountains. The jurors were not willing to give Grathagh the benefit of the doubt on this occasion, and she was found guilty of spying and executed.[33] This shift in attitude may have had much to do with the general deteriorating conditions of the colony at this time. The great European famine of 1315–18 would have been tumultuous enough in itself, but it also led to increased raids from the Irish of the mountains. Moreover, the unrest created by the Bruce invasion at exactly the same time may also have motivated the Irish to raid the manors closest to the mountains. Grathagh may have posed a real threat to the security of this manor, however, and there is no evidence that she was in any way typical of the Irish living on the manor, or that her punishment was in any way representative of how the Irish were treated by their neighbours. Petitions emanating from the royal manors were sent on behalf of both the king's Irish and his English tenants. Therefore, it would appear that, for the most part, the Irish tenants were as concerned by these raids as their English counterparts.[34]

Consequently, the evidence would suggest that the Irish living on the royal manors and their environs were just as beleaguered by the Irish living in the mountains as the rest of the community. In 1306, an Irishman named Oconyl was forced to move from Kilmesantan to Tathmothan, both of which were on the manor of Tallaght, to avoid providing the O'Tooles with food and drink. The jurors in his case included tenants on all four of the royal manors, namely Martin Long of Saggart, Adam Jordan and W. White of Newcastle Lyons, John Kissok of Esker and John Crumlin. They vouched for him and confirmed that Oconyl never gave the O'Tooles food and drink except when they were in the king's peace, and they stressed that even then he only did so under duress. In spite of their support, he was fined 100s. Here is an example of community unity that crossed not only ethnic but also possibly social divisions too. Moreover, not only did the jury accept that Oconyl was an unwilling receiver, but two other local men who were probably of English extraction – Hugh Canoun and Simon Bailiff of Clondalkin – stood as his pledges.

While acknowledging that evidence for solidarity between both races living on the royal manors does exist, it is also true that the courts often meted out different punishments depending on the defendant's ethnic origins. Certainly, Englishmen accused of the crime that led to Grathagh's conviction and execu-

33 Lydon, 'Medieval Wicklow', p. 14.   34 For an example of a petition from both English and Irish tenants, see *Affairs Ire.*, §41

tion were treated more leniently. In 1306, John Jordan, a brother of Adam Jordan of Newcastle Lyons, was fined £20 for receiving the Irish and spying for them.[35] One assumes that these malefactors were English outlaws and perhaps even the Tyrels of Lyons, who are discussed below. In his case, there is no evidence that the jury thought him innocent of these crimes – in fact, the heavy fine would suggest otherwise. Also in 1306, a monk of St Mary's Abbey, Dublin, was charged with receiving Cormok de Carrickbrenan, and it is likely that the monk was English. He was found not guilty, but the fact that he was charged in the first place would suggest a prior association between these two men. The evidence in the justiciary rolls proves that there was a great deal of interaction between both races, even in an area as heavily colonized as south Co. Dublin, and much of this interaction was positive.

The justiciary rolls yield other examples of interactions between the different ethnic groups within Co. Dublin. In 1308, for example, William Bernard, probably an Englishman, was accidentally stabbed by John McCorcan, who was almost certainly Irish, during a game of ball in the town of Newcastle Lyons.[36] The entry makes it clear that both men were 'fast friends' and after he paid William damages of 5s. John was pardoned. Surprisingly, there is little hint of tension between the two ethnic groups, and, in fact, most of the evidence for violent crime was between the English themselves. Moreover, when the Irish committed crimes against other Irish, they were usually just fined; for example, a group of men including Dermot McBride were fined 40s. for robbing Finyn, the clerk of Bryaneston,[37] a follower of John de Balygodman. Both Dermot and Finyn appear to be Irish, but many Irishmen would have adopted English names and it is not always easy to locate them in the sources. It is possible, therefore, that others received similar leniency from the courts. In most cases, where men who were clearly Irish were involved in acts of violence, it was usually as followers of members of the gentry. Certainly, the statutes passed at the parliament in Kilkenny in 1297 suggest that a high degree of interaction and assimilation was occurring between the races. It would also indicate that the administration was uncomfortable about this interaction. This acculturation was demonstrated when Englishmen adopted the dress of Irishmen and wore a distinctive Irish hairstyle known as the *cúlán*.[38] This led to many unfortunate incidences where Englishmen were murdered on the mistaken assumption that they were Irish!

---

35 Adam Jordan, a king's serjeant, appears to have held lands in the manor of Newcastle Lyons, because in 1309 John Lympit, who was provost of this manor, forgave him part of his rent due to the fact that Adam did not make the tenants of Newcastle Lyons serve on inquisitions and juries while he was in office: NAI, EX 2/3, pp 475–8.   36 *CJR, 1308–14*, p. 103. Note that the source refers to Newcastle Lyons as a town; this may signify its borough status.   37 *CJR, 1305–7*, p. 484.   38 *Stat. Ire., John–Hen. V*, p. 211; Philomena Connolly, 'The enactments of the Dublin parliament of 1297' in Lydon (ed.), *Law and disorder* (1997), p. 159.

Criminal behaviour and attitudes towards outsiders

For the English to survive with any degree of success on the royal manors, particularly the outer ones, they had to be able to interact and negotiate with the Irish. Day-to-day existence here exposed the impracticalities of the statutes passed in 1297. This may explain why evidence of violence against the Irish by tenants of the royal manors is scarce. There is, however, a case where William Sampson and Richard Lagheles of Newcastle Lyons and others were charged with attacking a group of men, including Irishmen, who were lodging in the Coombe with Maurice Carew while they were on their way to Scotland to fight for the king. In spite of the fact that some of the Irishmen were killed in the affray, William and Richard succeeded in escaping prosecution without even paying a fine, thanks to a legal technicality. Maurice Carew was compelled to withdraw the charges he made against them because he did not specify in his writ if the Irishmen were his *hibernici*. These Irishmen, however, were just passing through Dublin on their way to Scotland and were not locals. It is unlikely that they even knew their attackers on any sort of personal level. Moreover, it is unlikely that the jurors knew these slain men either, and the degree of leniency displayed towards William and Richard – whom they all probably knew well – is hardly surprising.

The jurors may have been showing natural wariness of the outsider. There are other occasions when the sources seem to reveal this distrust; with jurors being less inclined to show the same sympathy to a stranger as they would extend to a neighbour. Though the Irish were as likely to be acquitted of their crimes as their English counterparts were, the same could not be said of those who came from outside the locality. Outsiders and foreigners accused of breaking the law were far more likely to be found guilty by jurors. Unfortunately, the primary sources often do not indicate where individuals came from, and it can be difficult to ascertain if they were locals or not, but occasionally surnames can offer some clues as to their origins. For example, Gilbert Whithavene mentioned in the justiciary rolls in 1311 is probably a foreigner. This assumption is reinforced by the additional information that two of his companions, Robert Goderd and Richard Faber, were from Sandwich and Liverpool respectively. They, along with three others, were charged with assisting Thomas White, a mariner, in the murder of Robert Thursteyn. It is likely that all these men were sailors and all of them, apart from William Rede, were found guilty. It is not made clear in the sources why William was acquitted, but it is possible that he came from Ireland or had friends among the jurors, one of whom was John Marshal of Newcastle Lyons. The other men were hanged, but Robert Goderd and Richard Faber, who were presumed dead when they were cut down from the gallows, revived in the cart taking them to Kilmainham for burial. They took shelter in a church there and were subsequently pardoned.

THE CRIMINAL BEHAVIOUR OF THE ENGLISH ON THE ROYAL MANORS

Introduction

Indisputably, the criminal activities of the English of Ireland had an adverse effect on the fortunes of the lordship. This accelerated in the troubled years of the fourteenth century. Is it fair, however, to assume that the criminal behaviour of the English meant that they were 'turning native'? The petitions sent to the king by his 'faithful English' in Ireland complaining about the 'rebel English' as well as the Irish, might suggest that the process of Gaelicization was a factor in the criminal activity of these individuals.[39] Did the lawless behaviour of some elements of Irish society influence the behaviour of the English or were they simply taking advantage of the unsettled conditions that existed from the last quarter of the thirteenth century? Did the Irish and English commit felonies for the same reasons, and did ethnic divisions even matter? The English were unquestionably affected by the behaviour of their Irish neighbours – even in an area as heavily colonized as Dublin – but other motives came into play too. The poor and destitute must have had very different motives for stealing than those more comfortably off, regardless of their ethnicity.

Rather than beingt degenerate, this behaviour may in fact reveal a shared identity between the communities of Ireland and England. The pressure exerted by Edward I on the Irish revenues to fund his military expeditions has been suggested as a contributing factor to the lawlessness of his subjects on both sides of the Irish Sea. James Lydon maintains that the frequent taxes levied by the crown contributed to the lawless conditions of the colony.[40] Though the Irish colony was financially crippled by King Edward's wars, his subjects in England were experiencing the same problems too. The increase in numbers of commissions of oyer and terminer (to hear and determine) that occurred in the 1290s would suggest that crime was becoming an increasingly serious issue here as well.[41]

While the criminal activities of some of the native Irish living in or near the royal manors of Dublin must have had some influence on their neighbours, an examination of England in the same period demonstrates a high involvement by members of the gentry in illegal activities.[42] The evidence suggests that social status was an important factor in the types of crimes committed and, indeed, how particular individuals were treated by the courts. Therefore, it might be

---

39 For a discussion on degeneracy, see Seán Duffy, 'The problem of degeneracy' in Lydon (ed.), *Law and disorder* (1997), pp 87–106.   40 James Lydon, 'The years of crisis' in *NHI*, ii, pp 156–78, 202.   41 Prestwich, *Plantagenet England*, p. 518. These courts were presided over by judges of assize, with the help of commissioners chosen from the county where the cases were heard.   42 For general surveys of crime in medieval England, see J.C. Bellamy, *Crime and public order in the later Middle Ages* (London, 1973), passim; B. Hanawalt, *Crime and conflict in English communities, 1300–1348* (Cambridge, 1979), passim.

more beneficial to compare the criminal activities of the gentry in Ireland to their counterparts in England rather than just focus on degeneracy and Gaelicization.

While the subject of crime in medieval Ireland does appear in the secondary literature, it is often in a peripheral way. Seldom has this topic been closely examined on its own merits, either for the lordship as a whole, or within specific localities. Significantly, more focus is given to the political repercussions of this lawless behaviour than the behaviour itself.[43] While it would be a mistake not to take the political instability of the colony into account, it would be equally naïve to imagine that these conditions were a prerequisite for crime. To shed some light on this subject, criminal activities among tenants on the royal manors – from the perspective of both perpetrator and victim – are examined. Moreover, since it can be difficult to establish with any certainty from where some of the criminals originated, court cases that involved tenants on the royal manors as jurors are analysed, as it is more than likely that the criminals themselves were locals too. Additionally, how criminals were treated by the courts is assessed below.

The murder of William Brun

While serious crime was not an everyday occurrence, tenants on the royal manors were occasionally its victims or perpetrators. An early example of this is the case of William Brun, murdered in the city of Dublin sometime before 1200. The Brun family held lands in Newcastle Lyons.[44] After his murder, his son Owen brought an appeal against Richard Gille Michel, Warin London and Elias Fitz Philip for their alleged involvement in this crime.[45] Thomas Norreys and Robert de Winchester were also accused of participating in William's murder. He evidently had previous negative dealings with these men, for they had been bound to keep the peace against him at the Dublin county court.

An unnamed man struck William with a hatchet beside Dublin Castle. He fell into the dyke of the castle and died of his injuries. The men against whom his son took an appeal were charged with aiding and abetting his attacker. As a means of proving their innocence all but one of the accused men agreed to undertake a trial by battle. Warin London was injured during William Brun's attack and therefore it was decided that he would undergo trial by iron.[46] Incidentally, a Warin London appears on a witness list where Owen Brun

---

43 Some local studies that include examinations of lawless behaviour – though not specifically criminal behaviour – among the gentry have been done: for Waterford, see Parker, 'The politics and society of County Waterford', p. 334; for Louth, see Smith, *Colonisation and conquest*, pp 104–5.   44 *CDI, 1171–1251*, §§114, 116; *RDKPRI*, 36, p. 50; see also ch. 3 for an investigation of this family.   45 *CDI, 1171–1251*, §§114, 116.   46 The first criminal trial jury was not introduced in England until around 1220; therefore, William le Brun's attackers could not have chosen to be tried by jury: see Roger DeGroot, 'The early thirteenth-century criminal jury' in J.S. Cockburn and T.A. Green (eds), *Twelve good men and true: the criminal trial jury in England, 1200–1800* (Princeton, 1988), p. 3.

granted lands near Kilmainham to the citizens of Dublin.[47] No precise date is provided with this charter, but it is dated to after William Brun's death. This would suggest, at least if it is the same Warin, that he was pardoned or acquitted of the murder. Warin is mentioned as a juror in a charter relating to the abbey of St Thomas dating to 1219;[48] if this were the same individual, it would be reasonable to assume that this charter is close in date to Owen Brun's.[49]

The 'rebel English' and the lawless behaviour of the gentry
All too often, the Irish were blamed for the slow disintegration of the colony, and yet this case appears to have only involved Englishmen. Brendan Smith's study of Louth has highlighted that the English were the main perpetrators of some of the most horrifying atrocities to have occurred in the lordship and that their victims were more often than not their fellow Englishmen. When the English of Louth had their own resident magnate in the form of John Bermingham foisted upon them, they reacted by murdering him and most of his followers. Some of the men suspected of taking part in this massacre were among the leading gentry of the locality and even included the then sheriff of Louth, John Cusack.[50] Many petitions sent to the king lump the Irish and rebel English together, and the implication seems to be that these Englishmen had 'gone native'. An examination of the justiciary rolls, however, which survive from the end of the thirteenth century, offers a different perspective. These are the most important documentary source for criminal behaviour in the late thirteenth and early fourteenth centuries and they emanated from the royal court presided over by the chief governor of Ireland. By their very nature, these records contain a wealth of information about offenders and their crimes. They survive in published calendar form for the years 1295 until 1314 (and unpublished up to 1318). The period they cover offers a snapshot of a colony metamorphosing from a once prosperous enterprise into a financial liability for the English crown. This selective survival of material, with its limited chronology, means tracing long-term trends is challenging and can leave us with the erroneous impression that the first years of the fourteenth century were particularly lawless. Nevertheless, for these few years, the justiciary rolls serve as an invaluable window on society and can be informative concerning attitudes towards crime. They reveal that the Irish were often on the periphery of the criminal world and were frequently victims of, not participants in, crime. Certainly, in terms of the royal manors, most people involved in criminal activity or affected by it were English.[51]

---

47 *CARD*, 1, p. 163.   48 *RAST*, p. 146.   49 The Brun family were indirectly involved in another murder case almost two centuries later. When an Augustinian monk called Richard Dermot died in mysterious circumstances in 1379, his body was hidden by his fellow monks, and probable murderers, in the well in the garden of Adam Brun, a citizen of the city: see F.X. Martin, 'Murder in a Dublin monastery, 1379' in Gearóid Mac Niocaill and Patrick Wallace (eds), *Keimelia: studies in medieval archaeology and history in memory of Tom Delaney* (Galway, 1988), pp 468–98.   50 Smith, *Colonisation and conquest*, pp 113–16.   51 It may be the case, however, that

The types of crime committed by members of the gentry were quite different from those committed by those of lower social status and this is because, as a rule, their motivations were different. Moreover, they had the ways and means to steal larger and more valuable property. They were in a position to steal not only movable goods but land too, the main source of power in the medieval period. The early fourteenth century was a period when outlaw gangs, whose exploits were similar to those described in the legends of Robin Hood, reigned supreme in England. Outlaws like the Coterels of Derbyshire and the Folvilles of Leicestershire have received much attention from social historians.[52] Their lawless deeds reveal many similarities to the activities of criminal gangs in Ireland. Surprisingly, the criminal groups that existed have received less attention, even though their exploits are described in great – and sometimes lurid – detail in contemporary judicial records. These outlaw bands were created either to extend their own control over their locality or to maintain and extend the power of an overlord. In this section, the activities of Henry and Thomas Tyrel, and their respective outlaw gangs, are surveyed. They were based in north Co. Kildare and south Co. Dublin in the first two decades of the fourteenth century, and their proximity to the royal manors meant that they touched the lives – often adversely – of those living there. As members of the gentry, they were individuals who, to borrow Barbara Hanawalt's phrase, committed 'fur collar crime'.[53]

It appears that crime escalated in England in this period;[54] therefore, it would not be surprising to find a similar phenomenon occurring in Ireland. Both countries experienced population growth during the thirteenth century, which put pressure on the availability of land. With less hope of inheriting property, it was hardly surprising if some turned to crime as a career option to maintain their social status. In terms of wealth, little separated a petty knight from a prosperous peasant,[55] and it would have been easy for a knight of more limited means to lose his position in society. Alternatively, criminal activity may have been more carefully recorded at this time because of changing attitudes. People may have become increasingly unwilling to tolerate crime.[56]

crimes against the Irish were generally not reported. **52** E.L.G. Stones, 'The Folvilles of Ashby-Folville, Leicestershire, and their associates in crime', *TRHS*, 5th ser., 7 (1957), 117–36; J.G. Bellamy, 'The Coterel gang: an anatomy of a band of fourteenth-century criminals', *EHR*, 79 (1964), 698–717. **53** B. Hanawalt, 'Fur-collar crime: the pattern of crime among the fourteenth-century English nobility', *JSH*, 8:4 (1975), 1–18. **54** Barbara A. Hanawalt, 'Economic influences on the pattern of crime in England, 1300–1348', *American Journal of Legal History*, 18:4 (1974), 292. **55** Scott L. Waugh, 'The profits of violence: the minor gentry in the rebellion of 1321–1322 in Gloucestershire and Herefordshire', *Speculum*, 52:4 (1977), 844. **56** Richard W. Kaeuper, 'Law and order in fourteenth-century England: the evidence of special commissions of oyer and terminer', *Speculum*, 54:4 (1979), 737.

Violent crime

Compared with the relative paucity of evidence for conflict between the different ethnic groups in south Dublin, there are many incidences where Englishmen were killed or injured by their fellow Englishmen. The early example of William Brun's murder has been illustrated above. The high incidence of violent crime is not surprising, considering that most men carried weapons of some sort. Indeed, many deaths and injuries must have been the result of accidents like that involving William Bernard and John McCorcan of Newcastle Lyons, discussed above. The possession of weapons meant that many criminal acts were not premeditated. The sources dealing with the royal manors appear to indicate that, though crime was not an everyday occurrence, it did touch the lives of all tenants living here. Members of prominent families appear to have found themselves to be either victims or perpetrators of crime at some point in their lives. For example, in 1299, Simon Locumbe was fined one mark for wounding William, son of Thomas, on the head, and in 1306, John Crumlin accused Robert Taaf, William Babe and Philip Dieugrace of beating him and stealing his cattle.[57]

With regard to medieval England, John Bellamy made the point that it was possible to commit relatively serious crimes and be rehabilitated back into society. Indeed, many of these reformed felons subsequently acquired judicial offices and, consequently, became responsible for maintaining law and order themselves.[58] In Dublin, there are several instances of men with previous lives of crime later serving as jurors. Thomas Crumlin, for example, was fined on several occasions and yet he appears prominently on several jury lists and as a witness to charters, as well as serving as a tax collector. Obviously, in medieval Dublin, there was no long-lasting stigma attached to having a criminal past and the courts did not see a problem with the same men who had once broken the law subsequently upholding it. Of far more consequence to the courts and royal officials were those 'repeat offenders' who lived primarily on the fruits of their crimes. Particularly important to this study are the criminal gangs roaming in and around the vicinity of the royal manors who stole, murdered and intimidated for both material reward and control over the locality. In 1305, a jury gathered in Shanganagh near Shankill to hear the case of William, son of John, charged with committing robberies in this locality and elsewhere in Co. Dublin, declared that 'they dared not indict him'. Even the sheriff feared bringing this man to justice. There is no indication in the sources of his social status, but it is possible he was a member of the gentry. The evidence would suggest that most leaders of criminal gangs in Ireland, as in England, were members of the gentry. Bellamy observes that gentle blood within the outlaw gang was as valued within this group as it was to the world at large.[59]

57 NAI, EX 2/1, p. 12.   58 Bellamy, *Crime and public order*, p. 30.   59 Ibid., p. 75.

Gerald Tyrel

Henry Tyrel, a member of a prominent family in Co. Dublin, led a criminal gang active in the environs of the royal manors in the early fourteenth century. His brother, Thomas, may have been a member of Henry's gang, as he was outlawed when Henry was brought to justice. Their father, Gerald, was a knight and a close associate of two important men: John Fitz Thomas, lord of Offaly and later the first earl of Kildare, and Ralph Pipard.[60] Pipard, who, as well as owning extensive lands in Co. Louth and Monaghan, also owned the manors of Leixlip, Oughterard and Castlewarden in Co. Kildare, which were situated close to the royal manors of Saggart and Newcastle Lyons.[61] These manors were originally granted to Adam de Hereford by Strongbow after the invasion and came into the Pipard family's possession when Adam's daughter Auda married William Pipard.[62] Although he was a major landholder in Ireland, by the early fourteenth century, Ralph Pipard was spending all of his time in England and Gerald Tyrel served as marshal, and later seneschal, of his lands in Ireland. It is clear that Gerald also had property on the royal manors of Newcastle Lyons and Saggart, because he granted land here to Maurice Tyrel.[63] Maurice was probably Gerald's son, but instead of emulating his brothers, he became an administrator and was seneschal of the royal demesne in the early fourteenth century.[64]

Gerald first appears in the records in the 1280s as 'a youth distinguished for nobility, probity and arms', who, after an attack, was taken prisoner by the Irish and eventually traded for an Irish hostage.[65] Unfortunately, the source does not distinguish who the Irish were. Still, as a member of John Fitz Thomas' retinue, Gerald certainly would have had plenty of interaction with the Irish of Offaly and Kildare. Fitz Thomas often found himself on the wrong side of the law. For example, in 1294 he carried out the audacious act of capturing the most powerful noble in Ireland, Richard de Burgh, earl of Ulster, imprisoning him for several months.[66] His actions led to a period of widespread disturbance across the country and he proved such a thorn in the side of the administration that he was packed off to Scotland to fight.[67] In 1297, he was on the king's service in Flanders, and Gerald Tyrel almost certainly accompanied him because he was given a writ reprieving all pleas and assizes before the justiciar until April of 1298 while he was overseas with Fitz Thomas.[68] Tyrel also appeared as a witness in several charters issued by Fitz Thomas, along with many other prominent residents of Kildare, and he seems to have maintained this association while he served as Ralph Pipard's seneschal.[69]

---

60 *CDI, 1293–1301*, §834. **61** For a list of the Irish possessions of Ralph Pipard, see *Ormond deeds, 1172–1350*, pp 129–30. **62** *Knights fees*, p. 207. **63** NAI, RC 8/5, pp 275–7. **64** See ch. 4. **65** *CDI, 1285–92*, §828. **66** Lydon, 'The years of crisis', p. 187. **67** *CJR, 1295–1301*, p. 176; Lydon, 'The years of crisis', p. 188. **68** Lydon, 'The years of crisis', p. 198; *CDI, 1293–1301*, §461. **69** Gearóid Mac Niocaill (ed.), *The red book of the earls of Kildare* (Dublin, 1964), pp 32, 92, 95.

It is likely that either Fitz Thomas or Pipard granted him the manor of Lyons, which lay adjacent to the royal manor of Newcastle Lyons. John Fitz Thomas granted John Hotham lands in nearby Maynooth; therefore, he could have granted lands to Gerald as well. On the other hand, the location of the manor, sandwiched between Pipard's manors of Leixlip, Oughterard and Castlewarden, might make him a more likely candidate as Gerald's benefactor. It is not clear how long the Tyrel family held these lands, and consequently it is possible that the Pipards granted them to one of Gerald's ancestors. The Tyrels had originally come over to Ireland with the de Lacys and were granted lands in Co. Louth by King John; later, in 1227, Hugh Tyrel became sheriff of Louth. The Pipards were a major presence in the county from the late twelfth century onwards, and it is likely that these families had close ties from an early date.[70] Having virtual control over these manors made Gerald one of the most important people in the locality. In his study of Co. Louth, Brendan Smith has observed that the gentry were more likely to involve themselves in illegal activity in places where there was no permanent magnate present, and therefore Pipard's absence meant that the Tyrels had no one to whom to answer.[71] When Leixlip, Castlewarden and Oughterard came into royal hands, this locality came under the scrutiny of royal officials. As Ralph Pipard's seneschal, Gerald had free rein, but after Pipard's conveyance of his lands in Ireland to the king in 1302, the power balance here potentially shifted.[72]

Attitudes towards lawlessness in the medieval period were markedly different to those of today, and a certain degree of leniency was shown towards illegal activity. Some members of the nobility encouraged their followers to break the law as a means of extending their personal power and influence in a locality. Moreover, the crown was dependent on the gentry as administrators within local government and, consequently, it ignored much of the lawless behaviour of this class.[73] Gerald was considered important enough to receive a letter from the king requesting that he supply men-at-arms for the war against Scotland. Indeed, grants of land made to him on the royal manors of Saggart and Newcastle Lyons are another indication of his significance to the crown. He also deputized as constable of Roscommon Castle on behalf of John Fitz Thomas. Furthermore, in a dispute over the narrowing of the Liffey by weirs, he was one of the few men on the jury who was described as a knight.[74]

The Tyrel brothers

Gerald had at least three sons: Roger, Henry and Thomas, with Maurice being a potential fourth son.[75] Roger does not appear in the justiciary rolls, apart from

70 Smith, *Colonisation and conquest*, p. 48.   **71** Ibid., p. 105.   **72** Ibid., p. 95.   **73** W.R. Jones, 'Keeping the peace: English society, local government and the commission of 1341–4', *American Journal of Legal History*, 18:4 (1974), 307–20.   **74** *CJR, 1305–7*, pp 255, 257–9. Though the source does not state it explicitly, he was probably sheriff of Roscommon too.   **75** NAI, RC 8/9,

one brief entry that mentions his involvement in a trespass with Richard Tyrel of Castleknock.[76] No details are given as to the nature of the crime. He was probably the eldest son, who could look forward to inheriting his father's property. He seemingly did not have the motivations his brothers had to embark on a life of crime. Likewise, the eldest brother of the Folville gang in England also inherited from his father, thus becoming a country gentleman while the rest of his brothers became criminals.[77] Roger's partner-in-crime, Richard Tyrel, became one of the largest and wealthiest landowners in Dublin when he succeeded his father Hugh to Castleknock in 1299.

Henry Tyrel's criminal activities do not appear to have extended beyond his own locality. The justiciary rolls reveal that most of his crimes were committed between Lyons and Oughterard. He must have been a well-known figure among the tenants of the adjacent royal manors of Newcastle Lyons and Saggart. Bellemy has observed that most criminal gangs in England operated in the locality from which their leader either originated or in which he held lands. Obviously, this was their comfort zone. They understood the locality, and their supporters and followers lived there too. Additionally, Lyons lay close to the border between Kildare and Dublin and thus it is probable that when Tyrel's gang committed crimes in Dublin, they could quickly escape across the border to Kildare. County officials in one county did not have jurisdiction in the next, which made it easy for criminal gangs located close to where two or more counties met to escape justice. In 1351, a statute was passed that ordered sheriffs and officers in one county to pursue felons escaping into another county, and it permitted them to apprehend these felons.[78] The passing of this statute would suggest that there had been problems with felons escaping into other jurisdictions. It also compelled the sheriff of the county to which the felon escaped to provide aid in his capture. This would suggest that there had been little cooperation between sheriffs in the past, thus enabling criminals to use county borders as places where they could commit crimes in relative freedom. There is clear evidence in England of criminal gangs establishing themselves where two or more counties met and escaping into one county after committing felonies in another.

Certainly, to men of reasonably high social status with little land and fewer prospects, the life of an outlaw had its attractions. An alternative for a younger son was to fight for the king, and it is possible that the Tyrel brothers had served the king overseas. Nonetheless, when men came home, some would have found it hard to settle back into normality after growing used to the looting and other criminal behaviour so intrinsic to the life of a soldier. Of course, the Tyrel brothers may have simply become outlaws because they were attracted to the

p. 548.   76 *CJR, 1295–1303*, p. 449.   77 Barbara Hanawalt Westman, 'The peasant family and crime in fourteenth-century England', *Journal of British Studies*, 13:2 (1974), 16.   78 *Stat. Ire., John–Hen. V*, p. 381.

lifestyle. In the justiciary rolls, Henry is described as a 'common robber'.[79] According to Hanawalt, robberies, unlike burglaries, were usually violent and committed by strangers.[80] Tyrel was obviously a dangerous individual. The type of goods he stole marked him out as a member of the gentry, because, whereas peasants were more likely to steal small objects that would be easy to conceal, Henry stole livestock. He also extorted money from those travelling between Lyons and Oughterard; undoubtedly, he did this both for material reward and to extend his influence in the locality. It is conceivable that he also expected locals – including tenants on the nearby royal manors – to seek protection from him, thereby considerably enhancing his control of the area.[81]

Arnald Penrys is the only victim of Henry's named in the sources and he was probably a tenant on the royal manor of Newcastle Lyons since he served as a pledge for this community when they were accused of sheltering Henry.[82] Tyrel was charged with wasting Arnald's goods, as well as committing adultery with his unnamed wife, and bringing her with him on his travels. He is not accused of abducting her, and she may have been his willing companion. Moreover, she may have been an Irishwoman. A fragmented entry in the justiciary rolls for 1306 describes a concubine named Mcnabyth associated with an outlaw called Henry.[83] James Mills was of the opinion that this was Henry Tyrel.[84] She was also an associate of the O'Tooles and, if she was Arnald's wife, he was not the only English tenant from the locality to marry a member of this family. Grathagh O'Toole, discussed above, was married to Andrew Deveneys of Saggart.

Henry Tyrel's trial and execution

Henry was tried on 14 December 1305, and the sources suggest that he had been detained before on similar charges but had received a pardon. Though the justiciary roll entry is in a very fragmentary state, it seems that his father Gerald served as his pledge and may even have personally delivered him up to trial. In the same year, Patrick Alta Ripa delivered his son Maurice, who was charged with robbery, to the king's prison, 'lest he should turn to worse crimes'.[85] Gerald may have had the same motivations. If Henry's activities were detrimental to Fitz Thomas' control of the area, his father may have felt under pressure to deliver him up to the courts. Moreover, if he was consorting with his father's enemies and threatening his position in the locality, Gerald may, indeed, have had few qualms about handing him over.

The justiciar ordered that he be remitted to prison in Dublin Castle, and he instructed the constable to allow Henry neither food nor drink. There is evidence of criminals being 'put on the diet', which meant being allowed little or

79 *CJR, 1305–7*, p. 477.   80 Hanawalt, *Crime and conflict*, p. 83.   81 Hanawalt, 'Fur-collar crime', 5–7.   82 *CJR, 1305–7*, p. 483.   83 Ibid., p. 500.   84 Ibid., p. 611.   85 *CJR, 1305–7*, p. 484.

no food and drink until they gave evidence in court or confessed their guilt. Nonetheless, for a royal court to use starvation as a mode of execution was extremely unusual, if not unique. The vast majority of criminals executed in Dublin recorded in the justiciary rolls were dispatched by hanging. In the Annals of Ireland for 1339, Friar John Clyn reports that Maurice Fitz Nicholas, a knight from Kerry, possibly the earl of Desmond's brother-in-law, died in prison on a starvation diet.[86] He had rebelled with the Irish against the earl. Fitz Nicholas was, however, executed by Desmond, his overlord, and not the crown. In Henry's case, the administration may have thought it wise to let him die in prison rather than risk a public execution and give members of his gang the opportunity to help him escape. Alternatively, Henry's mode of execution may have been related to his status in society. Most of those executed by hanging in the justiciary rolls appear to have been of low social status. This would seem to be true concerning one of Henry's associates, Adam, who was hanged. His surname was not recorded in the justiciary rolls. If he was of low social status, the court may have considered a detail like his surname too trivial to document.

The most remarkable thing about this case may have been the fact that Henry Tyrel was executed at all. He was not a typical recipient of such rough justice. Henry was well-connected, and his father was a powerful individual in the locality. Henry was unequivocally a member of the gentry and most men of his social status who broke the law would have expected to escape with no more than a fine. His cousin, Richard Tyrel of Castleknock, for example, received just a fine when he admitted to the rape of Eva London and this 'punishment' was considered the norm.[87] Certainly, elsewhere in Europe when members of the gentry and nobility were executed at this time, the method was usually decapitation.[88] This makes Henry Tyrel's mode of execution extraordinary, as starvation would have been a slow, painful death. The court was clearly making an example of Henry. Highway robbers were considered particularly reprehensible and, in addition to this, Tyrel was a repeat offender. Yet it is possible that it was his association with the O'Tooles that ultimately sealed his fate.

Several of the men who served as jurors for his trial and decided his fate came from south Dublin and some held lands on the royal manors. Walter Fox was granted land in Saggart in 1306, and he possessed lands in Ballymackelly and Greenoge in Rathcoole.[89] Another juror, John Oweyn, had land in Saggart in the early fourteenth century.[90] Martin Long and John Marshal would have felt the brunt of the Tyrels' illegal activities as major tenants on the royal manors.[91] John Godman was possibly related to Hugh Godman, who served as provost of

86 Clyn, *Annals of Ireland*, p. 226. 87 *CJR, 1308–14*, pp 154–5. 88 Trevor Dean, *Crime in medieval Europe* (Harlow, 2001), p. 109; decapitation was usually reserved for treasonous crimes; this perhaps highlights how rare execution was among members of the gentry and nobility who committed murder and other violent acts. 89 NAI, EX 2/1, p. 174; *Alen's reg.*, pp 163–4, 185–9. 90 NAI, EX 2/1, p. 174. 91 *Exchequer payments*, p. 264.

Newcastle Lyons sometime before 1304.[92] The other jurors who took part in this case obviously had lands in the vicinity too, since they often appear in association with the above-mentioned individuals.

Henry's followers

Some of Tyrel's other followers tried that day were more fortunate than their leader. Thomas Norreys was charged with robbery and being in Henry's company, but the jury decided that he had been taken by force and he was therefore acquitted. Other individuals who shared his surname were tenants on or had associations with the royal manors. In 1277, Roger Crumlin was charged with the rape of Sarah Norreys. She may have been a relative of John, son of William, Norreys, who lived in Dublin at this time.[93] In 1306, William Norreys served as a pledge for William Kissok, who owed £10 of the arrears of the farm of the royal manor of Esker.[94] Three years later, David Norreys is identified as coming from Ballydowd, a grange on this same manor, and in the following year, he served as reeve of Esker. He also appears to have had ties with the Kissoks of Esker.[95] Furthermore, many of David's known associates also were tenants or held offices on the royal manors. These included Thomas Beg, who served as provost of Esker around 1321.[96] Thomas was also provost of Crumlin at some point before 1318 and is likely to have been a member of the Beg family of Saggart.[97] They paid the farm and arrears of the rent of this manor on multiple occasions in the thirteenth century, and Richard Beg served as provost there in 1314–15.[98] Thomas may also be related to Nicholas Beg, who served as provost on the royal manor of Crumlin sometime before 1313.[99] Adam Norreys, who, along with several other men, owed William Douce twelve marks in 1306, may have also been a royal tenant.[1] William owned extensive property on the royal manors of Newcastle Lyons and Saggart, and it is likely that the money Adam owed William was for land he held of him here.[2]

The Norreys were a prominent family on the royal manors and, though this investigation of the network of connections that existed between them and other tenants on the royal manors has been limited to just a few members of this family – and is certainly not exhaustive – it does seem to reveal a tightly knit community. Certainly, a close communal bond would have developed through sharing tenancies on the same manors and through serving in administrative office together. David Norreys, who was probably a relative of the outlaw Thomas,

---

92 *RDKPRI*, 38, p. 84; NAI, EX 2/1, p. 65.   93 NAI, RC 8/1, pp 350, 602.   94 NAI, EX 2/1, p. 153.   95 NAI, RC 8/4, p. 835; RC 8/6, p. 286; RC 8/7, p. 439.   96 *RDKPRI*, 42, p. 30; *RDKPRI*, 43, p. 29.   97 *RDKPRI*, 42, p. 27.   98 *CDI, 1285–92*, §§215, 271, 1078, 1148; *CDI, 1293–1301*, §§4, 21, 41, 329, 363, 408, 587; *CDI, 1302–7*, §72; *RDKPRI*, 36, pp 42, 67; *RDKPRI*, 37, p. 25; *RDKPRI*, 38, pp 68, 84, 94; *RDKPRI*, 39, p. 56.   99 *RDKPRI*, 39, p. 50.   1 NAI, EX 2/2, p. 228.   2 NAI, EX 2/2, p. 294; RC 8/5, p. 538; RC 8/8, pp 62–4; TNA, SC 8/105/5250; *IEMI*, §175.

served as reeve of Esker and, through this office, he would have developed ties with his fellow tenants. The judicial system developed these links further, since these men served as jurors together. For example, many of the jurors who decided Thomas Norreys' fate were tenants on the royal manors. These included – but were not limited to – men like Walter Fox, John Marshal, John Oweyn and Martin Long. Some of the other men listed as jurors may have held lands on the royal manors; but the shortcomings of the sources and the common surnames of some of the jurors mean that this cannot always be established with any certainty. These jurors accepted the somewhat implausible story that Norreys was a member of Henry's gang under duress. Norreys was charged with stealing from Rosyna, daughter of Dermot the smith, and he was found in possession of a horse that did not belong to him.[3] The evidence would suggest that he was inclined to a life of crime. Thomas Norreys likely knew many of the jurors and that they had close ties with other members of his family. Naturally, these men would have been very reluctant to send a neighbour's son to the gallows. Certainly, in England, most judicial cases led to acquittals, because the jurors were hesitant to condemn a friend or neighbour to death.[4] Thomas Norreys' trial and verdict demonstrates a community that protected its own and a judicial system that could bend and adapt to practical considerations.

Not only were the jurors loath to punish Thomas Norreys severely, they were in fact reluctant to punish him at all. He did not even pay a fine. This was in stark contrast to the fate met by his leader. Undoubtedly, one of the reasons they considered Tyrel to be so dangerous was that he was such a bad influence on others within the English community. Hence, even though the statutes passed as recently as 1297 were concerned with the seemingly negative influence of the Irish, the judicial records of the time reveal that often it was other Englishmen who were the prime instigators when their compatriots broke the law. That is not to say that the Irish could not be a negative influence on their English neighbours – and certainly, the Irish can be found living on the royal manors, particularly the outer manors of Newcastle Lyons and Saggart. Yet this was not the case with Thomas. If Norreys associated with the Irish at all, it is likely that Henry Tyrel was the intermediary. Tyrel may have been more severely punished because he did interact far too closely with the O'Tooles for the administration's comfort. Indeed, they may have considered him beyond rehabilitation. This close association with a group, who, even by this early date, were attacking the royal manors, may have alienated Tyrel from the rest of the community. Moreover, his father's association with some of the greatest magnates in the land may have served in creating a social gap between him and the rest of the gentry of the locality. If the community felt he was beyond their control, they may have welcomed this opportunity to take him out of the picture entirely.

3 *CJR, 1305–7*, p. 477. 4 Paul Strohm, 'Trade, treason and the murder of Janus Imperial', *Journal of British Studies*, 35:1 (1996), 3.

Richard, son of Richard le Shepherd, was another follower of Henry Tyrel.[5] The jurors agreed that he was an associate of Tyrel's, but they did not feel that he had taken part in some of the most serious offences. Although his life was spared, the jurors decided that he was more culpable than Thomas Norreys and he had to pay a substantial fine of ten marks. One of Richard's pledges had the surname 'de Athgo', which indicates that he came from Athgoe Hill, on the royal manor of Newcastle Lyons. It is likely that Richard came from the same locality. It seems likely that he also received some support from his leader's family, because Maurice Tyrel served as one of his pledges. Richard's surname may indicate his – or his father's – occupation, and it is possible that his association with the Tyrel family was related to his line of work. Athgoe Hill was adjacent to Lyons Hill, which was within the manor of Lyons and was held by the Tyrels at this time. Moreover, the twelve acres of moor that Gerald Tyrel held in nearby Castlewarden could only be practically used as pastureland, which suggests that this family invested significantly in livestock.[6] Richard could have been a shepherd working for the family in this locality. Certainly, the terrain of this area lent itself to pastoral rather than tillage farming. If Richard or his father was a servant of this family, they may have felt responsible for him and helped pay his fine. The composition of Henry's gang shared many similarities with that of James Clinton, a member of the gentry of Warwickshire, who terrorized his locality in the 1280s.[7] Clinton had twenty-four followers, including some relatives and a cleric who also happened to have a smaller gang of his own. The judicial records reveal that robbery and violence instigated by the gentry and the clergy were common at this time. Undoubtedly, the majority of the followers that made up this gang, like Tyrel's supporters, were of humbler social station, and some may well have been Clinton's servants.

Residents of the area also helped Henry Tyrel in his criminal activities. An individual whose name does not survive in the sources was fined 100s. for sheltering Henry Tyrel. One of his pledges was Reginald Athgo, probably the same person who served as a pledge for Richard Shepherd. It is worth noting that all of the other pledges who can be identified share the same surnames as known tenants of the royal manor of Newcastle Lyons. Yereward Athgo, who paid rent for lands in Newcastle Lyons in 1296, is possibly father to Richard, son of Yereward, who was one of these pledges.[8] Moreover, Hugh Yereward, who served as provost of Athgoe before 1328, may be this Richard's son.[9] Thomas del Rath is the merchant Thomas Marshal, who held lands in Newcastle Lyons at this time. There are also two men listed with the surname Blund, and though this is a common surname, there was a prominent family called Blund living on the same manor during this period.[10] Moreover, John and Reginald Hyne may

---

5 *CJR, 1305–7*, p. 476. 6 *SCSMI*, p. 268. 7 Hilton, *Medieval society*, p. 253. 8 *CDI, 1293–1301*, §329. 9 *RDKPRI*, 43, p. 29. 10 *CDI, 1252–84*, §§1740, 1814, 1834; *CDI,*

be members of the family that gave Hynestown – a townland just north of the main settlement at Newcastle Lyons – its name. Even though the name of the person who sheltered Henry Tyrel is not known, it can be established that he was a tenant on this royal manor. Ironically, it appears that Henry hid out on the king's lands in order to escape the justice of his courts.

This individual was not the only person on this manor accused of sheltering Henry Tyrel; in fact, the entire town of Newcastle Lyons, as well what seems to be Oughterard, were fined for receiving him.[11] It is not clear whether these towns sympathized with the felon and his gang or whether they sheltered him out of fear. One of the pledges for these two settlements was Arnald Penrys and, since Henry made off with his wife, it is unlikely that he would have supported those who helped these felons. Hence, it is likely that these two communities sheltered Tyrel's gang under duress. A community had genuine reason to fear the outlaws who lived among them. That is not to say that some members of these communities did not have any sympathy for Henry, particularly taking into account the fact that many who came from the locality joined his gang.

Possible motives for Henry Tyrel's criminal activities

Even though the full extent of his criminal activity is not known, Henry's crimes described in the justiciary rolls do not appear to be as serious as those committed by his brother, and some are examined below. It is possible that his gang were the local representatives of a more powerful local lord. Certainly, in England, there is evidence of criminal gangs, including the Coterels and Folvilles, working for the nobility. Alternatively, Henry may have simply been attempting to maintain and extend his father's control of this area. Gerald used the judicial system to uphold his rights and probably to intimidate lesser tenants; his son's criminal acts were possibly committed ultimately with the same objective in mind. With Ralph Pipard no longer having a presence in Ireland, the most obvious candidate for noble patron was John Fitz Thomas, who was certainly the most powerful magnate in the locality. Moreover, Fitz Thomas also had a long-standing associ-ation with Henry's father, Gerald. Nonetheless, if Henry, and his brother Thomas, were under the earl's protection, then it seems surprising that Henry, and perhaps Thomas too, were executed. It is possible that Gerald's sons had become a liability to Fitz Thomas. Though Fitz Thomas had been a thorn in the side of the Irish administration in the last decade of the thirteenth century, by 1310 he was a reformed character. By this time, he retained a ward of men to keep the peace in the area between Rathmore and Saggart. Not only was he commissioned to keep down the rebellion of the Irish, but he was also respon-

---

1285–92, §§309, 330, 371; *CDI, 1293–1301*, §§139, 206, 226, 264, 279, 289, 408, 550, 587, 613, 637, 748, 825; *CDI, 1302–7*, §§4, 72.   11 *CJR, 1305–7*, pp 481, 483. The source describes the settle-ment of Newcastle Lyons as a town, though it was certainly more rural in nature. Only a fragment of the name of the other settlement survives, but it seems to be Oughterard.

sible for dealing with the felons of Leinster, and this, presumably, included the English enemies of the king.[12] He could not afford to allow the likes of the Tyrels have the run of the area, as this would be proof that he was not in control.

Thomas Tyrel

In fact, the evidence suggests that Thomas Tyrel was an associate of Arnold Poer, a magnate who may have been an enemy of Fitz Thomas. When Thomas was tried 1311, he was accused of the murder of John Bonevill, the king's seneschal in Kildare and Carlow, and a close associate of Fitz Thomas.[13] John Bonevill's marriage to the heiress of Naas may have been a result of his connection with this magnate.[14] His wife, Matilda, was the granddaughter of David Fitzgerald, the last baron of Naas. She was also the widow of Thomas London, possibly grandfather to Eva, the young girl raped by Richard Tyrel of Castleknock. This act may suggest animosity between the Tyrels and Bonevill.[15] In 1310, Arnold Poer was acquitted of the murder, arguing that the deed had been done in self-defence.[16] This did not necessarily mean he was innocent, however; just that he had the power to avoid the consequences of his actions.

Thomas Tyrel was declared an outlaw on the same day his brother was sentenced to death.[17] While Thomas Tyrel's activities in Carlow are beyond the scope of this book, the career of this outlaw is also worth examining, as it seems that some of his followers also had close associations with the royal manors. Thomas, like Henry, was described as a common robber and, like his brother, it appears that he committed most of his crimes in Cos Kildare and Dublin. The justiciary roll entry for Thomas' trial states that he was so feared 'no one dared to come to the parts of Dublin to bring victuals there'.[18] Thomas was brought to trial in 1311, six years after his brother's execution. If he and his gang were active for all this time, one can only imagine the extent of control they had over the communities of both these counties.

Thomas claimed benefit of clergy and refused to answer the charges laid against him. There are many examples of accused men claiming to be clerks in the justiciary rolls, and certainly, in England, it was a legal loophole much used and abused. Men claimed to be clergy to have their case moved to an ecclesiastical court, where they would receive a much lighter punishment. It is not clear if Thomas was a clerk, but it was certainly plausible. Although one of the Folville brothers was in religious orders, he also happened to be one of the most

---

12 *Exchequer payments*, p. 597.   13 *CJR, 1308–14*, p. 168; C. Ó Cléirigh, 'John fitzThomas, fifth lord of Offaly and first earl of Kildare, 1287–1316' (PhD, TCD, 1996), p. 73; *CJR, 1295–1303*, pp 191, 203–4.   14 Bernadette Williams, 'The "Kilkenny chronicle"' in T. Barry, R. Frame, K. Simms (eds), *Colony and frontier in medieval Ireland: essays presented to J.F. Lydon* (London, 1995), p. 83.   15 *Knights fees*, 87; *CJR, 1308–14*, pp 154–5. Matilda Fitzgerald's husband died in 1302, but he had a son of the same name who may be this Thomas London.   16 *CSMA*, 2, p. 339.   17 *CJR, 1305–7*, pp 484–5.   18 *CJR, 1308–14*, p. 217

violent members of the gang and was eventually murdered outside his own church. In Thomas Tyrel's case, the jurors seemed unconvinced by his claims, as he was not found in clerical garb. Since he continued to refuse to answer the accusations laid against him, he was put on the diet. The constable of Dublin Castle was ordered to guard him and, it is presumed, make sure he did not receive food or water. It does not record if the case was moved to an ecclesiastical court or whether Thomas met the same end as Henry. If he did succeed in convincing the court of his clerical status, it is likely that he avoided his brother's fate.

Two of Thomas' accomplices stood trial with their leader. One of them, Richard Mora, was a chaplain, which may lend some credence to Thomas' claims of being a cleric himself.[19] A jury cleared Richard of robbing a horse, but found him guilty of breaking into a church at Aderrig, which is a small parish to the west of Esker and Lucan, and stealing goods from a chest belonging to a Robert Fedan. The jury also declared that he was responsible for stealing Hugh de le Felde's oxen and burning down Jordan Mouner's house, but he was only fined 40s. Adam Squer was also accused of being a follower of Tyrel's, and he was charged with the death of Nicholas Penbrigge and sentenced to death.[20] The entry informs us that he had neither chattels nor free land. Richard Mora may have escaped execution because he was a clergyman, but one has to wonder if Adam Squer could have avoided his fate for the sake of 40s.?

Thomas Tyrel had no jurors because he claimed benefit of clergy, but the jurors listed for Richard Mora's case again seem to have been tenants in the immediate locality. Thomas Kent held the castle of Leixlip in 1304. In the following year, he had the pleas and perquisites of Saggart and Newcastle Lyons, and he was seneschal of demesne of the royal manors by 1308.[21] Warin Owen possessed a meadow in Greenoge near Rathcoole, and, if he was related to John Oweyn, probably had lands in Saggart and Esker too. John Lung was the son of Martin Lung, who was a tenant in Saggart.

Petty crime and the peasantry
The participation of members of the gentry in criminal behaviour has been examined above and many of the examples given deal with major crime. That is not to say that the courts dealt exclusively with the gentry or with serious crimes. As has already been demonstrated, the tenants on the royal manor of Newcastle Lyons were charged with receiving Henry Tyrel.[22] This meant they supplied him with food and shelter or aided and abetted him in other ways. These receivers probably came from all levels of manorial society. Even though their participation in crime was passive, it is fair to say that without the support of these locals it would have been difficult for notorious criminals like Tyrel to

---

19 Ibid., p. 218.   20 Ibid., pp 218–19.   21 Ibid., p. 18.   22 *CJR, 1305–7*, pp 481, 483.

function. Indeed, members of Henry and Thomas Tyrel's gang may have been of peasant stock. It is unlikely that Richard Shepherd, for example, was a member of the gentry.

The justiciary rolls also record incidents of petty crime. Although men like the Tyrels committed acts of violence to acquire their ill-gotten gains, most incidents of robbery did not involve assault. Many accused of thievery were probably opportunists rather than hardened career criminals. This was especially true of those who stole small items that could be easily concealed on their person and removed from the scene. It was also more likely that those who stole less valuable items were of lower social status. For example, in 1305, Philip del Logh was fined for stealing various items including hoods and gloves from Adam Bras. Philip probably came from the same area as his pledges, who included Reysel of Newcastle, and Richard Gras and Roger Beg from Milltown, a grange on the royal manor of Newcastle Lyons. Indeed, Philip could have been a tenant on this royal manor too.[23] Del Logh does not seem to appear elsewhere in the sources, and people who shared his surname do not feature as jurors or administrators, and therefore he may have been of peasant stock. He may have been related to Richard Lough, whose property was taken into the hands of the king's serjeant, Adam Jordan, in 1310.[24] Adam had lands in Newcastle Lyons and, sometime prior to 1309, John Lympit, the reeve of this royal manor, reprieved his rent here.[25] Moreover, one of the granges of this manor was called Jordanstown and it is likely that it derived its name from Adam's family. Richard Lough may have held lands on this manor too. Richard had renounced the king's land, which may indicate that he had become an outlaw. His chattels were only worth 40*d*. and this may indicate that, like Philip, he was a member of the peasantry.

Incidentally, Adam Jordon had felons in his own family. He appropriated items belonging to his brother, John, who had recently escaped from Dublin Castle. John had been found guilty of spying on behalf of the Irish felons. He had the resources to pay the heavy fine of £20, which indicates that he, and by extension his family, was well off.[26] The goods seized by his brother further established his place in society. This included seven crannocs of corn, oats and barley, ten sheep and six lambs, four pigs, one brewing cup, one hogshead and a pair of irons for a plough. The value of his accumulated goods would have far exceeded the 40*d*. that made up the whole of Richard Lough's property, and marks him out as someone of higher social status than Richard. This information about Richard survives because Adam Jordan, in his capacity as king's serjeant, appropriated it for his own use. Matters dealing with forfeited lands and chattels, particularly when they were worth so little, were usually handled in the manor court.

23 Ibid., p. 486.   24 *CJR, 1308–14*, pp 153–4.   25 NAI, EX 2/3, pp 475–8.   26 *CJR, 1305–7*, p. 509.

CONCLUSION

The evidence would suggest that, certainly in the thirteenth and early fourteenth centuries, the English lived more or less in harmony with their Irish neighbours on the royal manors. Even though they were technically outside the law, there is evidence that they intermarried with their English neighbours. Indeed, some of the Irish who had the means acquired English law in order to enjoy the same legal benefits and privileges as their English neighbours. The case of Grathagh Deveneys, however, may display a hardening in attitudes towards the Irish that grew more acute as the fourteenth century progressed. As the raids by the O'Tooles and O'Byrnes intensified, it is possible that the Irish living on the manors became negatively and erroneously associated with these raiders. Two incidents at Newcastle in 1370 highlight this negative attitude. Thomas Snitterby, who may have been related to the cleric of the same name who held lands in Newcastle Lyons in the previous century,[27] captured the Irishman Richard McAoohye and his two sons on the same manor on St Patrick's Day. In addition, Lorcan O'Bouye, another Irishman, was beheaded in Newcastle at around this time as well.[28] Nevertheless, an examination of the court rolls of Esker and Crumlin dating from the late sixteenth century confirms that a large proportion of the population of these manors was still Irish. This would suggest that, in spite of the difficulties and ethnic tensions, the Irish were not driven away from the manors. In fact, it would appear that they had eventually lost the taint of betaghry and were now on a more level footing with their English neighbours.[29]

Not only were tenants on the royal manors tolerant of the Irish, particularly during the prosperous thirteenth century, the evidence would suggest that they often turned a blind eye to criminal behaviour of the English in their own community. Certainly, the sources appear to indicate that the tenants of the royal manors looked after their own. When the jurors – many of whom were also landowners on the royal manors – found Thomas Norreys innocent of any wrongdoing, they were banding together to protect one of their own. Instead of sharing the same grisly fate as his leader, Thomas was acquitted. This is not to say that they were always willing to tolerate the behaviour of the more lawless elements of society, as the case of the Tyrel brothers confirms. When the stability of the royal manors and their environs was threatened, the locals were more than capable of meting out tough justice.

Even though they operated on the margins of society, an examination of the Tyrel brothers and their associates, as well as the other criminal behaviour between the English, can be illuminating in regards to the social order of the royal manors. This particular case reveals the various ways in which people from

27 NAI, RC 8/8, pp 664–5. 28 *CCM, 1515–74*, 5 [Book of Howth], p. 169. 29 Curtis, 'Court book' (vol. 60), 143.

different levels of society were treated by the courts. There is some truth in the saying that 'rich man be hanged by the purse, poor man by the neck'.[30]

Henry Tyrel seems to have had close associations with the Irish of the locality; with this in mind, can his behaviour be described as a symptom of degeneracy? Contemporary sources can be misleading when one attempts to answer this question, as the 'wild Irish' and 'rebel English' usually appear in the same petitions sent to the king. This would imply that they were in league with each other, but appearances can be deceptive. Clearly, the behaviour of the Tyrel brothers bore more resemblance to the behaviour of their counterparts in England than the Irish. When the Irish were involved in criminal activity with the English, it was usually in the guise of follower rather than instigator. Certainly, no member of the Tyrel gang appeared to be Irish, though it cannot be discounted that some may have been Irish hiding behind English names. The Tyrels themselves, however, were English, and, even if some of their followers were native Irish, it is obvious that they were the degenerating influence and not the other way around! Rather than being influenced by the increasing lawless-ness of the Irish, they used the disorder to mask their own activities. A colony bled dry by the crown could be forgiven for feeling a certain amount of umbrage, and younger sons with no inheritance were bound to become desperate. Moreover, a bad harvest meant that many were often forced to steal. It could even be the case that some simply preferred the lifestyle of an outlaw. Therefore, although the increasingly disturbed state of the lordship of Ireland from the late thirteenth century might well be attributed to the concept of degeneracy among the colonists and the economic tribulations facing the colony as a whole, it could perhaps be argued with equal validity that such lawlessness was an everyday aspect of a typical English gentry society now manifesting itself in the 'Little England' that lay on the other side of the Irish Sea.[31]

---

30 John Stow, *A survey of London* (London, 1842), p. 96. 31 Phrase taken from F.W. Maitland, *The history of English law before the time of Edward I*, 2 (Cambridge, 1898), p. 688.

7

Crisis and continuity: the royal manors in the fourteenth and fifteenth centuries

INTRODUCTION

The trials and tribulations that marked the fourteenth century were not, of course, unique to the royal manors of Co. Dublin, or even to the colony at large. The whole of Western Europe suffered from a combination of famines and plagues throughout this century, which contributed to a serious and widespread economic slump, following several centuries of relative prosperity. In England, these changes can be traced back to the last decade of the thirteenth century, and parallels can be drawn with Ireland, where the crisis that affected the colony can, more or less, be dated to this period as well.[1] Though Michael Prestwich acknowledges that the poor harvests that plagued this decade were partly to blame for the situation in England, he believes that the heavy taxations and purveyances imposed on the population to support the wars of Edward I were the main trigger to this economic depression. This situation was exacerbated by the great European famine of 1315–16.[2] In Ireland, too, the financial pressures caused by Edward's wars were acutely felt and the exploitation of the colony not only led to economic difficulties, but also affected society and undoubtedly played a part in the escalating crime rates.[3] While the rest of Western Europe recovered from this recession to varying degrees during the 1330s and 1340s, Ireland does not seem to have experienced a similar resurgence and this was mainly because of the warfare that was becoming increasingly endemic from the time of the Bruce invasion.[4] In Dublin, the two outer royal manors of Saggart and Newcastle Lyons were particularly vulnerable to the threat of war from the Irish.

The importance of the royal manors in the defence of the city of Dublin and its environs was recognized as early as the third quarter of the thirteenth century. Much of the land in the hinterland of the city not taken into royal hands was held by the church. Aside from these ecclesiastical lands and the four royal manors, the rest of the land around the city was formed into small knights' fees. Those granted fees on the royal demesne were expected to see to the defence of

---

1 For an overview of conditions in Ireland, see Lydon, 'The years of crisis', pp 179–204. 2 Prestwich, *Plantagenet England*, p. 439. 3 Lydon, 'The years of crisis', pp 195–6. 4 Maria Kelly, *A history of the Black Death in Ireland* (Stroud, 2004), p. 95.

the city at its heart. The crown also expected tenants holding lands on the four royal manors, particularly the strategically located manors of Saggart and Newcastle Lyons, to play a part in the defence of the area. Even though the importance of the royal manors as defensive outposts was recognized almost from their inception, it was in the late medieval period that their function as a buffer zone became vital for the security of the rest of the county, as well as the city. This responsibility of protecting the surrounding area put tremendous pressure on the tenants of the royal manors, and this is demonstrated clearly in the sources through the debts that began to mount up from the end of the thirteenth century.

The crisis that ensued in the fourteenth century is made evident in the spiralling arrears owed by the tenants on the royal manors. Debts began to accumulate initially on the two outer manors, which were more exposed to raids from the Irish in the mountains. In 1278–9, the royal manor of Saggart, the land closest to the march, was in debt to the sum of £1,005 8s. 6d.[5] This debt had been accumulating for the previous seven years, which indicates that the manor had started to run into difficulties at the beginning of this decade. It was at precisely this time that Roger Owen described his lands in Saggart as being next to the land of war. The unsettled conditions of the colony in this period had as much to do with the discord between various English magnates, as raids from the Irish. Moreover, a serious famine at this time may have been the spark that led to mounting debts on this manor. There was a recovery in the 1280s, when the tenants succeeded in reducing their debts. In 1283–4, the debt stood at £702 11½d.[6] This recovery, however, was short-lived, and by 1301–2 they owed £1,162 7s. 10¾d.[7] Over the next few years, the debts of this manor continued to mount, reaching a high watermark in 1305, when the tenants owed the staggering sum of £1,175 13s. 8¾d.[8] In 1313–14, this large debt is no longer recorded in the pipe rolls, and there is simply a reference made to very large arrears.[9] The assumption here surely must be that the administration had long given up any hope that this debt would ever be paid.

Though the royal manor of Newcastle Lyons also accumulated large debts, it was usually able to clear them, unlike Saggart. These debts appear to have started to mount up at an earlier date on this manor, because in 1266 the tenants owed £598 1s. 8d.[10] In 1279–80, they owed £883 14s., which constituted the accumulated debts of the previous six years.[11] The situation here was similar to Saggart, where the tenants were unable to pay any of their rent for most of this decade. Even so, the tenants of Newcastle managed swiftly to pay off this large sum, and by 1281–2, they owed the tiny sum of 4s. ½d. in arrears.[12] Though the amounts owed rose again throughout the rest of the century, the sums of money involved were never at the same level as the debts owed on the manor of

5 *RDKPRI*, 36, p. 42.   6 Ibid., p. 77.   7 *RDKPRI*, 38, p. 68.   8 Ibid., pp 84, 94. 9 *RDKPRI*, 39, p. 50.   10 *RDKPRI*, 35, p. 46.   11 *RDKPRI*, 36, p. 50.   12 Ibid., p. 66.

Saggart.[13] In 1301–2, the tenants of Newcastle Lyons owed £979 12s. 10¾d., but they were able to pay off £523 11s. 7d.[14] Their debts stayed around the £500 mark in 1304–5 and 1312–13.[15] In 1314–15, just before the great European famine hit, they had managed to reduce these fees to £364 10s. 11d.[16] This drop in the amount of arrears owed may be no more than a decision not to record these large unpaid debts, as had been done on the manor of Saggart. The amount outstanding recorded in the following decade is not large, however, suggesting that the situation on the manor of Newcastle Lyons had not deteriorated to the same extent as that on the manor of Saggart.[17]

The two manors furthest from the mountains and more securely within the land of peace fared better, and their debts did not spiral to the same extent. Part of the explanation is that they were smaller manors and would not have been expected to generate the same amount of income in any case. In 1275–6, when the two outer manors were already in serious financial difficulties, the manor of Esker owed only £5 10s. 6d. to the exchequer.[18] Three years later, the manor was £33 12s. 6d. in arrears, but this sum was quickly paid off and arrears did not accumulate in the 1280s.[19] The manor, however, was in difficulties in the 1290s, and by 1301–2 its tenants were in debt to the sum of £168 for twelve years arrears, as well as owing £14 5s. rent for that year. They succeeded in paying off all but £30 7s. 6d. of the sum owed. This was the largest amount of arrears owed by the tenants of Esker recorded in the pipe rolls. The situation in Crumlin was more similar to Esker than the other royal manors. Its proximity to the city of Dublin meant that it was much more secure than any of the other royal manors and it was probably easier to retain tenants here than on the manors near the mountains, which were much more vulnerable to raids. At the turn of the fourteenth century, when Saggart and Newcastle Lyons were in debt to the tune of hundreds of pounds, Crumlin owed the relatively small sum of £66 17s. 2¾d.[20]

THE DEFENCE OF THE ROYAL MANORS

The strategic importance of the royal manors

The royal manors of Newcastle Lyons and Saggart lay particularly close to the mountains, and attacks on both these manors from the thirteenth century onwards were a localized expression of the deteriorating conditions of the colony at large. By 1272, Saggart was beside the marches, and, as previously noted, Roger Owen described his lands here as being near the land of war.[21] A

---

13 Ibid., p. 77; *RDKPRI*, 37, p. 31. 14 *RDKPRI*, 38, p. 69. 15 Ibid., p. 94; *RDKPRI*, 39, p. 37. 16 *RDKPRI*, 39, p. 56. 17 *RDKPRI*, 42, pp 32–4, 52; *RDKPRI*, 43, p. 30. 18 *RDKPRI*, 36, p. 30. 19 Ibid., pp 42, 66, 77; *RDKPRI*, 37, pp 26, 32. 20 *RDKPRI*, 38, p. 68. 21 *CDI*, *1252–84*, §930.

key reason for maintaining and retaining the royal manors in this frontier zone was to aid in the defence of the city and surrounding county. Together with the archiepiscopal manors of Rathcoole and Tallaght, the royal manors of Saggart and Newcastle Lyons formed part of the defensive barrier between the mountains and the rest of Dublin. The royal manors of Esker and Crumlin were less important strategically, but the profits of these manors were sometimes used to aid in the defence of the region. In 1430, the revenues of all four royal manors were used to help defend this area from attacks being made on it by both the king's Irish enemies and English rebels.[22] The importance of these outlying manors was further demonstrated in 1470, when Saggart was described as being one of the 'keys' to Dublin.[23]

Petitions

Certainly, the petitions sent to the king from the tenants on the royal manors reflect these worsening conditions. One of the earliest was dated by Sayles to 1274–85 and originates from the manor of Saggart.[24] Significantly, both the Irish and the English tenants on this royal manor were included among the petitioners and they complained of being greatly impoverished due to attacks by thieves and malefactors. In fact, these attacks had proved so catastrophic that the tenants were driven out of their homes. They were so calamitous that some tenants moved away permanently and at least thirteen carucates lay uncultivated. The petition does not give the ethnicity of these attackers, though it is likely that they were the Irish in the nearby mountains. A serious famine occurred in Ireland in the early 1270s, and the deteriorating conditions experienced by the Irish dwelling in the economically disadvantaged mountainous region may have been the motivation behind the raids on Saggart.[25] The royal tenants complained of family members being killed, as well as the destruction of their homes and property, and emphasized that that this was because of their proximity to the mountains. Concerning the escalating attacks on the Irish, they were on the frontline. It was at this time that Roger Owen, the king's sergeant, petitioned for an exchange of his land in Newcastle Lyons – in the land of peace – for land in Saggart, which was even then adjacent to the land of war.[26] It is not made clear why Owen would want to exchange lands in a relatively secure area for lands in Saggart, but the exchange may have involved him ending up with a larger portion of land. It could be argued that this would have cost the crown nothing, because a large area of this manor was laying waste anyway, and there were, according to the petition, thirteen carucates of land available here. In another petition from this manor, dating to around the same time, the tenants complained of one particular raid by the Irish, audaciously carried out during

22 D'Alton, *History of County Dublin*, p. 650.   23 *Stat. Ire., 1–12 Edw. IV*, p. 665.   24 TNA, SC 8/197/9811; *Affairs Ire.*, §41.   25 James Lydon, 'A land of war' in *NHI*, ii, p. 257. 26 *Admin. Ire.*, p. 230.

daylight hours, which resulted in the deaths of forty men.[27] Though conditions were to deteriorate further, it was certainly the case that, by the end of the thirteenth century, the raids carried out by the Irish were already seriously affecting the lives of the tenants on the royal manors.

The Book of Howth records that the O'Tooles and O'Byrnes attacked the settlements of Saggart and Rathcoole on 26 June 1311.[28] Since the raid was so early in the year, the motive was obviously not to steal their harvest. Nevertheless, the tenants were concerned that the Irish would return after the harvest, because an expedition was organized at this time to attack and drive the Irish out of Glenmalure, where they maintained a base from where they could attack Dublin. Both the Great Famine of 1315–18 and the Bruce Invasion, which occurred at the same time, exacerbated the concern experienced by the tenants on the royal manors. These new problems resulted in further petitions being sent to the king, seeking relief from rent and aid against these attacks. One difference between these and previous petitions was that the blame for these attacks was now being laid with the Scots, as well as the Irish in the mountains. One petition that originated from the poor tenants of the demesne lands of Saggart and Leixlip cannot be dated with any degree of certainty, but it may have been issued between 1327 and 1341, when the manor of Leixlip, which had previously been leased to the prior of Kilmainham, was in royal hands.[29] It was not the only occasion on which tenants from two different royal manors had jointly sent a petition to the king; for example, in around 1317, the tenants of Newcastle Lyons and Saggart complained that the sheriffs of Co. Dublin were taking fees in their courts.[30] In the petition emanating from Saggart and Leixlip, the tenants requested that their rent arrears be remitted on account of their great poverty. Their lands were waste from war, and they had been robbed by both English and Irish felons. The wars referred to may have been the Bruce invasion. Edward and Robert Bruce passed through Leixlip in the spring of 1317 and spent four days burning and looting the settlement. It may have been this episode that was the motivation behind sending the petition. Certainly, one royal tenant suffered at the hands of the Bruces. William Holebourn, a clerk, petitioned for remission on the rent he owed for his land on the royal manor of Esker because he had been captured, imprisoned and robbed by the Scots.[31]

The Scottish threat

The tenants of Newcastle Lyons also blamed the Scots for attacking their manor, and sent a petition requesting that they be pardoned their rent.[32] It was probably sent shortly after the Bruce invasion, when the impact of their visit was still

27 TNA SC 1/20/200. 28 *CCM, 1515–74*, 5 [Book of Howth], p. 159. 29 TNA SC 8/118/5882; Robin Frame, 'English policies and Anglo-Irish attitudes in the crisis of 1341–2' in idem, *Ireland and Britain* (1998), pp 116–23. 30 TNA SC 8/131/6509. 31 TNA SC 8/83/4116; *Affairs Ire.*, §134. 32 TNA SC 8/86/4296; *Calendar of documents relating to*

being felt. Another petition, sent by the tenants of the same royal manor in the 1330s, was still blaming the Scots for their impoverishment.[33] While the idea that the manor had not yet recovered from the Scottish invasion fifteen or more years after the fact appears somewhat implausible, the petition does state that the tenants owed £200, which may have been arrears of rent that had accumulated since that time. The crown at least partially accepted the merits of their petition, and they were pardoned £100 of their rent. Yet the real and constant threat with which the royal tenants had to contend lived permanently on their own doorstep. In 1332, the O'Tooles attacked and burned Newcastle Lyons and the petition may have been sent as a direct result of this raid.[34] The O'Tooles and the O'Byrnes had taken advantage of the panic created by the Scottish invasion by embarking on a campaign of attacks around Dublin. They attacked the royal manors of Bray and Newcastle McKynegan, but the king's lands on the other side of the Dublin Mountains were not spared some of their unwelcome attention.[35] Of course, the raids of the Irish may have had more to do with the famine that had gripped the country at the time of the Bruce invasion rather than the invasion itself.

Another petition from the tenants of Saggart, the original of which does not survive, claimed that their debts dated back to the war of Art Mac Murchadha.[36] This petition was sent to the king in the 1340s, but MacMurrough had been murdered in 1282.[37] It is remarkable that the tenants still had a memory of him sixty years after his death, but their contention that their debts began to accumulate at about that time is not entirely off base. Their debts began to mount up in the 1290s, just a decade after MacMurrough's murder, though the problem did not become chronic until the early years of the following century. While these debts cannot be directly related to MacMurrough's raids more than half a century earlier, they may have mistakenly associated this traumatic period as the beginning of their financial woes. Moreover, they were well aware of the MacMurroughs, and Art's son Domhnall – who did not die until 1339 – achieved a role of great prominence among the Irish of Leinster and proved to be a thorn in the side to the English of the area.[38]

Scotland, 1307–1357 (London, 1888), p. 586.   **33** TNA SC 8/118/5888; *CPR, 1330–4*, p. 551. **34** *CCM, 1515–74*, 5 [Book of Howth], p. 159.   **35** Duffy, 'The Bruce invasion of Ireland', pp 31–2, 36.   **36** *RDKPRI*, 53, p. 22.   **37** For a detailed account of the murder of Art Mac Murchadha, see Robin Frame, 'The justiciar and the murder of the MacMurroughs in 1282' in idem, *Ireland and Britain* (1998), pp 241–7.   **38** Emmet O'Byrne, *War, politics and the Irish of Leinster, 1156–1606* (Dublin, 2003), pp 89–94.

THE BLACK DEATH AND SUBSEQUENT PLAGUES

The devastation caused by famine and raids was exacerbated by the arrival of the Black Death in Ireland in 1348. It had entered Europe through Messina in September 1347 and, in less than a year, it had reached the ports of Ireland, bringing desolation in its wake.[39] The population of the Continent was decimated by this epidemic, even if it is difficult to assess with any degree of certainty what proportion of the populace died. There are widely varying estimates of between 10 and 50 per cent.[40] In England, some sections of society were affected more greatly than others. Among the clergy, the death rate was particularly high and, in the archdeaconry of Stow in Lincolnshire, over 57 per cent died.[41] It is estimated that 30–45 per cent of the general population of England perished in this first visitation of the plague.[42] The manorial court rolls have provided an insight into how the Black Death affected rural society in medieval England and the evidence seems to suggest that there was significant local variation; some manors were completely wiped out, while others got off much more lightly.[43] On the royal manor of Havering in Essex, for example, there is no evidence whatsoever of the shattering effects of the plague and, in an extent taken shortly afterwards, no mention is made of there being any empty, untenanted holdings.[44] Nonetheless, it is extremely unlikely that Havering escaped completely unscathed, considering its close proximity to the city of London.

Just like on Havering, there is very little evidence of how the lives of the tenants on the royal manors of Dublin were affected by the first wave of this pandemic, apart from a petition that no longer survives, but is referred to in a patent letter dating to 1354.[45] The tenants of Newcastle Lyons, Saggart and Crumlin – as well as the tenants of Oughterard and Castlewarden, the royal manors in Co. Kildare – petitioned for relief on the excessive extortions of food made on them by some of the king's ministers. They complained that the recent pestilence, as well as the enforced appropriation of their goods had left them impoverished. Though there was a tendency for petitioners to exaggerate the severity of their situation, the Black Death undoubtedly had catastrophic consequences for the inhabitants of the royal manors. According to Friar John Clyn, the Black Death entered Ireland through Dublin, through the port of either Howth or Dalkey, and devastated the population of the city.[46] It is inconceivable that the tenants living on the nearby royal manors were not affected by its arrival.

---

39 Christine Klapisch-Zuber, 'Plague and family life' in Michael Jones (ed.), *The new Cambridge medieval history*, 6: *c.1300–1415* (Cambridge, 2000), p. 131. 40 George Holmes, *Europe: hierarchy and revolt, 1320–1450* (London, 1975), p. 107. 41 Prestwich, *Plantagenet England*, p. 543. 42 John Hatcher, *Plague, population and the English economy, 1348–1530* (London, 1977), ch. 2. 43 Prestwich, *Plantagenet England*, pp 544–5. 44 McIntosh, *Autonomy and community*, p. 127. 45 *CPR, 1354–8*, 91. 46 Clyn, *Annals of Ireland*, p. 246.

Moreover, their problems did not end there, as there were several recurrences of the plague throughout the rest of the medieval period. In July 1362, the seneschal of demesne, Walter Somery, was ordered to lease land on the royal manors of Crumlin, Newcastle Lyons and Saggart that had been vacated through the most recent visitation of the plague.[47]

Another outbreak of the plague at the end of the fourteenth century resulted in the deaths of sixteen tenants in Colmanstown on the manor of Newcastle Lyons, leaving just three in this township.[48] Even before this devastating recurrence of the plague, Colmanstown appears to have been under-populated. The tenants informed the king's council that, although this grange contained in the region of 3½ carucates, only one carucate and thirty acres was under cultivation at that time. Even though most of the land was waste, the tenants were paying rent on all of it. Their difficulties were exacerbated by attacks from the king's enemies, who burned the settlement and killed the inhabitants. The council agreed that a new extent of the lands would be made so that the occupants would only pay rents on the lands they were actually farming. Undoubtedly, the administration appreciated the challenges faced by the tenants living in this frontier area, and was willing to make compromises to keep them on these lands. The Annals of the Four Masters report that in 1439, almost a century after the first outbreak of the Black Death, the plague raged virulently in Dublin from the beginning of spring to the end of May, and within that time, three thousand people succumbed to it.[49] It is unthinkable, considering the high death rate, that those living on the royal manors did not feel the effects of wave after wave of this epidemic. Indeed, later in the fifteenth century, matters had improved little. In 1479, the reeve and community of Saggart complained that their rent was assessed on 3½ ploughlands of land that they held, even though almost half of this land was waste, in mountain and wilderness. It was agreed that the tenants would be discharged the subsidies, tallages and taxes on this wasteland until such time as other tenants were found to occupy and till it.[50] Clearly, there was difficulty in finding tenants to occupy this outlying manor.

GOVERNMENT RESPONSE TO THE YEARS OF CRISIS

Introduction
Throughout the fourteenth century, the government was perpetually concerned with maintaining an adequate number of tenants on the royal manors. The strategic importance of the royal manors in Dublin was not lost on those inhabiting the city and the rest of the county, particularly as the colony started to contract and disintegrate in the fourteenth century. The other great landowner

47 NAI, RC 8/28, pp 309–10. 48 *PKCI, 1392–3*, pp 138–40. 49 *AFM*, 1439. 50 *Stat. Ire., 12–22 Edw. IV*, p. 721.

in south Dublin in the medieval period was the archbishop of Dublin. In 1460, a statute acknowledged that the archbishops of Dublin had in the past been great defenders and maintainers of the marches, where much of their property lay.[51] The statute went on to say that much of the archbishop's land there had been lost, and not just because of the Irish enemies and English rebels, but also because it had been alienated to others. For example, by this time, the prior of Kilmainham held Shankill but he was not obliged to defend the area, as he rendered no service to the archbishop. Moreover, the archbishop was having problems with his own officials, who were meant to be protecting his lands. Even though Thomas Walshe, the constable of the manor and lordship of Tallaght, was receiving the fees, wages, rewards and land pertaining to his office – amounting to £12 – he was not using this money to defend the area. Instead, he was investing it in land he held in peaceable areas. Clearly, Thomas' actions, though understandable, were damaging to the security of the area.

The crown faced the same problems, and the security of the royal manors – and by extension the rest of Dublin – was dependent on the men appointed to defend it. This problem was addressed exactly a century earlier, when another statute stipulated that the seneschal of the king's demesne lands, as well as lesser officers, had to be appointed on the advice of the chancellor, the treasurer and the council.[52] This would suggest that unsuitable men had been granted these offices in the past. It is likely that the office of seneschal of demesne reverted back to being a sinecure during the fifteenth century. The crown's policy in 1360 of granting this office to military men was not sustained for very long. Therefore, other means had to be found to defend these manors from incursions by the Irish. It is likely that at least some of the military responsibilities, originally belonging to the seneschals, were shifted onto the reeves of the various different manors, or in some cases to the seneschals appointed to individual manors. Additionally, the leading members of the gentry of Co. Dublin were expected to play their part in protecting the marches. The greatest burden was laid on the shoulders of the sheriff, but many of the leading gentry and merchant families in Dublin were also tenants of the king and therefore they had a personal stake in ensuring that these lands would not be subsumed into the land of war.

John Bennett

In the fifteenth century, one of the men responsible for organizing this defence was John Bennett, a merchant who served as mayor of Dublin and constable of its castle towards the end of Henry VI's reign.[53] Subsequently, during Edward IV's reign, he was granted the manor of Ballinteer in south Dublin, and this grant was held by grand serjeanty.[54] Ballinteer was part of the external lands belonging to the royal manor of Saggart. In 1337, Simon de la Sale, Saggart's

51 *Stat. Ire., Hen. VI*, pp 769–73. 52 *Stat. Ire., John–Hen. V*, p. 425. 53 *Stat. Ire., Hen. VI*, p. 729; *CARD*, 1, pp 275, 291. 54 Tenure of grand serjeanty meant that he held the lands in

extern provost, was also responsible for accounting for the rent of this settle-ment.[55] It is possible that Ballinteer had previously been a part of the royal manor of Okelly, which was located in the mountainous area just south of Tallaght and was incorporated into the manor of Saggart when the mountainous manor, vulnerable to attacks from the Irish, was swallowed up into the land of war or was granted out to other men. By the time Bennett was granted lands in Ballinteer, it too was in danger of falling into the hands of the Irish. Indeed, the O'Byrnes and the O'Tooles had already been using it as a base from which to attack the surrounding area. A century earlier, the English tried to drive the O'Tooles out of Glenmalure, but now they were able to establish strongholds much closer to the manors they were raiding. In 1431, both these septs were involved in a devastating raid on Dublin led by Donnchadh Mac Murchadha, where many English were killed and their goods stolen. On this occasion, the English community pursued their attackers, killing some and taking the leader of the O'Tooles prisoner.[56] This episode was out of the norm for Mac Murchadha, who was usually content to keep the peace with the English as long as they were prepared to pay him.[57] Of course, any peace arranged was bound to be volatile, with both sides constantly at odds with one another. Moreover, the payment of black rent to the Irish was financially crippling to the English community. Therefore, other ways and means had to be found to ensure that this area remained under English rule.

In order to maintain control of Ballinteer, Bennett built a tower there, and restored the town.[58] Bennett's mercantile pursuits meant that his chief interests were in the city, but the grant of lands in the marches gave him a stake in protecting this area and seeing to its continued security. As sometime mayor of Dublin,[59] Bennett was one of the city's elite, and he would have had the resources necessary to regenerate this outlying area and, indeed, he did restore Ballinteer to his great cost. Unfortunately, his efforts were ultimately in vain. By 1470, after Bennett's death, Edmund mac Theobald Ó Tuathail was receiving protection money from the inhabitants of Saggart. After they were subsequently compelled by the government to stop paying this money, the O'Tooles laid waste to half of this manor.[60] Clearly, the death of John Bennett had left a vacuum, and with apparently no one energetic or resourceful enough to pick up where he had left off, the Irish had moved back in to the area again to continue their attacks on the locality.

return for some specified service, in this case probably to aid in the defence of the region: *Stat. Ire., 1–12 Edw. IV*, p. 563; *Stat. Ire., 12–22 Edw. IV*, p. 445.   **55** *RDKPRI*, 45, p. 56.   **56** *AFM*, 1431.   **57** Art Cosgrove, 'The emergence of the Pale, 1399–1447' in *NHI*, ii, p. 544.   **58** The source describes Ballinteer as a town.   **59** Hill, 'Mayors and lord mayors', p. 553.   **60** O'Byrne, *Irish of Leinster*, pp 138–9; *Stat. Ire., 1–12 Edw. IV*, p. 665; *Stat. Ire., 12–22 Edw. IV*, p. 445.

Construction of ditches and the establishment of the Pale

Bennett appears to have willingly seen to the defence of his lands on the royal manors, but in most cases, it seems that the government had to step in and compel the local populace to defend the manors skirting the Dublin Mountains. In 1459, the Irish parliament commanded that dykes and ditches were to be made in the marches of Newcastle and Rathdown.[61] It was ordered that one man out of every household in these two baronies, as well as the church crosslands, was to be summoned with a spade, a barrow or a pickaxe annually in order to facilitate this construction. By this time, the problem of raiding by the Irish had become so acute that a physical barrier was created between the land of war and the land of peace. The dyke and ditch system constructed within the barony of Newcastle was a small part of that larger network of defences known as the 'Pale'. The earliest reference to this boundary dates to 1446–7,[62] just a decade before the statute ordering the construction of ditches in south Co. Dublin. By this date, the colony had contracted to such an extent that the two outer royal manors in this study lay at its southernmost edge, with the nearby mountains serving as a natural frontier. The proliferation of tower houses that still dot the landscape is testament to the frontier mentality adopted by the inhabitants of this locality.

In 1471, in reaction to raids on the royal manor of Saggart, labourers from all over Dublin were ordered to go there to enclose it with ditches and fosses.[63] The town of Saggart had been lately burned by the O'Tooles and O'Byrnes and they successfully destroyed the settlement due to it not being properly enclosed. The Commons were concerned by the vulnerability of this strategic location, and declared that the destruction of Saggart would result in the ruin of much of the rest of the county. Therefore, its fortification was a huge operation that involved eighty labourers from Balrothery, with the same number coming from the barony of Coolock and eighty more from the barony of Castleknock. These men were ordered to work for three days on this construction. The fact that labourers were drawn from north Dublin suggests that the government was anxious to re-fortify this area and put the onus of defending it squarely on the shoulders of the county community. Moreover, they also genuinely feared the consequences of it falling to the Irish. Eighty labourers from the barony of Newcastle were also ordered to assist in the building of this enclosure, but they were to work for six days because they had the most to lose from the Irish attacks. Clearly, the burden put on their shoulders was heavier because they lived closer to the land of war. Since much of this barony was within the march, it might have been harder to find sufficient men here to undertake this task. It was the sheriff's responsibility to muster these labourers, and if any of them proved reluctant to help in the

61 *Stat. Ire., Hen. VI*, pp 757–9. 62 Cosgrove, 'The emergence of the Pale', p. 533. 63 *Stat. Ire., 1–12 Edw. IV*, p. 809.

construction they would be fined. The amount of the fine rose from 4*d*. to 8*d*. if they did not turn up a second time, and they were fined 12*d*. if they did not turn up for the third day. This large workforce of over three hundred men was expected to provide its own tools and food, and therefore, though they were concerned about fortifying Saggart, they were not willing to have it as a drain on the administration's finances.

The Irish response

The physical barrier of ditches and tower houses that sprung up from the middle part of the fifteenth century did little to stem the tide of Irish raids. In fact, these raids escalated, and the Irish enemies made deep inroads into the land of peace. The known petitions sent to London from the royal manors in the thirteenth and fourteenth centuries all originated from Newcastle Lyons and Saggart. By the fifteenth century, Crumlin, which was close to the city and had previously been relatively distant from the marches, was now under attack. In 1465, Piers Cruys of Crumlin was taken prisoner by the O'Byrnes and was only released on payment of a large ransom. This impoverished him to such a degree that he was unable to pay the rent for his land in Crumlin or maintain his property here, causing it to become waste.[64] Five years later, much of the barony of Newcastle, where all four royal manors lay, was described as being within the march.[65] In the following year, Thomas Sharpe was excused 40*s*. of the yearly rent of 45*s*. he paid for sixty acres, also on the manor of Crumlin, for twenty years.[66] One of the reasons he was granted this reduction was that his tenants were being oppressed by marchers near the manor. Cruys and Sharpe both had difficulties finding sub-tenants to whom to let their land. Therefore, by this time, Crumlin was experiencing the same sort of problems as the outlying manors of Saggart and Newcastle Lyons concerning finding and maintaining tenants.

John Chevir and the mill of Esker

The scenario was similar on the royal manor of Esker, and one solution implemented by the administration was to offer prospective tenants special incentives to take up land there. On 26 March 1451, John Chevir was granted a lease of the land where the mill had once stood.[67] By the mid-fourteenth century, the water mill there was in ruins and the rent on Chevir's fifty-year lease was reduced for the first twenty years on the condition that he would rebuild the mill. The mill was usually a much sought-after grant because of the revenues it could generate. The grange of Milltown Regis on the royal manor of Newcastle Lyons was considered valuable because the mills of the manor were situated there. The seneschal of demesne often held this tenement and this potentially profitable appurtenance might have been one of the perks of this office. Richard, duke of

64 Ibid., pp 321–3.   65 Ibid., pp 667–9.   66 Ibid., pp 761–3.   67 Ibid., pp 93–7.

York, revoked the grant of the mill in Esker to Chevir in 1460, during his term as lord lieutenant. As a consequence of this confiscation, the mill once again went out of operation. Though the millstones remained, both the inner and the outer wheels of the watermill were broken. After this destruction, the mill was rendered of no value. In 1463, Edward IV re-granted the mill to Chevir on the same terms. It is not known how or why the mill was destroyed in the interim. It was out of Chevir's hands for only three years, and thus it seems unlikely that it would have deteriorated simply through abandonment. The mill may have been destroyed on purpose, though there is no evidence that the Irish were responsible, because in spite of occasional attacks – and their proximity to the march – both Crumlin and Esker were still firmly within the land of peace. This case highlights once again that the tenants on the royal manors were not only at the mercy of the Irish and criminal elements within their own community, but they also had to suffer the vagaries of the crown and its administrators.

Coyne and livery and the marcher lineages

One onerous burden put on the shoulders of the tenants of the royal manor of Newcastle Lyons was the imposition of coyne and livery. This was essentially a Gaelic Irish custom that had been adapted by the English for quartering armies within a community, and putting the responsibility of feeding and maintaining this army onto its inhabitants.[68] In 1475, the tenants on this manor complained of being oppressed by this enforced maintenance of men and horses.[69] The administration's response to their complaint is evidence that they were anxious to accommodate them. They were aware that these burdens could force tenants to abandon their holdings and they set about remedying the situation. The parliament decreed that the inhabitants would from this time forth be free of coyne and livery. Moreover, if anyone tried to billet their troops on the manor, the tenants were allowed to resist them and drive them out. As a further recognition of the tenants' importance to the security of the locality, purveyors could not levy their goods without their permission. Still, the administration expected something back, and these concessions were granted on two conditions: firstly, that the tenants maintained their ditches, and, secondly, that the king's purveyor would always have first option to buy any produce they had for sale.

The situation in Saggart and Newcastle Lyons continued to be tumultuous, not only because of the Irish, but also because of the English marcher lineages that had established themselves in south Dublin. The Harolds were one of these lineages, and their main base was in the vicinity of Kilgobbin, just south of Dundrum.[70] Yet, their influence expanded beyond this area. The swathe of land

---

68 Cosgrove, 'The emergence of the Pale', pp 541–2. 69 *Stat. Ire., 12–22 Edw. IV*, p. 301. 70 For an investigation of the Harolds and the other marcher lineages who inhabited south Dublin, see Christopher Maginn, 'English marcher lineages in south Dublin in the later Middle Ages', *IHS*, 34 (2004), 113–36.

that extended from Saggart to Kilmashogue was described in 1470 as Harold's Country. These extended family lineages often interacted with the Irish, and against the English, in a manner that was detrimental to the security of the locality. They were not always interested in accommodating the Dublin administration, which meant that it was difficult to collect subsidies granted by parliament. There was a fear that anyone sent in to collect taxes would be taken prisoner by the Harolds and delivered up to the Irish. The solution was to discharge those appointed from collecting subsidies in the rest of the barony of Newcastle, and appoint two collectors especially to collect subsidies within this area.[71] The marcher lineages would prove a double-edged sword, for while they could be an added headache for the English in Dublin, their presence there also meant that the Irish were contained within the march and were less likely to send raids into the land of peace.[72]

Occasionally, the tenants themselves could be the cause of endangering the security of the area. In 1475, parliament complained that the dyke that labourers from the four baronies of Castleknock, Balrothery, Coolock and Newcastle had constructed was being destroyed, and the locals, as well as the Irish and the king's English enemies, were responsible for this destruction.[73] This damage was not malicious on their part, but their use of the dyke as a roadway – as well as cutting into it for ease of passage – was also making it easier for potential raiders to gain access. The dyke had to be repaired, and, as in 1471, the labour and costs for this were the responsibility of the county community of Dublin. An act of parliament was passed to the effect that, if, in the future, this ditch should be breached again, the guilty party would be fined 20s. for its damage. Moreover, if the domestic animals of the locals broke the dyke through rooting and grazing, they were to be forfeited and sold, and the revenues received would be used to repair the dyke. Undoubtedly, the government took this matter seriously, because it was ordered that each quarter of the year the justices of the peace would hold an inquisition to check that the dykes had not been broken. Furthermore, the justices had the authority to apprehend those found guilty of destroying the fortification and bring them to Dublin Castle, where they would remain until they paid the fine.

CONCLUSION

By the late fifteenth century, both Newcastle Lyons and Saggart straddled the Pale boundary. The concentration of tower houses known to have existed in this area in the late medieval period is testament to the fact that this was indeed a

---

71 *Stat. Ire.*, *1–12 Edw. IV*, pp 667–9.   72 Maginn, 'Marcher lineages', 132.   73 *Stat. Ire.*, *12–22 Edw. IV*, pp 443–5.

frontier zone. The statutes of the Irish parliament confirm that the onus of defending these manors rested squarely on the shoulders of the tenants living there and the county community at large. The fact that even the inhabitants of north Co. Dublin were expected to help their neighbours in south Dublin with the construction and funding of these defences acknowledges the importance of these manors to the general security of the whole county. The safeguarding of these manors was important not only for local security, but also to ensure that the revenues from these manors continued to flow into the exchequer to make sure that the payments of annuities to local officials and royal favourites would continue. Though there is evidence that the royal manors spiralled into debt in the late thirteenth and early fourteenth centuries, there is not much proof that annuities were not paid. One example can be found in the late fourteenth century, when Reginald Lovel was owed £11 of an annuity of 1s. a day from the manor of Esker.[74] It is likely that the seneschals and reeves of the manors ensured that this money was usually paid.

The petitions originating from these manors during the tumultuous fourteenth century suggest that life there could be hard, and that the threat of raids from the nearby mountains was all too real. Nevertheless, while taking all this into account, there is a possibility that this aspect of the royal manors as strategic strongholds always under threat of attack has been overstated. This picture of a locality under constant pressure of attack has been built upon the evidence of a handful of petitions and parliamentary statutes. Nonetheless, these same records also reveal proof of a hardy population determined not to be pushed off its land. Though there may have been many petitions that did not survive, it is unlikely that the tenants were complaining to the king on a constant basis about raids from the mountains. Most that do survive appear to coincide with periods of crisis for the colony at large. Moreover, if the Irish were constantly raiding these manors, it would have been impossible to keep tenants there. In fact, the opposite is true – at least in regard to the safer manors of Esker and Crumlin – because throughout the medieval period, some of the leading county families and merchants from the nearby city became tenants there. What is more, this trend tended to escalate rather than slow down during the difficult fourteenth century, and by the late sixteenth century, the evidence from the court rolls of Esker and Crumlin confirms that some of the leading members of both the city and the county community considered it desirable to hold lands on the royal manors. Furthermore, some of the most important magnates in the colony had interests on the royal manors too. In 1528, Gerald Fitzgerald, ninth earl of Kildare, held four messuages and twenty-six acres in Newcastle Lyons; he also held a hundred acres and a castle in Athgoe, a grange on the same manor, and he had another castle in Crumlin, along with one messuage and a hundred acres.[75]

74 TNA, E101/246/5, §44. 75 *CICD*, p. 43.

In 1593, there was land in Crumlin called 'Earl's ground', and this is likely to have been the property previously belonging to Gerald Fitzgerald.[76] It is possible that this land in Crumlin is the 122 acres that was part of the king's original royal demesne. Gerald's immediate forebears, the seventh and eighth earls of Kildare, made a conscious effort to both strengthen and consolidate their power in Kildare and expand their influence into south Dublin and in the process, they brought order to the marchlands, including the outer royal manors.[77] Obviously, the construction of castles in Athgoe and Crumlin helped to solidify their control of the locality.

Clearly, there were advantages in holding lands there that belie the petitions. Rents remained low, even in the late sixteenth century, and this must have been an incentive to stay. People also had more personal and emotional reasons not to give up and move away – these manors were their homes. They invested in their property; the large number of tower houses that still exist or are known to have existed is evidence of this. In the mid-seventeenth century, the Civil Survey recorded seven castles in Newcastle Lyons alone, and this number did not include castles on some of the other granges, but merely those within the main settlement, close to the church.[78] Colmanstown, Milltown and Athgoe also had tower houses and, though an inscribed stone at Athgoe Castle dates it to 1579, the building is much older and it is likely to have been the same one that belonged to Gerald Fitzgerald.[79] As well as the tower houses, there is evidence that walls enclosed some of the settlements on the royal manors during the medieval period. The manors of Saggart and Crumlin may have had defensive walls, for example.[80] Certainly, locals built the ditches around the settlement at Saggart. The order to summon labourers from north Dublin to lend a hand in the construction of these ditches was probably an unusual one. The tenants may have had some help in the initial construction of the ditches, but they were expected to maintain these barriers themselves. Clearly, if they were willing to invest in walls and other defensive measures, there were advantages to living there.

76 Curtis, 'Court book' (vol. 59), 138–9. 77 Maginn, 'Marcher lineages', 132–3. 78 R.C. Simington (ed.), *The civil survey, AD1654–6* (10 vols, Dublin, 1931–61), vii, pp 304–5. 79 Tadhg O'Keeffe, 'Medieval architecture and the village of Newcastle Lyons' in O'Sullivan (ed.), *Newcastle Lyons*, p. 60. 80 Avril Thomas, *The walled towns of Ireland* (2 vols, Dublin, 1992), 1, p. 169; 2, pp 225, 243.

Conclusion

In the aftermath of the English invasion, the lands around Dublin were transformed by the introduction of the manor. The archbishop of Dublin already owned a significant amount of property in this locality, and it would appear that an agricultural system akin to the manorial system was already in place. Nonetheless, even though pre-existing land divisions may not have changed radically, the way in which the lands were administered was transformed beyond all recognition. The introduction of the manor brought with it a new order. This institution possessed a complex hierarchical organization, unlike anything that had been seen in the locality before, and it was a major factor in the transformation of society there. The manor, which was introduced to Ireland in the aftermath of the English invasion, was arguably the most important factor in dictating how the rural community in the conquered areas developed.

Crown intervention in the locality dictated to a large degree how society developed there. Those who had travelled over in the entourages of clerics and royal officials colonized the royal manors. There is evidence that many of those who came over and later held lands on the royal manors originated from Bristol and its broader provincial hinterland. This is unsurprising, considering this city's close ties to Dublin. The Russell family of Crumlin can probably be traced back to a cleric who arrived shortly after the invasion, and their ties to Worcester endured for at least another century. The clerics that provided the backbone to the administration of the new colony also played a significant role in its colonization. Ties of service and shared experience that bound this clerical class together may have meant that a sense of kinship already existed within this group when they came over to assist in the administration of the colony. The merchant class also played an important role in the colonization process, and many were early beneficiaries of royal patronage. Servants and extended families accompanied those who settled here and within this group, too, there could have been a pre-existing communal bond. Gillespie noted that a significant number of tenants with land on the royal manors in the early modern period came from the merchant community.[1] This was not an innovation. In fact, this process began almost as soon as the English king became lord of Ireland. The city was dependant on its hinterland for resources, but the merchants did not just affect the area on an economic level, they were also part of the social fabric of the locality.

1 Gillespie, 'Small worlds', p. 202.

Families like the Owens, who were once part of the city's elite, became leading members of the county community and played a vital part in the defence of the royal manors and their environs in the later medieval period.

Though the influx of new settlers had played a significant part in shaping post-invasion society in south Dublin, a considerable proportion of the populace living there were the original Gaelic Irish inhabitants. Dublin was more heavily settled with English colonists than most other areas of Ireland, but it is likely that the majority of tenants living on the royal manors – particularly the outer manors of Newcastle Lyons and Saggart – were native Irish. According to Ball, most of the tenants living on the manor of Lucan were betaghs, and it is likely that the population of the royal manors was largely composed of this putatively servile Irish class too.[2] This category of tenant may have shared many similarities with villeins in England, and most of them probably belonged on a relatively low rung of the manorial ladder.[3] Like their English counterparts, their daily lives were controlled by the wealthier tenants, who usually held the various offices associated with the manor and also served as jurors.[4] Unfortunately, less is known about the Irish compared to their English counterparts, because they do not appear in the administrative records in anything like the same frequency. Since they were mostly members of the peasantry, they are mostly invisible in the sources. They do appear with some frequency in the justiciary rolls, however, where they mostly feature as the victims of criminal activity. Not all of the Irish living on the royal manors belonged to this betagh class, as some of them purchased English law, indicating their willingness to be a part of the new social order and their desire to embrace an English identity, with the legal rights that entailed.

The evidence would suggest that, as the medieval period progressed, the tenants living on the four royal manors in this study – both English and Irish – increasingly identified themselves as a distinct community within the larger county community of Dublin. This sense of solidarity was helped in no small part by the privileges they enjoyed as holders of royal lands. When speaking of the sixteenth-century occupants of Crumlin and Esker, Curtis believed that the tenants here were a community that had 'some responsibilities but many profits and privileges in common and holding fertile pieces of land on easy terms'.[5] These advantageous conditions had not sprung up suddenly in the early modern period; they were a result of several centuries of tenants first establishing and then maintaining their tenurial rights. Their status as tenants of the ancient demesne would have made them a particularly advantaged group within this county society, and it was not something they would relinquish willingly. At least three (and probably four) of these manors were part of the king's ancient

2 Ball, *Dublin*, 4, p. 36.   3 It is unlikely that the betaghs were originally unfree tenants, but they increasingly became associated with this form of tenure.   4 Hilton, *Medieval society*, p. 152. 5 Curtis, 'Court book' (vol. 60), 147.

demesne, and they appear to be the only manors belonging to the ancient demesne that have been identified in Ireland.[6] The tenants of ancient demesne lands in England were an exceptionally privileged group, and the same could be said of their counterparts in Dublin. The benefits offered to Englishmen to come over and settle in Ireland – and perhaps to the Irish to induce them to remain on these lands – helped shape the identity of those living on the royal manors. Their position as king's tenants must have fostered a communal spirit, if for no other reason than to protect the privileges that came with this status.

Their status as king's tenants gave some of them access to patronage, and the constant stream of officials coming from England to take up administrative posts in Dublin created a bond between core and periphery. Those whose salaries were supplemented by revenues from the royal manors often used locals as their attorneys when they travelled back and forth from England. Many of those who received pensions and annuities but who may never have come to Ireland undoubtedly nominated attorneys in the locality to ensure they would continue to enjoy these revenues. The evidence suggests that many of these attorneys were substantial tenants on the royal manors. Some of them may even have travelled to England on their client's business. For example, in 1375–6, Robert Kissok of Esker and John Beg of Saggart served as attorney for Reginald Lovel, an English courtier. Both Kissok and Beg must have proved ineffectual as attorneys, however, because in 1377 Lovel was owed over £11.[7] Nonetheless, this constant interaction between London and Dublin also created another layer of community by defining the 'Englishness' of the colonists living here. During the fourteenth century, they never lost their sense of identity. They remained part of that larger community that enveloped both kingdoms.

The officials who came over from England to serve in the Irish administration must have established ties with the locality. In the fifteenth century, Giles Thorndon, the treasurer of Ireland, was granted £30 per year from the manor of Crumlin.[8] He became constable of Dublin Castle and keeper of the castles of Drogheda and Wicklow. Thorndon could have used these grants to reward followers who came over with him, or he may have granted these posts to locals and established a network of loyalties in Dublin.[9] Involvement in government at all levels helped to shape the identity of the king's tenants, and was as vital as the ownership of land in the development of a gentry class here. It is hardly an exaggeration to say that the royal manors became 'a nursery of royal administration and justice' and the tenants there filled positions in both local and central government.[10] The level of office held by an individual can inform us as to their

6 It is probable, however, that the city of Dublin and the other royal cities here were considered to be part of the Irish demesne in the medieval period, because they were listed as being so in the late fifteenth century, as was the royal manor of Esker: TNA, SP 46/183/41. 7 *CIRCLE*, PR 49 Edw. III, §156; TNA, E101/246/5, §44. 8 *CPR, 1436–41*, p. 361. 9 Ibid., pp 197, 240. 10 Wolffe, *Royal demesne*, p. 30.

place in the social hierarchy of manor, county and colony. The fact that two generations of the Crumlin/Russell family were involved in county administration informs us that they were members of the gentry. The Beg family of Esker, on the other hand, only held office at manorial level and therefore were more likely to be prosperous peasants. Members of both these families and their fellow tenants on the royal manors were all beneficiaries of royal patronage, albeit in some cases on a local level. While their landholdings and the privileges associated with being a royal tenant defined them, the holding of royal office also shaped their identity and made them leaders in their own communities.

In England, one of the chief benefits of residing on the ancient demesne was that rents were low, and the same was true of the four royal manors in Ireland.[11] Even as late as the mid-sixteenth century, the tenants of Crumlin were paying just 9*d.* an acre for their holding, while the tenants of Esker paid the modest sum of 7*d.* for each acre. Richard Stanihurst presented an interesting theory as to why the tenants of Crumlin were paying marginally more for their lands. He claimed that it was in punishment for murdering their seneschal. This account of the tenants dispatching the seneschal in their own manor court could be considered rather grisly proof that they functioned as a community, yet there is no actual evidence that it ever happened. Without a date or contemporaneous source, it is impossible to verify it.[12] In fact, the rent paid by the tenants at this time was substantially reduced from the sum they were paying three hundred years earlier: at the end of the thirteenth century, the tenants were paying a rent of 15*d.* on each acre of land.[13]

Nevertheless, even if there is little substance to Stanihurst's story, there is evidence that the tenants were energetic when it came to maintaining their rights, and their actions were similar to those of communities living on royal manors in England. For example, in the thirteenth century, the abbot of Halesowen in Worcestershire, in his capacity as lord of the manor, took away some the rights of the tenants of Halesowen. Consequently, the community there took the abbot to court and tried to argue that the manor was part of the ancient demesne. Yet, even though it was once a royal manor, it was not one at the time the Domesday Book was compiled, and therefore was not part of the ancient demesne. Therefore, the case went largely in the abbot's favour.[14] Even though they failed, the process of going to court to fight their case would have played a significant part in developing a sense of solidarity and communal spirit between the tenants of this manor. The same is of course true of the royal manors of Dublin. In the 1290s, when the crown decided to grant the demesne lands of Crumlin to Henry Compton, the tenants there put up a strong resistance. Moreover, because they could prove that the manor of Crumlin was

---

11 Hilton, *Medieval society*, p. 142.   12 Gillespie, 'Small worlds', p. 200.   13 *CDI, 1285–92*, §855.   14 Hilton, *Medieval society*, pp 159–61.

ancient demesne, they did eventually win their case against Compton. Though his grant of this property was only going to inconvenience one tenant – Thomas Crumlin – it appears that the entire community of not only Crumlin, but also Newcastle Lyons and Saggart, stood up against the crown. By protecting their neighbour's rights, they were protecting their own rights and this undoubtedly created a sense of solidarity among the tenants. Even when it was no longer of any real benefit to the crown, except as an instrument of patronage, the legal privileges associated with being a royal tenant remained, because the inhabitants of these lands now had the weight of custom behind them and they would not willingly allow these rights to be eroded away.

The same inquisition from 1290–1 established that the men of Crumlin had held the king's demesne lands there for the yearly farm of £20 from at least 1253–4. The tenants themselves claimed that they had held this farm since the time of King John.[15] Moreover, the evidence from the sixteenth century manorial court book of Crumlin establishes that this manor was still in the hands of its tenants three hundred years later. The manor of Esker was also in the hands of its tenants at the end of the sixteenth century.[16] Once this custom of farming the land directly to its occupants had been established, it proved impossible to change these tenurial conditions. Though the tenants resisted any change to the status quo, it should not be assumed that the crown was constantly struggling with these communities to remove their privileges. After failing in its attempt to grant the demesne lands of Crumlin to Henry Compton, the crown seemed content to leave the manor in the hands of its occupants. Though local officials were often granted these manors throughout the rest of the medieval period, they were obviously granted the revenues derived from the farm of the manor, not the land itself. In England, it was not unusual for the small tenants to hold the farm of a royal manor and, in fact, it may even be the case that the crown preferred leaving the farm in their hands.[17]

The reason that tenants wanted to hold the farm was that it gave them a greater degree of independence from external forces, particularly the king and his officials.[18] The act of farming out the manors to their tenants offered the opportunity of 'communal action and responsibility'.[19] If there is any truth to the story of the tenants of Crumlin assassinating the seneschal of the royal demesne, they may have done so because he was overstepping his authority, at least as far as they were concerned. In the thirteenth century, the tenants of Crumlin also held the pleas and perquisites of their own manor court, which would have probably resulted in even less interference from external authority. This meant that the inhabitants of Crumlin – and probably the other three royal manors in this study – were responsible for governing themselves. By holding

15 *CDI, 1285–92*, §855. 16 Curtis, 'Court book' (vol. 60), 143–4. 17 Hoyt, *Royal demesne*, p. 160. 18 Hilton, *Medieval society*, p. 219. 19 Hoyt, *Royal demesne*, p. 138.

the farm of the manor and being responsible for the administration of the manor court, the tenants must have exercised considerable autonomy.

The manorial court was the place where the community could reprimand and fine petty criminals and other public nuisances. Moreover, the leading tenants could use it in other ways as a means of controlling the rest of the populace of the manor. The court book of Esker and Crumlin may be an early modern source, but the operation of the manor court had undoubtedly changed little over the previous centuries. Therefore, it is useful in illuminating how this institution helped promote a sense of community in an earlier period too. All tenants owed suit of court and were expected to attend the court and participate in its operation. Jurors were elected by the rest of the tenants, as were the manorial officials. Aside from the reeve, constables, serjeants and appraisers were elected each year.[20] Other officials on the royal manor at the end of the sixteenth century included the keeper of the common and a common herdsman.[21] These offices, or ones similar to them, undoubtedly existed in previous centuries too, indicating that the entire community, through their courts, regulated employment on the manors.

The manor court affected all aspects of day-to-day life. Ordinances were issued by the manorial court to ensure, for example, that watercourses were not stopped and that common lands were not overgrazed. It would have been impossible for the court to enforce these ordinances without the general consent of the entire community. The court was also a place where disagreements could be resolved and tenants of the manor arbitrated many cases. The courts could also be used to deal with nuisance neighbours. In 1596, for example, Nicholas Tailor was fined for harassing his neighbours with writs. Though the larger landholders on the royal manors tried to control the rest of the populace through the manor court, this does not necessarily mean that the other tenants were always amenable to this level of social control. In 1600, Nicholas Enghill was fined the substantial sum of 6s. 8d. on two different occasions for assaulting the constable of Esker manor, Brian O'Coffye.[22] Yet, the fact that the jury, made up of his fellow tenants, issued these fines would suggest that the community at large were not prepared to tolerate this assault on their constable.

The court book of Esker and Crumlin, as noted, is a late source, and our knowledge of the tenants of the royal manors from an earlier period is significantly impoverished because we do not have similar information about their everyday lives. Since most records dealing with these communities emanate from central government, the tenants were usually only observed from the outside. The petition is one source that did originate from the tenants, but these documents are not representative of tenants' everyday lives, as they were usually

---

20 Curtis, 'Court book' (vol. 59), 47.   21 Curtis, 'Court book' (vol. 60), 146–7.   22 Curtis, 'Court book' (vol. 59), 47, 58, 135.

composed during times of crisis on the manors. These petitions catalogue the attacks from the Irish of the mountains, as well as the threat of Scottish invaders. They also describe the mounting debts that the communities of the royal manors were unable to pay, due to the increasingly volatile conditions of the region. These are direct communications from the tenants to the king, and it is clear that the petitioners represented themselves as a community. Petitions sometimes emanated from more than one royal manor, which indicates that the concept of community transcended the confines of individual manors. In 1317, the tenants of Newcastle Lyons and Saggart sent a petition to the king complaining that the sheriff was taking fees from their courts.[23] In this case, both communities united to air their grievances and supported each other against the activities of the sheriff. This case seems to have much in common with that involving Henry de Compton, where the communities of Newcastle Lyons and Saggart supported the tenants of Crumlin in impeding the royal official from enjoying his grant.

Petitions offer us some of the only clues that survive as to how the tumultuous fourteenth century affected the tenants on the royal manors. In 1354, not long after the first outbreak of the Black Death, the tenants of Newcastle Lyons, Saggart and Crumlin sent a petition complaining that the king's ministers were impoverishing them by appropriating their goods.[24] Again, they were coming together as a community to defend themselves against external interference. Though there is no evidence of how many people perished on the royal manors because of this first visitation of the plague, it must have been a significant proportion of the community. Having to suffer the excessive extortions of royal officials could only have made a bad situation worse. Subsequent visitations of the plague decimated the populations of the royal manors; for example, in 1362, the seneschal, Walter Somery, had to find new tenants for the manors of Newcastle Lyons, Saggart and Crumlin.[25]

A petition that probably dates to around 1274–85 from the manor of Saggart includes both Irish and English tenants among its petitioners.[26] This would suggest that communal bonds and solidarities transcended ethnic divisions, at least in the thirteenth century. Moreover, there is good evidence for intermarriage between both races on the royal manors, at least up to the early years of the fourteenth century. For example, in 1305, a justiciary roll entry reveals that Andrew le Deveneys of Saggart, an Englishman, was married to an Irishwoman named Grathagh, who was a kinswoman of the O'Tooles.[27] Just five years later, another court case reveals that the Englishman John Fangoner was married to Ostina Otrescan, whose father was a betagh from Saggart.[28] It is also possible that the outlaw Henry Tyrel's concubine was an Irishwoman who was married to a tenant living on the royal manor of Newcastle Lyons.[29] Even though this

23 TNA SC 8/131/6509.   24 CPR, *1354–8*, p. 91.   25 NAI, RC 8/28, pp 309–10.   26 TNA, SC 8/197/9811; *Affairs Ire.*, §41.   27 *CJR, 1305–7*, pp 480–1.   28 NAI, EX 2/3, pp 488–9. 29 *CJR, 1305–7*, pp 483, 500.

evidence is rather slim, it is probably only the tip of the iceberg in terms of inter-marriage between these two ethnic groups. The fact that Englishmen were married to, or involved with, Irishwomen did not appear to be in any way remarkable in these records.

There is other proof of concord between the Irish and English living on the royal manors. For example, when William Bernard was accidently stabbed by John McCorcan during a game of ball in Newcastle Lyons in 1308, the records declare that both men had been 'fast friends' in the past and at the time of the incident. John, who was almost certainly an Irishman, got off with just a fine.[30] Clearly, both ethnic groups within the manor of Newcastle Lyons interacted with each other; they shared common pastimes and acknowledged bonds of friendship. John accidently stabbed his friend while running for a ball – evidently there was no ill feeling there. Unfortunately, court records often highlighted the animosity between the ethnic groups and not the bonds that frequently held them together. Though the statutes of 1297 admonished Englishmen for wearing Irish dress and adopting the Irish hairstyle known as the *Cúlán*, there is no hint here that the administration was promoting the kind of segregation found in later statutes. In fact, the evidence suggests close ties and integration between the ethnic groups, even in an area of the colony as heavily settled as Dublin.[31]

The records confirm that the rights of Irish tenants were protected, even to the detriment of their English neighbours. In 1310, David Otrescan complained that his brother-in-law, John Fangoner, an Englishman, had illegally ousted him from his lands in Saggart. John argued that he inherited these lands through his wife, Ostina, and while the court did not dispute this, David received seisin of the property. David won because he was a 'true betagh of the king'. Arguably, it would have been difficult for the administration to uphold David's rights unless the majority of the English tenants living on the royal manor of Saggart had not accepted the court's ruling. David's father, Nicholas, had held the lands before him, and, logically, the other tenants would have known him well. John Fangoner may have come from outside the manor and therefore the tenants may have been more concerned in seeing a neighbour's rights being upheld, regardless of ethnic origins. The Irish living on the royal manors had privileges that were not available to those Irish living elsewhere. Certainly, by the sixteenth century, betaghs were no longer to be found living on the royal manors, even though they still existed on the archbishop of Dublin's manors. It is possible that the Irish of the royal manors, with their favourable tenurial terms, lost the taint of villeinage early on. By the end of the medieval period, the small farmers of both Crumlin and Esker, and probably Newcastle Lyons and Saggart too, were allowed to commute their services to a small rent.[32]

30 *CJR, 1308–14*, p. 103. The source refers to Newcastle Lyons as a town, indicating its borough status.　31 *Stat. Ire., John–Hen. V*, p. 211.　32 Curtis, 'Court book' (vol. 60), 143–4.

There is evidence that some of the Irish on the royal manors bought English law. Richard Pudding is an interesting example of an Irishman living on the manor of Newcastle Lyons who was clearly not a betagh, as he had burgess status even before applying for English law. Pudding must have been accepted as an equal among the other leading tenants of this manor, even before acquiring the legal status of an Englishman. It is even possible that this sort of assimilation was encouraged. In 1292, William, son of Donald Clerk of Newcastle Lyons, and his children were granted the use of English law.[33] This patent roll entry is the only indicator of his ethnic origins. Donald is probably an anglicized version of Domhnall, but he gave his son an English name, perhaps because he wanted his family to assimilate into English society. It is likely that there were many other native Irish living on the royal manors who purchased English law, and the loyalties of men like Richard Pudding and Donald Clerk would have been with their fellow tenants, English and Irish. The petitions confirm that they had as much reason to fear attacks by the Irish of the mountains as the rest of the community.

Though the Irish and English appear to have coexisted in a relatively harmonious way during the prosperous years of the thirteenth century, the records suggest that there was a shift in attitudes during the fourteenth century. In 1305, when Grathagh, wife of Andrew le Deveneys, was accused of sheltering one of the O'Tooles, the jury, which was made up of locals, acquitted her.[34] Some years later, Grathagh was accused of spying on the men of Saggart on behalf of the Irish in the mountains. On this occasion, the jurors decided not to give her the benefit of the doubt, and she was executed.[35] The increased frequency of attacks by the Irish in the mountains may have soured relations between Irish and English tenants living on the royal manors. On the other hand, this apparent shift in attitude may have more to do with the type of records that survive than a perceived change in opinion towards the Irish of the manors. The evidence from the sixteenth-century court book confirms that, even by this late date, a large proportion of the tenants were still Gaelic Irish in origin, and therefore, even if attitudes did harden, most of the animosity felt was probably reserved for the Irish living in the mountains.[36]

What can be said for certain is that the judiciary, as a rule, treated the Irish more harshly than they treated the English. An Irishman found guilty of robbery or murder was much more likely to be executed than his English neighbour. For example, in 1306, when John Jordan, an Englishman, was found guilty of spying on behalf of the Irish, he was fined £20. As mentioned above, Grathagh le Deveneys, an Irishwoman, was executed for the same crime.[37] While the courts do appear to have displayed a bias towards the English, it is fair to say that social

---

33 *CDI, 1285–92*, §1096.   34 *CJR, 1305–7*, pp 480–1.   35 Lydon, 'Medieval Wicklow', p. 14.
36 Curtis, 'Court book' (vol. 60), 148.   37 *CJR, 1305–7*, p. 509; Lydon, 'Medieval Wicklow', p. 14.

status was probably as important as ethnicity when it came to deciding how wrongdoers were treated by the courts. While the types of punishment being meted out can be informative with regard to social status, it is also possible to identify hierarchy on the manors through the type of crimes being committed by their tenants. As a rule, those who were wealthy enough were able to avoid serious retribution, and the poorest members of society were generally treated more harshly by the courts.

On the royal manors, it is possible to identify a social pecking order based on criminal activity. Members of the gentry tended to steal more substantial goods than their peasant neighbours. Thomas Norreys, who was a member of Henry Tyrel's gang, for example, was charged with robbery. Robbery, as opposed to burglary, usually indicated that violence was involved. He was a kinsman of many prominent tenants on the royal manors, and it is likely that he was a member of the gentry. Conversely, at around the same time, Philip Logh, who probably came from Newcastle Lyons, was fined for stealing small items like hoods and gloves.[38] Philip was probably a peasant, as they tended to steal smaller items that could easily be concealed on their person. The gentry had the ways and means to perform audacious criminal acts, while poorer tenants usually stole due to need.

What is clear from the records emanating from the judiciary is that the community of these four manors were able, at least to some degree, to regulate and control criminal activity there. The jurors who served in the Thomas Norreys court case, for example, were all leading members of county society, and many were tenants on the royal manors. These men were the representatives of their community. They decided that his leader had led Norreys astray, and he escaped without even having to pay a fine. This was in spite of the fact that Henry Tyrel and other members of his gang were executed. The jurors would have found it difficult to send a neighbour's son to the hangman's noose, and this probably resulted in many criminals not receiving any sort of punishment. It was certainly a problem in England at this time, and it was of great concern to the crown that local jurors preferred that strangers be robbed than offenders punished, because they often knew the offenders or their protectors.[39] Nonetheless, the Dublin jury was not prepared to allow Henry Tyrel to get away with his crimes, even though he was the son of a neighbouring knight and must have been well known to many of the jurors. There is evidence that Tyrel compelled at least some of the community of Newcastle Lyons to shelter him, and undoubtedly many there were the victims of his crimes. Other people in the locality may have willingly facilitated his activities, to the detriment of the entire community. The courts tended to blame entire communities for receiving

38 *CJR, 1305–7*, p. 486.   39 Bernard William McLane, 'Juror attitudes toward local disorder: the evidence of the 1328 Lincolnshire trailbaston proceedings' in Cockburn and Green (eds), *Twelve good men and true*, p. 36.

outlaws, even though it is unlikely that everyone condoned their activities. This assumption of collective responsibility must also have fostered a sense of unity within communities. Certainly, the jurors in this case did not pardon Henry Tyrel's crimes, and they did not show him any leniency, in spite of his elevated social status and ties to the rest of the community. Ultimately, they decided that he was too much of a disruptive influence on the rest of the local populace and they dealt with him accordingly.

Though the tenants had much to fear from those who originated on the manors, a more serious threat came from the mountains. The responsibility of defending this area was left almost entirely on the shoulders of those living there. During the fourteenth century, the seneschal of the royal demesne was responsible for the defence of the royal manors, but, during the fifteenth century, the entire community of Co. Dublin was expected, on certain occasions, to come to the marches of Newcastle and Rathdown to construct ditches. This was a huge undertaking, involving hundreds of men, and it could not have been done without a high degree of community cooperation. Certainly, the various crises that marked the end of the medieval period meant that the tenants on the royal manors had to depend on each other. This responsibility of protecting the surrounding area put tremendous pressure on them, and this is demonstrated most clearly in the sources through the debts that began to mount from the end of the thirteenth century.

The proof of decline within the colony from the fourteenth century onwards is irrefutable. Yet, this must be tempered with the persuasive evidence that tenants on the royal manors not only survived but also prospered to some degree, particularly in the fifteenth century. Corroboration of this can still be seen on the landscape. The tower houses dotted around the royal manors suggest that at least some of the inhabitants of these manors were individuals of considerable means. The size and architectural quality of the parish church in Newcastle Lyons indicate that significant wealth and resources were available on this manor. Its construction reveals that the community living here was tightly knit and highly organized. It also served as a memorial for those who had perished in the famines, plagues and war that marked the fourteenth century. Harold Leask estimated that this church was constructed in the early years of the fifteenth century and judged its large curvilinear window in its east wall to be the finest in the country.[40] Its elaborate tracery was certainly carved by a professional artisan, which is evidence of the care and investment the locals put into the construction of this building. It is remarkable that this finely carved and delicate window survived the ravages of time and the raids of the Irish. Much like the tenants that lived there and on the other royal manors, its apparent vulnerability belies its resilience.

---

40 Leask, *Irish churches*, 3, pp 18–9.

Appendix

Seneschals of the demesne

Name and title	Term of office	Other offices and associations[1]
William Gernet – had custody of the king's Irish manors but no title is given[2]	c.1278	
William Deveneys – keeper of the king's demesne[3]	c.1281	Engrosser of the great rolls of the exchequer; remembrancer of the exchequer; marshal of the exchequer; prothonotary; keeper of the *Originalia* (before 1284–5);[4] baron of the exchequer (c.1300);[5] justice itinerant (1301); justice of the common bench (c.1303–5)[6]
John Kent – no title given[7]	1285	Baron of the exchequer (1280–93)[8]
Robert Mouncens – seneschal[9]	1307	
Thomas Kent – seneschal	1 August 1307[10]– c.26 July 1314[11]	Constable of Leixlip (1304);[12] keeper of Baliogary and Ballysax (1307);[13] coroner for Dublin county (1320);[14] king's coroner for Fingal (1326–7)[15]
Maurice Tyrel – seneschal	c.26 July 1314[16]– at least July 1316[17]	Described as seneschal of Newcastle Lyons in 1315;[18] probably the son of Gerald Tyrel, knight, owner of the manor of Lyons in co. Kildare[19]

1 Dates given denote the first time the individual concerned is recorded as being in office. 2 *CDI, 1252–84*, §1496; he was paid 50s. for custody of the king's manors in the Vale of Dublin. 3 Ibid., §1835, *Exchequer payments*, pp 69, 71, 75, 79. 4 *CDI, 1285–92*, §2. 5 *Admin. Ire.*, p. 106, §1. 6 Ibid., pp 26, 143, 151; NAI, RC 8/4, p. 71. 7 *CDI, 1285–92*, §149. In 1285 John de Kent paid £4 18s. 63/4d. of the arrears of his account of the king's manors. 8 *CDI, 1292–1301*, §730; *Admin. Ire.*, p. 105. 9 NAI, EX 2/2, pp 329, 330, 348, 370; *CFR, 1307–19*, pp 20, 23. 10 NAI, EX 2/2, p. 248. 11 By this date, Maurice Tyrell was seneschal of Demesne: see NAI, RC 8/9, p. 548. The termination date given is usually the earliest date that the succeeding seneschal is mentioned; it does not necessarily indicate that the previous seneschal served up to this date and, indeed, there may have been other seneschals who served between the terms of those listed here. 12 NAI, EX 2/1, p. 118. 13 Ibid., pp 203, 210. 14 *CSMA*, pp 6, 7–8. 15 *CARD*, pp 154–6. 16 NAI, RC 8/10, p. 729. This is the last mention of Maurice Tyrel as seneschal, though he may have remained in office as late as 1319, at which time John Beneger was described as seneschal. Tyrel was named as seneschal of Newcastle in 1315 (see next note), though it is hard to say if this was a separate appointment from that of seneschal of the royal demesne. 17 NAI, RC 8/12, p. 259. 18 NAI, RC 8/10, p. 485. 19 NAI, RC 8/5, pp 275–7.

Name and title	Term of office	Other offices and associations
John Beneger[20] – seneschal	After July 1316[21]– before Hilary term 1320[22]	Justice of the Common Bench (1312)[23]
Haket de la Sale – seneschal	Before Hilary 1320[24]– 30 June 1321[25]	Possibly the son of John de la Sale, a tenant on the royal manor of Saggart
Henry Nasshe – seneschal	30 June 1321[26]– at latest 6 July 1327[27]	Ship's master?[28]
John Baddeby[29] – possible seneschal	c.1324–5	Constable of Leixlip Castle (1324–5)
Thomas Warilowe[30] – seneschal	6 July 1327[31]– 17 March 1332[32]	Constable of Leixlip Castle (1330–1);[33] clerk of wages (1327–31);[34] engrosser of exchequer (1321)[35]
Thomas Dent – seneschal	Trinity term 1332[36]– before 21 August 1334[37]	Clerk of wages (1332–3);[38] second justice of the pleas (1337);[39] chief justice of the pleas (1341);[40] chief justice of the common bench (1344);[41] justice at the court of the justiciar (1348–9);[42] commissioner of oyer and terminer (1347);[43] king's pleader (1331–2)[44]

20 John Beneger spent time in Scotland in the company of Edward, prince of Wales, in 1301–2 and he was paid £98 14s. 4d. from the exchequer to cover his expenses incurred on this expedition, including the wages of men-at-arms as well as the cost of transporting these men and their horses to and from Scotland: *Exchequer payments*, p. 170.   21 NAI, RC 8/10, p. 729.   22 NAI, RC 8/12, p. 259.   23 Ball, *Judges*, 1, p. 63; *Exchequer payments*, p. 218.   24 NAI, RC 8/12, p. 259.   25 Ibid., p. 741.   26 Ibid.   27 *RDKPRI*, 43, p. 66.   28 Between 31 August and 29 September 1301, Henry del Nasshe, the ship's master of the *Godale* of Rye, was paid £20 wages for himself, two constables and forty-eight sailors going from the port of Dublin to Scotland in aid of the king's war there: *Exchequer payments*, p. 162.   29 *RDKPRI*, 42, p. 52. Baddeby was constable of Leixlip Castle in 1324–5; he was also described as seneschal. Since Leixlip did not appear to have a seneschal, it is possible that he held the office of seneschal of the royal demesne in tandem with the constableship.   30 In 1331–2, Thomas de Warilowe was paid £20 from the exchequer in compensation for expenses incurred while he was in the king's service and to recoup the ransom he had to pay when he was captured by O'Toole: *Exchequer payments*, p. 342.   31 *RDKPRI*, 43, p. 66.   32 Ibid., p. 66.   33 *RDKPRI*, 43, p. 39; *Exchequer payments*, p. 325.   34 *Exchequer Payments*, p. 334; Warilowe was responsible for paying the wages of the men going in the company of Roger Outlawe, deputy justiciar, to Munster to subdue the O'Briens and other enemies of the king. Outlawe was prior of Kilmainham; it is possible that Warilowe was one of his fellow Hospitallers.   35 Ibid., pp 280, 286, 343.   36 NAI, RC 8/16, p. 411.   37 NAI, RC 8/18, pp 442–3.   38 *Exchequer payments*, p. 351.   39 *CPR, 1334–8*, p. 477.   40 *CPR, 1340–3*, p. 252.   41 *CPR, 1343–5*, p. 316.   42 *Exchequer payments*, p. 427.   43 *CPR, 1345–8*, 464; *CPR, 1348–50*, pp 590, 591.   44 *Exchequer payments*, pp 341, 345, 349, 356, 362, 613.

Name and title	Term of office	Other offices and associations
William Barthelby (Bardelby) – possible seneschal of Newcastle Lyons, Crumlin and Saggart	*c.* 1333?[45]	Keeper of the rolls (1334)[46]
Walter Coumbe – seneschal	Before 21 August 1334[47]– 12 March 1343[48]	Chamberlain of the exchequer(1331–2)[49]
Thomas Smithe (probably Smothe?) – possible seneschal of Newcastle Lyons, Crumlin and Saggart?	*c.* 1336?[50]	Remembrancer of exchequer (1320–1)[51]; keeper of the stores of Dublin castle (1324–5)[52]; Clerk of wages (1336)[53]
William Epworth – seneschal	12 March 1343[54]– 21 October 1345[55]	Baron of the exchequer (1341)[56]
Thomas Pippard – seneschal[57]	21 October 1345[58]– 18 October 1352[59]	Royal official (1347)[60]
William Botte (Butler?)[61] – seneschal	18 October 1352[62]– 7 December 1353[63]	Clerk of the exchequer? (1356–8)[64]

45 According to D'Alton, *History of Dublin*, p. 696, William de Barthelby was made seneschal of the manors of Newcastle Lyons, Saggart and Crumlin in 1333. 46 Ball, *Judges*, 1, p. 36. 47 NAI, RC 8/18, pp 442–3. 48 NAI, RC 8/22, p. 649. 49 *Exchequer payments*, p. 347, passim. 50 According to D'Alton, *History of Dublin*, p. 696, Thomas de Smithe was made seneschal of the manors of Newcastle Lyons, Saggart and Crumlin in 1336. He may be a kinsman of Thomas Smothe, who served as seneschal in 1360. 51 *Exchequer payments*, pp 277, 280, 409, 423, 617. 52 Ibid., pp 306, 325, 329, 334, 337. 53 Ibid., p. 325. 54 NAI, RC 8/22, p. 649. 55 NAI, RC 8/23, p. 449. De Epworth stepped down because he was unable to discharge his office personally; it is possible that his responsibilities as a baron of the exchequer caused him to give up this office. 56 *Exchequer payments*, pp 399, 409, 411, 414, 422; NAI, RC 8/22, p. 649; *Admin. Ire.*, pp 110–11. 57 *Exchequer payments*, p. 428: between 9 December 1346 and 9 June 1348, Pippard was paid £7 10s. for his office as seneschal at the exchequer. His fee was £5 per annum; this is the only time a fee for the office of seneschal of demesne is recorded within the exchequer rolls. 58 NAI, RC 8/23, p. 449. 59 NAI, RC 8/26, p. 41. 60 Between 10 April and 23 August 1347, Thomas Pippard, accompanied by Roger Haward, went to Calais on very urgent business concerning the king: *Exchequer payments*, p. 420. This was in the middle of his term as seneschal of the royal demesne and, though he had originally been granted the office on the stipulation that he would perform the duties himself, they were carried out by a deputy: see NAI, RC 8/23, p. 449. 61 This surname does not appear elsewhere in the records of the period; however, he is likely to have been the clerk of the exchequer called William Butler (le Botiller), who accompanied Thomas Mynot, baron of the exchequer, to Munster on the king's behalf in 1356–8: see *Exchequer payments*, p. 485. 62 NAI, RC, 8/26, p. 41. 63 Ibid., pp 1236–46.

Name and title	Term of office	Other offices and associations
William Barton[65] – seneschal	7 December 1353[66]– 30 January 1360[67]	Purveyor (1354–5);[68] senior clerk of the chancery (1337–8); chief engrosser of the exchequer (1350); chamberlain of the exchequer (1354);[69] clerk of wages;[70] keeper of works of Dublin castle (1341–3)[71]
Thomas Smothe – seneschal	30 January 1360[72]– 6 April 1360[73]	May be the remembrancer of exchequer (1320–1);[74] keeper of the stores of Dublin castle (1324–5);[75] Clerk of wages[76] mentioned above under 1336 but since this exchequer clerk was not active after the mid 1340s it is much more likely that the individual serving as seneschal in 1360 was a kinsman.
Thomas Maureward – seneschal	6 April 1360[77]– 1 December 1361[78]	Mayor of Dublin (1389–90);[79] sheriff of Co. Dublin (1399);[80] seneschal of Crumlin (1385)[81]
Walter Somery[82] – seneschal	1 December 1361[83]– at least up to 29 October 1376[84]	
Geoffrey Vale – seneschal of Esker, Newcastle Lyons and Saggart	From 1388[85]– unknown	Sheriff of Carlow (1375)[86]
Stephen Scrope, knight[87] – possible seneschal, received the manors that had been in Vale's hands.	From 1407[88]– unknown	
Thomas Walleys – seneschal	15 July 1420[89]	Usher of the exchequer (1420);[90] chief engrosser of the exchequer (c.1431–6)[91]

64 Ibid., 8/26, p. 41.   **65** Previous to his appointment as seneschal, Barton held lands of the king in Crumlin, and during his term of office he acquired extensive property on the royal manors of Newcastle Lyons and Saggart: see *CIRCLE*, CR 18 Edw. III, §111; TNA, C 47/10/22/7.   **66** NAI, RC 8/26, pp 1236–46.   **67** NAI, RC 8/27, p. 579.   **68** *Exchequer payments*, pp 464, 468, 472.   **69** *Admin. Ire.*, pp 18, 123.   **70** *Exchequer payments*, p. 468.   **71** Ibid., pp 403, 413.   **72** NAI, RC 8/27, p. 579.   **73** Ibid., p. 579.   **74** *Exchequer payments*, pp 277, 280, 409, 423, 617.   **75** Ibid., pp 306, 325, 329, 334, 337.   **76** Ibid., p. 325.   **77** NAI, RC 8/27, pp 578–9.   **78** NAI, RC 8/28, p. 91.   **79** Jacqueline Hill, 'Mayors and lord mayors of Dublin from 1229', *NHI*, ix, p. 553.   **80** D'Alton, *History of Dublin*, p. 29.   **81** Ibid., p. 681.   **82** In 1365–6, Somery was paid £10 for capturing felons in Munster: *Exchequer payments*, pp 522–3.   **83** NAI, RC 8/28, p. 91.   **84** NAI, RC 8/32, p. 588.   **85** *CPR, 1385–9*, p. 533; D'Alton, *History of Dublin*, pp 649, 681.   **86** NAI, 999/217/1iii.   **87** *CPR, 1413–16*, p. 31.   **88** D'Alton, *History of Dublin*, p. 677.   **89** NAI, RC 8/38, pp 15–16.   **90** *Exchequer payments*, p. 550.   **91** Ibid., p. 574.

Name and title	Term of office	Other offices and associations
John Seys[92] – seneschal	From 1450[93]– before 1458	Justice of the common bench (1435)[94]
John Burnell – seneschal (duties of office carried out by his deputy Thomas Rede)[95]	According to Statutes was serving as seneschal in 1458 but date of his appointment unknown	Baron of the exchequer (1478)[96]

---

92 His sister Janet married John Arthur of Crumlin: Ball, *Judges*, 1, p. 172.   93 D'Alton, *History of Dublin*, p. 681.   94 Ball, *Judges*, 1, p. 177.   95 *Stat. Ire., Hen. VI*, p. 627.   96 Ball, *Judges*, 1, p. 159.

Bibliography

MANUSCRIPT SOURCES

Ireland
Dublin: National Archives of Ireland
EFP   Lindsay Papers
EX 2/1–3   PROI Calendar of Irish memoranda rolls
RC 8   Record Commission of Ireland Calendar of memoranda rolls (31 vols)
999/217   Copies of documents concerning Balthasar–Francois Wale's claim to nobility, 1747 and the history of the Wall family in Ireland, 1170–1691

United Kingdom
Kew: The National Archives of the United Kingdom
C 47   Chancery: Chancery miscellanea
C 143   Chancery: Inquisitions ad quod damnum, Henry III to Richard III
E 28   Exchequer: Treasury of the receipt: council and privy seal records
E 101   Exchequer: King's remembrance: accounts various
SC 1   Special Collections: Ancient correspondence of the chancery and the exchequer
SC 8   Special Collections: Ancient petitions
SC 11   Special Collections: Rentals and surveys: rolls
SC 12   Special Collections: Rentals and surveys: portfolios
SP 46   State papers domestic: supplementary

PRIMARY SOURCES

Bain, Joseph (ed.), *Calendar of documents relating to Scotland*, iii, 1307–57 (London, 1888).
Berry, Henry F. (ed.), *Register of wills and inventories of the diocese of Dublin in the time of archbishops Tregury and Walton, 1457–1483, from the original manuscript in the library of Trinity College, Dublin* (Dublin, 1898).
Best, R.I., Osborn Bergin, M.A. O' Brien and Anne O'Sullivan (eds), *Book of Leinster* (Dublin, 1954–83).
Brooks, Eric St John (ed.), *Register of the hospital of St John the Baptist without the New Gate* (Dublin, 1936).
Brooks, Eric St John, *Knights' fees in Counties Wexford, Carlow and Kilkenny* (Dublin, 1950).
Calendar of entries in the papal registers relating to Great Britain and Ireland: papal letters, 1198–1304 (London, 1893–).

Calendar of the Carew manuscripts preserved in the archiepiscopal library at Lambeth, 1515–74 [etc.] (6 vols, London, 1867–73).

Connolly, Philomena (ed.), *Irish exchequer payments, 1270–1446* (Dublin, 1998).

Connolly, Philomena, and Geoffrey Martin (eds), *The Dublin guild merchant roll, c.1190–1265* (Dublin, 1992).

Cotton, Henry (ed.), *Fasti ecclesiae Hibernicae, the succession of the prelates and members of the cathedral bodies of Ireland* (Dublin, 1848).

Crooks, Peter (ed.), *A calendar of Irish chancery letters, c.1244–1509* [*CIRCLE*].

Curtis, Edmund (ed.), *Calendar of Ormond deeds, 1172–1603* (6 vols, Dublin, 1932–43).

Dryburgh, Paul, and Brendan Smith (eds), *Handbook and select calendar of sources for medieval Ireland in the National Archives of the United Kingdom* (Dublin, 2005).

Dryburgh, Paul, and Brendan Smith (eds), *Inquisitions and extents of medieval Ireland* (Kew, 2007).

Empey, Adrian (ed.), *Proctors' accounts for the parish church of St Werburgh, Dublin, 1481–1627* (Dublin, 2009).

Fasti ecclesiae Anglicanae, 1066–1300, vii (Bath and Wells, 2001).

Gilbert, John T. (ed.), *Calendar of ancient records of Dublin* (19 vols, Dublin, 1889–1944).

Gilbert, John T. (ed.), *Chartulary of Saint Mary's Abbey, Dublin* [...] (2 vols, London 1884–6).

Gilbert, John T. (ed.), *Register of the abbey of St Thomas* (Dublin, 1889).

Gilbert, John T., *Historic and municipal documents of Ireland, 1172–1320* (London, 1870).

Giraldus Cambrensis, *Expugnatio Hibernica*, ed. A.B. Scott and F.X. Martin (Dublin, 1978).

Giraldus Cambrensis, *The history and topography of Ireland*, ed. J.J. O'Meara (Mountrath and London, 1982).

Griffith, Margaret C. (ed.), *Calendar of inquisitions formerly in the office of the chief remembrancer of the exchequer prepared from the mss of the Irish record commission* (Dublin, 1991).

Hardy, Thomas Duffus (ed.), *Rotuli Litterarum Clausarum* (2 vols, London, 1833).

Haydn, Joseph, *The Book of Dignities; containing rolls of the official personages of the British Empire, civil, ecclesiastical, judicial, military, naval and municipal, from the earliest period to the present time; compiled chiefly from the records of the public offices; together with the sovereigns of Europe, from the foundation of their perspective states; the peerage of England and of Great Britain; and numerous other lists* (London, 1851).

Lennon, Colm, and James Murray, *The Dublin city franchise roll, 1468–1512* (Dublin, 1999).

Mac Niocaill, Gearóid, *Crown surveys of lands, 1540–41: with the Kildare rental begun in 1518* (Dublin, 1992).

Mac Niocaill, Gearóid, *The Red Book of the earls of Kildare* (Dublin, 1964).

McEnery, M.J., and Raymond Refaussé (eds), *Christ Church deeds* (Dublin, 2001).

Mills, James (ed.), *Account roll of the priory of Holy Trinity, Dublin, 1337–1346* (Dublin, 1891; repr. 1996).

Mills, James (ed.), *Calendar of the justiciary rolls ... of Ireland ...: Edward I* [*1295–1307*] (2 vols, Dublin, 1905–14).

Palgrave, Francis (ed.), *Rotuli Curiae Regis, 1194–99* (London, 1835).

Richardson, H.G. and G.O. Sayles (eds), *The administration of Ireland, 1172–1377* (Dublin, 1963).

Riley, H.T. (ed.), *Registrum abbatiae Johannis Whethamstede* (London, 1872).

Riley, H.T. (ed.), *Registrum Abbatiae Johannis Whethamstede* (London, 1872).

Sayles, G.O. (ed.), *Documents on the affairs of Ireland before the king's council* (Dublin, 1979).

Simington, R.C. (ed.), *The civil survey, AD1654–6* (10 vols, Dublin, 1931–61).

Sweetman, H.S., and G.F. Handcock (eds), *Calendar of documents relating to Ireland . . .,* *1171–[1307]* (London, 1875–86).

Victoria County History, Worcestershire, ii (London, 1906).

Victoria County History, Worcestershire, iii (London, 1913).

Victoria County History, Worcestershire, iv (London, 1924).

Williams, Bernadette (ed.), *The Annals of Ireland by Friar John Clyn* (Dublin, 2007).

Wood, Herbert, and A.E. Langman (eds), rev. M.C. Griffith, *Calendar of the justiciary rolls . . . of Ireland: I to VII years of Edward II (1308–14)* (Dublin, 1956).

SECONDARY SOURCES

Acheson, E., *A gentry community: Leicestershire in the fifteenth century, c.1422–c.1485* (Cambridge, 1992).

Bailey, Mark, *The English manor, c.1200–1500* (Manchester, 2002).

Bailey, Mark, *Medieval Suffolk: an economic and social history, 1200–1500* (Woodbridge, 2007).

Ball, F.E., *A history of the county of Dublin* (6 vols, Dublin, 1902–20).

Ball, F.E., *The judges in Ireland, 1221–1921* (2 vols, London, 1926), ii.

Barber, Madeline, 'John Norbury (*c.*1350–1414): an esquire of Henry IV', *EHR*, 68 (1953), 66–76.

Barrow, G.W.S., *Kingship and unity: Scotland, 1000–1306* (London, 1981).

Barry, T.B., Robin Frame and Katharine Simms (eds), *Colony and frontier in medieval Ireland: essays presented to J.F. Lydon* (London, 1995).

Bartlett, Robert, *The making of the Middle Ages: conquest, colonisation and cultural change, 950–1350* (London, 1993).

Bartlett, Robert, *England under the Norman and Angevin Kings, 1075–1225* (Oxford, 2000).

Bateson, Mary, 'Irish exchequer memoranda of the reign of Edward I', *EHR*, 18 (1903), 497–512.

Bellamy, John G., 'The Coterel gang: an anatomy of a band of fourteenth-century criminals', *EHR*, 79 (1964), 698–717.

Bellamy, John G., *Crime and public order in the later Middle Ages* (London, 1973).

Benedictow, Ole J., *The Black Death, 1346–1353: the complete history* (Woodbridge, 2004).

Bennett, H.S., *Life on an English manor* (Cambridge, 1937; reissued 1971).

Bennett, Michael, *Richard II and the revolution of 1399* (Stroud, 1999).

Bennett, Michael J., *Community, class and careerism: Cheshire and Lancashire society in the age of Sir Gawain and the Green Knight* (Cambridge, 1983).

Berry, Henry F., 'History of the religious gild of St Anne in St Audoen's Church, Dublin, 1430–1740, taken from its records in the Haliday Collection, RIA', *PRIA*, 25C (1904–5), 21–106.

Berry, Henry F., 'Some ancient deeds of the parish of St Werburgh, Dublin, 1243–1676', *JRSAI*, 45 (1915), 32–44.

Berry, Henry F., 'Catalogue of the mayors, provosts and bailiffs of Dublin City, AD1229 to 1447' in Howard B. Clarke (ed.), *Medieval Dublin: the living city* (Dublin, 1990), pp 153–62.

Bradley, John, 'The interpretation of Scandinavian settlement in Ireland' in John Bradley (ed.), *Settlement and society in medieval Ireland: studies presented to F.X. Martin OSA* (Kilkenny, 1988), pp 49–78.

Bradley, John, 'The medieval boroughs of Dublin' in Conleth Manning (ed.), *Dublin and beyond the Pale: studies in honour of Patrick Healy* (Bray, 1998), pp 129–44.

Bradley, John, 'Rural boroughs in medieval Ireland: nucleated or dispersed settlements?' in Jan Klápště (ed.), *Ruralia III* (Prague, 2000), pp 288–93.

Bradley, John, 'A tale of three cities: Bristol, Chester and Dublin and "the coming of the Normans"' in Howard B. Clarke and J.R.S. Phillips (eds), *Ireland, England and the Continent in the Middle Ages and beyond* (Dublin, 2006), pp 51–66.

Brand, Paul, 'Chancellors and keepers of the great seal (A) 1232–1534' in *NHI*, ix, pp 500–8.

Britnell, Richard, *Britain and Ireland, 1050–1530: economy and society* (Oxford, 2004).

Brooks, Eric St John, 'Archbishop Henry of London and his Irish connections', *JRSAI*, 60 (1930), 1–22.

Brooks, Eric St John, 'The de Ridelesfords', *JRSAI*, 81 (1951), 115–38; 82 (1952), 45–61.

Campbell, Bruce, 'The land' in Rosemary Horrox and Mark Ormrod (eds), *A social history of England, 1200–1500* (Cambridge, 2006), pp 179–237.

Carpenter, David, *The struggle for mastery* (London, 2004).

Clarke, Howard B., 'The 1192 charter of liberties and the beginnings of Dublin's municipal life', *Dublin Historical Record*, 46:1 (1993), 5–14.

Clarke, Howard B., '*Angliores ipsis Anglis:* the place of medieval Dubliners in English history' in Clarke, Prunty and Hennessy (eds), *Surveying Ireland's past* (2004), pp 41–72.

Clarke, Howard B., Jacinta Prunty and Mark Hennessy (eds), *Surveying Ireland's past: multidisciplinary essays in honour of Anngret Simms* (Dublin, 2004).

Clarke, Howard B., 'External influences and relations, *c.*1220 to *c.*1500' in John Crawford and Raymond Gillespie (eds), *St Patrick's Cathedral, Dublin: a history* (Dublin, 2009), pp 73–95.

Cockayne, G.E., *Complete peerage of Great Britain and Ireland*, iii (London, 1937).

Connolly, Philomena, 'The enactments of the Dublin parliament of 1297' in James Lydon (ed.), *Law and disorder in thirteenth-century Ireland: the Dublin parliament of 1297* (Dublin, 1997), pp 139–61.

Connolly, Philomena, 'The rise and fall of Geoffrey de Morton, mayor of Dublin, 1303–4' in Seán Duffy (ed.), *Medieval Dublin, 2* (Dublin, 2001), pp 233–51.

Connolly, Philomena, *Medieval record sources* (Dublin, 2002).

Cosgrave, Art, 'The emergence of the Pale, 1399–1447' in *NHI*, ii, pp 533–56.

Cosgrave, Art, 'Chief governors, (A) 1172–1534' in *NHI*, ix, pp 469–85.

Coss, Peter, *The origins of the English gentry* (Cambridge, 2003).

Cotton, Henry, *Fasti Ecclesiae Hibernicae* (4 vols, Dublin, 1851–78).

Crooks, Peter, '"Divide and rule": factionalism as royal policy in the Lordship of Ireland, 1171–1265', *Peritia*, 19 (2005), 263–307.

Crooks, Peter, 'Factionalism and noble power in English Ireland, c.1361–1423' (PhD, TCD, 2007).

Crooks, Peter, 'The Lecky professors' in idem (ed.), *Government, war and society* (2008), pp 23–53.

Crooks, Peter, 'Medieval Ireland and the wider world', *Studia Hibernica*, 35 (2009), 167–86.

Crooks, Peter (ed.), *Government, war and society in medieval Ireland, essays by Edmund Curtis, A.J. Otway-Ruthven and James Lydon* (Dublin, 2008).

Curtis, Edmund, 'The court book of Esker and Crumlin, 1592–1600', *JRSAI*, 59 (1929), 45–64, 128–48; 60 (1930), 38–55, 137–49.

Curtis, Edmund, 'Janico Dartasso, Richard the Second's "Gascon esquire": his career in Ireland', *JRSAI*, 63 (1933), 182–205.

Curtis, Edmund, 'Rental of the manor of Lisronagh, 1333, and notes on "betagh" tenure in medieval Ireland', *PRIA*, 43 (1936), 41–76.

Curtis, Edmund, *A history of medieval Ireland* (New York, 1938).

Curtis, Edmund, 'The English and Ostmen in Ireland' in Crooks (ed.), *Government, war and society* (2008), pp 287–96.

Curtis, Edmund, 'The clan system among the English settlers in Ireland' in Crooks (ed.), *Government, war and society* (2008), pp 297–301.

Curtis, Edmund, 'The spoken languages in medieval Ireland' in Crooks (ed.), *Government, war and society* (2008), pp 302–16.

D'Alton, John, *A history of the county of Dublin* (Dublin, 1838).

Davies, Robert Rees, 'Kings, lords and liberties in the March of Wales, 1066–1272', *TRHS*, 5th ser., 29 (1979), 41–61.

Davies, Robert Rees, *Domination and conquest: the experience of Ireland, Scotland and Wales, 1100–1300* (Cambridge, 1990).

Davies, Robert Rees, *The Age of conquest: Wales, 1063–1415* (Oxford, 1991).

Dean, Trevor, *Crime in medieval Europe* (Harlow, 2001).

DeGroot, Roger, 'The early thirteenth-century criminal jury' in J.S. Cockburn and T.A. Green (eds), *Twelve good men and true: the criminal trial jury in England, 1200–1800* (Princeton, 1988).

Dolley, Michael, *Anglo-Norman Ireland, c.1100–1318* (Dublin, 1972).

Down, Kevin, 'Colonial society and economy in the high Middle Ages' in *NHI*, ii, pp 439–91.

Duddy, Cathal, 'The role of St Thomas' Abbey in the early development of Dublin's western suburb' in Seán Duffy (ed.), *Medieval Dublin*, 4 (Dublin, 2003), pp 79–97.

Duffy, Seán (ed.), *Medieval Dublin*, 1 (Dublin, 2000), pp 69–83.

Duffy, Seán, 'Irishmen and Islesmen in the kingdoms of Dublin and Man, 1052–1171', *Ériu*, 43 (1992), 93–133.

Duffy, Seán, 'The Bruce invasion of Ireland: a revised itinerary and chronology' in idem (ed.), *Robert the Bruce's Irish wars, the invasions of Ireland, 1306–1329* (Stroud, 2002), pp 9–43.

Duffy, Seán, 'The problem of degeneracy' in James Lydon (ed.), *Law and disorder in thirteenth-century Ireland: the Dublin parliament of 1297* (Dublin, 1997), pp 87–106.

Duffy, Seán, 'Town and crown' in Michael Prestwich, Richard Britnell and Robin Frame (eds), *Thirteenth century England, X: proceedings of the Durham conference, 2003* (Woodbridge, 2005), pp 95–117.

Duffy, Seán, 'A reconsideration of the site of Dublin's Viking Thing-mót' in Tom Condit and Christiaan Corlett (eds), *Above and beyond: essays in memory of Leo Swan* (Dublin, 2005), pp 351–60.

Dyer, Christopher, *Standards of living in the Middle Ages* (Cambridge, 1989).

Ellis, S.G., *Ireland in the age of the Tudors, 1447–1603* (Harlow, 1998).

Ellis, S.G., 'FitzEustace, Roland, first baron of Portlester (d. 1496)', *ODNB*, www.oxforddnb.com/view/article/8938, accessed 1 July 2008.

Empey, C.A., 'Medieval Knocktopher: a study in manorial settlement', *Old Kilkenny Review*, 4 (1982), 329–42; 5 (1983), 441–52.

FitzPatrick, Elizabeth, and Raymond Gillespie, 'Preface' in idem (eds), *The parish in medieval and early modern Ireland: community, territory and building* (Dublin, 2006), pp 15–18.

Flanagan, Marie Therese, *Irish society, Anglo-Norman settlers, Angevin kingship* (Oxford, 1989).

Flanagan, Marie Therese, *Irish royal charters: texts and contexts* (Oxford, 2005).

Foley, Áine, 'Violent crime in medieval Dublin: a symptom of degeneracy?' in Seán Duffy (ed.), *Medieval Dublin*, 10 (Dublin, 2010), pp 220–40.

Foley, Áine, 'Chieftains, betaghs and burghers: the Irish on the royal manors of medieval Dublin', Seán Duffy, *Medieval Dublin*, 11 (Dublin, 2011), pp 202–18.

Foley, Áine, 'The king's favourites and royal officials: patronage and the royal manors' in Seán Duffy and Susan Foran (eds), *The English Isles: cultural transmission and political conflict in Britain and Ireland, 1100–1500* (forthcoming).

Frame, Robin, *Colonial Ireland* (Dublin, 1981).

Frame, Robin, 'Two kings in Leinster: the crown and the MicMhurchadha in the fourteenth century' in Barry, Frame and Simms (eds), *Colony and frontier in medieval Ireland* (1995), pp 155–75.

Frame, Robin, 'Ireland and the Barons' Wars' in idem (ed.), *Ireland and Britain, 1170–1450* (London, 1998), pp 59–69.

Frame, Robin, 'English policies and Anglo-Irish attitudes in the crisis of 1341–42' in idem (ed.), *Ireland and Britain, 1170–1450* (London, 1998), pp 116–23.

Frame, Robin, 'The justiciar and the murder of the MacMurroughs in 1282' in idem (ed.), *Ireland and Britain, 1170–1450* (London, 1998), pp 241–7.

Gilbert, J.T., *A history of the city of Dublin* (Dublin, 1854).

Gillespie, Raymond, 'Small worlds: settlement and society in the royal manors of sixteenth-century Dublin' in Clarke, Prunty and Hennessy (eds), *Surveying Ireland's past* (2004), pp 197–216.

Gillingham, John, *The Angevin Empire* (2nd ed., London, 2001).

Gillingham, John, *The Wars of the Roses: peace and conflict in fifteenth-century England* (London, 2001).

Given-Wilson, Chris, *The royal household and the king's affinity* (London, 1986).

Goodman, A., *The Wars of the Roses: military activity and English society, 1452–97* (London, 1981).

Gorski, Richard, *The fourteenth-century sheriff* (Woodbridge, 2003)

Graham, Brian, 'Foreword' in James Lyttleton and Tadhg O'Keeffe (eds), *The manor in medieval and early modern Ireland* (Dublin, 2005), pp 11–14.

Green, Judith A., *The government of England under Henry I* (Cambridge, 1986).

Griffith, Margaret, 'The Talbot–Ormond struggle for control of the Anglo-Irish government', *IHS*, 2 (1940–1), 376–97.

Griffith, Margaret, 'The Irish record commission, 1810–30', *IHS*, 7 (1950), 17–38.

Griffiths, R.A., *King and country: England and Wales in the fifteenth century* (London, 1991).

Gwynn, Aubrey, 'Medieval Bristol and Dublin', *IHS*, 5 (1946–7), 275–86.

Gwynn, Aubrey, 'Archbishop John Cumin', *Reportorium Novum*, 1 (1955–6), 285–310.

Hall, D.N., Mark Hennessy and Tadhg O'Keeffe, 'Medieval agriculture and settlement in Oughterard and Castlewarden, Co. Kildare', *Irish Geography*, 18 (1985), 16–25.

Hanawalt, Barbara, 'Economic influences on the pattern of crime in England, 1300–1348', *American Journal of Legal History*, 18:4 (1974), 281–97.

Hanawalt, Barbara, 'Fur-collar crime: the pattern of crime among the fourteenth-century English nobility', *JSH*, 8:4 (1975), 1–18.

Hanawalt, Barbara, *Crime and conflict in English communities, 1300–1348* (Cambridge, 1979).

Hanawalt, Barbara, 'The peasant family and crime in fourteenth-century England', *Journal of British Studies*, 13:2 (1974), 1–18.

Harris, Gerald, *Shaping the nation: England, 1360–1461* (Oxford, 2005).

Hartland, Beth, 'Reasons for leaving: the effect of conflict on English landholding in late thirteenth-century Leinster', *Journal of Medieval History*, 32:1 (2006), 18–26.

Hatcher, John, *Plague, population and the English economy, 1348–1530* (London, 1977).

Hennessy, Mark, 'Manorial organization in early thirteenth-century Tipperary', *Irish Geography*, 29:2 (1996), 116–25.

Hennessy, Mark, 'Manorial agriculture and settlement in early fourteenth-century Co. Tipperary' in Clarke, Prunty and Hennessy (eds), *Surveying Ireland's past* (2004), pp 99–117.

Hill, Jacqueline, 'Mayors and lord mayors of Dublin from 1229: (A) 1229–1447' in *NHI*, ix, pp 548–52.

Hilton, R.H., *A medieval society: the West Midlands at the end of the thirteenth century* (Cambridge, 1983).

Holmes, George, *Europe: hierarchy and revolt, 1320–1450* (London, 1975).

Horrox, Rosemary, 'The urban gentry in the fifteenth century' in John A.F. Thomson (ed.), *Towns and townspeople in the fifteenth century* (Gloucester, 1988), pp 22–44.

Hoyt, Robert S., *The royal demesne in English constitutional history, 1066–1272* (New York, 1950).

Jacob, E.F., *The fifteenth century, 1399–1485* (Oxford, 1961).

Johnson, P.A., *Duke Richard of York, 1411–1460* (Oxford, 1988).

Jones, W.R., 'Keeping the peace: English society, local government and the commission of 1341–44', *American Journal of Legal History*, 18:4 (1974), 307–20.

Jotischky, Andrew, *Crusading and the crusader states* (Harlow, 2004).

Kaeuper, Richard W., 'Law and order in fourteenth-century England: the evidence of special commissions of oyer and terminer', *Speculum*, 54:4 (1979), 734–84.

Kelly, Maria, *A history of the Black Death in Ireland* (Stroud, 2004).

Klapisch-Zuber, Christine, 'Plague and family life' in Michael Jones (ed.), *The New Cambridge Medieval History*, 6: *c.1300–1415* (Cambridge, 2000), pp 124–54.

Lawlor, H.J., 'The monuments of the pre-Reformation archbishops of Dublin' in Howard B. Clarke (ed.), *Medieval Dublin: the making of a metropolis* (Dublin, 1990), pp 227–51.

Leask, Harold G., *Irish churches and monastic buildings* (3 vols, Dundalk, 1960), iii.

Lydon, James, 'The years of crisis, 1254–1315' in *NHI*, ii, pp 179–204.

Lydon, James, 'A land of war' in *NHI*, ii, pp 240–74.

Lydon, James, 'The Dublin purveyors and the wars in Scotland, 1296–1324' in Mac Niocaill and Wallace (eds), *Keimelia* (1988), pp 435–48.

Lydon, James, 'Medieval Wicklow: "A land of war"' in Ken Hannigan and William Nolan (eds), *Wicklow, history and society: interdisciplinary essays on the history of an Irish county* (Dublin, 1994), pp 151–89.

Lydon, James, 'Dublin in transition: from Ostman town to English borough' in Seán Duffy (ed.), *Medieval Dublin*, 2 (Dublin, 2001), pp 128–41.

Lydon, James, *The lordship of Ireland in the Middle Ages* (Dublin, 2003).

Lyons, M.C., 'Manorial administration and the manorial economy of Ireland, *c.*1200–*c.*1377' (PhD, TCD, 1984).

Lyttleton, James, and Tadhg O'Keeffe (eds), *The manor in medieval and early modern Ireland* (Dublin, 2005).

MacCotter, Paul, *Medieval Ireland: territorial, political and economic divisions* (Dublin, 2008).

McFarlane, K.B., *The nobility of later medieval England* (Oxford, 1997).

McGrath, Gerard, 'The shiring of Ireland and the 1297 parliament' in James Lydon (ed.), *Law and disorder in thirteenth-century Ireland: the Dublin parliament of 1297* (Dublin, 1997), pp 107–24.

McIntosh, M.K., *Autonomy and community: the royal manor of Havering, 1200–1500* (Cambridge, 1986).

McLane, Bernard William, 'Juror attitudes toward local disorder: the evidence of the 1328 Lincolnshire trailbaston proceedings' in J.S. Cockburn and T.A. Green (eds), *Twelve good men and true: the criminal trial jury in England, 1200–1800* (Princeton, 1988).

Mac Niocaill, Gearóid, 'The origins of the betagh', *Irish Jurist*, new ser., 1 (1966), 292–8.

Mac Niocaill, Gearóid, and Patrick Wallace (eds), *Keimelia: studies in medieval archaeology and history in memory of Tom Delaney* (Galway, 1988).

Maginn, Christopher, 'English marcher lineages in south Dublin in the later Middle Ages', *IHS*, 34 (2004), 113–36.

Maitland, F.W., *The history of English law before the time of Edward I* (2 vols, Cambridge, 1898), ii.

Martin, F.X., 'Allies and an overlord' in *NHI*, ii, pp 67–97.

Martin, F.X., 'Murder in a Dublin monastery, 1379' in Mac Niocaill and Wallace (eds), *Keimelia* (1988), pp 468–98.

Matthew, Elizabeth, 'The governing of the Lancastrian lordship of Ireland in the time of James Butler, fourth earl of Ormond, *c.*1420–52' (PhD, University of Durham, 1984).

Matthew, Elizabeth, 'Talbot, Richard (d. 1449)', *ODNB*, www.oxforddnb.com/view/article/26939, accessed 1 July 2008.

Mills, James, 'Tenants and agriculture near Dublin in the fourteenth century', *JRSAI*, 21 (1890), 54–63.

Mills, James, 'The Norman settlement in Leinster: the cantreds near Dublin', *JRSAI*, 24 (1894), 161–75.

Mitchell, Frank, and Michael Ryan, *Reading the Irish landscape* (Dublin, 2001).

Nicholls, K.W., 'The land of the Leinstermen', *Peritia*, 3 (1984), 535–58.

Nicholls, K.W., 'Three topographical notes', *Peritia*, 5 (1986), 409–15.

Ní Mharcaigh, Máirín, 'The medieval parish churches of south-west County Dublin', *PRIA*, 97C (1997), 245–96.

O'Byrne, Emmet, *War, politics and the Irish of Leinster, 1156–1606* (Dublin, 2003).

Ó Cléirigh, C., 'John fitzThomas, fifth lord of Offaly and first earl of Kildare, 1287–1316' (PhD, TCD, 1996).

Ó Corráin, Donnchadh, 'The career of Diarmait mac Mael na mBó', *Journal of the Old Wexford Society*, 3 (1970–1), 22–5; 4 (1972–3), 17–24.

O'Keeffe, Tadhg, 'Medieval architecture and the village of Newcastle Lyons' in O'Sullivan (ed.), *Newcastle Lyons* (1986), pp 46–61.

O'Loan, J., 'The manor of Cloncurry, Co. Kildare, and the feudal system of land tenure in Ireland', *Eire*, 58 (1961), 14–36.

O'Sullivan, Peter, 'Place-names, fieldnames and folklore' in O'Sullivan (ed.), *Newcastle Lyons* (1986), pp 25–43.

O'Sullivan, Peter (ed.), *Newcastle Lyons: a parish of the Pale* (Dublin, 1986).

Oftedal, Magne, 'Scandinavian place-names in Ireland' in Bo Almqvist and David Greene (eds), *Proceedings of the Seventh Viking Congress* (Dublin, 1976), pp 125–33.

Ormrod, W. Mark, Gwilym Dodd and Anthony Musson (eds), *Medieval petitions, grace & grievance* (Woodbridge, 2009).

Orpen, G.H., 'Liamhain, near Newcastle-Lyons', *JRSAI*, 36 (1906), 76–80.

Orpen, G.H., 'The castle of Raymond Le Gros at Fodredunolan', *JRSAI*, 36 (1906), 368–82.

Orpen, G.H., 'Castrum Keyvini: Castlekevin', *JRSAI*, 38 (1908), 17–27.

Orpen, G.H., *Ireland under the Normans* (4 vols, Oxford, 1911–20; new ed. 4 vols in 1, Dublin, 2005).

Otway-Ruthven, A.J., 'Anglo-Irish shire government in the thirteenth century' in Crooks (ed.), *Government, war and society* (2008), pp 121–40 [first published in *IHS*, 5 (1946), 1–28].

Otway-Ruthven, A.J., 'Knight service in Ireland' in Crooks (ed.), *Government, war and society* (2008), pp 155–68 [first published in *JRSAI*, 89 (1959), 1–15].

Otway-Ruthven, A.J., 'The mediaeval church lands of Co. Dublin', *Medieval Studies presented to Aubrey Gwynn SJ* (Dublin, 1961), pp 54–73.

Otway-Ruthven, A.J., 'The partition of the de Verdon lands in Ireland in 1332', *PRIA*, 66C (1968), 401–55.

Otway-Ruthven, A.J., *A history of medieval Ireland* (2nd ed., Dublin, 1980).

Otway-Ruthven, A.J., 'The character of Norman settlement in Ireland' in Crooks (ed.), *Government, war and society* (2008), pp 263–74 [first published in J.L. McCracken (ed.), *Historical studies V: papers read before the sixth conference of Irish historians* (London, 1965), pp 75–84].

Parker, Ciaran, 'The politics and society of County Waterford in the thirteenth and fourteenth centuries' (PhD, TCD, 1992).

Phillips, Jonathan, 'The Latin East, 1098–1291' in Jonathan Riley-Smith (ed.), *The Oxford history of the Crusades* (Oxford, 1999), pp 112–40.

Pollard, A.J., 'Talbot, John, first earl of Shrewsbury and first earl of Waterford (*c.*1387–1453)', *ODNB*, www.oxforddnb.com/view/article/26932, accessed 1 July 2008.

Pollock, Frederick, and Frederic William Maitland, *The history of English law* (2nd ed., Cambridge, 1923).

Poole, Astin Lane, *From Domesday Book to Magna Carta, 1087–1216* (2nd ed., Oxford, 1955).

Powicke, Maurice, *The thirteenth century, 1216–1307* (Oxford, 1962).

Prestwich, Michael, 'Royal patronage under Edward I' in P.R. Coss and S.D. Lloyd (eds), *Thirteenth century England, I* (Woodbridge, 1986), pp 41–52.

Prestwich, Michael, *Plantagenet England, 1225–1360* (Oxford, 2005).

Price, Liam, 'The antiquities and place-names of south County Dublin', *DHR*, 2:4 (1940), 121–33.

Price, Liam, 'The manor of Bothercolyn', *JRSAI*, 74 (1944), 107–18.

Price, Liam, 'The grant to Walter de Ridelesford of Brien and the land of the sons of Turchil', *JRSAI*, 84 (1954), 72–7.

Price, Liam, 'A note on the use of the word *baile* in place-names', *Celtica*, 6 (1963), 119–26.

Price, Liam, 'The origin of the word *betagius*', *Ériu*, 20 (1966), 185–90.

Quinn, D.B., 'Aristocratic autonomy, 1460–94' in *NHI*, ii, pp 591–618.

Radulescu, Raluca, and Alison Truelove (eds), *Gentry culture in late medieval England* (Manchester, 2005).

Razi, Zvi, and Richard Smith, *Medieval society and the manor court* (Oxford, 1996).

Reynolds, Susan, *An introduction to the history of English medieval towns* (Oxford, 1977).

Reynolds, Susan, *Fiefs and vassals* (Oxford, 1994).

Reynolds, Susan, *Kingdoms and communities in Western Europe, 900–1300* (2nd ed., Oxford, 1997).

Richardson, H.G., and G.O. Sayles, 'Irish revenue, 1278–1384', *PRIA*, 52C (1961–3), 87–100.

Richardson, H.G., and G.O. Sayles, *The administration of Ireland, 1172–1377* (Dublin, 1963).

Simms, Anngret, 'Rural settlement in medieval Ireland: the example of the royal manors of Newcastle Lyons and Esker in south County Dublin' in B.K. Roberts and R.E. Glasscock (eds), *Villages, farms and frontiers* (Oxford, 1983), pp 133–52.

Simms, Anngret, 'Newcastle as a medieval settlement' in O'Sullivan (ed.), *Newcastle Lyons* (1986), pp 11–23.

Simms, Anngret, 'The geography of Irish manors: the example of the Llanthony cells of Duleek and Colp' in John Bradley (ed.), *Settlement and society in medieval Ireland* (Kilkenny, 1988), pp 291–326.

Simms, Anngret, K.J. Edwards and F.W. Hamond, 'The medieval settlement of Newcastle Lyons, Co. Dublin: an interdisciplinary approach', *PRIA*, 83C (1983), 351–76.

Simpson, Linzi, 'Anglo-Norman settlement in Uí Briúin Cualann' in Ken Hannigan and William Nolan (eds), *Wicklow, history and society* (Dublin, 1994), pp 191–235.

Simpson, Linzi, 'Dublin's southern frontier under siege: Kindlestown Castle, Delgany, County Wicklow' in Seán Duffy (ed.), *Medieval Dublin*, 4 (Dublin, 2003), pp 279–368.

Smith, Brendan, *Colonisation and conquest in medieval Ireland: the English in Louth, 1170–1330* (Cambridge, 1999).

Smith, Brendan (ed.), *Ireland and the English world in the late Middle Ages: essays in honour of Robin Frame* (Basingstoke, 2009).

Smyth, Alfred P., *Celtic Leinster: towards an historical geography of early Irish civilization, AD500–1600* (Blackrock, 1982).

Southern, R.W., 'The place of the reign of Henry I in English history', *Proceedings of the British Academy*, 48 (1962), 127–70.

Stokes, G.T., 'The antiquities from Kingstown to Dublin', *JRSAI*, 25 (1895), 5–15.

Stones, E.L.G., 'The Folvilles of Ashby-Folville, Leicestershire, and their associates in crime', *TRHS*, 5th ser., 7 (1957), 117–36.

Stow, John, *A survey of London* (London, 1842).

Strohm, Paul, 'Trade, treason and the murder of Janus Imperial', *Journal of British Studies*, 35:1 (1996), 1–23.

Stubbs, William, *The constitutional history of England in its origin and development* (3 vols, Oxford, 1896).

Swan, Leo, 'Newcastle Lyons: the prehistoric and early Christian periods' in O'Sullivan (ed.), *Newcastle Lyons* (1986), pp 1–10.

Thomas, Avril, *The walled towns of Ireland* (2 vols, Dublin, 1992).

Thomas, Hugh, *Vassals, heiresses, crusaders and thugs: the gentry of Angevin Yorkshire, 1154–1216* (Philadelphia, 1993).

Thrupp, Sylvia, *The merchant class of medieval London, 1300–1500* (Chicago, 1962).

Titow, J.Z., *English rural society, 1200–1350* (London, 1969).

Tout, T.F., 'Firearms in England in the fourteenth century', *EHR*, 26 (1911), 666–702.

Tout, T.F., *Chapters in administrative history*, 2 (Manchester, 1920).

Tout, T.F., *Chapters in administrative history*, 4 (Manchester, 1928).

Tuck, Anthony, *Richard II and the English nobility* (London, 1973).

Tuck, J.A., 'Richard II's system of patronage' in F.R.H. Du Boulay and Caroline M. Barron (eds), *The reign of Richard II: essays in honour of May McKisack* (London, 1971), pp 1–21.

Twomey, Valerie, 'St Mary's, church of Ireland parish church, Leixlip, Co. Kildare' in Linda Curran, Valerie Twomey, Patricia Donohoe and Suzanne Pegley (eds), *Aspects of Leixlip: four historical essays* (Dublin, 2001), pp 29–61.

Tyrell, Joseph Henry, *A genealogical history of the Tyrrells* (Dublin, 1904).

Ua Broin, Liam, 'Rathcoole, Co. Dublin, and its neighbourhood', *JRSAI*, 73 (1943), 79–97.

Ua Broin, Liam, 'Clondalkin, Co. Dublin, and its neighbourhood', *JRSAI*, 74 (1944), 191–218.

Valante, Mary, 'Dublin's economic relations with hinterland and periphery in the later Viking age' in C.T. Veach, 'Henry II's grant of Meath to Hugh de Lacy in 1172: a reassessment', *Ríocht na Mídhe*, 18 (2007), 67–94.

Veach, C.T., 'A question of timing: Walter de Lacy's seisin of Meath, 1189–94', *PRIA*, 106C (2009), 165–95.

Walker, S., 'Janico Dartasso: chivalry, nationality and the man-at-arms', *History*, 84 (1999), 31–51.

Warren, W.L., *The governance of Norman and Angevin England, 1086–1272* (London, 1987).

Waugh, Scott L., 'The profits of violence: the minor gentry in the rebellion of 1321–1322 in Gloucestershire and Herefordshire', *Speculum*, 52:4 (1977), 843–69.

Wedgewood, J.C., *Biographies of the members of the commons house, 1439–1509* (London, 1936).

Williams, Bernadette 'The "Kilkenny chronicle"' in Barry, Frame and Simms (eds), *Colony and frontier in medieval Ireland* (1995), pp 75–95.

Wolffe, B.P., *The royal demesne in English history: the crown estate in the governance of the realm from the Conquest to 1509* (London, 1971).

Glossary

appraiser	an individual who assesses the value of property
appurtenance	a right, privilege or property that is considered incident to the principal property
betagh	an unfree tenant of Irish origin
borough	settlements, often urban but sometimes rural, that were granted some self-government
carucate	a unit of land representing how much could be cultivated by a single plough in a year. There is a great deal of variation in the size of this unit according to the sources, though 120 acres was typical
chace or chase	exclusive hunting reserve, i.e. a private forest
chattels	private property that is movable, as opposed to real estate
coyne and livery	the provision of food and accommodation for soldiers, exacted from the people whose lands they passed through
crannoc	a measurement, usually of grain
crosslands	church or monastery lands that were exempt from the crown control
distrain	seizure of property to obtain payment of rent or other money owed
enfeoff	receive possession of land in exchange for a pledge of service
extent/to extend	valuation of property, especially for taxation
farm/fee farm	land held at an annual fixed rent, without homage, fealty or any service other than that mentioned in the feoffment
fortalice	a defensive structure, a small castle
girdler	primarily makers of girdles, but they also made other leather items
grand serjeanty	lands held in return for some specified service, to aid in the defence of the locality, for example
heriot	a tribute paid to a lord out of the belongings of a tenant who died
hibernici	individuals who were Irish in origin

knight's fee	a measure of a unit of land deemed sufficient to support a knight
march	refers to a border region similar to a frontier, the territory between English- and Irish-dominated lands
messuage	a dwelling house with outbuildings and land assigned to its use
oyer and terminer	a court authorized to hear certain criminal cases
pipe roll	an annual record of the accounts of a sheriff or other minister of the crown kept at the exchequer
pleas and perquisites	profits of a court
prisage	a toll levied on wines
prothonotary	a chief clerk of any of various courts of law
provost	an overseer, steward or bailiff of a manor
reeve	an overseer, steward or bailiff of a manor
seisin	possession of land by freehold
seneschal	an agent or steward in charge of a lord's estate
sinecure	a position requiring little or no work but giving the holder status or financial benefit
suit of court	any proceeding by one person or persons against another or others in a court of law
vill	in England, this word signified the parts into which the territorial division known as the hundred was divided
ward and marriage	a person who is under the protection or in the custody of another; the custodian could marry ward off to whomsoever they chose

Index

Adam, an associate of Henry Tyrel 161
Aderrig, Co. Dublin 167
Adgo, Yerward 116
administrators 58–65, 189–90
Albert of Livonia, bishop 115
All Hallows, priory of 24
Alta Ripa, Maurice, son of Patrick 160; Patrick 160
Alwyne, Peter, provost of Crumlin 85
ancient demesne 6, 9–10, 40, 87, 92, 145, 147, 188, 190, 191
Angerston [Aungierstown], sub-manor of Newcastle Lyons 106
Annals of the Four Masters 33, 178
Aquitaine, France 46
Archer, John 144
Arklowe, Co. Wicklow 130
Artane, Co. Dublin 72
Ashbourne, Andrew 129; Elias, knight 107
Athgo, Reginald 164; Yereward 164
Athgoe, sub-manor of Newcastle Lyons 3, 84, 128, 164, 185
Athgoe Hill 164
Athlone Castle, Co. Westmeath 122
Attewelle, John, of Crumlin 91
Aylmer, family 84; Adam, reeve of Colmanstown 84; John, reeve of Colmanstown 4, 84; Robert, provost of Newcastle Lyons 84

Babe, William 156
Baddeby, John, constable of Leixlip Castle 104, 199
Bagot family 5
Bailiff, Simon, of Clondalkin 149
bailiffs 37
Bakehouse of the Rame, the, parish of St Audoen, Dublin city 127
Balally, Co. Dublin 25
Balbriggan, Co. Dublin 61
Baldoyle, Co. Dublin, manor 24
Balimony [unidentified but probably Co. Dublin] 99
Baliogary [Garristown], Co. Dublin, manor 93
Balitened [Powerscourt], Co. Wicklow 98

Ballinteer, Co. Dublin 4, 15, 25, 56, 144, 179–80
Ballybother [Booterstown], Co. Dublin 99
Ballycorus, Co. Dublin 128
Ballydowd, sub-manor of Esker 5, 62, 162
Ballyfermot, Co. Dublin, manor 44, 61, 63, 89, 130, 149
Ballyhaueny [Owenstown], Co. Dublin 62
Ballymaguire, Lusk, Co. Dublin 136
Ballymakelly, Rathcoole, Co. Dublin 72, 161
Ballymadun, Co. Dublin, manor 34, 67, 119
Ballyowen, sub-manor of Esker 5, 135
Ballysax, Co. Kildare, manor 93
Balrothery, Co. Dublin 67, 89, 181
Balscadden, Co. Dublin 61
Balygodman, John de 150
Barby, Richard 95
Bardelby, William, seneschal of the royal demesne 105, 200
Barnewall, family 63, 121–2, 137; Reginald 121, 148, 149; Wolfran, sheriff of Dublin 34, 89
Barton, William, seneschal of the royal demesne 106, 108–9, 201
Bas, David 60
Bath, family 135
Baughton, Worcestershire 68
Bauzan, Stephen 9
Beg, family 81, 83–4, 85; Adam 83; John, of Saggart, seneschal of Newcastle Lyons 49, 81, 83, 88, 101; John, provost of Esker and reeve of Newcastle Lyons 83, 85, 189; Nicholas, son of Richard 102; Nicholas, provost of Crumlin 83, 162; Reginald, of Saggart 82; Richard, provost of Saggart 62, 83, 102; Robert, of Clondalkin 83n; Roger, of Milltown 168; Thomas 83, 162
Belgard, Co. Westmeath 50
Belgree, Co. Dublin 100n
Beneger, John, seneschal of the royal demesne 101, 103, 198
Bennett, John, mayor of Dublin and constable of Dublin Castle 179–80
Berkshire, England 35